THE FUTURE
OF
PSYCHOANALYSIS

HEINZ KOHUT

THE FUTURE
OF
PSYCHOANALYSIS

Essays in Honor of
Heinz Kohut

Edited by
Arnold Goldberg

International Universities Press, Inc.

New York

Library of Congress Cataloging in Publication Data

Main entry under title:

The Future of psychoanalysis.

   Bibliography: p.
   Includes index.
   1. Psychoanalysis—Addresses, essays, lectures.
2. Kohut, Heinz. I. Kohut, Heinz. II. Goldberg,
Arnold, 1929-   . [DNLM: 1. Psychoanalysis—Trends.
WM 460 F996]
BF173.F94   1983   616.89'17   83-251
ISBN 0-8236-2105-7

Manufactured in the United States of America

Contents

Part III

DREAMS, TECHNIQUE AND CLINICAL THEORY

Part IV

DEVELOPMENT

Part V

APPLIED PSYCHOANALYSIS

Preface

Our happy idea suddenly became sad when Heinz Kohut died on October 8, 1981. Our planned Festschrift for his seventieth birthday became a memorial, and the faces that had looked to the future turned back to the memories of what had been lost.

The papers in this volume are addressed to a man whose vigor and vitality as an intellectual leader in psychoanalysis were unmatched. They should be read in that spirit of life. Someday a proper memorial volume will address the significance of Kohut's work. That will require a little time and distance; but for now, he is too much with us. Our book is alive with his presence.

The preparation of this book was financed by funds from the Harry and Hazel Cohen Research Fund. Mrs. Chris Susman and Ms. Ellen Bilofsky provided secretarial and editorial assistance.

Contributors

George E. Atwood, Ph.D.—Associate Professor of Psychology, Livingston College, Rutgers University.

Michael Franz Basch, M.D.—Training and Supervising Psychoanalyst, Chicago Institute for Psychoanalysis; Attending Psychiatrist, Michael Reese Hospital, Chicago; Clinical Professor of Psychiatry, Pritzker School of Medicine, University of Chicago.

Bernard Brandchaft, M.D.—Training and Supervising Analyst, Los Angeles Institute for Psychoanalysis.

Arnold M. Cooper, M.D.—Professor of Psychiatry and Director of Education, The New York Hospital-Cornell University Medical Center.

Lawrence Friedman, M.D.—Clinical Associate Professor of Psychiatry and Member of the Section on the History of Psychiatry, Cornell University Medical College.

Arnold Goldberg, M.D.—Training and Supervising Analyst, Chicago Institute for Psychoanalysis; Clinical Professor of Psychiatry, Pritzker School of Medicine, University of Chicago; Attending Psychiatrist, Michael Reese Hospital.

James S. Grotstein, M.D.—Associate Clinical Professor of Psychiatry, UCLA; Training and Supervising Analyst, Los Angeies Psychoanalytic Institute and Society; Attending Staff Physician, Cedars-Sinai Medical Center; Director, Interdisciplinary Group for Advanced Studies in Psychotic, Borderline, and Narcissistic Disorders, Los Angeles.

Mark Kanzer, M.D.—Past Director and Clinical Professor of Psychiatry Emeritus, Division of Psychoanalytic Education, State University of New York (Downstate).

Peter H. Knapp, M.D.—Professor of Psychiatry, Boston University School of Medicine.

Joseph D. Lichtenberg, M.D.—Editor-in-Chief, *Psychoanalytic Inquiry;* Faculty, Washington Psychoanalytic Institute; Faculty, Baltimore-D.C. Institute for Psychoanalysis.

Bonnie E. Litowitz, Ph.D., Dean, Erikson Institute; Adjunct Associate Professor, Northwestern University.

Norman S. Litowitz, M.D.—Faculty Chicago Institute for Psychoanalysis.

Nathaniel J. London, M.D.—Director, Psychoanalytic Foundation of Minnesota; Training and Supervising Analyst, Chicago Institute for Psychoanalysis; Clinical Professor of Psychiatry, University of Minnesota.

W. W. Meissner, S. J., M.D.—Clinical Professor of Psychiatry, Harvard Medical School; Training and Supervising Analyst Boston Psychoanalytic Institute.

Robert Michels, M.D.—Barklie McKee Henry Professor and Chairman, Department of Psychiatry, Cornell University Medical College, Psychiatrist-in-Chief, The New York Hospital; Training and Supervising Analyst, Columbia University Center for Psychoanalytic Training and Research.

Arnold H. Modell, M.D.—Associate Clinical Professor of Psychiatry Harvard Medical School, Psychiatrist, Beth Israel Hospital, Training and Supervising Analyst, Boston Psychoanalytic Institute.

Anna Ornstein, M.D.—Professor of Child Psychiatry, University of Cincinnati College of Medicine Faculty, Cincinnati Psychoanalytic Institute.

Evelyne Schwaber, M.D.—Institute of New England East, and Boston Psychoanalytic Institute.

Robert D. Stolorow, Ph.D.—Professor, School of Professional Psychology, Albert Einstein College of Medicine; Training and Supervising Analyst, Institute of the National Psychological Association for Psychoanalysis.

Charles B. Strozier, Ph.D.—Associate Professor of History, Sagamon University.

Marian Tolpin, M.D.—Training and Supervising Analyst and Faculty Member, Institute for Psychoanalysis, Chicago; Faculty Member, Child and Adolescent Psychotherapy Program, Institute for Psychoanalysis, Chicago.

Paul Tolpin, M.D.—Training and Supervising Analyst Chicago Institute for Psychoanalysis, Associate Attending, Michael Reese Hospital, Chicago.

Robert S. Wallerstein, M.D.—Chairman, Department of Psychiatry, University of California, San Francisco, School of Medicine.

Ernest S. Wolf, M.D.—Faculty Training and Supervising Analyst, Chicago Institute for Psychoanalysis, Assistant Professor of Psychiatry, Northwestern University Medical School.

Introduction

As a candidate in analytic training I had the extreme good fortune to have Heinz Kohut as the supervisor on my first case. A colleague had told me that this was a rare opportunity, and I was frightened accordingly. My fear did not prevent me from recognizing that some of the things my renowned supervisor told me made no sense to me at all, and some of the things that he was interested in seemed perfectly outlandish to me. The supervision helped with the case, however, and I did not complain. I do not intend to describe what it was like to be supervised by Kohut, but rather to highlight one particular moment of that experience, which occurred after the patient had terminated. I returned to review the case with Dr. Kohut and to discuss the supervision in general, and I had stored up a small list of puzzles and grievances, which I planned to put in the form of searching questions. I cannot now recall the particular point of my most worrisome query, but it ended with my wanting to know why my supervisor had not explained something to me much earlier. He matter-of-factly answered that he himself had not understood the point at the time. I can now confess that I was dumbfounded. I thought that my supervisor, like my analyst, knew everything and was just doling it out for reasons of time, money, and an assumed limitation in my capacity to assimilate it. What a jolt to find out that he, too, was learning on the job!

And that is the essential point I wish to make about Heinz Kohut and the future of psychoanalysis and why it seemed appropriate and necessary to join the two. A combination of dissatisfaction, puzzlement, curiosity, and joy in discovery make the field of psychoanalysis one of scientific inquiry rather than a closed technology of accepted tenets. These same qualities in Kohut demonstrated to all of us that there are still problems to be solved, that our field is too young to be concerned with issues of orthodoxy, and that a proper spirit of ignorance is the best insurance of future discoveries. We are, all of us, still learning on the job.

Psychoanalysis is so keenly tuned to its past, so heavily enmeshed in the history of its patients and of itself, that it sometimes neglects to look to the future. Not only does this emphasis on the past tend to encourage complacency in our practice and in our training of future analysts, but it also encourages a form of participation more appropriate to a trade or perhaps a guild rather than to a pursuit of problems and puzzles.

Regardless of how one feels about the truth or necessity of self psychology, it *has* made psychoanalysis exciting once again. Issues have been raised, arguments have flourished, and a whole new breed of criticism based on heresy has developed. The contributors to this volume have all shared in that excitement, though they by no means share a common perception of its value. There are proponents and dissidents in attendance here. Thus, no brief is made for self psychology as *the* future of psychoanalysis. Rather, self psychology *demonstrates* the future of psychoanalysis. This takes form in three areas: theory, clinical psychoanalysis, and applied psychoanalysis.

Theory

Discussions and arguments about the theoretical status of psychoanalysis date from the inception of scientific work on it. In fact, a recent book on the subject (Farrell, 1981) says that psychoanalysis has a "vision of promise." The debate about theory ranges from the comparison of analytic theories with those of the natural sciences to an attempt to find a home for psychoanalysis in the social sciences. Positions cover the spectrum, from judging analysis capable of satisfying the hypothetico-deductive method to enlisting it as a member of the hermeneutic disciplines. The debate examines problems of testability, verifiability, and falsification as well as considering validity as a narrative belonging to the field of discourse. All these arguments are welcome and healthy tests for judging the scientific status of psychoanalysis in contrast to according it a place as an art form or a "pseudoscience" or, as the obviously brilliant and equally uninformed Nobel prize winner P. Medawer says, a gigantic hoax.

That a new way of looking at clinical material, a new form of clinical theory could be developed within the methodology of psychoanalysis seems to me to speak volumes for the scientific status of psychoanalysis. Notwithstanding the sturdy voices of our own orthodoxy, the perception of the selfobject and the selfobject transferences by scores of analysts in diverse geographical settings and the parallel study of the resolution of such transferences in varied settings is testimony to the fact that ours is a scientific pursuit, regardless of how we may characterize an ideal for scientific knowledge. We have seen a problem, we have devised a theory about it and we have changed our way of looking at the world because of it. No more could be asked for qualification in the scientific enterprise. There is no one way of "doing" science, nor can anyone dictate what is proper for science, save an effort to expand our knowledge of the world.

Whether or not self psychology can in itself answer some of the questions about the status of psychoanalysis, its position in the family of science, and its capacity to generate further questions and answers is a matter for the future. Self psychology holds some promise of carrying out the task, but that self psychology could come about at all is satisfaction enough for the present.

The first two sections of this volume include papers that review and criticize the theoretical status of self psychology. They properly address the question of how we use theory and whether our present theories are adequate to help us understand our clinical data. Above all, they are written in the spirit of inquiry and with an outlook toward a future theory for analysis. They are diverse in scope but honestly reflect the learning process that Kohut so clearly exemplified in his own work.

Clinical Psychoanalysis

Self psychology originated as an expansion of the treatment of patients, a widening of analytic technique to include the so-called narcissistic personality disorders. Kohut's description of the transference and countertransference phenomena observed in and with these patients had an inevitable "ripple effect." Narcissistic issues were not only acknowledged, but soon became part of a wave of popularity.

Much of the general practice of clinical psychoanalysis was changed by awareness of and sensitivity not only to these transferences but to all the implications of the role of the selfobject for normal and abnormal development, technical interventions, and the analytic concept of cure. The ambience of the analytic setting was felt to be altered (Wolf, 1976), the nature of interpretation was reconsidered (Ornstein and Ornstein, 1975), and the problem of termination was reevaluated (Kohut, 1977). Hardly an area of psychoanalysis was left unmodified by this initial attempt to broaden its scope.

All these developments speak for the recognition of the need to continually reevaluate just about everything that is taken for granted in clinical psychoanalysis. Whether or not one is committed, for example, to the self psychologist's position of permitting various non-interpretive responses to the patient, ranging all the way from a greeting on the street to a measure of sympathy at the death of a loved one, there is now a rationale for alternative forms of behavior. Areas of clinical practice can no longer escape scrutiny because of tradition or explanation based on shaky clinical theory.

This is not to say that self psychology would alter much of clinical analysis, but it does indicate that we may see many things in a new light. A simple and accepted issue such as the "Monday morning crust," which was described by Freud and encountered by generations of analysts, has now been given a new consideration (Wolf and Wilson, 1980), not in an effort to alter clinical practice but rather to enrich our perception of the analytic commonplace. On the other hand, a proposed new way of making diagnostic assessments of borderline disorders (Brandchaft and Stolorow, 1981), may lead either to marked changes in indications for analysis or perhaps to equally powerful changes in our use of the diagnostic manual.

All of these insights and others being put forth have one crucial implication for clinical psychoanalysis: It is not stagnant, it does not run the danger of a rote exercise, and no single bit of clinical practice is sacred. As difficult as it is for some to accept, this is the true mark of a science and the true assurance of a vigorous future for our clinical work. The clinical sections of this book continue the effort to avoid taking our practice for granted and emphasize the forward-looking aims of psychoanalysis.

Applied Psychoanalysis

Extension of psychoanalytic knowledge to fields outside the clinical setting was encouraged by Freud's writing and by generations of psychoanalysts. The most optimistic appraisal of its success would characterize it as mixed. Some fields felt enriched by analysis, some ignored it entirely, and some ridiculed it. So much of this involvement in other fields was sterile because it focused on applying analytic formulas to nonanalytic material to the point of neglecting the opportunity for mutual enhancement. There seemed to be an accepted principle of investigation, first enunciated by Hartmann (1944), that analytic study in other disciplines mainly served to corroborate what was already known in analysis. As the findings of self psychology began to serve as a bridge to other disciplines, they offered a variety of options to scholars who heretofore had only variations on the theme of the oedipal complex to consider. Another beneficial product was an emphasis on the analytic method of empathy as a major form of data-gathering in other disciplines. But still another result has been to enable analysts to reach out to other disciplines in order to rethink and reexamine many of their concepts and conclusions. A reciprocal relationship has developed.

In the field of infant study we have been able to effect a marriage of sorts between the examination of the mother-infant unit and the self-selfobject unit. However, this goes way beyond the simple correlation of two allied fields to the whole study of open systems with feedback regulation. This is a far cry from the closed-system thinking of early psychoanalysis.

In the field of psycholinguistics, analysts inspired by Lacan had already returned to the study of language, from Saussure to Chomsky. Now the field of self psychology can begin to study the nature of the linguistic tie to the selfobject as well as the development of the self via language. We can return to Freud and language, but we can also use our knowledge of the development of language to study the development of the self. The selfobject is a bridge to a theory of communicative discourse.

In many other fields, as diverse as literature, history, anthropology, and music, we can begin to see a mutual enrichment of each discipline with psychoanalysis. Our psychology allows us to ask questions best answered with the aid of other disciplines and enables us to help those disciplines with their own questions. The field of applied psychoanalysis cannot be an effort to "apply" analytic knowledge to nonanalytic settings but must be an effort to initiate a dialogue with nonanalysts. Self psychology can and does hope to be in the frontier of such a partnership of learning. The spark of recognition that so many disciplines have felt with regard to self psychology makes for a mutuality of learning that is vital for applied psychoanalysis.

The last section of the book is representative of the best work in applying analysis beyond the boundaries of the clinical setting. But again, this is not so much an application but a series of efforts at mutual enrichment.

The plan of this book was a simple one. A group of distinguished analytic scholars was invited to contribute to a volume with the title of *The Future of Psychoanalysis,* and this was intended to be a birthday gift for Heinz Kohut. Of those who accepted the invitation, most seemed to want more to write about Kohut's work than about the suggested title. However, reading and studying these papers leaves little doubt that the title has been realized. These are not papers that review the literature, present a case or two, and confirm once again what the reader already knows. Nor are they lengthy descriptions of clinical and theoretical material with a minor variation that offer little cause for alarm. These papers are all products of a thoughtful concern that would be the best sort of gift for Heinz Kohut, who was so familiar with that particular psychic state.

Part 1 is clinical and consists primarily of various critiques of self psychology. Arnold Cooper reviews much of the previous work on devising a place for the self in psychoanalysis. Robert Wallerstein's paper is perhaps the most thorough and dispassionate examination of the "fit" of self psychology and classical analysis. W.W. Meissner takes this a step further with his own reformulation of self phenomena, while Robert Stolorow and George Atwood clearly go further in their statement for a new theoretical stand that recasts much of our clinical data in a new form, emphasizing a shared meaning achieved between participants. Arnold Modell gives us a historical perspective on the nature of narcissistic disorders. The second section on theory follows naturally from these clinical discussions, as Robert Michels sets the stage for the particular role and use of theory for the clinician. Lawrence Friedman suggests a model for considering the new perceptions of self psychology. James Grotstein demonstrates how one schooled in British object relations grapples with the findings of self psychology. Joseph Lichtenberg reexamines one of the most basic issues of psychoanalysis in terms of its delivering a world view of its own.

Part 3 returns to clinical material, focusing here on technique and dreams. Mark Kanzer continues his study of the "specimen dream" of Freud, and Paul Tolpin presents his work on self-state dreams. Evelyne Schwaber reviews her work on clinical listening, and Arnold Goldberg offers a self-psychological perception of a character disorder. The papers by Ernest Wolf and Bernard Brandchaft are outstanding examples of the revisiting of familiar material with a new set of ideas; one is on countertransference and the other on the negative therapeutic reaction. The fourth section, on development, is brief but thorough. Marian Tolpin discusses the development of the selfobject; Anna Ornstein discusses the dilemma of assessing fantasy versus reality in the etiology of psychopathology; and Bonnie and Norman Litowitz discuss the development of verbal expressions of the self.

The final section on application of self psychology deals with the topic that was probably nearest and dearest to Kohut's own interests. It is introduced by Michael Basch's paper linking the psychology of the self to the other behavioral sciences. Demonstration of this ranges from Peter Knapp's work on research in free association, to Nathaniel London's on literature, to Charles Strozier's on cults and history.

The book ends with a summary statement from Ernest Wolf whose eloquence speaks for itself. We hope that our volume in turn speaks for a recognition of the significance of such a forum for new ideas. More than anything else, that opportunity for a fluid and flexible exchange of thinking opens a future path for our field. Ideas are meant to be debated, discussed, and digested, and we hope that our readers will do that with this book. The essays that lie ahead for the reader should ignite a spark of enthusiasm for psychoanalysis. Such a spark enables us all to foresee a rich and meaningful future for our science and connects us to the feeling that Heinz Kohut had for our field all of his professional life.

References

Brandchaft, B., & Stolorow, R. (1981), unpublished manuscript.

Farrell, B.A. (1981), *The Standing of Psychoanalysis*. New York: Oxford University Press.

Hartmann, H. (1944), Psychoanalysis and Sociology. In: *Essays on Ego Psychology*. New York: International Universities Press, 1964, pp. 19–36.

Kohut, H. (1977), *The Restoration of the Self*. New York: International Universities Press.

Ornstein, A., & Ornstein, P.H. (1975), On the interpretive process in psychoanalysis. *Internat. J. Psychoanal. Psychother.*, 4:219–271.

Wolf, E. (1976), Ambience and abstinence. *The Annual of Psychoanalysis*, 4:101–115. New York: International Universities Press.

Wolf, E.S., & Wilson, J.W. (1980), The "Monday crust" in the disorders of the self, *The Annual of Psychoanalysis*, 8:197–214. New York: International Universities Press.

Part I

CLINICAL CRITIQUE OF SELF PSYCHOLOGY

The Place of Self Psychology in the History of Depth Psychology

Arnold M. Cooper

Introduction

No topic in psychoanalysis has received such breadth and intensity of discussion so quickly after its introduction as has self psychology. Furthermore, it is unique in the history of the psychoanalytic movement that ideas put forth so clearly as alternatives—as better than or opposed to—classical ideas have been debated within the analytic movement rather than relegated to a nonanalytic purgatory. We are all familiar with the fate of major dissenters or innovators in the past; they were either invited to explore their ideas outside the Freudian bailiwick or they were permitted to wither away in an atmosphere of analytic silence. Neither of these fates has befallen self psychology, and this may be an indication that there is no longer a psychoanalytic "movement." Rather there is psychoanalysis, a body of thought no longer the property of any small group, but broadly explored by people of varied backgrounds with different conceptions of what psychoanalysis should be.

I have elsewhere (Cooper, in press) discussed some of the reasons for the change in the psychoanalytic climate that has permitted Kohut's ideas in particular, and what have been referred to (Calef and Weinshel, 1979) as "revisionary" ideas in general, to be tolerated and debated

3

within mainstream psychoanalysis. It may help introduce my discussion of the place of self psychology in the history of depth psychology to review briefly some of the factors that make our present analytic debate possible.

We are now approaching the completion of a half century of psychoanalytic work without Freud's living presence. This may have been the time required for the analytic community to complete its mourning and to gather the strength to consider changes in identity without fearing either the loss of a needed tie to a powerful father or a disloyalty to a beloved father. I think it is not mere coincidence that the psychoanalytic community is pursuing the discussion of self psychology at the same time that it has developed the capacity to welcome a fuller, unbowdlerized picture of Freud the man, warts and all, aware that this deeper biographical knowledge can only enrich psychoanalysis, not weaken it.

Another important factor is the change in cultural climate between the time of Freud's greatest productivity and now—for example the change in family structure and role, the effects of postindustrial consumer culture, the knowledge of nuclear destruction and the holocaust, the changed nature of literature, art, and music. This social change presumably is responsible for the change that most analysts perceive in the problems of analytic patients from symptom neuroses to the more severe character pathologies. This change in population and consequent changes in practice and outcome require a reexamination of our modes of analytic thought. Finally, I suggest that before we began our discussions of self psychology and despite the inroads of European object relations theory, psychoanalysis in America was experiencing a diminution of scientific productivity and a loss of intellectual excitement, although we continued to mine ego psychology to good effect.

Against this background of professional maturation, cultural and characterologic change, and slowing of scientific progress, self psychology appropriately engages our thought and passion because it challenges cherished ideas, claims to be attuned to our modern culture and scientific method, and takes a stance on long-standing, major scientific tensions of psychoanalysis. These are the tensions around which the various schools of depth psychology have organized themselves in the past, the areas of undying dispute in psychoanalysis. Some examples are the following:

1. Self psychology claims to be the next logical step in the search for the basic concept or concepts that underlie secondary theoretical propositions. The large purview of self psychological theory in the broad sense allows, for example, for the structural point of view to be seen as a set of derivative rather than basic propositions.

2. Self psychology gives clear precedence to the importance of preoedipal events in determining the course of the development of the patients we see. What Freud (1905, p. 226, n. 1) referred to as a shibboleth—that the nucleus of neurosis is the Oedipus complex—is for Kohut a historical view, retaining usefulness for a minority of patients. We might observe that Freud also noted in his paper on female sexuality (1931) that the centrality of the Oedipus complex was no longer a tenable proposition, but he did not thereafter abandon it.

3. In place of the central role of the drives in determining the unfolding of human development, Kohut has asserted the central role of the self in its matrix of self objects. The real environment and the role of culture are far more determining for Kohut than for Freud, and the drives, per se, become a focus of attention only in certain forms of pathology.

4. In place of Freud's inevitably and perpetually ambivalent and conflicted individual, Kohut has envisioned a basically unified person who is more likely to suffer deficit than conflict, whose tragic defeat in pursuit of his or her guiding vision is the consequence of humanity's puny place in the universe, rather than a guilt-engendered neurotic self-defeat.

5. Whereas Freud tried his best to maintain psychoanalysis within the framework of science and its always reductionist methodology, Kohut's model blurs the lines between hermeneutic and scientific inquiry.

6. Whereas traditional analysis has advanced interpretation as the psychoanalyst's basic therapeutic action, Kohut emphasizes the analyst's creation of a new kind of experience for the patient within the transference relationship, of which interpretation is only a facet.

I could mention other issues, but I think it is clear that when a view as radically different as self psychology is from classical psychoanalysis is discussed seriously in psychoanalytic scientific forums, then the traditional psychoanalytic "movement" has passed out of existence. In its place we begin to see a situation more like that prevailing in the rest of science, where differing views are argued not only with data—which are usually inadequate early in the development of a point of view, although they may one day be decisive—but with passion, persuasion, and politics. Furthermore, as in natural science, every effort is made to keep newer theories out of the realm of debate until the weight of evidence or the number of converts no longer permit that exclusion. Scientific debate has never been noted for its politeness or orderliness. A series of national conferences on self psychology testify to the clear intent of the self psychologists to use all the means at their disposal to gain adherents, to spread the good word, and, presumably, to advertise the evidence of the usefulness of their theories and the richness of their data with the hope that we all will come to share their views.

While this style of debate is to be welcomed as a way of speeding the advance of analytic knowledge, one should note one danger involved in the loss of the analytic "movement." Freud spoke of the possible need to alloy the pure gold of psychoanalysis with the copper of psychotherapy. I think we must also show some concern for the alloy of psychoanalysis with whatever metals make the disciplines of philosophy and the humanities. Because psychoanalysis deeply affects the intellectual and often personal lives of such a broad range of professional and paraprofessional groups, including all who work in the humanities. We must take care that our theories remain linked to the chain of ideas that go back to the clinical situation of psychoanalysis. I believe the professionalism of self psychology is beyond reproach; but because its value system of optimism, joyful creativity, enlarged human potential, and belief in the individual's core strength gives self psychology such a seductive appeal, it risks attracting adherents because of its philosophic outlook rather than its scientific standing. The very language of self psychology lends itself to a quick sense of familiarity and perhaps conviction for individuals who lack the experience of the clinical situation.

Depth Psychology

What is depth psychology? According to Ellenberger (1970), Bleuler coined the term, and it became popular during the time that psychoanalysis was equated with the psychology of the unconscious. Ellenberger says

> It might have seemed, in 1896, that Freud had now reached his goal of building a new theory of neuroses, explaining every detail of the symptoms and origins. . . . For Freud, however, this was just the starting point for the creation of what came to be called Depth Psychology. Depth Psychology claimed to furnish a key to the exploration of the unconscious mind, and through this a renewed knowledge of the conscious mind, with wider application to the understanding of literature, art, religion, and culture [p. 489].

Ellenberger suggests that Freud's depth psychology was built upon four contributions. The theory of hysteria proposed that forgotten early traumatic sexual experiences were revived by later events, which activated the memory chain leading back to the original trauma. The second contribution to depth psychology was dream theory, in which an elaborate, conscious production of the mind could be understood through the linkage of day residue to infantile libidinal wishes that disturbed the resolution of the Oedipus complex, which in turn led to the construction of the latent dream underlying the manifest content. *The Psychopathology of Everyday Life* (1901) was Freud's third contribution to depth psychology, with its message that all life activities are characterized by the tension of forbidden wishes and repressing forces. The fourth pillar of depth psychology was the book on jokes (1905) in which Freud maintained that whereas dreams express wish fulfillment, jokes satisfy the need for pleasure in play; and whereas dreams regress from language to pictorial thought, jokes are the regression from logical thought to playful thought.

In this view, Freud's great contributions to depth psychology include the concepts of repression; the continuity of behaviors from adulthood back to adolescence and childhood and the underlying universe of instincts; the explanation of the creative act, whose prototypes are the dream and the joke; and the assumption that every action simultaneously includes within it past and present, wish and defense, infantile and adult ways of thinking and feeling.

In effect, then, Freud's depth psychology claimed to provide the avenues to understanding both the everyday and the creative act, goal-directed and playful behavior, the waking and the sleeping mind, the unconscious routes to conscious behaviors, the reconstructable living past of each individual's present, and the techniques for curing some types of mental illness and improving one's existential state. These are ambitious claims for any psychology. They are, nonetheless, the program of depth psychology, with minor amendments here and there, as put forth not only by Freud, but by Jung, Rank, Adler, Klein, Sullivan, Horney, Rado, Kardiner, Lacan, and many others whom I am leaving out—and now by Kohut.

Self psychology can now be discussed as a system of depth psychology that has advanced to the status of an *alternative* psychology to classical psychoanalysis, a view I believe consistent with the most recent work of Kohut (1980) and Ornstein (1980). As did Adler, Rank, and Jung before him, for example, Kohut has renamed his depth psychology, reassessed the value system and scientific status of psychoanalysis, redefined the psychic elements of interest to depth psychology, and revised the technical procedures of the treatment of patients. Two issues will serve as examples of the thrust of self psychology: the view of human nature and the content of the psychic depths.

Human Nature

One of the major sources of dissidence among depth psychologists has been dissatisfaction with Freud's description of human nature. While it is a great oversimplification to think of Freud's view as simply pessimistic, there can be little question that the human creature he envisioned was inevitably ambivalent and conflicted, even in his or her most loving relationships; divided rather than unified; more determined by the past than self-determining by strivings toward the future; and capable of being investigated and understood by the reductionistic, objective methods of traditional science. For Freud the distinction between health and illness was blurred—to be not too neurotic was the best one could hope for. Evil, in the sense of socially unacceptable and destructive desires, was built into the nature of the beast; the conflict of individual and society could be controlled but not removed, and the cost of that control was a quantum of happiness. Freud understood well that this view of humanity was not easily accepted, and he referred to psychoanalysis as the third great narcissistic injury. As Copernicus discovered that we are not the center of the universe, and as Darwin revealed that our species is subject to all the laws of evolution, enjoying no special status, psychoanalysis revealed that we are not even masters of our own selves; rather, we are carrying out a predetermined program, whose roots and aims are unknown to us. We are merely the actors, directed by unknown forces.

One can understand important aspects of the work of the early alternative schools of depth psychology—Adler, Jung, and Rank (Progoff, 1956)—as a rejection of this view of humanity. In contrast to the determinism of Freud, Jung's construction of the self conveyed the sense of individuals as open-ended, guiding their fate by their own vision of their own future, and capable of transcendent religious experience. Adler insisted that his individual psychology was subjectivist in its scientific stance, emphasizing individual assertiveness toward health, wholeness, and social concern and the realization of personal goals in the style of life. Rank's idea of the Will was an expression of his belief in the individual's striving toward and capacity for creativity and the achievement of uniqueness. Each of these theorists explicitly rejected what they perceived to be Freud's materialistic view of the psyche and the implied denigration of individuality that accompanied this view. This critique of Freud's value system is also present in the work of Heinz Kohut.

Kohut is explicit in rejecting Freud's views on human nature and development from infancy to adulthood. When Kohut speaks of Tragic Man in contrast to Freud's Guilty Man, he rejects the human nature that Freud assumed. Kohut (1980), speaking of at least one group of classical analysts, refers to "the conceptions of those who emphasize the primacy of hostility and destructiveness in human nature and, consequently, man's propensity to be beset by conflict, guilt, and guilt-depression" (p. 478). These terms contrast with the views of self psychology in which the entire course of development from infancy to adulthood is seen as the movement of an "independent, assertive, strong" creature who is "psychologically complete so long as it breathes the psychological oxygen provided by contact with empathically responsive selfobjects'' (p. 481). This view of the infant as strong, assertive, and complete within its appropriate environment of selfobjects is in the strongest contrast to the view of classical analysis in which the baby is incomplete, symbiotically dependent, fearful of separation, and inevitably subject to anxiety because of its helplessness in both the real world and the inner world of its own libidinal and aggressive drive. What Freud saw as the inevitable, fantastic, mental content of an immature ego apparatus striving to cope with drive demands, Kohut views as an avoidable disintegration product of failures of self-cohesion. Kohut sees the joy of creative achievement as a clear human potential; Freud saw that joy as always tempered by the reproaches of an insatiable superego.

On questions of such complexity as the nature of being human, we are usually unable to distinguish which portions of any psychoanalyst's views are determined by objective data and which reflect the personal apperceptive lens through which all clinical experience and data are filtered and altered. Infant research seems to demonstrate that the infant is born into a more comfortable world than Freud envisioned. Drives or affects are generally quantitatively and qualitatively attuned to both the average expectable environment and to the infant's developmental timetable. Affects, rather than requiring taming, grow in hierarchic complexity. The relation of mother and child is a two-way channel of intricate communication rather than a simple funneling of welfare handouts from a ''have'' to a ''have-not.'' None of these altered views of childhood, however, dictates Kohut's view of adult human nature. Moreover, Kohut may be doing Freud an injustice in contrasting Tragic with Guilty Man. Surely, the Freudian baby's infantile omnipotence assures the human being's constant search for greatness and immortality as well as his tragic failure in the quest. In Freud's view, our misery and our greatness are inextricably interwoven, and guilt is only one index of the outcome.

Intrinsic to the views of all those depth psychologists who chose to see humanity's potential as open-ended is the notion of the human being as unified. The Freudian individual's acts are seen as a deterministic result of at least three vectors of conflicting command—id, ego, and superego; Kohut's individual acts out of the inherent goals of its self, which is perceived as an ''independent center of initiative.''

Once the self has crystallized in the interplay of inherited and environmental factors, it aims towards the realization of its own specific programme of action—a programme that is determined by the specific, intrinsic pattern of its constituent ambitions, goals, skills and talents, and by the tensions that arise between these constituents. The patterns of ambition, skills and goals; the tensions between them; the programme of action that they create; and the activities that strive towards the realization of this programme are all experienced as continuous in space and in time—they are the self, an independent centre of initiative, an independent recipient of impressions [Kohut and Wolf, 1978, p. 414].

It is clear that the self, the only psychological structure that Kohut describes, is in all its aspects, an integrating, self-motivating force. Instincts do not lie behind it pushing it on. The self aims to fulfill a future-oriented program, which it develops itself. While the psychic structures and functions that Freud described can be understood in widely disparate ways and through differing frames of reference, depending on how one chooses to interpret aspects of Freud's conceptual scheme, there is clearly a radical difference between Freud and Kohut. (Difficulties that may be inherent in the concept of "self" are beyond the scope of this discussion. There are problems with a construct that simultaneously belongs to a person, is the motivator of the person, judges its self, feels and is aware of feeling, etc.)

As this dispute has been waged in the history of depth psychology, each side has made the predictable charges against the other. Those seeing the unified, creative individual have charged that Freud applied the wrong philosophy of science to his brilliant observations. Humanity should be understood either in terms of hermeneutic principles or at least with a scientific world view more attuned to that of modern physics, with its central uncertainty principle and union of observer and observed. On the other side, self psychology and its precursors have been accused of trying to blink away the evidence for the darker side of humanity—its destructiveness, primitiveness, and drivenness. While classical analysis is accused of reductionism, self psychology is accused of adopting a holistic view that interferes with scientific analysis and the deep understanding produced by a hierarchical systems organization. Interestingly, each side claims that its vision of human nature provides more freedom for the individual. The unitary theorists, from Jung to Kohut, have decried the concept of individuals as prisoner of their drives. On the other hand, in the book *Freud or Jung,* Glover (1956) attacked Jung's concept of the collective unconscious as depriving individuals of freedom. And Lionel Trilling (1955) refers to Freud's view of the innate opposition of individual drives and cultural demands as an ennobling, freedom-enhancing view, since it limits the extent to which individuals can be tamed by society. Their innate nature—their drives—will assure their discontent and their capacity to struggle against cultural taming. In contrast, Kohut's vision requires no such dissonance; the individual is potentially entirely harmonious with the culture.

Whether questions such as these will be settled by knowledge or whether the prevailing view will always oscillate according to the personality of the theorist and the cultural needs of the time is beyond this writer's ability to guess.

What Lurks in the Depths of Depth Psychology?

There is renewed interest today in the reasons why Freud abandoned his original seduction theory of the etiology of neurosis in favor of a theory of drive-motivated sexual fantasy leading to neurosis. Apparently (Blumenthal, 1981), some of the newer material emerging from Freud's letters indicates his clinical findings did not require this switch. Historically, however, it seems clear that had Freud not made the shift from seduction to fantasy, the development of psychoanalysis would have been impossible. It was essential that the etiology of neurosis somehow be located in the individual psyche to insure that the investigator's microscope would be focused there. The seduction theory, an essentially environmental point of view would have led logically to a sophisticated sociology, but not, at that stage of knowledge, to depth psychology, that is, to psychoanalysis. The issue is one of necessary scientific strategies rather than one of correctness of data.

The history of depth psychology includes the long-standing effort of many depth psychologists, beginning with Adler and including Sullivan, Rado, Horney, Kardiner, and now Kohut, to restore the role of the environment in understanding behavior. Of course, Freud never entirely relinquished the environment as a significant determinant of behavior. Throughout his writings it is clear that he did not believe the disposition of instincts alone determined developmental fate; rather it was the mixture of instincts, "accidental events," and the individual's constitution that together determine the course of development. Although the emphasis in Freud's theoretical writings is on the strength of the predetermined course of instinctual tendencies, his clinical examples always indicated with great clarity that any individual's life could be understood only in terms of the interactive consequences of drive and environment.

Within the mainstream of psychoanalysis, it was principally Hartmann who attempted to find a place in the theory for culture and society; but not until the impact of research in child analysis and the increasing influence of the object relations point of view were felt did interpersonal or cultural determinants of behavior begin to achieve a significant role in analytic theory.

The emphasis of self psychology on the determining role of empathic responsiveness throughout the entire course of development, but most significantly in the earliest years, represents a major shift toward the environmental, cultural, or interpersonal point of view. It is clear in Kohut's writings that, although his major interest is in the infant as a locus of experience, he and his followers believe the infant's experience represents a reasonably accurate response to the actual environment of empathic objects that the infant encounters. In fact, Kohut has ascribed the characterological shift in our time toward narcissistic personalities to a cultural change in the nature of the family and the amount and timing of stimulation given to the infant by the infant's selfobjects. Furthermore, as I understand the nature of the infantile bipolar self, its strivings and tendencies are conceived in the broadest terms, without specific content; it follows that the environment must be a profound shaper of the psyche, since self psychology has no equivalent of the drives and their developmental sequence.

The depths of the mind as revealed by self psychology will reflect the embeddedness of the infant in its selfobject matrix, in contrast to the psychic depths of classical analysis, which reveal the distortions of infantile wishes, body perceptions, and internalized object relations. The extent of the difference is illustrated by Kohut himself in his example of agoraphobia (1980, pp. 521–523). He makes it clear that in his view the agoraphobic's conscious need for a reassuring companion is the key to what lies in the psychic depths—namely, the lack of stable self-selfobject configuration and continued yearning for a maternal merger. The repressed prostitution fantasy discovered by Freud may indeed be present, but it is regarded as a more superficial content, the result of disintegration products of an earlier lack of self-cohesion. Paradoxically, then, Kohut's emphasis on the importance of preoedipal events leads to a clinical conclusion that the surface phenomena of the symptom or, even more important, of the transference, may be a clear guide to the individual's depth psychopathology, not requiring the detours of multiple wish-defense layers. This is a logical and necessary conclusion from Kohut's view of the self as the supraordinate organizer of behavior, and his emphasis on maturational arrest and deficit rather than a pathological maturational course. This view necessarily deemphasizes the repressed, distorted, pathological, sexual, and aggressive fantasy.

Lurking in the depths of self psychology, then, are not the strange, distorted, grotesque, forbidden desires and perceptions of classical psychoanalysis; rather there are the yearnings for a fulfillment of needs that seem eminently reasonable in the light of the infant's actual empathic experience with its selfobjects. This deep content certainly seems readily comprehensible; it fits our intuitive ideas of the needs of ''his majesty the baby,'' as Auden referred to it. Moreover, it brings psychoanalytic depth psychology closer to those who have long maintained that the psychoanalytic focus on sex and aggression has missed the issues of dependency, autonomy, and the maintenance of some form of omnipotent fantasy.

Returning briefly to Kohut's example of the analysis of agoraphobia, we might ask what has become of the concept of repression in self psychology. The issue is clearly drawn by contrasting Brenner's (1976) definition of psychoanalysis as the study of man in conflict, with that of Kohut, who describes it as the study of complex mental states. The unraveling of a complex mental state may not involve the undoing of repression and the emergence of dynamically potent unacceptable wishes as we know them in classical psychodynamics. It may rather be an undoing of disavowals and vertical splits, and the recovery of infantile yearnings that are not so much repressed as preconscious or unidentifiable in their intertwining with compensatory behaviors. The concept of compensatory behavior, similar to Rado's reparative behavior and Adler's compensations, differs significantly from the concepts of dynamic repression and additional defense mechanisms. In the classical view, the superego regularly plays a part in determining what and why and how mental contents are buried, whereas conscience would seem to have no necessary role in the depth content of self psychology. That self psychology seems simpler does not in itself tell us whether it is more or less true.

The emphasis of self psychology on preoedipal events is accompanied by the belief that empathic responsiveness in the transference will foster a regression back to the early fixation points. This conviction of the aliveness of the past and its continuing influence on the present is a return to a view of psychopathology that was, in different ways, abandoned by Jung and Horney and more recently by Gill (1979) and Emde (1981). It seems somewhat contradictory that a psychology so emphatically directed toward humanity's unrestricted potential also sees the past as actively determining the present through the continuation of unchanged, unsatisfied needs. In his work on transference, Gill (1979) has made the perhaps extreme suggestion that only the psychoanalytic here-and-now situation is therapeutically relevant, and reconstruction is of little therapeutic importance. In reviewing child research, Emde (1981) suggests that the actual or reconstructed past as a determinant of present behavior has been overemphasized and that the structures operating at later points of maturation are new syntheses no longer reducible to their formative elements. The understanding and alteration of those structures and how they function is a different task from that of retracing their synthesis. The difference is analogous to comparing the tasks of physiology with that of embryology. In this view, self psychology would be victim of the genetic fallacy. At any rate, the classical and self psychological views of the role of the deep past on current behavior seem to be proceeding on divergent paths.

Must we make a choice between the depth content of self psychology and that of classical analysis, or are both correct, both requiring analytic attention in the majority of cases? Wallerstein (1981) has suggested the views may be complementary; M. Stein (1979) has asserted they are incompatible. I will not attempt a verdict.

Conclusion

Depth psychology is the creative product of Freud's genius. Self psychology engages us so deeply in part because it contains within it so much of the history of depth psychology. I have tried to indicate some of the changes in the culture of psychoanalysis that now permit a discourse rejected by the earlier psychoanalytic "movement." Some of the specific issues of this discourse go back almost to the beginnings of psychoanalysis and involve values and cultural biases as well as clinical data. I have chosen to discuss the views of human nature and the buried contents of the mind as examples. Because the psychoanalytic method of investigation is so heavily burdened by the investigator's biases or empathic preferences, distortions or limitations, we do not have a sure method for refereeing our differences. We may not be touching the same parts of the elephant. It is a virtue of self psychology that as its theory has grown in sweep and elegance, it has required us to reexamine even our most cherished and basic psychoanalytic beliefs. History teaches, to paraphrase Socrates, that the unexamined belief is not worth holding.

References

Blumenthal, R. (1981), Scholars seek the hidden Freud in newly emerging letters. *The New York Times,* August 18, p. C-1.

Brenner, C. (1976), *Psychoanalytic Technique and Psychic Conflict.* New York: International Universities Press.

Calef, V., & Weinshel, E.M. (1979), The new psychoanalysis and psychoanalytic revisionism. *Psychoanal. Quart.,* 48:470–491.

Cooper, A. (in press), Psychoanalytic inquiry and new knowledge. In: *Reflections on Self Psychology,* ed. J. Lichtenberg and S. Kaplan. New York: International Universities Press.

Ellenberger, H.F. (1970), *The Discovery of the Unconscious.* New York: Basic Books.

Emde, R.N. (1981), Changing models of infancy and the nature of early development: remodeling the foundation. *J. Amer. Psychoanal. Assn.,* 29:179–220.

Freud, S. (1901), The psychopathology of everyday life. *Standard Edition,* 6. London: Hogarth Press, 1960.

———— (1905), Three essays on the theory of sexuality. *Standard Edition*, 7:125–245. London: Hogarth Press, 1953.

———— (1905), Jokes and their relation to the unconscious. *Standard Edition*, 8. London: Hogarth Press, 1960.

———— (1931), Female sexuality. *Standard Edition*, 21:223–246. London: Hogarth Press, 1961.

Gill, M. (1979), The analysis of the transference. *J. Amer. Psychoanal. Assn.*, 27:263–288.

Glover, E. (1956), *Freud or Jung?* New York: World.

Kohut, H. (1980), Summarizing reflections. In: *Advances in Self Psychology*, ed. A. Goldberg. New York: International Universities Press, pp. 473–554.

———— & Wolf, E.S. (1978), The disorders of the self and their treatment: An outline. *Internat. J. Psycho-Anal.*, 59:413–426.

Ornstein, P.H. (1980), Self psychology and the concept of health. In: *Advances in Self Psychology*, ed. A. Goldberg. New York: International Universities Press, pp. 137–160.

Progoff, I. (1956), *The Death and Rebirth of Psychology*. New York: Julien Press.

Stein, M. (1979), Review of Kohut's *The Restoration of the Self. J. Amer. Psychoanal. Assn.*, 27:665–680.

Trilling, L. (1955), Freud: Within and beyond culture. In: *Beyond Culture*. New York: Viking Press, pp. 89–118.

Wallerstein, R.S. (1981), The bipolar self: Discussion of alternative perspectives. *J. Amer. Psychoanal. Assn.*, 29:377–394.

Self Psychology and "Classical" Psychoanalytic Psychology: The Nature of Their Relationship

ROBERT S. WALLERSTEIN

For almost a decade now the psychoanalytic world has been explicitly and self-consciously confronted with the evolving articulation of the contributions to its theory and its technique offered by Heinz Kohut and his many colleagues. At first these ideas were presented under the rubric of concern with the problems of narcissism and of the narcissistic disorders as the emergent prototypical personality formation of our time. More recently, Kohut and his followers have adopted the declaredly more encompassing rubric of the psychology of the self. The major landmarks in this progressive unfolding have been Kohut's two books: *The Analysis of the Self* (1971), and *The Restoration of the Self* (1977). The first was subsequently declared to be the expression of the psychology of the self in the narrower sense. In it the self is portrayed as contents of the agencies of the mental apparatus, that is, as mental representations *within* the id, ego, and superego. Kohut's second book elaborates the psychology of the self in the broader sense;

This paper was presented in condensed form at the Boston Psychoanalytic Society and Institute Symposium on The Psychology of the "Self," Boston, Massachusetts, November 1, 1980.

19

the self is depicted as a *supraordinate* constellation, with the drives and defenses (the central ingredients of classical psychoanalytic conceptions of psychic functioning) subsumed as constituents of this self. This is the view of what is called the bipolar self, in which, with maturation, normally self-assertive ambitions crystallize as one pole and attained ideals and values as the other—the two poles then being connected by a tension arc of talents and skills.

In December 1979 the American Psychoanalytic Association held its first panel on the bipolar self (Meyers, 1981), which focused on the issues raised by Kohut's (1979) elaborate clinical description of his two ways of analyzing Mr. Z—the old in accord with the tenets of classical psychoanalytic psychology, and the new according to the precepts of self psychology. As one of the participants on that panel, I developed at some length—in the context of my discussion of Kohut's clinical material—my own *clinical* perspectives on the nature of the contributions of the self psychology approach, my view of its reach and of its limitations (Wallerstein, 1981). I will here attempt to articulate a more *theoretical* critique of this most significant and controversial new development in the psychoanalytic corpus offered to us by Heinz Kohut and his followers.

For this effort I have broadened my sources from the narrow base of the case report on Mr. Z., which was set as the springboard for the deliberations of the 1979 panel. My present review is based on a wide ranging and, I trust, adequately representative, if not totally comprehensive, consideration of the central writings from within self psychology, as well as on certain of the discussions and reviews, both sympathetic and critical, from psychoanalytic authors outside it. And yet, so much has the interest in and the controversy around self psychology grown during the past decade, and so much has the literature around it burgeoned, both here and abroad, that I feel the need for a note of apology to the many other contributors to this debate whose work I do not draw upon in my synthesizing critique. Incidentally, Ernest Wolf (1979), in his introduction to the New York panel on the bipolar self, made specific reference to some of the most salient and influential of these contributions from and about this psychology of the self, in our own country and abroad, in our own field of analysis and in the cognate realms of social, behavioral, and humanistic intelligence of man.

Let me begin my own contribution now to this subject with a schematic statement of what I see as the essence of Kohut's contribution to the body of psychoanalytic concept and endeavor. Most simply and directly, it is what Kohut took as his own clinical starting point: the focusing of our psychoanalytic awareness on the psychological as well as the psychopathological phenomena of narcissism as representing a most central and salient aspect of the psychological functioning, normal and abnormal, of *all* people. This aspect, which previously had not been regularly and systematically conceptualized and explicated, is of overriding clinical and therefore technical importance with certain people in particular—the so-called narcissistic personalities or characters, the prototypical individuals of Christopher Lasch's (1978) new age or "Culture of Narcissism."

By this I am not referring to the proposal of a separate developmental line for narcissism apart from that for object relatedness and object love. This proposal, which splits apart and expands Freud's original conceptualization of the line of developmental stages proceeding from autoerotism through narcissism to object love, did seem to be clearly set forth in Kohut's first book (1971) as the centerpiece of his new views on narcissism. Though some theoretical controversy did arise around this suggestion,[1] this issue of separateness of developmental lines is not the point on which the most searching critiques of the evolving directions of self-psychology have rested their main case. Indeed, I have sensed widespread agreement among analysts, even to some extent among those committed to the perspectives of self psychology, that this particular aspect of Kohut's formulations is neither that new nor, by itself, that important.

As I stated in the 1979 panel, in terms of both clinical and theoretical conceptualizations of the phenomena with which psychoanalysis deals, I *have* found it eminently useful to see narcissistic investments and object-related investments as parallel, complexly interlocking developmental processes, each originating in the most archaic mental dispositions and each being successively transmuted in

[1] See, in this context, Hanly and Masson's (1976) spirited attack on this position and their equally spirited defense with clinical adumbration, of Freud's original "unitary" conceptualization of developmental progression. See also Loewald's (1973), p. 446) milder, demurring statement in his review of Kohut's book.

the crucible of life experience into more mature, ego-syntonic, and socially valued mental states and propensities.

But I also stated that I did not regard this particular aspect of Kohut's self psychology to be as revolutionary a contribution as Paul Ornstein (1981), speaking on that same panel, seemed to imply that it was. In principle it seems no different than Anna Freud's (1965) work in separating out various developmental lines along many drive- and ego-related axes, or than Mahler's similar focus on the developmental unfolding from the autistic through the symbiotic onto separation-individuation (Mahler, Pine, and Bergman, 1975). In all of this, to quote directly from my statement, "psychoanalytic clinical and theoretical thinking has long transcended its initial formulations by Freud that had assumed the unitary centrality of the psychosexual developmental ladder as a comprehensively satisfactory framework within which to view genetically life course and development, the influence of past on present, or said for different purpose, the incremental transformation of past into present" (Wallerstein, 1981, p. 381). As I went on to state, I felt that psychoanalysts today, including Kohut himself (more in the spirit of his second book), seem to be in general accord with a conceptualization of a unitariness and an overall coherence of development. Within this perspective, for purposes of heuristic and conceptual highlighting, we can focus on varieties of drive-, ego-, and object-related developmental lines. Division among us would be much more likely to arise around the question of the specific value of Kohut's particular conceptualization of the *self* as the supraordinate or overarching, unifying perspective on the personality.

Furthermore, I do not regard as the major issue, import, or even novelty of Kohut's formulations on narcissism his clear emphasis on the primacy of the libidinal over the aggressive component in emotional interaction and development. This issue has of course been a major focus of Kohut's theoretical differences with Otto Kernberg. Kernberg has consistently called attention to the deemphasis in Kohut's "empathic" and "soothing" clinical approach of the roles of the primitive aggressive drives, the hateful, preoedipal maternal transference imagoes, and the vicissitudes of infantile oral envy and rage (Kernberg, 1974, 1978). In fact, Kernberg points to a failure of "a basic resolution of what I consider the pathological structure of the grandiose self"

(1974, p. 238). He links this failure to "re-educative elements" in Kohut's approach that he believes are the inevitable results, if not the intent, of helping patients rationalize their aggressions as "a natural consequence to the failure of other people in their past" (1978, p. 17).

This kind of criticism has of course been joined by others. Segel (1981), in his reasoned and even-handed critical assessment of the work of both Kohut and Kernberg, scores Kohut for viewing aggressive outbursts as well as libidinally based acting out mainly (or even solely?) as disintegration products of an insufficiently consolidated self in response to difficult frustration or empathic failure. Rather, Segel indicates, these outbursts should be considered at least equally as drive manifestations whose unconscious meanings must be explored. Rothstein's (1980) critique also attacks this declared deemphasis on the aggressive drives, on sadism and sadistic pleasure in narcissistic characters,[2] and on the analytic management of rage and shame, which are seen only as secondary to frustration and deficit in parental empathy. Carried to its extreme implications for child-rearing and clinical technique, he argues, that this "paradigm facilitates the illusion that rage can be disavowed or even avoided [in development] if the optimal 'restorative' self-object can be found" (p. 435).

A related but separate point is that a consistent (if unintended) devaluation of the drive- and object-related origins of the superego emerges throughout self psychology. In Kohut's second book (1977), in which the concept of the bipolar self, with its pole of ambitions and pole of ideals and values, is fully unfolded, the word "superego" is used but a half-dozen times (see index, p. 344). Moreover, in each instance the word appears in the context of a brief statement of the formulations of classical "structural psychology," always by way of contrast with the perspectives of self psychology on the mental phenomenon being viewed (see, for example, p. 112). Although most analysts would view the pole of "ideals and values" in some relation to the approving and loving aspects of superego development, this relationship is nowhere drawn by Kohut. In fact, it is specifically disavowed:

It will now be obvious, too, why self psychology does not assign

---

[2] See, in this regard, Wilhelm Reich's (1933) original formulation of the sadistic pleasure gain in phallic narcissistic characters.

> a person's basic ambitions and basic ideals to his mental apparatus,
> specifically, to id and superego, but considers them, as I said,
> the two poles of his self. As seen from the point of view of the
> psychology of the self in the broad sense of the term, they are
> the essential constituents of that nuclear tension-arc which, having
> become independent of the genetic factors that determined its
> specific shape and content, strives only, once it has been formed,
> to live out its intrinsic potentialities [Kohut, 1977, pp. 242–243].

This separation of superego (and also id) as "constituents of the mental
apparatus of Guilty Man" (p. 243) from nuclear ambitions and ideals
as poles of the self, the "center of the pursuits of Tragic Man" (p.
243) in effect both downplays the entire role of the superego as an
organizing focus in mental life (thus the scarce mention of it in the
second book) and strips it away from psychic elements (ideals and
values) that are usually explained in relation to superego structuralization. Altogether, this seems to be an unhappy skewing of emphasis
as well as an unfortunate confusion of meaning-structure (in removing
ideals and values totally from superego structure).

Yet, again, I do not regard such issues as the most central to
Kohut's contribution to (or departure from) the theory of psychoanalysis. Rather, as with Kohut's drawing of a totally separate developmental line for narcissism, I see these positions as reflecting the kind
of temporary one-sidedness and overemphasis that seem, unfortunately, almost inevitable in any new conceptual position. Equally
inevitably, such exaggerations tend to be gradually moderated over
time to a more accommodating and ultimately reasonably consensual
return of the pendulum to a more central conceptual resting place.

Given these disclaimers, where do I then center my main statement
of the nature of Kohut's contributions to our psychological understanding? In my opinion, his most important contributions lie in the *clinical*
realm—in his careful delineation and highlighting of the significance
and meaning within the psychoanalytic situation of certain interactional
modes (which Kohut first called the narcissistic transferences [1971]
and subsequently [1977] termed the selfobject transferences) as well
as the counteractive and countertransference responses they characteristically evoke. Again, there is widespread enough agreement with

these ideas in the psychoanalytic world, even among those who have been most sharply critical of Kohut's formulations (see Stein, 1979).

Of course, not all, or perhaps not even many, would follow Kohut all the way in according these formulations such overriding centrality and primacy in explaining human psychological functioning. In his long summarizing remarks at the 1978 Chicago Conference on the Psychology of the Self, Kohut went so far as to state: "In the view of self psychology, man lives in a matrix of selfobjects from birth to death. He needs selfobjects for his psychological survival, just as he needs oxygen in his environment throughout his life for physiological survival" (1980, p. 478). (By contrast, Kohut declared that every other psychological view assumed a natural movement through life from helpless dependence to proud autonomy, with the concomitant hidden value system—not shared by self psychology—of a "maturation morality" or a "developmental maturity.") This extreme, somewhat fanciful, and tendentious metaphor aside, I think we analysts can (almost all of us) agree on the importance of Kohut's clinical formulations of the selfobject transferences, the varieties of mirroring and idealizing transferences, and their characteristic colluding countertransferences. In addition, we can agree, I think, on the elegance of the beautiful outline by Kohut and Wolf (1978) of psychopathological types and the behavioral typologies into which they sort themselves, considered from the standpoint of selfobject transference formulations. These are indeed significant and enduring additions to and widenings of our psychoanalytic vistas and our therapeutic armamentaria.[3]

Rothstein (1980) has also called this aspect "Kohut's most original and heuristically beneficial contribution" (p. 429). He points out as a corollary of Kohut's view—that part and parcel of the selfobject concept is an intensified emphasis on the real relationship with the mother during the earliest developmental phases, as well as on the real relationship with the analyst during the analytic process. This highlights the "reparative role of the analysand's experience of the analyst as

---

[3] Actually, one of the chief clinical fruits of Kohut's work lies in our universally sharpened *clinical* perspective on the various clinical manifestations of the cohesive and the fragmenting self. The interpretive work that we used to do more intuitively or haphazardly can now, in the light of the clinical formulations of self psychology with regard to selfobject transferences, be much more precisely focused.

new object in the metamorphosis of his or her psychic structure'' (pp. 428–429).[4] But these points are of course not new with Kohut, either. There is a vast literature in both child analysis and developmental psychology, and in behavioral pediatrics now as well, on the overwhelming importance of the early mother-infant interaction for the lifetime developmental course. In addition, much has been written on the nature of the relationship between analyst and analysand and its influence on the mutative psychoanalytic process (see the seminal contributions of Loewald [1960] and Stone [1961], and, from a quite different and not entirely acceptable perspective, Alexander and French [1946]).

Thus far, I trust I have traced a path that can be traveled by both the proponents and the critics of the new self psychology that is evolving within psychoanalysis. At what point, then, does this consensus dissolve and do I offer a different, critical perspective on the nature of the contribution and the ultimate place of self psychology in relation to the tenets of classical psychoanalysis? Briefly, it is at the point of translating a broadly clinical into a broadly theoretical contribution. This transition is perhaps marked by the shift from what Kohut calls the psychology of the self in the narrower sense (1971), to what he terms its broader sense (1977). As I have indicated, the first perspective views the self as *contents* or representations within the classically established mental apparatus of id, ego, and superego. The second, by contrast, is a psychology in whose theoretical framework the self—further elaborated in the conceptualizations of the bipolar self—occupies the central, encompassing and supraordinate position. In the latter view, the expressions of the drives (and the defenses?) are seen as *breakdown products* emerging under fragmenting pressures stemming from improper and "disempathic" interactions, rather than as primary component manifestations of the malfunctioning psyche,

---

[4] Kohut himself has formulated this point as follows: "Because psychological health was formerly established through the solution of inner conflicts, cure, whether in a narrow or in a broad sense, was then seen exclusively in terms of conflict solution through the expansion of consciousness. But because psychological health is now achieved with ever-increasing frequency through the healing of a formerly fragmented self, cure, whether in a narrow or in a broad sense, must now also be evaluated in terms of achieving self-cohesion, particularly in terms of the restitution of the self with the aid of a re-established empathic closeness to responsive self-objects" (1977, p. 281).

whose unconscious *meanings* are surfacing for exploration and elucidation. This is what Ornstein (1978, 1981) calls the "revolutionary" step to the third paradigm of psychoanalysis; he sees self psychology as the successor to the two prior paradigms created by Freud—first drive psychology and then ego psychology. In his discussion at the Chicago Conference of this "new scientific paradigm," Ornstein referred approvingly to Stolorow's "aptly and courageously" hailing this new paradigm as the "Restoration of Psychoanalysis."

Here I would like to elaborate on a point of contention. At the New York panel, I started my discussion by explaining the semantics of my use of the word "paradigm" in the sense propounded and given widespread currency by Kuhn (1962). In that sense, psychoanalysis clearly has had and still has but one basic paradigm of how the mind works—that devised by Freud, which rests on the fundamental postulates of psychic continuity and unconscious psychic processes (see Rapaport, 1944). My use of the word paradigm is explicitly *not* that of Eissler (1969), who trivialized it in his paper on the present and the future of psychoanalysis, in which he practically equated each conceptual and theoretical advance by Freud with the addition of yet another paradigm.

It is in Eissler's sense, I think, that the word was taken up by Ornstein and then has been attacked, for example by Rothstein (1980). Rothstein argues against the unhealthy aspects of what he calls "paradigm competition"—although, *pari passu,* true paradigm competition can have extremely healthy consequences for the ultimate advancement of science (cf. Kuhn, 1962). Rothstein, however, sees paradigm competition as fostering an "overvaluation" of paradigms and notes that "in the process of such overvaluation the related contributions of others are consciously ignored or deemphasized" (p. 424). Less *ad hominem,* and more appositely, Rothstein argues that "a second disadvantage of unnecessary paradigm competition is that the theoretician often creates new terms without defining their advantage over or relationship to the terms they are intended to replace" (p. 425).

This is off the main point of this essay which is that we are not dealing with a new paradigm at all, but rather with a substantial addition to our clinical insights into psychoanalytic phenomena and into the nature of the psychoanalytic process. These new insights have to do

with the play of narcissistic or selfobject transferences and the countertransferences they evoke. I believe that this most impressive clinical
contribution can be incorporated into the main body of classical psychoanalysis without the need for either new or separate theory. Only
time will tell whether Kohut's particular theoretical accents, such as
his concept of the structure of the bipolar self, will prove to be useful
as *additions* to our classical conceptualizations of the mental apparatus.[5]

I shall begin the thread of my own main argument by picking up
some surprisingly little-noted internal inconsistencies within the formulations by Kohut and others of the new psychology of the self. To
start with, let us look at some condensed statements by Ornstein (1980).
Ornstein quotes Kohut's own claim that psychoanalysis will come
closer to being a general psychology if it "expands its border and
places the classical findings and explanations within the *supraordinate*
framework of a psychology of the self" (Kohut, 1977, p. 230, italics
added). Further on, however, Ornstein notes that Kohut "put self
psychology side by side with ego psychology in a *complementary*
relationship and demonstrated that the new paradigm of self psychology
can *encompass* certain aspects of mental health and illness that could
not be adequately accounted for within the previous paradigm" (p.
157, italics added). At issue here is the reversal of the older (classical)
hypotheses of the primacy of the drives, and the defenses that come
to be erected against them, as organizers of the psychic functioning
and the psychic apparatus. In other words, self psychology denies that
the drives, in interaction with the environment and with experience
(and, since Hartmann, with the maturational unfolding of inborn ego
apparatuses), are the primary developers of the maturing coherent ego
and/or self. Instead, self psychology hypothesizes the opposite view:

---

[5] I am puzzled in trying to follow Kohut's way of using the phrase and concept,
"mental apparatus." A typical quotation, this one from the case write-up of the two
analyses of Mr. Z. (Kohut, 1979a, p. 65), is the following: "I have referred to a
concept that belongs to the armamentarium of classical metapsychology wherein the
human psyche is seen as a mental apparatus." Kohut is referring by this to the usual
formulations of id, ego, and superego—as if the conceptualization of two poles within
the self and a tension arc between, around which transferences, object precipitates,
and mental representations cluster, is not in itself a species (Kohut's species) of mental
apparatus psychology.

the primacy of the organizing, cohering self organization, with drive expressions seen as the breakdown products of the vulnerable self under fragmenting pressures. This formulation of the self as a *supraordinate* constellation, with the classical drives and defenses subsumed as its constituents, is precisely what Ornstein and others properly point to as the revolutionary effort at metapsychological reformulation that is the essence of the psychology of the self in the *broader sense*.

Given this perspective, on the all-encompassing nature of self psychology, then in what sense is the word "complementary" being used, for example, in Ornstein's remarks quoted earlier, or in Kohut's own statement that a comprehensive "depth-psychological explanation of psychological phenomena in health and disease requires two *complementary* approaches: that of a conflict psychology and that of a psychology of the self" (1977, p. 78, italics added). In their discussions, Kohut and Ornstein make clear that they use this word in the sense derived from the physicist Niels Bohr's conceptualization of different perspectives, each having primary explanatory power in relation to some (but not other) mental phenomena.

For example, Ornstein and Ornstein (1980) claim:

> Structural change through conflict resolution is of greater significance and at the center of the resolution of the transference neurosis, with structure building as a not insignificant, but silent accompaniment of the analysis. Structure building through "transmuting internalization"—the filling in of structural deficits—is of greater significance and at the center of the resolution of the selfobject transferences, with structural change as a silent accompaniment of the analysis" [p. 206].

Here the dichotomy imposed by the complementarity of the approach is between structural *change* and structure-*building*. In Kohut's second book (1977), it evolves theoretically into the counterposed psychologies of Tragic Man—the struggle with the issues of primary cohesion and integrity of the self—and Guilty Man—the struggle of psychic instances in conflict within a sufficiently consolidated self. And in Kohut's (1979b) major clinical description from the perspective of self psychology, he counterposes the two analyses of the same patient. In the first period of analysis, the central clinical focus is on the oedipal conflicts, with the narcissistic entitlement demands seen only as regressive defenses against oedipal anxieties, to be interpretively confronted. In the second period of analysis, however, the central conceptualization entails the same narcissistic imperatives, seen now as analytically valuable replicas of childhood conditions being revived in the analysis, to be analytically nurtured.

The inconsistency here is the simultaneous, vigorous thrust within self psychology in two incompatible directions. Conceptually central to the first direction is the broad view of self psychology as the putatively more *encompassing* framework, which will improve our explanatory and therapeutic power in relation to the narcissistic personality disorders (upon whose treatment its claims were first built). It will presumably also enable us to reconceptualize profitably many if not most of our heretofore central classical metapsychological formulations (such as the nature and position of the Oedipus complex in human mental development). Moreover, as an extension of this claim, proponents of self psychology raise as an issue for open-minded empiric scrutiny that the treatment of classical neurotic conflict as it evolves within the transference neurosis in classical psychoanalysis can also be enhanced in range and effectiveness when considered within the more encompassing self-psychological framework. The other and incompatible thrust is toward complementarity, meaning separateness and dichotomization. This is exemplified in the first analysis of Mr. Z. in the older, "classical" way, with its only partial result, followed by the second analysis of Mr. Z. in the newer, self-psychological way with its declaredly much more complete result. Following this thrust, Ornstein (1980) can ask, "Do these . . . observations, therefore, not suggest that an integration of conflict psychology within the new paradigm of self psychology is the logical next step in psychoanalysis? The answer to this question is a decisive no" (p. 145, n. 4). Rather than an integration, which should not be forced, Ornstein opts for "Leaving them unintegrated—and maintaining thereby the duality of 'Guilty Man' and 'Tragic Man' " since "the complementary [i.e., separate] use of conflict psychology and self psychology is closer to the available clinical data" (p. 145, n. 4).

And here is where I feel that the theorists of self psychology have created unnecessary inconsistency and a specious dilemma. In opposition to the dichotomization that devolves from the framework of complementarity is the position that I undertook to develop in my own discussion paper at the New York panel (1981) that, most simply put, we are not dealing with an "either/or" situation but rather with a "both/and." Let us grant that Kohut's central clinical contribution may well be in seeing so many aspects of the psychopathology of pregenital development, not as regressive defenses against the emergence of oedipal transferences *alone,* but also as recreations of deficient and impoverished childhood constellations within mirroring and idealizing selfobject transferences. Granted all this, it is the qualifying word "alone," that is to me the crux of this particular issue. For in the flow and flux of analytic clinical material we are always in the world of "both/and." We deal constantly, and in turn, both with the oedipal, where there is a coherent self, and the preoedipal, where there may not yet be; with defensive regressions and with developmental arrests; with defensive transferences and defensive resistances and with recreations of earlier traumatic and traumatized states.

Of course, all this is not new. It is simply the application once again of the psychoanalytic principle of overdetermination, and in Waelder's (1930) terms, of multiple function. This central point has been made in several of the critiques of self psychology offered to this juncture (Jacobson, 1978; Rothstein, 1980; Treurniet, 1980; and Segel, 1981).

Segel (1981) decries Kohut's setting up of the self as a "separate kingdom" as opposed to "the constant interrelatedness developmentally of a sense of self-identity and of object constancy, even while being cognizant of the rapprochement crisis of the separation-individuation state" (p. 470). Rather than opposing two psychologies—a psychology of the self, where empathy prevails, and a psychology of drive and structure, where conflict prevails and where interpretation of transference and resistance is the vehicle—Segel underlines that these realms of self and structure, of preoedipal and oedipal, are continuous with one another. In his opinion, psychic phenomena need to be looked at not in terms of one framework or the other—of defect in self or conflict, preoedipal or oedipal, developmental arrest or defensive regression—but from both (and all) perspectives at the same

time, to see what each contributes at the particular time. This is an
enlargement, through the addition of the self-psychological perspective, of our familiar metapsychological way of thinking simultaneously
from multiple vantage points and multiple perspectives. With clinical
references, Segel points out that, after all, narcissistic reactions and
phenomena may well represent regressive resistances to oedipal conflicts, especially in developmental histories where an overstimulated
child has been unbearably painfully deflated by traumatic primal scene
experiences. Regressive attempts to solve the resulting anxieties may
well take the form of compensating grandiose, exhibitionistic wishes
or intense narcissistic rage. Jacobson (1978), in his thoughtful discussion of Segel's paper, makes the additional useful point that in such
situations Kohut's dichotomizing either/or approach puts an undue
strain on our capacity for differential diagnosis by forcing us to designate the narcissistic expression either as a reflection of a developmental arrest or as a defensive regression—each requiring its exclusive
technical handling. By contrast, Segel's both/and approach has the
technical advantage of allowing the analyst to respond to a patient's
themes and conflicts as they become apparent, without being forced
to make a final commitment to a particular view (and a particular
technical approach) before the data have crystallized in a fully convincing way. I would add that using multiple and shifting vantage
points to direct the analyzing instrument as the clinical material shift-
ingly surfaces and resonates with our empathic and introspective capacities can allow the harmonious reconciliation of the many solid
clinical advances offered by the framework of self psychology with
the already established clinical wisdoms of classical analytic psychology.

Treurniet had exactly this in mind when, in the course of his very
similar critique of Kohut's work he states: "I would be the last person
to deny a creative scientist his right to temporary one-sidedness. It is
understandable that self-psychology needed a temporary discontinuity
with the existing matrix of psychoanalytic theory in order to safeguard
its process of individuation. Too early demands for integration are
phase-inappropriate. . . . But the reality of rapprochement is inevitable
also for a scientific theory" (1980, p. 327). This same issue, which
Segel calls the setting up of the self as a "separate kingdom" and

Treurniet calls self psychology's need for a "temporary discontinuity" has also been explicitly stated by Hanly (1982). He said: "The problem with the psychology of the self as a theoretical orientation for therapy is that it *disconnects* the treatment of narcissistic conflicts from the concurrent and sequential treatment of object libidinal conflicts" (pp. 40–41, italics added).

This discussion—of separateness versus relatedness, of distinct psychologies, each with its separate domain of transcendent explanatory power and therapeutic applicability, as opposed to conceptualizations of the continuity of and the explanatory and therapeutic trafficking between phenomena from both the earlier and the later childhood developmental phases—leads directly to what I consider the heart of the challenge posed by self psychology to classical psychoanalytic metapsychology. This has to do with the posited distinction between self psychology as a theory of psychological formation born not out of conflict but out of states of psychological defect or deficiency, and classical psychoanalysis, which prototypically has been a psychology of conflict.

Let us put aside for the moment the major thrust of the work of Hartmann (1964) and his colleagues (Hartmann, Kris, and Loewenstein, 1964) as well as of Rapaport (1944) in the development of modern-day ego psychology, in trying to make psychoanalysis a truly general psychology that embraces all the phenomena of mental functioning, normal as well as abnormal, and that elaborates as part of that, the concepts of the conflict-free sphere of ego functioning. Putting these theoretical conceptualizations aside, we can say that psychoanalysis has, in its clinical and therapeutic activity, never ceased to base its endeavor centrally on the mobilization and resolution of conflict. In Ernst Kris's (1947) famous aphoristic definition, its subject matter is defined as nothing but "human behavior viewed as conflict" (p. 6). Brenner (1979) gives a more current and more detailed statement of the same basic, and quintessentially psychoanalytic, theme:

> The goal of psychoanalysis is to alter conflict. . . . Both the normal and the pathological arise from psychic conflicts that originate in the same childhood instinctual wishes. . . . All that we enjoy and prize in mental life—all that we rightly call nor-

mal—is as closely related to the same or similar conflicts originating in childhood instinctual wishes as is what we call
pathological. The normal and neurotic are different in degree but
not in kind. The practical difference to the person involved is
immense. The relation to conflict and the dynamics and origin
of the conflict to which they are related are identical [pp.
562–563].

Whether or not one accepts Brenner's narrowly "traditional" way of
formulating the nature of psychic conflict, or his insistence that all
mental development and mental life can be conceptualized as derived
from conflict formulated in that way,[6] his words do underline a broad
consensus among practicing psychoanalysts about the centrality of
conflict as a (or as *the*) explanatory principle governing psychopathology and its psychoanalytic treatment.

By contrast, Ornstein in an explanatory letter properly pointed to

what makes *The Restoration* more revolutionary or more explicitly
revolutionary than *The Analysis of the Self* was. This is because
The Restoration introduces the new paradigm of the bipolar self
that is *not* born out of conflict. Psychoanalysis has been a conflict
psychology par excellence, as derived from the neuroses and
neurotic character disorders. That has not changed. We will have
to maintain it, side by side, with a self psychology, born out of
our new understanding of primary self-pathology, based not on
conflict but on psychological defect or deficiency (the basic fault,
as Balint [1968] called it). The empirical question then is whether
concepts and theories of self pathology, first and foremost among
them the concept of selfobject and the selfobject transferences,
offer us a better therapeutic handle for the treatment of non-neu-
rotic conditions or not [1979, personal communication].

I summarized this juxtaposition of psychological perspective—and
consequent therapeutic intervention strategies—in my discussion paper
in New York (1981):

---

[6] I shall indicate shortly the basis for another, broader, way of formulating the
nature of conflict.

Kohut and his followers propound as their major clinical insight that, in contradistinction to the neurotic problems that stem from the intrapsychic conflicts of the developmentally more structured and integrated personalities, where attention to the opposition of drive and defense, i.e. to *conflict*, and to the attendant regressive neurotic transference or transference neurosis is the key to resolution and cure, with the narcissistic problems of those with unintegrated selves vulnerable to fragmenting pressures under stress, it is attention to the unfolding of selfobject (or narcissistic) transferences that stem from earlier and more archaic (more undifferentiated) experiences of failure of maternal (or parental) empathy, i.e., experiences of emotional *deficit,* that becomes the central key to analytic amelioration—and *restoration* [pp. 382–383].

This led me to propose a series of questions: "How much this altered clinical emphasis for the treatment of the narcissistic characters is that vital, how much it is so preponderantly or one-sidedly vital, how much it is that fundamentally new, and incidentally how much this is truly a distinction between focus on conflict and focus on deficit are all matters of sharply divided opinion among us" (p. 383).

This brings me to the very crux of my argument—the usefulness of this distinction between deficit and conflict, which I regard as the very centerpiece of the claim of self psychology to being a different psychology, alongside of, complementary to, but not (or not yet anyway) to be integrated with so-called "classical" psychoanalytic metapsychology (which is avowedly centered on conflict). At the same time, it should be noted again, the self psychology theorists also confusingly claim the one framework to be supraordinate to the other, able to encompass and subsume it.[7] But first I must elaborate what I mean

---

[7] I will not enter here into the closely related theoretical controversy concerning the nature of the pathology in the schizophrenic disorder—whether it is to be conceptualized by a deficit or conflict model. For a good discussion of the pros and cons of this argument, see Gunderson (1974). For myself, I would only point here to the parallel considerations in my development of a broadened conceptualization of the nature and meaning of conflict and the resolution thereby of this central dilemma created by self psychology theory. These same considerations will, *pari passu,* be equally appropriate and applicable to the understanding of the schizophrenic disorder and its treatment.

by the concept of conflict, since my definition differs from what is inherent in Brenner's interpretation.

I shall take as my point of departure the formulations advanced by Sandler (1974, 1976) in a recent statement of what is to me a modern and broadened psychoanalytic conceptualization of the nature of conflict. Basically, his thesis is that what is essential to conflict is what can be called the "unconscious peremptory urge" (1974, p. 53). Such urges are neither to be confined to nor equated with the id, the instincts, or the drives; nor are they to be limited to conflict with superego standards or the sense of reality alone. True, there is such intersystemic conflict (between established and consolidated psychic instances), but there is also intrasystemic conflict between, for example, different instinctual tendencies (heterosexuality and homosexuality, activity and passivity, love and hate, etc.) or between conflicted ego impulses.

Anna Freud (1965) has described three main types of conflict: between child and environment, between ego and superego, and between drives and affects of opposite quality. More broadly, Sandler goes back to the logical development of Sigmund Freud's (1894) original statement of the individual's need to defend against any incompatible idea. He then brings within this orbit our by now familiar ideas about "defenses against defenses" (1974, p. 60) and "conflict over previous solutions to conflict" (p. 57)—in fact, every situation in which there is any opposition between any kind of peremptory urge and any impulse to delay, involving any aspect of psychic functioning in any form. He specifically rejects "the equation of the idea of 'peremptoriness' with drive impulses in one form or another in the structural theory . . . [as but] a legacy of earlier phases of psychoanalysis" (p. 58). Instead, he favors the statement: "Peremptory impulses are not always the manifestations of instinctual wishes alone, but may arise as a consequence of stimuli from any part of the mental apparatus or from the outside world" (p. 60). In his 1976 paper, Sandler sums this up simply: "We can regard all conflict as being a conflict of *wishes of one sort or another*" (p. 61, italics added). This general postulate can then be circled back to an earlier quotation and viewed specifically in its relevance to the perspectives of self psychology. In his 1974 paper, Sandler stipulates that the concept of conflict "includes as well compelling urges of a different, non-instinctual character, as for example the automatic and impelling unconscious tendency for an adult to use a childhood defensive manoeuvre in particular circumstances, or the automatic and imperative ego response of anger or rage in circumstances of externally aroused frustration" (p. 53).

Also relevant here is the new emphasis, spurred by child psychoanalysis and by psychoanalytic child developmental psychology (Mahler, Pine, and Bergman, 1975) on the developmental point of view as a major metapsychological psychoanalytic perspective. Settlage, in a historical overview of what he calls "Psychoanalytic Developmental Thinking" (1980), cites the variety of innate, environmental, and experiential forces propelling the developmental progression. He then states that "throughout the developmental progression, at each stage the same generic issues are confronted—namely, new intrinsic phase-specific biological changes and developmental tasks; new extrinsic demands for adaptation with related interpersonal *conflicts*; new intrapsychic *conflicts*; and reactivated past intrapsychic *conflicts*" (p. 151, italics added). Just this kind of thinking underlies Dorpat's (1976) excellent discussion of the same issue in his article, "Structural Conflict and Object Relations Conflict." He defines structural conflict as conflict between the psychic instances in the developed, structurally differentiated personality (the established tripartite structure), whereas he defines object relations conflict as conflict "between the subject's wishes and the ideals, injunctions, and prohibitions that are not experienced as his own, but rather as represented in primary- or secondary-process representations of some (usually parental) authority" (p. 856). Dorpat gives examples of the kinds of conflicts that are not structural but are rather "object relations conflicts," as these reflect the unresolved issues of differing oedipal and preoedipal developmental phases.

Given such a conceptualization of the nature of conflict, how can we view the self-declared revolutionary claim of self psychology in the broad sense that it is a psychology and yields a therapy that is born not of experience of conflict but rather of deficit? In my earlier presentation (1981) I described the insistence on this distinction as "puzzling and to me fundamentally unhelpful" (pp. 388–389). Let me elaborate on what I mean by citing the writings of self psychology

theory. I shall start with the excellent summary paper by Kohut and
Wolf (1978), which they call an "outline" of the disorders of the self.
The authors state in summary form that the firm and consolidated self
develops, out of optimal interplay with the selfobjects, into three major
constituents:

> (1) one pole from which emanate the basic strivings for power
> and success; (2) another pole that harbors the basic idealized goals;
> and (3) an intermediate area of basic talents and skills that are
> activated by the tension-arc that establishes itself between am-
> bitions and ideals. Faulty interaction between the child and his
> selfobjects results in a damaged self—either a diffusely damaged
> self or a self that is seriously damaged in one or the other of its
> constituents [p. 414].

I would underline here that "tension arc" and "faulty interaction" to
me connote, in some fashion, the concept of something out of kilter—
in other words, conflicted.

But let me follow further the argument of Kohut and Wolf. They
go on to talk of the normal developmental process, stating: "The self
arises thus as a result of the interplay between the new-born's innate
equipment and the selective responses of the selfobjects through which
certain potentialities are *encouraged* in their development while others
remain *unencouraged* or are even actively *discouraged*" (p. 416–417,
italics added). In this context the authors refer constantly to optimal
(i.e., minor and nontraumatic) failures in maternal empathic response,
that is, frustration; at the same time, they speak of optimal gratification:
"Such optimal frustrations of the child's need to be mirrored and to
merge into an idealized selfobject, hand in hand with optimal gratifications, generate the appropriate growth-facilitating matrix for the
self" (p. 417). Again, one wonders how all this essentially differs
from the parental response to the play of impulse, of affect and drive
(both libidinal and aggressive), in terms of allowing and thwarting,
of setting the parameters and requirements for accommodation, which
we call, in classical metapsychology, compromise formation and conflict accommodation or amelioration. Isn't this what conflict—using
Sandler's conceptualization of the term—is all about? What then makes

one a psychology to be understood in terms of conflict and not the other?

To pick up again with Kohut and Wolf's description of the psychopathology and symptomatology of the disorders of the self, they state:

> If it was the grandiose-exhibitionistic pole of a person's self that had been exposed to unempathic overstimulation in childhood, then no healthy glow of enjoyment can be obtained by him from external success. On the contrary, since these people are subject to being flooded by unrealistic, archaic greatness fantasies which produce painful tension and anxiety, they will try to avoid situations in which they could become the center of attention. . . . The creative-productive potential will be diminished because their intense ambitions which had remained tied to unmodified grandiose fantasies will frighten them [p. 419].

The same holds for overstimulation of the pole harboring the ideals. The need for merger with the external ideal will threaten the equilibrium of the self: "Since contact with the idealized selfobject is, therefore, experienced as a danger and must be avoided, the healthy capacity for enthusiasm will be lost" (p. 419). Here we note the use of words like "tension," "anxiety," "avoidance," "frighten," and "danger"—all from the classical vocabulary of conflict and its management. Taking one last statement from this overview article by Kohut and Wolf, I would refer to the authors' description, under the heading of "characterology," of the "mirror-hungry personalities" (p. 421), and the "contact-shunning personalities" (p. 422), among others. They point to the intensity of the psychic needs and to the suppression that stems from the fright and the shame these patients feel—once again the language of conflict.

In even more explicit support of this main point that I am trying to make vis-à-vis self psychology from the position of the paradigm of classical psychoanalysis as a conflict psychology, I shall quote from Ornstein's (1980) paper at the Chicago Conference: "The point is that our usual interpretive focus on the compromise formations made necessary by the unresolved conflicts now has to be extended to a consideration of how such conflicts hamper the expression of ambitions, talents and values as conceptualized from the standpoint of the bipolar self" (p. 151). Moreover, in his final sentence, Ornstein singles out "the introduction of the bipolar self as a supraordinate constellation and especially . . . the differentiation of *primary, defensive,* and *compensatory* structures within it" (p. 157-158, italics added). Here again, should one not see this as a statement of conflict, and of conflict compromise and resolution, within the "structure" of the self? Similarly, should not the poles of ambitions and values and ideals, with a tension arc between them of skills and talents, also be read as a structured delineation within which conflict is necessarily of the essence?

What emerges from this review of the propositions of self psychology from the point of view of conflict? Others, such as Treurniet (1980a) and Segel (1981), focus on the same point in their critiques of self psychology. I have already drawn attention to some of the specifics of Segel's position in discussing the issue of exclusivity and a "separate kingdom" versus relatedness and continuity within the framework of multiple vantage points and overdetermination. Treurniet clearly states his position that "conflicts and deficits are not necessarily antithetical. What self-psychologists call 'deficit' is not a real deficit (in Anna Freud's sense of an irreversibly lost function) but a reversible phenomenon originated in insufficient help to overcome the *conflicts* experienced by the preoedipal child. . . . Restoration phenomena of the Self can also be viewed as a defensive solution of unbearable depressive affects" (personal communication, 1979).

I hope that I have by now sufficiently elaborated two main points in the discussion of this fundamental issue of conflict versus deficit. The first is the need to counterpose a broadened construction of what is meant—or should be meant—by the concept of conflict in psychoanalysis against the self psychologists' overly narrow reading, which has unhappily set the stage for the unfortunate division (and divisiveness) between the notions of conflict and deficit. A corollary to this point is the obligation to conceptualize the terms of the conflict at each developmental level within the array (or lack) of disparate or opposed needs and fulfillments that are crystallized and expressed at that particular developmental stage (in sequence of increasing "structuralization," however we conceptualize the structures). My second major point is that conceptualizing conflict in this way renders unnecessary dichotomizing and opposing (with all that flows from it) of the realms of deficit as against the realms of conflict.

A fuller statement of my position on this centrally important issue, is found in my earlier paper (1981):

> I . . . see the life course or the life cycle as one of the successive facing and the adequate resolution—or not—of a sequence of phase-specific developmental tasks (conceptualized incidentally along each and any of the posited developmental lines), in each phase and in each instance, a task created by the unique conjunction of the innate maturational developmental unfolding of capacities and readinesses, together with the phase-linked normative societal expectations within that culture at that historic moment, and added to by the happenstance and timing of more or less traumatic and adventitious life experience. Seen this way the task (or *a* main task) of the earliest developmental phase in accord with the tenets of self-psychology is the development of a coherent and consolidated self-organization as an ultimately emerging "independent center of initiative" (Kohut's words) and the task in the later psychoanalytic treatment of disorders of the self that come out of the failures of this stage is that of completing an arrested or derailed development of such an integrated self, firming up and consolidating its cohesiveness and/or restoring its vitality. *Pari passu,* the task (or also *a* main task) of the oedipal developmental phase is . . . the appropriate and ego-syntonic mastery of the inevitable vicissitudes of triangular (and by extension, of all multilateral and mutual) human relationships within the context of the innate human propensities for ambivalence. And of course the task in the later psychoanalytic treatment of the structured neurotic disorders that come out of the failures of this oedipal stage is that of the resolution of the attendant intrapsychic conflicts that represent the structural embedding within the psychic agencies of the earlier pathological or nonhealthy oedipal resolutions.

At both levels, that of the earlier arena of primary development of the self and that of the later structuring of the personality under the impact of the emergence and resolution of the Oedipus complex, severe anxieties and other attendant dysphorias can arise that must be coped with to the best of the ability of the immature ego, or self, of that stage, given the resources, defenses and coping mechanisms available to it within, as well as the empathic supports and material and psychological nutriments available to it without. This coping will then have a more or less healthy *vis-à-vis* a more or less pathological outcome in specific character formation or deformation. I do not really see how it is therefore any more or any less a matter of developmental task or dilemma, of attendant anxiety and of its management, in short of psychic conflict, and its more or less healthy or pathological resolution, in either case" [p. 389–390].[8]

At this point, I want to turn to a related and equally vital issue stemming from the unnecessary confusion introduced by the overly narrow (and also, I think, quite idiosyncratic) conceptualization of conflict within the literature of self psychology. This is a concomitant, serious confounding of the distinction between conflict and pathology—conflict being the universal fundament of the human condition, and pathology being its centrally untoward outcome. Kohut (1977) and his followers may be correct in their assertion that the *pathology* of the oedipal phase, which results in the various disorders known to us from classical psychopathology, may not be as basic and as ubiquitous

---

[8] After preparing this manuscript, I became aware of Modell's paper, "Self Psychology is a Psychology of Conflict" (1981). After showing the real linkages of self psychology's conceptualizations to the contributions of Fairbairn, Melanie Klein, and Winnicott, as well as to his own, Modell makes the same central point that I do: The constructs of self psychology (like those of the other authors cited) are embedded in conceptions of *conflict* to the same extent, not more and not less, as are the constructs of classical psychoanalytic metapsychology. The effort to distinguish self psychology, as a psychology of states of deficit, from classical psychoanalysis, as a psychology of states of conflict, is consequently spurious and divisive. Modell elaborates from both a clinical and theoretical perspective his view of the role of anxiety, defense, and conflict in the developmental issues of central concern to self psychology. He also clarifies the role of unconscious guilt, not only in the transference neuroses (which Kohut designated the specific arena of Guilty Man), but also with the narcissistic disorders or disorders of the self (the arena of the so-called Tragic Man, where Kohut has tried to rule out guilt as a significant operative mechanism).

in human psychic functioning as many of us have thought. Indeed, to a considerable, and perhaps heretofore somewhat unappreciated extent, it may be a consequence of or rest on the kinds of earlier developmental failures to which the self psychologists have so convincingly drawn our attention.

To see the extreme lengths to which this viewpoint has been taken, let me turn to Ornstein's (1980) paper from the Chicago Conference just because of its precise focus on "Self Psychology and the Concept of Health." Ornstein describes the contribution of self psychology as a "decisive shift of emphasis away from a preoccupation with the pathological and toward a focus on the potentially healthy or more adaptive aspects of the personality" (p. 137). Quoting Kohut's (1966) own words, Ornstein cites Kohut's intention from the first to correct "a widespread 'negatively toned evaluation' of narcissism" and to focus on "the contributions of narcissism to 'health, adaptation and achievement' " (p. 138). In this regard, Ornstein speaks of fulfilling "the intrinsic patterns for creative expression laid down in the structure of the bipolar self" (p. 143). Turning to Kohut's formulation (1977, p. 63), Ornstein stresses the functional freedom of the healthily developed or the rehabilitated self " 'in which ambitions, skills and ideals form an unbroken continuum that permit joyful creative activity' " (p. 144). He then extends all this to Kohut's "reassessment of the form and content of the Oedipus complex" the evolution in normal (adequately empathically enveloped) development of a joyful Oedipus complex as a maturational achievement marked by "the essentially healthy and adaptive aspects of the oedipal period" (p. 147).

However, Ornstein further extends his argument to where the confounding of conflict and pathology becomes clear. He goes on to say that in classical theory "the positive qualities acquired by the psychic apparatus during the oedipal period were seen as the *result* of the oedipal experience and not as a *primary intrinsic aspect of the experience itself* (Kohut, 1977, p. 229). The contrast between the two theories is evident" (p. 147). That is, classical theory "could only conceive of health and the capacity for adaptation emerging out of pathology, i.e., out of the resolution of infantile oedipal conflicts. In self psychology, conversely, the potential for health and adaptation is seen as present *a priori* in any given empathic self-selfobject relationship'' (p. 148). Here the ''straw-man'' argument has been made explicit. It is infantile conflict, *not* infantile neurosis or pathology, that classical theory calls universal and ubiquitous. Health, then, clearly grows out of effective mastery of conflict; it does not arise of necessity out of the bedrock of pathology and neurosis—the perspective these theorists of self psychology attribute to classical theory and the imputed error from which they feel they rescue psychoanalysis.

And again, in explicitly capping this argument Ornstein puts forth a view of well-contained oedipal strivings as positive, enriching experiences that are not in and of themselves pathological. This exemplifies exactly the point that self psychologists miss completely. It is not that the ''oedipal strivings'' are pathological but that they are conflicted that is vital to their classical understanding and to the evolved psychoanalytic theory of development. Ornstein continues: ''Only when the nuclear self cannot maintain its firmness or cohesiveness will these oedipal strivings appear in isolated, intensified form as breakdown products expressing the underlying self pathology'' (pp. 148–149). This finally leads Ornstein to state: ''In this connection it should be stressed that it is quite likely that the customary view of the infantile Oedipus complex as highly conflict-laden and ubiquitously pathological [again, conflict-laden is automatically equated with pathological] is an artifact of erroneous reconstructions from the transference neurosis'' (p. 149).

At this extreme our classical formulations of the Oedipus complex as the universal psychological nodal point of the human developmental drama are indeed recast as the happenstance of traumatic and particular psychopathological outcomes or as the ''artifacts'' created out of ''erroneous reconstructions'' again from the pathological outcomes of the adult neurotics in our consulting rooms. This view unacceptably shades Freud's fundamental insight into the basic nature of oedipal *conflict* as an inevitable and central part of the vicissitudes of normal human development. By this I mean, of course, the central teaching of psychoanalysis that an integral component of healthy development is the appropriate mastery, within the Oedipal phase, of all the inevitable conflicts in triangular human relationships within the context of the innate human propensities for ambivalence. This achievement, of course, is constantly reworked throughout the successive stages of the life cycle. That such oedipal *conflict* (not necessarily its pathological manifestation or pathological outcome) retains a central and ubiquitous role in proper psychic development—even if the particular outcome be, in Kohut's words, joyful and creative—is exactly what gets lost in these recent writings on self psychology. This is perhaps an inevitable or at least a logical outcome of the unfortunate way self psychology has narrowly defined conflict itself as distinct from deficit, assigning each to its separate and specific arena of development and of psychic formation and deformation. I would prefer, within my own more encompassing conceptualization of conflict, to say that just as the Oedipus complex (and its normal or abnormal resolution) has its joyous, growth-enhancing, and not always or only conflict-based perspectives, so too the pathology of the self has its conflicted and conflict-based sides. This goes back one again to how one defines and understands conflict. And it is precisely in this dichotomization within self psychology—between the pathology of the transference neuroses that resides in conflict as opposed to the pathology of the narcissistic disorders that resides not in conflict but in something different, called deficit—that the ultimate disservice that self psychology theory poses to the clarity of our psychoanalytic thinking lies.

This very point is also the main critical thrust of Schwartz's (1978) review of Kohut's second book. He observes: "Kohut wonders if the classically described oedipus complex may be understood as the child's reactions to the parents' failure to enjoy and participate empathically in the child's growth. . . . The implication here is that castration anxiety and penis envy, related classically to conflicts concerning phallic narcissism, are imposed from outside, rather than being the consequences of the human being's constitutional heritage interacting with his or her human environment" (p. 440). In this reading, castration anxiety has become not a core human anxiety to be mastered but a neurotic creation imposed from the outside by trauma and environmental failure (ultimately, failure of empathy).

There is a logical corollary to self psychology's effort to reconceptualize the Oedipal drama as not necessarily pathological (i.e., conflicted, as they confound these terms), and therefore not necessarily problematic or "traumatic" as a developmental task. This is the curious concomitant deemphasis on the role of "gross events" or trauma in psychic development. Segel (1981) was among the first to remark on this as a point of theoretic concern:

It is also difficult for me to believe with Kohut (1977, p. 187) that "psychoanalysis will move away from its preoccupation with the gross events in the child's early life" towards the pre-eminence "of the child's needs to be mirrored and to find a target for his idealization." The difficulty stems from the inclusion as "gross events" of such things as births, illnesses, and deaths of siblings, the illnesses and deaths of parents, the breakups of families, the child's prolonged separations from significant adults, his severe and prolonged illnesses, observations of parental intercourse or sexual overstimulation [p. 470].

In their overview paper, Kohut and Wolf (1978) again make this same point central:

Psychoanalytic case histories tend to emphasize certain dramatic events—from the child's witnessing the "primal scene" to the loss of a parent in childhood. But we have come to incline to the opinion that such traumatic events may be no more than clues that point to the truly pathogenic factors, the unwholesome atmosphere to which the child was exposed during the years when his self was established. Taken by themselves, in other words, these events leave fewer serious disturbances in their wake than the chronic ambience created by the deep-rooted attitudes of the self objects, since even the still vulnerable self, in the process of formation, can cope with serious traumata if it is embedded in a healthily supportive milieu [p. 417].

What is troubling in all of this is the one-sidedness, the not so subtle devaluation of the conceptual importance of the kinds of life circumstances that we have, on the basis of cumulative clinical experience over time, come to consider developmental organizing foci. Once again, this view manifests an either/or quality, counterposing "grossly traumatic events" against "unwholesome atmosphere" and "chronic ambience." Of course, classical psychoanalysis itself has had its historical difficulties with its conceptualizations of "psychic trauma" and the role of the traumatic event (experiential vicissitude) in shaping the developmental process. There is no need to review Freud's own major reconceptualizations, so fateful for the development of both psychoanalytic theory and practice. We might simply recall the reformulation to which he was driven of the stories of childhood sexual excitement and trauma recounted by his adult patients. He came to see these tales not as memories of actual childhood sexual seduction but as recaptured childhood sexual fantasies powered by the evolving oedipal libidinal and aggressive drives—i.e., not as fact but as drive-triggered fantasy. This reformulation, of course, placed the drives and their vicissitudes properly at the center of the psychoanalytic under-standing of psychic development. It also, concomitantly, repositioned the role of reality (of circumstance and happenstance) as a determi-native force in development, reality assuming an uncomfortably less-ened, but never completely clarified, status. In recent years, however, psychoanalytic literature has, sadly, accumulated on the longstanding, profoundly deleterious psychic consequences experienced by the sur-vivors of the holocaust (carrying over even to successive generations); we also now have literature on the psychic residues of other events, less overwhelming to the human spirit only by comparison with the horrors of concentration camps, like that on survivors of nuclear dis-aster (Lifton, 1967), or destruction of communities by natural disaster (K. Erikson, 1976), or kidnapping and taking of hostages (Terr, 1979). Only with this accumulation of evidence from such extreme situations are we beginning to reassess the important and often enduring psychic impact of trauma, even if it occurs after the most vulnerable and formative childhood years and even in those whose earliest years have been embedded (in Kohut's terms) in the most "healthily supportive [empathic] milieu." In this sense, I find Kohut's downgrading of the importance in psychic development of what he calls trauma or the traumatic event (and he mostly means quite regular and commonplace life events, not extreme situations) to fly in the face of the current struggles in psychoanalytic conceptualizing to redress imbalances that have already gone too far in that downplaying direction. Nor does it help, from the point of view of increasing the conceptual clarity in this murky terrain that self psychology uses the same concept—trauma—to cover everything from the extremes of externally imposed events, even of the kinds just alluded to, to the excitements of drive-powered sexual overstimulation in the primal scene experience. Presumably, all of these are to be (comparably?) deemphasized in favor of ambience and milieu.

And yet, paradoxically, Kohut and self psychology can simultaneously be charged with overvaluing the importance of the external event (external trauma?) for the healthy unfolding of the self. They maintain an insistent, deep, and one-sided emphasis on the role of maternal empathy (which is what they basically mean by ambience and milieu) in the proper fulfillment of the developmental potential. There are many aspects to this issue of empathy. Certainly, we can agree on the powerful corrective emphasis that Kohut has given to *empathy* and *introspection* as central vehicles of the psychoanalytic endeavor. This view was initiated and signaled by his 1959 essay on that subject, which Ornstein properly declares to be "the first nodal point" (1978, p. 27) in the evolution of self psychology theory. And, of course, an emphasis on the role of empathy and introspection in the psychoanalytic undertaking is the counterpart of the emphasis on the role of maternal (parental) empathy in the promotion of a healthy developmental unrolling (the consolidation of a cohesive self). Certainly, this emphasis on empathy and introspection as vehicles of the analytic work stands as a corrective contrast to the widespread view rendered most articulately by Gill's (1954) widely influential article from the same period, in which he defines psychoanalysis in terms of the unfolding "of a regressive transference neurosis and the ultimate resolution of this neurosis by techniques of interpretation [leading to insight] *alone*" (p. 775, italics added).

However, Kohut's emphasis on empathy and introspection as vital components of the unfolding psychoanalytic process is neither that new nor that unique to self psychology theory. A number of converging psychoanalytic strands arose at the same time which emphasized the closely related issue of the nature and quality of the psychoanalytic relationship as a major factor in the mutative analytic process. These ranged from Alexander and French's (1946) strong but misguided[9]

---

[9] Misguided in the sense of distorting the essential nature of the psychoanalytic interaction in the ostensible service of facilitating it.

emphasis on the importance of the "corrective emotional experience," to Zetzel's (1956) elaboration of the concept of the therapeutic alliance, and Greenson's (1967) elaboration of the closely related concept of the working alliance as elements vital to the matrix within which a successful psychoanalytic resolution then becomes possible. In addition, Loewald's (1960) incisive and most influential article "On the Therapeutic Action of Psychoanalysis" conceptualized the empathically crafted "integrative experience" (p. 24) as a condition or explanation of change in psychoanalysis that is of at least equal importance as the process of interpretation leading to insight. All these constructs focus on relationship-oriented elements of analytic process and analytic change, as distinguished from the time-honored role of interpretation leading to insight. These constructs are not that different from the distinction that Ornstein (1981) draws when, for example, he describes Kohut's analytic work with Mr. Z. in the first analysis as being predominantly in the inferential (interpretive, insight-aiming) mode and his work in the second period of analysis as being predominantly in the empathic (relationship-centered) mode.

True, many analysts feel that Kohut has gone overboard in this one-sided emphasis, unnecessarily downgrading the at least equally vital role of interpretation and insight. This has been central to the criticisms of Treurniet (1980, 1983) and Kernberg (1979) among others. Treurniet (1983), stated this concern strongly: "By attempting to replace the concepts of transference and resistance with selfobject relations and empathic failure the equilibrium between what has been done to the child and what he does with what has been done to him has shifted nearly completely to the first part of the equation. This overvaluation of the person of the analyst and of the external event is technically very dangerous. The patient is deprived of his autonomy, as he is deprived of his drives" (p. 87).

Kernberg (1979) puts this equally forcefully: "The misinterpretation and overgeneralization of these findings imply that, for patients in regression, it is the therapist's empathic presence—rather than his interpretation—that is really helpful; that it is the patient's identification with this mothering function—rather than his coming to terms with his intrapsychic conflicts—that is important" (p. 231). "On the contrary," he continues, "an empathic and concerned attitude on the part of the analyst is a necessary precondition in all cases of psychoanalysis. And, as mentioned before, at levels of severe regression, the analyst has to be empathic not only with the patient's central subjective experience at any particular point, but also with what the patient cannot tolerate in himself and has to dissociate or project. Empathy is a prerequisite for interpretive work, not its replacement" (p. 232). Even Loewald, whose thrust in relation to analytic theory and technique seems in many ways sympathetic to that of Kohut, stresses this same issue that empathy is not enough and that undue emphasis on it can make for imbalance: "To my mind a not inconsiderable share of the analytic work consists in more or less actively and consistently confronting these freed narcissistic needs and narcissistic transferences with what Kohut calls the mature aspect of the reality ego of the patient. Granted that such confrontations too often are ill-timed or judgmentally tinged, there are also good times for them and a balanced attitude may be maintained" (1973, p. 447).

Overemphasis on one's own contribution is not a major fault, however, and time will no doubt be a corrective for this as it has been for so many fashions and accents within our field. Of more concern to me in the dominant role assigned to empathy and introspection in analysis are a variety of other considerations, I will list in some order of ascending significance. First, empathically derived knowledge can be quite wrong, as Treurniet (1980) says: "Empathy is supposed to bring forth certain experiences which are analogous to those of the other person, but in itself it contains no guarantee as to its own reliability or validity" (p. 328). Jacobson (1978), in his discussion of Segel's paper, makes this point even more dramatically: "While empathic use of our inner selves in psychological therapy has on this score highest value, opening us to the possession of incredibly intimate knowledge of the workings of the mind of another person, it harbors at the same time the potential of opening us to the most grievous errors; errors where while we think we are grasping a fundamental aspect of the patient, we may in fact be grasping a fundamental aspect of ourselves, of some object from our own history, or of a cherished belief" (p. 7). These are, of course, all the well-known risks of wild analysis.

A second, even greater danger in self psychology's elevation of empathy and empathic failure to guiding explanatory concepts in understanding analytic change rests in the implications for technique and for understanding the theory of technique in the analytic work. I am not referring to the concern, expressed by Rothstein (1980) that the emphasis on empathy and on the transmuting internalizations achieved over time within adequately empathic analytic interactions, leads to results that are psychotherapeutic, rather than psychoanalytic, even akin to the Alexandrian "corrective emotional experience" (an attribution of similarity unfairly leveled at Kohut's work by a number of his critics [see also, Stein, 1979]). Rather, I mean the more serious issue raised by Segel (1981) of a not so subtle shifting of the responsibility (and the blame) for therapeutic difficulty unfairly (i.e., one-sidedly) onto the interfering countertransferences of the analyst. At least, this *can* be one consequence of holding analytic progression to be dependent on a near perfect analytic empathy, and of seeing analytic setback as characteristically reflective of analytic empathic failure.

Segel (1981) put it thusly: "No interpretations are made of aggressive outbursts or libidinal acting out of a variety of perverse, sadistic, auto-erotic, or homosexual behavior except to understand what empathic failure by the therapist produced them. They are always seen as 'disintegration products' (Kohut, 1977, p. 77) rather than primary drive manifestations whose unconscious contents must be explored" (p. 467). He goes on to comment: "In fact, we might even be tempted to raise the question of whether the pendulum may now have reversed itself partially so that instead of punishing our patients, some self-flagellation is even subtly evident. I am referring to the widespread use of terms like 'empathic failures' of the therapist even where the demands of the patient, verbal and non-verbal, seem impossibly excessive, even when directed towards experienced therapists" (p. 469). In summarizing this point, Segel quotes Kohut's remark that our unavoidable failures of empathy should not produce *undue* guilt in us, a terminology that Segel finds pejorative and unfairly critical. "It is striking to me that while removing the demeaning label from the narcissistic patient, Kohut seems to have shifted it on to the parents and the therapists" (p. 469).

To point out the third (and potentially greatest) danger in Kohut's overemphasis on empathy, I will shift my focus from the implications for analytic technique to the wider implications for analytic theory.

This shifts the ground of concern from the conceptualization of the role of analytic empathy in psychoanalysis to the role of maternal empathy in psychic development—back to what I called the curiously paradoxical overvaluation of the external event for the healthy development of the self. This issue is central to the critical review by Stein (1979) of Kohut's second book: "The impact of Kohut's work is, paradoxically, far more literally deterministic than that of Freud, since it tends to ascribe an extremely complex set of disturbances and developments to what is essentially a single etiological factor: defects of maternal empathy" (p. 673). Stein makes this same point again, albeit too sharply, further on in the review: "It is regrettable that we find ourselves once again presented with an apparently easy solution for the extraordinarily complex problems of the origin of psychopathology: defects in maternal (or parental) empathy" (p. 677). The point is vital. The danger lies in the reductionistic theoretical oversimplification to which psychological explanation is all too readily prone; and part of the overdetermined complexity of psychoanalytic explanation is to guard against this. In fact, such an explanation is all too reminiscent of another explanatory framework once popular in our theorizing but now more properly incorporated within a wider explanatory net—the overly simple conception of the schizophrenogenic mother.[10]

I shall turn now to the statements of the proponents of self psychology itself, to illuminate what I feel to be the most fundamental issue for our conception of what psychoanalysis is all about, which self psychology theorists raise under the guise of considering the role of empathy in analysis. This to me is a matter of their essential re-

[10] As a sidelight to this discussion of the dominant role ascribed by Kohut to empathy and introspection as the fundamental vehicles of both psychoanalytic understanding and psychoanalytic process, it is curious that self psychology never seems to raise the question of the proper limitations of empathy, those that (conceptually) are there, and those that (technically) should be there. Treurniet (1983), has raised this as follows: "It is here that I find myself in the most fundamental, most basic opposition to Kohut's work. . . . A very important technical principle [is] that real empathy is only possible by sharp recognition of its limitations. I have stated elsewhere (Treurniet, 1980) that patients with gross traumatization often demand recognition by stating that the therapist can never really understand what they have been through. The only realistic and empathic answer is of course that this is true, recognizing the limits of one's capacity for empathy and thereby granting the patient the uniqueness of his experiencing self" (p. 87).

defining analysis, or at least its determining parameters. Although requiring considerable amplification and qualification, Freud's well-known and simple statement that whatever deals with the phenomena of transference and resistance can properly call itself psychoanalysis has nonetheless withstood the test of analytic usage over time. Kohut's evolving views on the nature and the role of empathy in psychoanalysis have led him to ask us to reconsider this fundamental conceptualization of the essence of psychoanalysis. In the epilogue to his second book, Kohut (1977) asks: "What Is the Essence of Psychoanalysis?" (pp. 298–312). He answers consistently and single-mindedly: "Psychoanalysis is a psychology of complex mental states which, with the aid of the persevering *empathic-introspective* immersion of the observer into the inner life of man, gathers its data in order to explain them" (p. 302, italics added). He goes on to specify that "the essence of psychoanalysis . . . [is] the fact that its subject matter is that aspect of the world that is defined by the *introspective stance* of the observer" (p. 303, italics added). Even more explicitly, he states "Empathy is not a tool in the sense in which the patient's reclining position, the use of free associations, the employment of the structural model, or of the concepts of drive and defense are tools. Empathy does indeed in essence *define* the field of our observations" (p. 306, italics added).

That this definition (redefinition) may indeed lead us ultimately to discard Freud's definition of the essence of psychoanalysis is a potential that Kohut himself admits: "I am not able to imagine how analysis could *at this time* do away with the two concepts—transference and resistance—that are the experience-distant distillate of [intra-analytic, interactive] activities. I would still insist that some future generation of psychoanalysts might discover psychological areas that require a novel conceptual approach—areas where even in the therapeutic realm these two now universally applicable concepts have become irrelevant" (p. 308). Ornstein, then, is certainly within bounds when in his own paper on the "Central Position of Empathy in Psychoanalysis" (1979) he claims: "When Kohut explicitly proposed introspection and empathy as the *key* observational tools of psychoanalysts in 1959, he also delineated the field itself, its content and subject matter, as that which is actually or potentially encompassed through introspection and empathy" (p. 100). The truly idiosyncratic as well as radical nature of this definitional transformation of psychoanalysis has been made most explicit in Schwaber's (1979) recent article. She redefines empathy itself in specifically self-psychological terms: "The object's inability, for whatever reason, to serve as the needed self-object supplying the missing structure or function, is experienced as a 'failure' in empathy. Empathy is here implicitly understood as the provision of a *self-object use*" (p. 469, italics added). And, even more explicitly, she stipulates "It is such a listening perspective that is considered to be the intrinsic aspect of what is meant by empathy. Empathy is herein viewed as an introspective awareness arising within the context of a *self-object phenomenon*" (p. 477, italics added).[11]

By this point, both psychoanalysis and empathy have been re-defined, equated, and made into self psychology theory. It is perhaps fair to say, then, that the issue is not just empathic failure as an explanatory tool for difficulties in technique in work with narcissistic (and other) patients, but, much more comprehensively, that *empathy* is made the central explanatory key to understanding the essence of our subject matter. Moreover, this central role given to empathy is as much a fundamental building block in the development of self psychology as a theory as is the more widely focused on and appreciated concern with the phenomena of narcissism. In line with this, let me circle back to the statement from Ornstein (1978, p. 27) quoted earlier that Kohut's (1959) essay on introspection and empathy can be taken as "the first nodal point" in the progressive evolution of self psychology. This paper appeared some seven years before Kohut's "Forms and Transformations of Narcissism" (1966), which Ornstein calls one of the "points of entry into the third period, the new territory of narcissism" (1978, p. 50). These conceptualizations of empathy and

[11] Schwaber, in a personal communication, has called my attention to counterbalancing remarks she makes in a subsequent statement of her views (Schwaber, 1981). She states that empathy is "a specific, scientifically-trained mode of perceiving the data . . . independent of the particular theory upon which the clinician draws" (p. 358); that "although I have found it particularly useful to conceptualize empathy within such a framework [one that draws upon the selfobject concept], this need not imply either a fundamental change in its meaning or that the theory employed will by itself determine the listening stance" (pp. 373–374); and that "empathy is not the domain of any one theoretical view. . . . Arguments between proponents of different theoretical systems do not, by themselves, address the fundamental issue of how the clinical data are being observed" (p. 374).

narcissism have coalesced and expanded into the new psychoanalytic psychology of the self. In the process, psychoanalysis has been potentially seriously altered.

The positioning of empathy in self psychology, as both a central theoretical explanatory construct and a central technical tool also raises a number of related questions about the therapeutic results, which can be considered under a variety of linked headings such as therapist's style and/or personality and/or experience. These questions have arisen most pointedly in several discussions of Kohut's fullest case description, "The Two Analyses of Mr. Z." (1979b).[12] In this paper Kohut lays out, side by side, two periods of his analytic work with the same patient. Each period was about four years in length, with an intervening five-year period of no treatment. The first analysis was conducted by Kohut in terms of his understanding of classical theory and technique. The result achieved seemed satisfactory enough at the time to both Kohut and his analysand, athough some questions about it arose in retrospect. The patient returned after five years with some familiar symptoms that had been reawakened by new life pressures. The second analysis was conducted in terms of the newly evolved understandings of self psychology. The total case report is a side-by-side discussion of the analytic issues in the first analysis, the kinds of understandings reached about them, the limitations that Kohut subsequently discerned in those resolutions, and the new understandings of the very same issues arrived at in the second analysis, with the sense of a far more substantial and enduring analytic result. Needless to say, the patient suffered from severe narcissistic problems.

How is the more thorough analytic cure that was finally achieved to be understood? To Kohut this is clearly an issue of the greater appropriateness to the patient's dominant narcissistic problems of the new theoretical perspectives of self psychology with their derived technical implementation. In my own review of this case material (Wallerstein, 1981, p. 390–392), I compared in some detail Kohut's tandem

---

[12] I myself have participated in two such discussions of this case: a discussion group at the International Psycho-Analytical Association Congress in New York in July 1979, co-chaired by Paul Ornstein and Anna Ornstein, and the panel discussion at the midwinter meeting of the American Psychoanalytic Association in New York in December 1979 (Meyers, 1981).

description of six nodal instances or critical configurations, contrasting his earlier understanding and interpretive endeavor with the later one. Kohut's format is in all cases the same: "In the first analysis, I saw it this way . . ." (basically, as defensive against oedipal pathology) "but in the second analysis, I came to see it this way" (basically, as an analytically valuable reenactment of childhood constellations revived in the selfobject transference). My main point is that Kohut put all this in terms of "either/or"—and, by implication, of "incorrect/correct." To me it seems rather a matter of "both/and"—the application once again of the principle of overdetermination and of multiple function. I believe that *each* of the explanatory perspectives adduced by Kohut in relation to each of the various aspects of the analytic material (as well as probably still other perspectives not mentioned) could play its appropriate role in understanding the total psychological picture and therefore could have its place as part of the total analytic work.[13] Where, at what point, with what emphasis, and how, would then become matters of tact and timing as well as clinical judgment—matters, that is, of the appropriate use of the tools of empathy and introspection that Kohut has been among the foremost in making self-consciously central to our clinical (and also theoretical) undertaking.

Considerations such as these have led different observers to wonder how much the more substantial and more enduring result that eventuated from Mr. Z.'s second analysis was indeed a matter of new and better theory, and how much was a matter of better empathy, guided perhaps to some extent by the enlarged perspectives for understanding that derived from the conceptual additions of self psychology. Some have pointed to issues of style and personality. Was Kohut's style more heavily authoritative in the first analysis, more

---

[13] Neither Kohut's perspective nor my own, incidentally, speaks specifically to the kinds of considerations raised by Erik Erikson in a personal communication concerning this case material and my own discussion of it. From *his* perspective of concern for the life cycle and the life trajectory, he asks: Since one analysis started a decade later than the other, what is the impact on the analytic work and the analytic result in each period of the fact that both the patient and the analyst are in different phases of their own life cycles and also at different points in historic time? In addition, one should consider the fact that the second analysis (no matter how differently conducted) took place with someone who already had experienced the first analysis, and therefore inevitably also built upon it.

benignly empathic in the second? Are the significant differences in approach to the same disorders between Kernberg and Kohut wholly reflections of differing conceptualizations of the primacy of the aggressive drives (the envy and rage directed at the hateful parental imagoes)? Or are they to some or perhaps an equal extent due to the difference between a precisely confrontative mode and an empathically soothing one? This question is reminiscent of another, similar controversy close to half a century ago. In "A Controversy about Technique," Herold (1939) convincingly related Wilhelm Reich's and Theodor Reik's diametrically different conceptualizations of the psychoanalytic interactive and mutative process to the differences in personality and working style of the two men.

We may, then, legitimately ask: How much of what Kohut takes issue with in the clinical work of others (or, as in the case of Mr. Z., in his own earlier work) is truly a matter of differing and altered conceptualizations, and how much is a quarrel with faulty (i.e., unempathic) technique? Let me quote two points from the overview paper by Kohut and Wolf (1978). First, "If the analyst responds to these [narcissistic] demands by *exhortations* concerning realism and emotional maturity, or, worse still, if he *blamefully interprets* them as the expression of their insatiable oral drive that needs to be tamed or of a primary destructiveness that needs to be neutralized and bound by aggression-curbing psychic structures, then, as we said, the development of the narcissistic transference will be blocked" (p. 423, italics added). This proceeding is then contrasted with the following: "If, however, the therapist can *explain without censure* the protective function of the grandiose fantasies and the social isolation and thus demonstrate that he is in tune with the patient's disintegration anxiety and shame concerning his precariously established self, then he will not interfere with the spontaneously arising transference mobilization of the old narcissistic needs" (p. 424, italics added).

Clearly, many will see this not as an opposition between interpretation, declared to be misplaced or inappropriate, and the (more proper) empathic acceptance of unfolding transference positions. Rather, it may be seen as an opposition between bad technique—exhortation, and blameful interpretation—and appropriate technique—explanation without censure. Again, one might then ask why a dichotomy, or rather a straw man, is being set up between "blamefully interpreting" the libidinal and aggressive drives (clearly not okay) and "explaining without censure" the narcissistic needs (clearly okay)? Can we not, rather, all agree that Kohut is placing an appropriate emphasis on the proper empathic posture in relation to all drives and all needs, an emphasis that we all share, albeit that he has indeed made all of us more mindful of it? In this same sense, then, perhaps the advocates of self psychology can in turn agree with the unifying view of "both/and," of overdetermination and multiple function, that I have been offering from within the perspective of the classical analytic position. As Rangell (1981) puts it: "The 'Two Analyses of Mr. Z.' reported by Kohut (1979) should have comprised one total classical analysis" (p. 133).

This emphasis on "one total classical analysis" brings me back to my central theme in this review of the contribution of self psychology to the theory and technique of psychoanalysis. I am stressing the wholeness of psychoanalysis within its one (Freudian) paradigm and the need to deal with its phenomena—complex mental states—from an overdetermined perspective and from multiple (metapsychological) points of view, according to the unifying language and thought conventions of "both/and," rather than the splitting and dichotomizing thrusts of "either/or."

On the other hand, those who, like Kohut, are truly significant contributors to the advance of psychoanalysis, or, for that matter, to the advance of any science, often frame their additions in ways that highlight and indeed overemphasize the new, while deemphasizing the clear links to the already established—at the expense of the overall balance of the whole. The reasons for this can be articulated several ways. In his *Introductory Lectures on Psychoanalysis* (1916–17) Freud puts it most simply, in human terms: "In scientific matters, people are very fond of selecting one portion of the truth, putting it in place of the whole, and of then disputing the rest, which is no less true, in favor of this one position" (p. 346). Schafer in a recent article dealing with "the construction of multiple histories" (1979), describes it from the perspective of the current philosophy of science: "Any question or any perspective implies a selective organization of the data specific to it; like an intellectual system, it enforces a figure-ground organization of the data. Thus it is that an individual analysis produces not one history but a set of more or less coordinated accounts of life history. And thus it is that different analytic approaches based on different assumptions produce different sets of *self-confirming* life histories'' (p. 15, italics added). From this it follows that "analytic case summaries purport to say what is true of the individual when they should say what is true according to the details of the different investigations that have been carried out. . . . For this reason, Kohut's (1977) data on the vicissitudes of the self are functions of the kind of analytic focus he develops'' (p. 14).

With Freud's admonition and Schafer's reminder clearly in mind, how would I, in overall summary, state my own view of the nature of Kohut's contribution to our science and its fit within the total psychoanalytic corpus? As I indicated earlier, I believe his contribution lies in the *clinical* realm—in offering a much more precise specification and delineation of the narcissistic phenomena than has been heretofore presented, as discerned in the specific narcissistic (or selfobject) mirroring and idealizing transferences that emerge in the psychoanalytic process, as well as in their counterpart, the countertransferences characteristically evoked by them. Kohut himself has described this major contribution in these very terms: "It is possible, from the viewpoint of the psychology of the self in the narrower sense—i.e., from the standpoint of a theory that considers the self as a content of the mental apparatus—to enrich the classical theory by adding a self-psychological dimension'' (1977, p. 227). It is just this salutory impact on our field of the new focus on the psychology and the pathology of the self as revealed in the selfobject transferences and countertransferences of the psychoanalytic situation, that I wish very much to acknowledge as a central dimension of our understanding of human mental functioning.[14]

---

[14] Of all the major writers in this realm, Treurniet comes closest to my own perspective of admiration for the clinical enrichment of our discipline that the contributions of Kohut have brought, while feeling that the proffered theoretical reconceptualizations are for the most part unnecessary and divisive. In his most recent paper, Treurniet (1983), has similarly stated: "If the psychology of the self remains within its original bounds, as a subordinate, auxiliary construct within the matrix of classical metapsychology I can foresee a very stimulating and productive exchange for the benefit of all of us. In this context the impressive contribution of Kohut to classical analysis could be expressed as an expertly refined improvement in the technical management of the impact of the real, i.e., the non-transference and non-resistance aspects of analyst and patient on the analytic process, of the vicissitudes of the idealization of self and object and of the corresponding under- and over-stimulation of the self experience and of the adaptive aspects of these vicissitudes in their mirroring and idealizing functions. . . .'' (p. 96-97).

By the same token, I have yet to be convinced that such enrichment and enlargement in the clinical realm requires a new theory, a new metapsychology—all the ramifications of the psychology of the self in the broader sense, including the theoretical reifications in the conceptions of the bipolar self and the special and separate new psychology of Tragic Man. The controversy generated in this metapsychological theoretical realm has (unnecessarily) tended to obscure somewhat our fullest appreciation of so major a set of additions to our clinical wisdom and our clinical capacities as has been offered to us by Heinz Kohut and his collaborators. And it has thereby forestalled their appropriate integration within the ever-growing mainstream of classical psychoanalysis.

References

Alexander, F., & French, T.M. (1946), *Psychoanalytic Therapy: Principles and Applications*. New York: Ronald Press.

Balint, M. (1968), *The Basic Fault: Therapeutic Aspects of Regression*. London: Tavistock.

Brenner, C. (1979), The components of psychic conflict and its consequences in mental life. *Psychoanal. Quart.*, 48:547–567.

Dorpat, T. (1976), Structural conflict and object relations conflict. *J. Amer. Psychoanal. Assn.*, 24:855–874.

Eissler, K. (1969), Irreverent remarks about the present and the future of psychoanalysis. *Internat. J. Psycho-Anal.*, 50:461–471.

Erikson, K.T. (1976), *Everything in its Path: Destruction of Community in the Buffalo Creek Flood*. New York: Simon & Schuster.

Freud, A. (1965), *Normality and Pathology in Childhood: Assessments of Development*. New York: International Universities Press.

Freud, S. (1894), The neuro-psychoses of defense. *Standard Edition*, 3:41–68. London: Hogarth Press, 1962.

——— (1916–17), Introductory lectures on psychoanalysis, Part 3. *Standard Edition*, 16:243–496. London: Hogarth Press, 1963.

Gill, M.M. (1954), Psychoanalysis and exploratory psychotherapy. *J. Amer. Psychoanal. Assn.*, 2:771–797.

Greenson, R.R. (1967), *The Technique and Practice of Psychoanalysis*, Vol. 1, New York: International Universities Press.

Gunderson, J.G. (1974), The influence of theoretical model of schizophrenia on treatment practice. Report of panel. *J. Amer. Psychoanal. Assn.*, 22:182–199.

Hanly, C. (1982), Narcissism, defense and the positive transference. Presented to San Francisco Psychoanalytic Society, San Francisco, February.
———— & Masson, J. (1976), A critical examination of the new narcissism. *Internat. J. Psycho-Anal.*, 57:49–66.
Hartmann, H. (1964), *Essays on Ego Psychology: Selected Problems in Psychoanalytic Theory.* New York: International Universities Press.
———— Kris, E., & Loewenstein, R.M. (1964), *Papers on Psychoanalytic Psychology* [Psychological Issues, Monogr. 14]. New York: International Universities Press.
Herold, C.M. (1939), A controversy about technique. *Psychoanal. Quart.*, 8:219–243.
Jacobson, J.G. (1978), Discussion of Nathan Segel's paper on Narcissism and adaptation to indignity. *Newsletter, Denver Psychoanal. Soc.*, 5(Fall):5–8.
Kernberg, O.F. (1974), Further contributions to the treatment of narcissistic personalities. *Internat. J. Psycho-Anal.*, 55:215–240.
———— (1978), Contemporary psychoanalytic theories of narcissism. Presented to a symposium at Columbia University College of Physicians and Surgeons Department of Psychiatry and Center for Psychoanalytic Training and Research, New York, October.
———— (1979), Some implications of object relations theory for psychoanalytic technique. *J. Amer. Psychoanal. Assn.*, 27:207–239.
Kohut, H. (1959), Introspection, empathy, and psychoanalysis: An examination of the relationship between mode of observation and theory. In: *The Search for the Self,* ed. P.H. Ornstein. New York: International Universities Press, 1978, pp. 205–232.
———— (1966), Forms and transformations of narcissism. In: *Search for the Self,* ed. P.H. Ornstein. New York: International Universities Press, 1978, pp. 427–460.
———— (1971), *The Analysis of the Self.* New York: International Universities Press.
———— (1977), *The Restoration of the Self.* New York: International Universities Press.
———— (1979), The two analyses of Mr. Z. *Internat. J. Psycho-Anal.*, 60:3–27.
———— (1980), Summarizing reflections. In: *Advances in Self Psychology,* ed. A. Goldberg. New York: International Universities Press, pp. 473–554.
———— & Wolf, E.S. (1978), The disorders of the self and their treatment: An outline. *Internat. J. Psycho-Anal.*, 59:413–425.
Kris, E. (1947), The nature of psychoanalytic propositions and their validation. In: *Selected Papers.* New Haven: Yale University Press, 1975, pp. 3–23.
Kuhn, T.S. (1962), *The Structure of Scientific Revolutions.* Chicago: University of Chicago Press.
Lasch, C. (1978), *The Culture of Narcissism.* New York: Norton.
Lifton, R.J. (1967), *Death in Life: Survivors of Hiroshima.* New York: Random House.
Loewald, H. (1960), On the therapeutic action of psychoanalysis. *Internat. J. Psycho-Anal.*, 41:16–33.
———— (1973), Review of *The Analysis of the Self. Psychoanal. Quart.*, 42:441–451.
Mahler, M.S., Pine, F., & Bergman, A. (1975), *The Psychological Birth of the Human Infant.* New York: Basic Books.
Meyers, S.J. (1981), The Bipolar Self. Report of panel. *J. Amer. Psychoanal. Assn.*, 29:143–159.

Modell, A.H. (1981), Self psychology as a psychology of conflict. Unpublished paper.
Ornstein, P.H. (1978), Introduction. In: *The Search for the Self*, ed. P.H. Ornstein.
New York: International Universities Press, pp. 1–106.
————— (1979), Remarks on the central position of empathy in psychoanalysis. *Assn.
Psychoanal. Med. Bull.*, 18:95–108.
————— (1980), Self Psychology and the concept of health. In: *Advances in Self
Psychology*, ed. A. Goldberg. New York: International Universities Press, pp.
137–159.
————— (1981), The bipolar self in the psychoanalytic treatment process: Clinical-
theoretical considerations. *J. Amer. Psychoanal. Assn.*, 29:353–375.
————— & Ornstein, A. (1980), Formulating interpretations in clinical psychoanalysis.
Internat. J. Psycho-Anal., 61:203–211.
Rangell, L. (1981), From insight to change. *J. Amer. Psychoanal. Assn.*, 29:119–141.
Rapaport, D. (1944), The scientific methodology of psychoanalysis. In: *Collected
Papers*. New York: Basic Books, 1967, pp. 165–220.
Reich, W. (1933), *Character Analysis*. New York: Orgone Institute Press, 1945.
Rothstein, A. (1980), Toward a critique of the psychology of the self. *Psychoanal.
Quart.*, 49:423–455.
Sandler, J. (1974), Psychological conflict and the structural model: Some clinical and
theoretical implications. *Internat. J. Psycho-Anal.*, 55:53–62.
————— (1976), Actualization and object relationships. *J. Phila. Assn. Psychoanal.*,
3:59–70.
Schafer, R. (1979), The appreciative analytic attitude and the construction of multiple
histories. *Psychoanal. Contemp. Thought*, 2:3–24.
Schwaber, E. (1979), On the ''self'' within the matrix of analytic theory—Some
clinical reflections and reconsiderations. *Internat. J. Psycho-Anal.*, 60:467–479.
————— (1981), Empathy: A mode of analytic listening. *Psych. Inquiry*, 1:357–392.
Schwartz, L. (1978), Review of *The Restoration of the Self*. *Psychoanal. Quart.*,
47:436–443.
Segel, N.P. (1981), Narcissism and adaptation to indignity. *Internat. J. Psycho-Anal.*,
62:465–476.
Settlage, C.F. (1980), Psychoanalytic developmental thinking in current and historical
perspective. *Psychoanal. Contemp. Thought*, 3:139–170.
Stein, M.H. (1979), Review of *The Restoration of the Self*. *J. Amer. Psychoanal.
Assn.*, 27:665–680.
Stone, L. (1961), *The Psychoanalytic Situation*. New York: International Universities
Press.
Terr, L.C. (1979), Children of Chowchilla: A study of psychic trauma. *The Psy-
choanalytic Study of Child*, 34:547–623.
Treurniet, N. (1983), On the relation between the concepts of self and ego in Kohut's
psychology of the self. *Internat. J. Psycho-Anal.*, 61:325–333.
————— (1983), Psychoanalysis and self psychology: A metapsychological essay with
a clinical illustration. *J. Amer. Psychoanal. Assoc. 31*:59–100.
Waelder, R. (1930), The Principle of multiple function: Observations on overdetermination. *Psychoanal. Quart.*, 5:45–62.
Wallerstein, R.S. (1981), The bipolar self: Discussion of alternative perspectives. *J.
Amer. Psychoanal. Assn.*, 29:377–394.

Wolf, E.S. (1979), Introduction to panel on the bipolar self. Presented to American Psychoanalytic Association, New York, December.
Zetzel, E.R. (1956), Current concepts of transference. *Internat. J. Psycho-Anal.*, 37:369–376.

Phenomenology of the Self

W. W. MEISSNER

Introduction

Ever since Heinz Hartmann's (1950) clarification of the distinction between the notion of self in psychoanalysis and the concept of the ego, there has been increasing interest in establishing and elaborating a psychology of the self. In the ensuing years, a number of competing points of view have emerged regarding the conceptualization of the self within the context of psychoanalytic theory.

Hartmann pointed to the appropriate oppositional context for the concept of self in relation to the notion of object, in contradistinction to the proper oppositional context for the concept of the ego in reference to the other intrapsychic agencies that compose the mental apparatus. However, Hartmann went no further than designating the notion of self as roughly equivalent to the concept of "person." Jacobson (1964) extended this formulation to include the whole person, including bodily manifestations. It should be noted, however, that in both cases the emphasis was placed on representational aspects. Both Hartmann and Jacobson essentially regarded the self as equivalent to self-representations based on the person as the unit of reference. Spiegel (1959) offered a somewhat more subtle formulation. He envisioned the self as an independent organizing principle—independent, that is, of the other acknowledged psychic agencies, but providing a unifying frame

65

of reference. This frame of reference applies in particular to the organization of perceptual experience, but is not restricted to that context.

Along similar lines and consistent with his notions of primary identity, Lichtenstein (1965) proposed that the self be regarded as "the sum total of all transformations which are *possible* functions of an early-formed invariant correlation of the various basic elements of the mental apparatus" (p. 126). Others have emphasized the structural aspects of the self (Levin, 1969; Saperstein and Gaines, 1973). Saperstein and Gaines (1973) emphasize the substantial characteristics of the self as opposed to its representational qualities, and identify the self as a supraordinate organization. This is synonymous with the sense of self-as-agent and is thus an equivalent formulation to the sense of personal agency that has been consistently criticized in analytic metapsychology (Guntrip, 1969, 1973; Schafer, 1976). I have previously expressed similar views in attempting to deal with conceptualizations of the self (Meissner, 1977).

One certainly cannot ignore the contributions of Heinz Kohut to the psychology of self, but unfortunately Kohut's clinical formulations have not contributed substantially to our theoretical understanding of the self. In his earlier work, Kohut (1971) settles for a descriptive account of the self as a low-level, experience-near abstraction, a sort of content of the mental apparatus. He does not regard the self as a psychic agency, but it nonetheless has structural characteristics. It is more a content than a constituent of the mind, somewhat analogous to object representations. In his more recent work, Kohut (1977) acknowledges the self to be a structure, but asserts that this structure is not knowable in essence, either by any form of observation or introspective experience. Nonetheless, the self allows the data of experience to be organized and related in terms of the subjective experience of the "I."

Basch's (1979) formulation takes this rather noncommittal stance regarding the theoretical status of the self a step further. He describes the self as a "form symbolic abstraction" of the developmental process, or, in other terms, the symbolic transformation of experience into an overall, goal-oriented construct. To this we can add the recent contribution of Gedo (1979), who describes the self organization as the cohesive structuring of goals and values into potentials for action.

In this sense, the "personality as a whole," which is synonymous with the self, "is most fruitfully understood as a hierarchy of potentials for actions, i.e., of both organismic and subjective goals, as modified by a system of values" (pp. 11–12).

In the flux of such theoretical perspectives, a consensus is obviously needed that would allow the formulation of a theoretically integrated concept of the self. This concept must be sufficiently specific to function adequately within the referential scheme of psychoanalytic theory and to be set apart from the more commonsense usage that adheres to the notion of the self. Nonetheless, stealing a leaf from the book of common usage with the prestigious support of Hartmann's formulation, we can suggest that a minimal conceptualization of the self would include the interaction between the self and its objects as a central feature. To this I would add a second important element based on common usage, namely, the connection between the notion of the self and subjectivity. The connection of the self-as-agent with the experientially grasped subject of the first person pronoun is more or less taken for granted. In this sense, the self can be taken as synonymous with the source of personal agency and identified and unified as such in conscious experience. I do not suggest that this commonsense basis for an approach to the concept of self in psychoanalysis will prove to be exhaustive, or that other conceptual aspects will not have greater valence in the psychoanalytic perspective, but at least these components provide a starting point for investigation.

An important aspect of defining the concept of self is the use of specific empirical references. Part of the problem with the diversity of viewpoints on the self is that this effort has been bypassed in favor of the articulation of the self in relation to other theoretical formulations and contexts. A necessarily antecedent step in this process of definition is finding a pretheoretical starting point that allows us to return with greater clarity to the clinical situation, where we can begin to delineate such an explicit experiential reference for the concept of the self.

In the present essay I would like to attempt such a return to a basic phenomenology of the self—that is, to the level of clinical description—in order to sort out the aspects of the self organization as they manifest themselves in concrete clinical terms. Underlying this strategy is the conviction that the psychology of the self is not only theoretically mandatory, but also brings into focus important aspects of the clinical situation and clinical experience that have been inadequately articulated. Thus, a return to the basic phenomenology of the self with a minimum of theoretical commitments can serve not only to focus important aspects of our clinical experience in a more meaningful and productive way, but also offers the basis for a more meaningful development of our theoretical notions regarding the self and its psychology. My specific aim in this undertaking is to describe aspects of the functioning of the self within the psychoanalytic situation—the privileged arena within which we as analysts have access to the relevant data.

Aspects of the Psychoanalytic Situation Related to the Phenomenology of Self

The various aspects of the psychoanalytic situation are so complex and interwoven into the more global tapestry of the analytic experience that it is difficult to single out for observation, description, and analysis one particular element without simultaneously touching most, if not all, of the others. It is possible, however, to focus on particular aspects with the understanding that their discussion must inevitably overlap with the description of the other aspects of the analytic situation with which it is so closely involved. The dimensions I will focus on here are familiar enough, and I will make no pretense at providing an exhaustive catalogue. We will also have to keep in mind that the overlapping and interactive quality of these descriptions is magnified by approaching them with reference to the central and globally inclusive concept of the self.

The first aspect of the psychoanalytic situation that I would like to focus on is the role of affects. There can be little argument that affective expression is one of the core dimensions of the analytic experience. From one point of view, affects may be taken as expressing important dimensions of the subject's relationship with objects. Whether the affect expressed is that of fear, anger, or sadness, the communication of affects is telling us something profoundly meaningful about the quality of the individual's experience of and relationship to specific objects. At the same time, in the very act of affective experience, the subject is telling us something about his experience of himself (Schwaber, 1979). Depressed patients, for example, may in their sadness and grief be expressing something quite meaningful about their relationship to the lost object, but in the same breath they are also expressing something even more profoundly meaningful about the way in which they experience themselves. Embedded in the depressive affective context may be components of a self experience in which the patient feels weak, helpless, dependent, vulnerable, worthless, frightened, and so on. These dimensions of the affective experience of depression are, in a way, direct readouts or transcripts from the inner contexts of self organization that form the basic components of the patient's experience of himself.

These affective components may be caught up in the patient's concern about relationships with specific objects to the extent that the patient is concerned with the ways in which other people experience or react to him, or the sorts of affective experiences that arise in the course of the patient's relationships with others. The analytic ear, however, is always tuned to the inner melody—the subtle harmonics that, in the crescendo of externally directed affective expression, are simultaneously playing a melody of internal reference and self-expression. Needless to say, these affective components play a major role in the analytic situation and contribute to almost all aspects of the analytic experience, including the other areas of the patient's experience in which some aspect of the self and its functioning comes into play.

The patient's resistances and the defensive organization to which they are related are similarly involved in every aspect of the analysis. Resistances are generally considered in the context of conflict and defense. That is to say, the activation of an impulse, usually unconscious, stimulates a defensive response whose purpose is in one way or another to keep the content connected with the impulse out of consciousness. In the classic view, then, the breakthrough of such instinctually laden material is a threat to the stability and functioning of the ego and must be defended against. From another point of view, however, the breakthrough of disruptive material can be seen as in some sense threatening to the organization and experiencing of the self. The defense, therefore, can also be seen as operating in the context of the defense and maintenance of the individual's sense of self. In this context, it may be more accurate to speak of the defense of the self against aspects of the self organization that are poorly integrated or are somehow divergent from the overall context of self functioning and thus pose a threat to it.

In the analytic situation, resistances can be viewed in a somewhat similar fashion. The patient's resistance to the analytic work may represent a fending off of the effort to unveil, discover, bring understanding to, or (in the persistent military metaphor) attack various aspects of the self that need to be kept distant from the individual's functioning sense of self. In some patients, particularly those with a noteworthy degree of narcissistic vulnerability, the need to maintain a certain view, attitude, or way of seeing and feeling about themselves may loom as a more significant and powerful motivating force than the related but somewhat different issue of defending against instinctual derivatives. It is not at all unusual in analytic experience that the self-image, which may lie at the core of such defensive and resistive efforts and which the patient struggles to maintain, may itself be pathological and, indeed, may lie at the heart of the patient's difficulties (Bach, 1977).

In this sense, then, the frame of reference provided by the self offers a motivational context within which the patient's resistances can be understood that is quite distinct from the notion of a defense against unconscious instinctual impulses, but is not unrelated. This understanding can make a difference with certain patients for whom the traditional interpretation may not carry much impact, but for whom the vulnerability they feel and the need to protect that vulnerability loom with considerably greater urgency. The patient who comes chronically late for her analytic hour may be carrying on an anal struggle for control, or she may be dealing with the difficult and recurrent issue of compliance and defiance in relation to important figures in her life who hold some position of authority over her. But in addition to these transparently applicable and relevant dimensions, we can add her vulnerable and threatened sense of herself, which continues to function behind the need to fend off and protect. This vulnerable and defective sense of self, however, is itself pathogenic and lies at the heart of many of the patient's neurotic difficulties, particularly those having to do with depression, dependency, and the need to strive counter-phobically and phallically for achievement. Regardless of the impediments and difficulties to which it gives rise, the patient nonetheless clings to this enfeebled and defective sense of self because it is the only self she has. Her resistance is ultimately an effort to maintain the status quo, which the analytic effort threatens.

The patient's self-image is particularly difficult to focus because it is reflected in practically everything that happens in the psychoanalytic situation. (The use of the term "self-image" in this context is merely a matter of convenience and is not intended to make any theoretical commitment. The term is used here only in the descriptive and phenomenological sense, referring to the way in which the patient feels about, thinks about, and portrays himself.) This is an aspect of what Rapaport (1967) referred to as the "projective hypothesis"—that in all segments of his behavior the patient is expressing some aspect of his inner self-image. In his verbal expressions, in his affective reactions, in his mannerisms and behaviors, in his way of relating to and dealing with the analyst, and in a host of other conceptual, affective, and cognitive behaviors, the patient is expressing some dimension, some aspect, of how he sees himself and feels about himself. The man in his mid-thirties who experiences successful intercourse for the first time is not simply expressing a libidinal drive or achieving a degree of libidinal gratification. He is simultaneously experiencing and expressing a central view, attitude, and set of feelings about himself as masculine. Masculinity, as opposed to biological maleness, is linked to gender identity and is a characteristic of the self (Rochlin, 1980).

Several points can be noted about the image of the self as it is projected within the analytic situation. The first is that the image of himself that the patient generates and maintains is usually quite complex, manifesting a multiplicity of aspects and characteristics that may be quite divergent and that are often poorly integrated into the individual's general psychological functioning and life experience. At different times and in different circumstances within the analysis, the patient will reveal different aspects of the organization of his sense of self. At one time he may present himself as self-assured and confident, at another time as doubtful and hesitant; at one point in the analytic work, he may seem somewhat shy and diffident, while at a later point, he may become peremptory and demanding.

However complex and multifaceted the images of himself that the patient provides, there is usually detectable over time a certain consistent motif or theme that more or less characterizes the core aspects of the patient's sense of himself. A set of qualities or characteristics emerge that often have surprising consistency and coherence. The patient may present a picture of himself as weak, dependent, and in need of care and sustenance, or the patient may see himself as defective and somehow repulsive. Other patients may have a sense of themselves as somehow worthless and devalued, as though nothing they ever did had any intrinsic merit to it, or conversely, that no matter what they did they would never be admired, respected, or valued by the important figures in their environment.

More often than not, the self-image and the sense of self that lies behind it is not readily apparent or available to the subject. Often, only after a significant amount of uncovering do the lineaments of the self-image become more available and begin to shape themselves into a coherent theme. These configurations of the self-image may not in themselves be unitary or consistent. Often patients will discover multiple aspects of themselves that at times seem to be set in divergent or contradictory patterns. The scenario is familiar, for example, in depressed patients, who present themselves as worthless, shameful, and depleted, with little of value or meaning to themselves or to the important others in their lives. One can take these expressions of self-devaluation as eloquent testimony to the pathological sense of self around which their personalities are organized and in terms of which the depression is focused. However, extension of the clinical investigation frequently reveals that behind the sense of depletion and devaluation, there is a more resilient narcissistic core that has embedded in it quite different characteristics of narcissistic entitlement—a sense of specialness and expectations of privilege and special treatment. This core provides a quite different and divergent set of characteristics, which are in opposition to the more consciously available and phenomenologically direct characteristics expressed in the depressive stance. It is not difficult to discern the dynamic and motivational connections between these divergent images, but it is worth noting that both images, in different ways and through different modes of expression, function as components of the individual's experience of how he is and how he functions as a person.

Certain aspects of the phenomenology of the self have been described by Kohut and Wolf (1978), with particular reference to the self-image and the style of self experience. They characterize the *understimulated self* as lacking vitality, feeling boring and apathetic, often seeking exciting stimulation to ward off the pain of inner deadness. The *fragmenting self* becomes disorganized, uncoordinated in various aspects of behavior and functioning, and loses the sense of internal cohesion and integration in the face of narcissistic deprivation. Fragmented states often manifest themselves in hypochondriacal preoccupations. The *overstimulated self* tends to find little satisfaction in external success, and the intense ambition and fantasies of greatness of such individuals tend to inhibit their capacity for creativity or productivity or cause them to draw back from any context in which they become the center of attention. The intensity of the exhibitionistic and grandiose fantasies tends to frighten and inhibit them. The *overburdened self* tends to view the world as hostile and dangerous and feels easily attacked or hypersensitive, even bordering on paranoia.

In addition to this catalogue of subjective states related to the quality of self-image, the same authors describe a variety of self organizations that express themselves in more object-related terms. These tend to follow the forms of narcissistic transference described by Kohut (1971). They describe *mirror-hungry personalities* who strive to evoke attention, recognition, and approval from others in an effort to counter their inner sense of worthlessness and diminished self-esteem. *Ideal-hungry personalities* are constantly on the lookout for others whose power, beauty, prestige, intelligence, or values they can admire. They feel good about themselves only to the extent that they are related to these others. The attachment to the object may sustain these individuals for a time, but the underlying neediness and emptiness in time assert themselves and precipitate a search for new objects. There are also *alter ego–hungry personalities* who need a relationship with another who serves as a twin, and whose conforming appearance, opinion, or values confirms and sustains the reality of the self. The more pathological *merger-hungry personalities* need to attach themselves to an object to such an extent that their own identity fuses with that of the other, and they lose the ability to discriminate their own thoughts and wishes from those of the object. Any independence or separation on the part of the other becomes intolerable. Finally, *contact-shunning personalities* find it necessary to avoid involvement with objects, not because of indifference but because their need for objects is so intense. They are exquisitely sensitive to rejection, but on a deeper level fear engulfment and destruction in the longed for union (Kohut and Wolf, 1978).

For the most part, these descriptions overlap with more generally recognized characteristics of personality types in relation to objects. The contact-shunning personality is recognizable as basically schizoid, for example (Guntrip, 1969, 1973), and the varieties of object-hungry personality have been variously described (for example, by A. Reich, 1953). Although these authors formulated their descriptions in a specific genetic context and with regard to narcissistic dynamics, their sheer phenomenological and descriptive validity suggests that other dynamic and structural issues may be involved. Contact-shunning and overburdened types would hardly seem adequately understood without an appeal to aggressive vicissitudes.

In addition to the variety and modes of expression of the self-image, it also seems safe to say that the self-image is highly affectively toned, particularly to the extent to which it functions in pathological ways, and that the affective coloring of the self-image reflects the categories of instinctual derivatives that analysts have been familiar with over the years. It is not surprising, then, that the primary lineaments of the self-image as they are experienced within the analytic context (and probably in most other contexts of the patient's life) are structured along the lines of instinctual derivatives, particularly those of aggression and narcissism. I suspect that aggression and narcissism have a primary role in determining the quality of self organization precisely insofar as they constitute those instinctual dimensions that play a role in the sphere of the self and its functioning.

Just as the narcissistic components of the self configuration can display themselves both in terms of inferiority or self-devaluation and through hypervaluation, superiority, and grandiosity, the aggressive components also can display themselves in terms of such polar opposite configurations. Thus, the image of the self in patients whose conflicts have to do with the vicissitudes of aggression can express itself in terms of the aggressive characteristics of destructiveness, hostility, powerfulness, evilness, and sadistic maliciousness. However, the opposite configuration may be seen in a sense of weakness, vulnerability, masochistic suffering and submission, and an overall sense of victimization.

Here again, these instinctually derived aspects of the patient's sense of self may function in different modalities within the patient's intrapsychic world. Depressive patients find it more comfortable in some sense to live in terms of their sense of vulnerability, victimization, and narcissistic depletion. However, further clinical investigation often reveals the opposite configuration operating at a different level of conscious awareness and intrapsychic availability. Thus, depressive patients are often found to harbor repressed and well-concealed hostility, aggressive and destructive wishes, wishes for vengeance, and impulses to inflict sadistic, hostile, and demeaning injury upon others. This aspect of the self-image is generally repulsive and undesirable to patients, a dimension of themselves they seek to deny, mask, repress, and otherwise dissociate from their functioning sense of themselves. In large measure, analytic work with such patients can be envisioned as gradually uncovering these hidden dimensions of the self and reworking them to modify their intensity and allow their gradual integration into a more harmonious and effectively functioning sense of self.

One other observation in this regard has considerable clinical relevance. I have never dealt with a patient on any level of intrapsychic organization and functioning in whom all of these polar configurations have not been operative to some degree. I have described these configurations in terms of the primary instinctual derivatives that seem to have reference to the patient's self organization. There may be other dimensions that I have overlooked, but in my experience the forming of the sense of self in terms of the derivatives of narcissism and aggression seem to be clinically adequate. The point I would like to emphasize, however, is that in both narcissism and aggression, both polar configurations play a role in the patient's sense of self in varying degrees and in varying modalities of expression.

In patients functioning at a more characteristically neurotic level, one or the other of the polar configurations may come to predominate, playing the primary role in the organization of these patients' sense of self insofar as it is available through their introspective experience and as it generally manifests itself in their external behavior. However, the opposite polar configuration can be unearthed by psychoanalytic investigation, and, insofar as it forms an essential part of the dynamic configuration that serves as the pathogenic core of the patient's neurosis, it too must be brought to a level of conscious awareness and availability for analytic processing. The sense of self as victim or as victimized does not stand on its own terms. Characteristically, it is organized in defensive terms to counter and maintain in its masked condition the more forthrightly aggressive and destructive aspects of the patient's self. Analysis of only half of this configuration is only half an analysis. One must retrieve, focus, articulate, analyze, and work through both aspects of this dichotomous configuration before the patient is effectively able to resolve the inherent aggressive conflicts and their implications for his intrapsychic life. The same argument holds for the parallel case of narcissism. The patient's sense of inferiority is inevitably matched by the components of grandiosity. The depressive core of the neurotic stance cannot be adequately dealt with or resolved unless both aspects have been thoroughly worked through and brought to some degree of harmonious integration. This aspect of the narcissistic components of the self organization has been well demonstrated in Kohut's Mr. Z. (1979).

As one descends the scale of psychopathology, however, the tendency for the polar configurations to exist with greater degrees of derepression and to play a more available and concurrent role in the psychic organization and functioning is also characteristic. This state of affairs has been consistently described by Kernberg and others (Kernberg, 1976; Nadelson, 1976) in terms of dissociated ego states, which may vacillate back and forth, for example, between a sense of victimization and aggressive destructiveness, or between a sense of depressive inferiority and pathological grandiosity; or they may operate simultaneously in the patient's sense of self and in the organization of the patient's inner world.

One of the important parts of the analytic work is the recovery of memories derived from various strata of the patient's developmental experience, particularly memories that may be repressed from earlier oedipal or preoedipal childhood strata. However, even in these early memories, the effects of the self-image as an integrating and organizing principle can be detected. Within certain limits, material of this kind can be examined through more than one frame of reference. The original position of psychoanalysis, largely influenced by Freud's early view of the recovery of traumatic memories, was that such revivified memory segments could be taken as veridical data representing the replication of the child's reality-based early experience.

However, as knowledge of memory functions became more sophisticated, it became clear that these accounts could not be given such straightforward credence. Such memories had to be regarded as in large measure selected, reorganized, and redefined in terms of the ongoing current of the subject's needs and interests. Freud's key realization in the abandonment of his seduction hypothesis was that such reminiscences could not be assumed to represent veridical accounts of real traumatic memories, but might reflect the fantasied productions of underlying libidinal impulses. Thus, the retrieved memory, even when recaptured from under the cloak of repression, can be taken only partly as a recounting of realistically remembered events; the other aspect is that the account given is in some measure a creation or a recreation on the part of the subject to serve certain needs and concerns in the patient's current life situation. An important organizing and motivating principle of this remembering is the patient's sense of himself and the self-image to which the patient is committed. Thus, the memory script is recast and rewritten to provide material that is consistent with and reinforces a certain view that the patient maintains of himself. The analyst may find in the content of the retrieved memory direct expression of aspects of the patient's self-image or indirect dramatic presentations that embody aspects of the self-image. Similar expressions are found in dreams, but dream material often expresses aspects of the patient's self that may otherwise be more solidly defended against or unconscious. Dream material, therefore, can often be a valuable resource in analytic work for uncovering aspects of the patient's self that would otherwise remain masked.

From a more commonsense perspective, one of the important dimensions of the functioning of the self is its continuous definition and expression in commerce with objects. The particular object relationships that assume major significance in expressing the functioning and characteristics of the patient's self are those of the greatest emotional importance to the patient. Thus, the accounts patients provide of their dealings and interactions with parents, siblings, and other family members, are of extreme importance not only for what they tell us about the interpersonal contacts in the patients' life experience as reflected in the personalities and behaviors of those around them, but also for the important information they provide about the patients' functioning self as expressed in the interactions and reactions to these important others. The context of such object relationships is not limited to the family, however, but may include other significant figures such as boyfriends or girlfriends, teachers, students, bosses, fellow workers—anyone with whom the patient has an emotionally significant and ongoing involvement.

The more intense and meaningful these relationships are, the more effectively they represent aspects of the patient's self-image. Consider, for example, the obsessional patient, who describes feelings of resentment, outrage, and anger when her boss makes decisions that affect her without seeking her advice and counsel, creating situations that impose on her sense of privacy and control over her environment. This patient is not only telling us a great deal about the manner in which she deals with such a figure in her life and the quality of her relationship with him, but also is expressing in a fairly direct manner important aspects of her own character structure and her experience of herself in action. It is worth noting that in discussing the interaction between the self and its objects, no new data are introduced beyond those that would be considered using an object-relations perspective. However, instead of focusing attention on the self's extrinsic frame of reference—that is, the frame of reference provided by the external objects—attention is focused in the opposite direction, namely, on the frame of reference provided by the patient's subjective sense and experience of himself in the process interacting with these same external objects. This difference in emphasis and perspective brings into focus different components of the same situation. We must remember that object relations have a dual perspective, one looking outward toward the objects, the second looking inward toward the self (Meissner, 1979).

If the dialectic of self and other has its place in the course of ordinary object relations, this interaction plays itself out with special intensity in the analytic process. We have grown accustomed to discussing the various aspects of this complex interaction in terms of the therapeutic alliance or the interplay of transference and countertransference. These components of the analytic interaction have been subject to various emphases and often quite divergent understandings (Gutheil and Havens, 1979). While factors related to the therapeutic alliance have been variously described and to various degrees either differentiated from or confused with aspects of transference, they nonetheless delineate a different dimension of the analytic experience than those typically ascribed to transference dimensions. The important point for the present discussion is that, both in terms of the alliance factors and transferential interactions, the therapeutic object relationship involves and expresses important dimensions of the sense of self and self organization of both patient and analyst.

What is to be noted here is that the descriptive aspects of both alliance and transference cannot be attributed exclusively to one of the psychic agencies (id, ego, and superego), as has so often been attempted. While the concepts of alliance and transference attempt to delineate different aspects of the complex experience of the analytic interaction, they both involve multiple and complex dimensions of the individual's functioning personality. We may address ourselves to some differential distribution or balancing of various aspects of the patient's functioning in relation to either alliance or transference, in the sense that the components contributed by the recognizable psychic agencies are quite different; nonetheless, they undergo a complex integration within the experience of the relationship that does not allow any one of these factors to be excluded. In other words, both alliance and transference are forms of experienced relationship to an object that involve specific forms of experiencing oneself in that relationship. Consequently, both the alliance and the transference are forms of engagements of the self with the other, viewed reciprocally from the perspectives of the patient and the analyst.

For purposes of the present discussion, we can regard the alliance aspect of the patient's participation in the analytic process as reflecting the more reality-oriented, reasonable, and realistic aspect of the patient's functioning, which allows the patient to engage with the analyst in a collaborative and productive process, a shared voyage of exploration and discovery of meaning and selfhood. This aspect of the patient's self organization expresses itself in the capacities for trust, autonomy and initiative and in the ability to set meaningful goals and undertake to achieve them. Implicit in these aspects of the patient's functioning is a constant dialectic and interaction with the analyst in which the respective selves of both are caught up in a process of constant interchange and mutual self-expression and self-definition. In other words, the individual's sense and experience of himself in this relationship are not only an expression of forces, capacities, and characteristics latent within himself, but are also shaped and modified by the ongoing quality of the interaction itself.

It is readily apparent that the same kinds of interactional issues also arise in the context of the transference. Nonetheless, the quality of the interaction and the kinds of issues it reflects can be markedly different than those implicit in the aspects of the alliance. As analysts have learned and continue to learn, the transference involvement between analyst and patient call up and revivify in often dramatic and forceful terms the more infantile, conflicted, and instinctually burdened aspects of the individual's personality functioning. Whether the transference involvement expresses aspects of the individual's erotic investment; whether it expresses the dynamics of the aggressive polarities of sadism and masochism, power and vulnerability, or aggressive destructiveness and powerless victimization; or whether it expresses the vicissitudes of narcissistic grandiosity, entitlement, specialness and idealization or their dialectical negatives, each of these components of the transference communication reflects vital aspects of the individual's sense of self, both as experienced and as operating.

Analytic experience suggests that one can emphasize the distinction between those aspects of the self that are experienced by the subject and those that operate beyond the realm of immediate experience. Often the transference interaction brings to a head certain dimensions of the individual's functioning personality that have been operating in subtle—or often not so subtle—ways, but have not been experienced as such by the individual. One of the contributions that the analytic process makes is to deepen and broaden the awareness of such aspects of the self that often may have remained hidden, or latent in the individual's behavior, but have not been available for conscious acknowledgment or processing.

It is important to note that the dimensions of the transference can express themselves in unique ways insofar as they reflect dimensions of the patient's self organization. It is crucial that the elements of the transference interaction be focused in the context of their relationship to the patient's inner world and its integration as a part of his functioning personality. I am here structuring my approach to classical displacement transference (Meissner, 1981a) in terms of the history of the patient's relationship to significant objects. For example, the somewhat obsessional patient who sees me as a rule-making, standard-setting, critical, and judgmental figure to whom she must respond with compliance and an attempt to placate and please is undoubtedly expressing the residues of her experience with her rather stern, demanding, and critically judgmental father. We can understand this phenomenon as displacement from the earlier object representation to the new context of the analytic relationship.

Traditionally, the focus of the analysis within this transference context is on the displacement; that is, the basis for interpretation is that the object representation reflects certain genetic vicissitudes and plays a distorting role in the analytic experience. Nonetheless, the way the patient organizes this set of experiences and its reproduction in the analytic situation expresses something about the patient's functioning self and her own sense of self. In this particular case, an important reflection of the patient's self was her sense of powerlessness, which put her in the position of constantly having to strive for perfection to prove her worth to a number of father figures in her life, including the analyst himself. Thus, while the transference in this instance may reflect issues of oedipal conflict and castration fears on an instinctual basis, a further dimension concerned with the patient's sense of self is implicated in these motifs.

The development of the transference can also take place in projective terms, however, and aspects of the displacement transference and the projective transference may be expressed differentially or may be intermingled in a variety of ways. Projective transference, refers specifically to the patient's projection onto the analyst of some quality or set of qualities that derive demonstrably from the patient's own self organization. I believe this aspect of the transference phenomenon may be involved in all forms of transference to a limited degree, but it is typical when the full intensity of the transference neurosis has developed and is expressed (Meissner, 1981a).

More often than not, the elements of projective transference are displayed in terms of the polar aspects of the self-image that has already been discussed. Thus, the young man who in the analytic relationship sees me as a powerful, threatening, and potentially destructive object and in his transferential relation to me feels himself to be weak, vulnerable, fragile, and easily defeated or hurt is, in fact, projecting onto me a segment of the polar configuration that characterizes his own self organization. In other areas of his experience, he plays out the role of the powerful one who can direct and influence others and force them to comply to his wishes. He is capable of becoming imperious and demanding in a variety of his relationships, particularly in his relationship to women, whom he wishes to see as weaker and more vulnerable than himself. Moreover, his fantasy life and dreams are replete with images of power and destructiveness, particularly images of forcing women to submit to a variety of perverse and humiliating acts in complete subjection to his irresistible will. Such fantasies of domination and subjection express the opposite part of his self organization that is hidden and, in fact, denied in his interaction with the analyst but is nonetheless projected onto the figure of the analyst. The interaction provides an unequivocal reading of this aspect of the patient's self organization as it plays itself out in a relationship to a significant object.

This projective transference experience also comes into play in the often subtle interactions that arise in the context of the transference-countertransference. Needless to say, the elements of the countertransference in the analyst can arise as a product of the analyst's own inner dynamics, more or less independent of the patient's activity (Chediak, 1979); but they can also arise from the dynamics of the interaction between the analyst and the patient as a result of projective elicitation of countertransference reaction. In other words, the patient's projection in the interaction can elicit a response in the analyst that at once confirms and reinforces the projection. For example, the patient may project the aspects of power and critical judgment onto the analyst while adopting the position of vulnerable submission and compliance. The projective process may interact with aspects of the analyst's own personality to induce the analyst to respond in a way that plays into the patient's need to feel weak, powerless, and victimized. The patient just described did, in fact, introduce this form of projective distortion, and this could easily have elicited the corresponding reaction, which would have constituted a form of countertransference on my part.

Such transference-countertransference interactions in normally well-functioning and neurotically structured personalities tend to be extremely subtle. They often either pass unnoticed or, when they reach the threshold of awareness, can be dealt with by the analyst's own inner reflective processing and monitoring of his manner of interacting with the patient. However, in more primitively organized personalities, the tendency for projective transferential distortion is much stronger and the potential for eliciting such countertransference reactions is proportionately greater and more problematic (Meissner, 1982). To take a historical example, it is more than likely that Freud's unconscious victimizing of Dora by his use of interpretations was expressing something that Dora had, in fact, elicited, but that had escaped Freud's awareness. This would have set the stage for Dora to turn the tables on Freud, making him her victim (Meissner, in press). One can think, therefore, that Freud and Dora played out this drama of victimization to the ultimate detriment of Dora's treatment. But from the point of view of our present concern, the dialectic of interaction that arose was, in fact, expressing vital components of the operative selves of both Freud and Dora as they entered into this interaction. On both sides of the interaction, the dynamic interplay between self and object was being expressed, bringing into play aspects of the self organization of each participant that neither had any sense of.

In both its alliance and transferential aspects, the analytic interaction is essentially a process of reciprocal influence and responsiveness between the respective self organizations of both patient and analyst. The analyst's self and sense of self are utilized not only as an important organ of perception in the ongoing interaction with the patient, but also constitute a vital component within the analytic field of action. That field is defined by the interaction of the participating selves. We must constantly remind ourselves that the analytic relationship is not only influenced by input from the patient, but is also shaped and modified by the input from the analyst. Moreover, the influences from the side of the analyst are cast in both alliance and transference terms. The analyst's self, then, is not only a receptive and perceptive organ in the process of listening and responding to his patient, but is also a transmitting organ that enters into and determines the flow and the quality of analytic material. Thus, the analyst's self is a determining force in modifying the course of the analytic process itself. Conceptualizing aspects of the psychoanalytic situation as a dialectic between the selves of patient and analyst in this reciprocal manner enlarges our understanding of the forces that shape the outcome of any analysis and bring about the conditions of change and growth in the patient.

Extending this point of view, anything that shapes or helps to constitute the organization of the personality and thus becomes a functioning part of the self can have a role in the analytic experience. As one of the descriptive aspects of the self organization that is rarely considered in the analytic situation, values must nevertheless be seen as playing a highly influential role. "Values" is used here in a loose sense to denote those beliefs, attitudes, interests, standards, or norms that the individual sets up as criteria for determining voluntary behavior and that therefore constitute some of the most important and influential dimensions of an individual's personality organization.

For the patient, values undoubtedly reflect a variety of important dynamic and genetic derivatives and thus form an important subject for analytic inquiry and processing. Values enter into the patient's analytic experience in a bewildering variety of ways and are expressed in all sorts of behavior, attitudes, beliefs, and so on. They are expressed in the details of how patients choose to lead their life, and values affect nearly all aspects of patients' experience. Values determine how they live and with whom, how they work and play, even how they pray. Within the analytic work itself, values are constantly expressed, not only as implicit conditions for patients' behavior and attitudes, but often explicitly in relation to the analysis and the analyst. In all these instances, patients are telling us something of vital importance about the way the self is put together and how it functions. Moreover, they are telling us in these value-impregnated contexts what about themselves they deem most important and value most.

There has long been a myth in psychoanalysis that the analyst operates in a value-free modality. Hartmann (1960) was acutely aware of the importance of moral values, as he called them, not only in the organization and functioning of the personality, but also in their role in the analytic process. Nonetheless, he emphasized the role of values primarily from the point of view of the patient and the patient's participation in the analytic effort. On the side of the analyst, however, Hartmann was unwilling to go much beyond an endorsement of what he called "health values"—the analyst's commitment to standards of healthy and adaptive psychological functioning. Anything beyond this was seen as an undesirable contamination of the analytic situation akin to countertransference. As already noted, however, the perspective of a self psychology makes it clear that values of all kinds, moral values included, play an extremely important role. Consequently, while values and related ethical systems cannot be taken to encompass the whole of the individual's self or personality organization, they nonetheless play an extremely important part in the organization and direction of the individual's life experience and the functioning of his personality. They thus must be regarded as central factors in the organization of the self and deserve a place in the psychoanalytic account of the self.

Phenomenology of Self in the Clinical Context

It will be useful to consider specific analytic material in order to focus some of these considerations. For this purpose, I will use an hour taken from the detailed account of the psychoanalytic process provided by Dewald (1972). My purpose here is solely to articulate in an empirical and descriptive way the manner in which aspects of the self are expressed in the analytic material and thus come to play a part in the analytic process. My concern here is not with any theoretical or conceptual issues, or for that matter with questions of how refocusing of the analytic material in terms of the self might influence our understanding of the patient or our clinical interventions. While the use of such transcripts precludes a variety of data pertinent to our interests in the psychology of the self that could only be obtained in the actual analytic situation, enough pertinent material may still be contained in the verbal record to allow us to gain a better focus on the phenomenology of the self.

The patient is a 26-year-old married woman with two children, whose primary complaints were a mixture of anxiety symptoms and depression, at times amounting to an acute panic and a fear of death. Her symptoms began in connection with her pregnancies. Diagnostically, she seems to present a variety of hysterical and perhaps borderline features. The quotations are from Dewald's published case material; the interspersed comments are my own.

Session 215
The patient comes in wearing high heels, and she has a sophisticated new type of hair-do.
P: I've felt more nervous than I ever have been about coming here.—I feel as if I'm going off to the big world all by myself and I feel like a baby. I'm scared to fly all the way to Florida by myself. I feel like a baby in a woman's world [p. 433].

Comment: From the moment the patient enters the office, there is something striking in her presentation of herself. Her dress is strikingly different and more feminine and attractive than is usual for her. In it, she is expressing something important about herself, something that stirs highly conflictual feelings. The session and the dressing up take place in the context of the patient's going on a trip, thus creating a separation from the analyst. Her first statement suggests that this connects with transference feelings, and she projects an image of herself as somehow helpless and vulnerable—a baby in a woman's world.

A: What's the detail of the anxiety about coming here today?
P: I don't know. I'm scared to death of something. I'm afraid of myself and of my own thoughts and when I get all dolled up like this, I'm afraid that I'll seduce men. This is a defense for me and it's just like nursing. I wear a sloppy dress and I don't really fix my hair when I come here every day. But in Florida I have to have my hair fixed, and I'll be wearing dresses and I feel so scared. These are all *my* thoughts, but I want to take you with me. I have a feeling that I'm evil and I want to escape back to being a child [pp. 433–434].

Comment: The patient quickly admits that dressing up in a more sexual and attractive manner stirs her own sexual wishes to seduce, which are terrifying for her. Her normally less attractive and sloppy appearance is a way of fending off these impulses. The wish to be a child is her defense against these seductive wishes, which are connected with a sense of evilness. The defense is mobilized against the impulses connected with an underlying view that the patient maintains about herself. Sexuality is connected with the feelings of destructiveness and reflects the patient's feelings that she is somehow evil and powerful, a seducer and destroyer of men. The separation stirs anxieties about being on her own in an adult world. Her wishes to remain attached to and dependent on the analyst are intensified. One option is to be dependent like a helpless child, another is to make the analyst depend on her by sexual seduction. Both these aspects play a role in her view of herself. In the face of the patient's turmoil and conflict, we can note the analyst's attempt to be dispassionate, a paragon of objectivity in the face of the patient's emotionality.

A: You're dressed up here today and you have a new hairdo. You must have had some fantasies about this.

P: I'm so embarrassed. I had the thought that I'll destroy them and seduce the hell out of them.

A: What effect did you think the dressing up would have on me?

P: It all sounds so stupid. But I got myself all worked up coming here.

A: It's as if this is a test situation here with me today. You got yourself all dressed up and you fixed your hair and for a little while you gave up the defense of sloppiness.

P: I'm dividing myself all up again. I'm much more afraid of the way that *I* am. For me to look nice is the same as being a bitch and it means that I want to destroy everyone. I *do not* want this. But I feel as if it is uncontrollable in me. So to be a baby again is like a defense against these thoughts. I want men to think that I am a baby. This is all so silly! Men do look at me. And then I fall apart and get scared to death. I feel as if I can't handle it and I can't handle myself and I have a sense of panic [p. 434].

Comment: The analyst calls attention to the patient's behavior and indicates its relevance to transference issues. The previous sloppiness was defensive in quality, but by indirection was expressing some important feelings the patient has about herself. These feelings are now being stirred and intensified both in relationship to the transference and by the circumstances surrounding her dressing up, namely, the looming separation. The patient articulates important feelings that have direct reference to her self-image. She is the destructive seductress, the Circe who turns men into swine, only to destroy them. This underlying aggressive and destructive image of herself is terrifying to her, so that she must retreat from it to the more tolerable counterwish that she would be helpless and impotent, like a baby. She is caught between the uncertainties of her feelings that men will somehow take advantage of her weakness and vulnerability, and her terror of her wishes to consume them and destroy them.

A: All of these thoughts and feelings about men are condensed into this relationship with me and the fantasies about coming here today dressed up, and the thoughts about what effects it will have on me. What comes to your mind?

P: If I really let myself go I'll seduce you and then I can take you with me.

A: What's the detail?

P: I want to feed on you and take the breast with me. So I'll take your penis with me, but then I destroy you. I'm a monster and so I just can't love you. I can only be either a baby or a bitch. And yet I can't run away from the fact that I'm a woman and that I *am* attractive to men. I just can't take a situation like this [p. 434].

Comment: The analyst focuses the patient's feelings and fantasies explicitly in relation to the transference. The patient is explicit about her sense of her power to seduce and destroy the analyst. She is the evil monster who devours and destroys men. The fusion of libidinal and aggressive drives plays an important role here. In addition, however, the affect is cast partly in terms of a self-image in which libidinal wishes are experienced as destructive and the self is regarded as evil, monstrous, destroying. The alternative to this is the image of herself as the helpless baby—she is either baby or bitch.

>A: Why not?
>P: We're by ourselves. I have to run away from what it is that I want. If I let you know how I feel, will you act out on my feelings? Will you take advantage of me? I was so scared about having my hair done. . . . Somehow this is related to Friday night. Tom and I made love and I was so embarrassed and it had never happened before. It was about a thought of mine and I had a fear that you'd find out. . . . I'm thinking now—I had my hair done and I'm really beautiful. Are you attracted to me? [pp. 434–435].

Comment: The patient expresses the fear and the wish that the analyst would act upon her feelings of vulnerability and thus become the aggressor to her victim. At the same time and in the same degree, if the analyst is attracted by her improved appearance, he becomes the victim of her seductive and destructive power.

>A: I think you are still censoring and editing the fantasies you had Friday night.
>P: I don't know! Friday night I had the thought, "I'm afraid to feel like a woman tonight." I don't want to talk about it! My love feelings are just like evil monsters. . . . They are destroying. I'm so afraid that I will. . . All my thoughts rush in on me! I'm so scared. I just can't think. I love you and you've helped me so much and I want to take you with me, and I know that I'll be so hostile toward you when I leave. I want something from you. . . . When I feel love for you then I have such sexual feelings and then I'm a woman. I think then maybe I can be able to take you. I just can't be separated from you when I love you so much. . . . I really need *you.* I started having my period this morning and I shouldn't! I'm on Enovid and it's not the time for me to have my period. I feel as if I am losing my mind [p. 435].

Comment: The analyst senses a retreat in the patient from the intensity of the transference feelings and their related conflicts. The patient's impulses stirred within the intensity of the transference are troublesome because they carry a self-image that is terrifying and repulsive to her. The analyst's effort to break through and to make contact with this underlying self-image unleashes a flood of intensely affective material expressing again the patient's sense of herself as monstrously evil and destructive, particularly in relation to libidinal feelings. At the same time, she expresses another aspect of her self-image in her intense need for and clinging dependency on the analyst.

> A: What's the detail about getting your period this morning?
> P: I've gone and done it and I've destroyed you. That's you! I think about my uncle!
> A: What are you referring to?
> P: A penis. I've eaten it and it's inside me and it's bleeding! I'm a woman and there is something inside me that is going to get bigger and bigger. What have I done? I've done something horrible. . . . I'm so worried about why my period would have started this morning [p. 435].

Comment: The patient is referring here to a previous incestuous episode with an uncle. The primitive fantasy is one of incorporation in connection with the wish to devour the man's penis. The fantasy is that she has devoured the penis and that it is bleeding within her. She suggests some connection with the issue of pregnancy. Taking in men's penises and becoming pregnant is something horrible and destructive; the pregnancy may even be a form of punishment for such horrible wishes. The wish is to devour the analyst's penis so that it becomes her possession, something that she can carry away with her.

> A: You have a fantasy that you have a penis inside of you and that it's bleeding. It seems as if you think that it is either your uncle's or mine. What comes to your mind about it?
> P: I'm a monster and I'm just wild! I'm a woman! Shit! I think of eating a penis and how it would be mean and hostile to do this and I want to!! It's all this love and hate and nursing and orgasm. It's all one thing. I've got to take your penis with me.

Goddamn it, I must do it! I sometimes feel as if I have already done it [p. 435].

Comment: The themes of libido and aggression are here intensely mingled and reach a thundering crescendo. The themes of penis envy and castration are obvious. But at the same time, the patient is expressing in an intensely affective way a view of herself as needy and deprived, and as only able to gain what she desires and needs by violently devouring and destroying what belongs to another. In the fantasy the wish is expressed as a wish to have and destroy the penis. But at the same time the fantasy expresses important aspects of the patient's sense of herself as devalued, deprived, and penisless, as well as articulating a set of feelings and attitudes that she attributes projectively to those who have penises.

A: The fantasy seems to be that you are going to use your vagina as though it were a mouth and you are going to bite the penis off. You're reacting to the blood this morning as if it was from my penis or your uncle's penis and as if you feel that it's still in there.

P: I feel as if I've done this. Why do I feel I've done it? I had a dream about the Evanston basement where all of this business went on and I meant to tell you about it and I forgot.

A: What's the detail?

P: I was a woman in the dream and I felt so good about it and the basement seemed so clean. . . . Our yardman was there and also my uncle. I feel as though I have actually done this and I do have a penis inside of me. . . . My vagina has teeth in it and I'll bite him off. Why do I believe this? I feel just like a child. . . . [pp. 435–436].

Comment: The analyst focuses on the instinctually derived aspects of the material and interprets it accordingly. It is clear that this instinctual material, which is largely aggressive in quality, is a powerful force in determining the patient's sense of herself. While the wish to possess the penis, the sense of deprived outrage at not having one, and the orally destructive wish to devour it are undoubtedly significant in their own right as determinants of the patient's conflicts, they also contribute strongly to an even more powerful and internally convincing theme in the patient's inner world. These feelings become the vehicle for the patient's pervasive and deeply embedded sense of herself as evil and destructive. One could imagine that this aggressively toned and negative sense of self that pervades this patient's experience is not solely based on these particular dynamic concerns. Consequently, the clarification and interpretation of the conflictual issues and their related defenses might not bring the analytic impact to bear on the level of the patient's underlying sense of herself. The issues presented in such analytic material may be separate and independent. The analyst here chooses to focus on the instinctual and conflictual aspects of the material, but makes no attempt to approach or deal with the elements having to do with the dimensions of the patient's self that are in play.

A: What comes to your mind about the yardman in the dream?

P: We had one who was an alcoholic. Most of the time our yardmen were bums, but his name was Frank. He had no teeth. . . . I wonder if I used to have fantasies about him? I know that I was scared of him, but in the dream he put his arms around my waist and he was drunk and he wouldn't let me go. He was very nice to me actually. I had an evil eye for any man who was nice to me and I used to have wild thoughts like they are nice to me and maybe I can get their penises. I used to think this about Bill and Frank and my uncle and Mr. Jones and all of the other men. I used to wish that I could just know their thoughts. But I *feel* as if something really happened and as if I am a monster. . . .

A: We'll stop here for today [p. 436].

Comments: The same motifs are processed into the dream material and reflect the same underlying feelings and attitudes that the patient has expressed toward herself previously in the hour. The dream fulfills the wish and the fantasy to seduce the helpless man and to get his penis. The patient goes on to describe herself at this earlier stage of her life. In her mind's eye she sees herself as having an evil eye for men and having wild thoughts about getting their penises. She then returns to the theme of herself as a monster. These memory fragments show a consistency with other aspects of her expressions about herself and with the dream material. All these elements are integrated around a core dimension of her self-image that is highly aggressively toned, particularly in her sense of deprived neediness and the motifs of orally aggressive devouring and destroying.

Conclusions

What emerges from these considerations is that the operation of the self seems to pervade every aspect of the psychoanalytic situation. Everything the patient does—the patient's behavior, feelings, verbalizations, and interactions with the analyst—in some measure, directly or indirectly, explicitly or implicitly, expresses some aspect of the patient's self. In addition, the patient is caught up in a continual interaction with the analyst in which the dialectic between self and other plays itself out. The perspective of the self embraces the full range of the data base of psychoanalysis and refocuses it specifically in its own frame of reference.

In this sense, the traditional range of analytic concepts have all in some measure articulated aspects of the overall functioning of the self. Whether expressed in topographical terms—that is, as conscious, preconscious, or unconscious—or in structural terms—in relation to id, ego, and superego functions—discriminable aspects of the organization and functioning of the self were constantly at issue. Moreover, the self is also a central organizing vehicle for expressing and integrating instinctual forces. It should be noted that, based on the phenomenological description provided here, the frame of reference of the self and its psychology is not adequately expressed by or determined by the forms and issues of narcissism. The attempt to confine a psychology of the self to a narcissistic base would be excessively constrictive and would run counter to a more broadly conceived phenomenology of the self (Meissner, 1981b).

Another recurring theme in this consideration that deserves particular emphasis is that the self perspective of any of the dimensions in the analytic experience we have been discussing is a separate focus and provides a separate direction for interpretation within the analytic work. Thus, to focus on the self aspect of affects, resistances, memories, dream fragments, and even aspects of the transference and countertransference is to deal with the patient's material from a different perspective than is obtained from the more traditional instinctual or structural emphases. In the analytic hour just discussed, the focus on the instinctually derived aspects of the patient's sense of deprivation and neediness, her castration anxiety and penis envy, and her devouring oral aggressive needs is a well-defined and familiar frame of reference established by theories of drive, conflict, defense, and structure. One could also approach the patient's material from a more specifically object relations perspective that would emphasize the quality of the patient's relationship to the analyst, the inherent aspects of her involvement with men, and the history of her relationship with significant objects that this reflects.

In either case, although the aspects of the patient's self and its own inherent psychology might be touched on tangentially or by indirection, they would not be explicitly or adequately addressed. The patient's deprived, needy, evil, and aggressively destructive sense of herself embodies a separate set of issues with a separate set of underlying motivations and concerns, which need to be addressed on their own terms. In other words, interpretation of the patient's instinctually derived conflicts may undercut the immediate conflict and indirectly may mitigate some of the pathogenic quality of her self-image, but they do not come to bear in an adequate or effective way on the pathogenic aspects of the self-image as such. This perspective suggests that a separate set of motives, interests, and investments is involved in the patient's shaping and maintaining of such a pathogenic self organization and self-image. They are to some degree independent of, although certainly not unrelated to, more specifically instinctual dynamics.

This discussion has attempted to specify the basic phenomenology of the self as it expresses itself within the analytic situation and the analytic process. It is hoped that this effort will contribute some greater degree of specificity to the discussion of the self and its psychology and will offer a firmer basis for its future theoretical elaboration.

References

Bach, S. (1977), On the narcissistic state of consciousness. *Internat. J. Psycho-Anal.*, 58:209–233.

Basch, M. (1979), An operational definition of "self." Presented at the Houston Psychoanalytic Society, April 27.

Chediak, C. (1979), Counterreactions and countertransference. *Internat. J. Psycho-Anal.*, 60:117–129.

Dewald, P. (1972), *The Psychoanalytic Process.* New York: Basic Books.

Gedo, J.E. (1979), *Beyond Interpretation: Toward a Revised Theory for Psychoanalysis.* New York: International Universities Press.

Guntrip, H. (1969), *Schizoid Phenomena, Object Relations, and the Self.* New York: International Universities Press.

——— (1973), *Psychoanalytic Theory, Therapy, and the Self.* New York: Basic Books.

Gutheil, T.G., & Havens, L.L. (1979), The therapeutic alliance: Contemporary meaning and confusions. *Internat. Rev. Psycho-Anal.*, 6:467–481.

Hartmann, H. (1950), Comments on the psychoanalytic theory of the ego. In: *Essays on Ego Psychology.* New York: International Universities Press, 1964, pp. 113–141.

——— (1960), *Psychoanalysis and Moral Values.* New York: International Universities Press.

Jacobson, E. (1964), *The Self and the Object World.* New York: International Universities Press.

Kernberg, O. (1976), *Object Relations Theory and Clinical Psychoanalysis.* New York: Aronson.

Kohut, H. (1971), *The Analysis of the Self.* New York: International Universities Press.

——— (1977), *The Restoration of the Self.* New York: International Universities Press.

——— (1979), The two analyses of Mr. Z. *Internat. J. Psycho-Anal.*, 60:3–27.

——— & Wolf, E.S. (1978), The disorders of the self and their treatment: An outline. *Internat. J. Psycho-Anal.*, 59:413–425.

Levin, D.C. (1969), The self: A contribution to its place in theory and technique. *Internat. J. Psycho-Anal.*, 50:41–51.

Lichtenstein, H. (1965), Towards a metapsychological definition of the concept of self. *Internat. J. Psycho-Anal.*, 46:117–128.

Meissner, W.W. (1977), Cognitive Aspects of the Paranoid Process—Prospectus. In: *Psychiatry and the Humanities*, Vol. 2: *Thought, Consciousness, and Reality.* ed. J. Smith. New Haven: Yale University Press, pp. 159–216.

——— (1979), Internalization and object relations. *J. Amer. Psychoanal. Assoc.*, 27:345–360.

——— (1981a), *Internalization in Psychoanalysis.* [Psychological Issues, Monogr. 50.] New York: International Universities Press.

——— (1981b), A note on narcissism. *Psychoanal. Quart.*, 50:77–89.

——— (1982), Notes on countertransference in borderline conditions. *Internat. J. Psychoanal. Psychother.*, to be published.

——— (in press), Studies on hysteria—Dora. *Internat. J. Psychoanal. Psychother.*

Nadelson, T. (1976), Victim, victimizer: Interaction in the psychotherapy of borderline patients. *Internat. J. Psychoanal. Psychother.*, 5:115–129.

Rapaport, D. (1967), *Collected Papers.* New York: Basic Books.

Reich, A. (1953), Narcissistic object choice in women. *J. Amer. Psychoanal. Assoc.*, 1:22–44.

Rochlin, G. (1980), *The Masculine Dilemma*. Boston: Little, Brown.

Saperstein, J.L., & Gaines, J. (1973), Metapsychological considerations on the self. *Internat. J. Psycho-Anal.*, 54:415–424.

Schafer, R. (1976), *A New Language for Psychoanalysis*. New Haven: Yale University Press.

Schwaber, E. (1979), On the "self" within the matrix of analytic theory— Some clinical reflections and reconsiderations. *Internat. J. Psycho-Anal.*, 60:467–479.

Spiegel, L.A. (1959), The self, the sense of self, and perception. *The Psychoanalytic Study of the Child*, 14:81–109. New York: International Universities Press.

Psychoanalytic Phenomenology:
Progress Toward a Theory of Personality

ROBERT D. STOLOROW
GEORGE E. ATWOOD

This paper is in the nature of a progress report on our ongoing efforts to construct the foundation for a new psychoanalytic theory of personality. These efforts have been guided by three general considerations. First, we feel that any new framework should be capable of preserving the contributions made by the classical analytic theorists and of translating these contributions into a common conceptual language. Second, it is our view that the theory of psychoanalysis should be formulated on an experience-near level of discourse, closely anchored in the phenomena of clinical observation. The third guiding consideration is found in our belief that an adequate theory of personality must be designed to illuminate the structure, significance, and origins of personal subjective worlds in all their richness and diversity.

Our studies in the foundations of psychoanalysis have accordingly led us to propose a "psychoanalytic phenomenology" that takes human subjectivity as its principal focus (Stolorow and Atwood, 1979). The goal of the present essay is to demonstrate that this framework provides a coherent perspective from which to view the issues and problems forming the traditional central concerns of personality theory. We shall discuss the methodology of psychoanalytic research, the notion of

97

personality structure, the relationship of conduct to experience, the concept of motivation, the idea of unconscious mental processes, the theory of psychological development, the problem of defining health and pathology, and the nature of the therapeutic action of psychoanalysis.

Methodology of Psychoanalytic Research

Psychoanalytic phenomenology is a depth psychology of human subjectivity, devoted to illuminating the meanings implicit in personal experience and conduct. Interpretation lies at the heart of its methods. Psychoanalytic interpretation is an activity in which empathy and inference are inextricably combined (Kohut, 1959, 1977). Empathy is implicit in the attempt to understand a person's actions and communications from the standpoint of that person's own subjective frame of reference. Its importance arises as a methodological consequence of the fact that one is observing and studying an experiencing subject, rather than a material object. The inferential component of interpretation consists in locating the act or expression under study within the nexus of personal meanings pervading the individual's life history and subjective world as a whole.

How does one arrive at knowledge regarding the structures of meaning in a person's experience, and how does such knowledge relate to more generally applicable psychological concepts and principles? Unveiling the dominant structures of an individual's subjective life involves a complex and extended interplay between empathic observation and inference. This process begins in a modest way, with a single instance of a person's behavior. One or more interpretive hypotheses are posed regarding the experiential and life-historical context within which that behavior has meaning. Further instances of the person's actions are then studied and further inferences made about the subjective and genetic contexts to which they belong. In this way a field of hypothesized meanings comes into being, and these meanings are compared, cross-linked and cross-validated, with the plausibility of particular inferences about the person being assessed by their degree of coherence with the analysis as a whole. This mode of investigation discloses structures of meaning in the form of invariant thematic configurations repeated in different sectors of the person's experience. In the interpretive science of psychoanalysis, the elucidation of such invariants is the counterpart to the replication of observations in the natural sciences.

Since case analysis is an interpretive procedure, the validity of its final results is evaluated in light of distinctively hermeneutic criteria. These criteria include the logical coherence of the argument, the consistency of the results with accepted psychological knowledge, the comprehensiveness of the explanation, and the aesthetic beauty of the analysis in illuminating previously hidden patterns of order in the material being investigated (Polanyi, 1958).

Interpretive case studies represent the central research methodology of psychoanalytic phenomenology and are associated with two mutually enhancing realms of knowledge. There is first of all the detailed *clinical* knowledge resulting from such studies, dealing with the life-historical sources and manifestations of all the varied structures that may crystallize in a human being's experience. This knowledge concerns specific personal worlds and their vicissitudes. The second area of knowledge is more abstract and pertains not to particular persons, but rather to the structure and development of personal experience *in general*. Here we encounter interpretive principles and ideas to guide our explorations of personal worlds, assumptions regarding the appropriate units of analysis for such investigations, and concepts applying to the evolution and transformation of experience throughout the life cycle. The remaining topics that will be considered in this paper pertain to this latter, more general realm of knowledge.

Personality Structure

From the perspective of psychoanalytic phenomenology, personality structure is the *structure of a person's experiencing*. Our particular focus has been the concept of the "representational world" (Sandler and Rosenblatt, 1962; Stolorow and Atwood, 1979)—the distinctive configurations of self and object that shape and organize a person's experiences. These representational structures are not to be viewed simply as "internalizations" or mental replicas of interpersonal events, as Kernberg (1976), for example, does. Nor should they be regarded as having an objective existence in physical space or somewhere in a "mental apparatus." Instead, we conceptualize these structures as systems of ordering or organizing principles (Piaget, 1970)—cognitive-affective schemata (Klein, 1976) through which a person's experiences of self and other assume their characteristic forms and meanings (Stolorow, 1978a). Thus, it is important to note, the term "representational world" is not equivalent to a person's subjective world of mental imagery. Rather, it refers to the *structure* of that world as disclosed in the thematic patterning of his subjective life.

In psychoanalytic phenomenology, the concept of character is coextensive with that of the representational world (Atwood and Stolorow, 1980). A person's character *is* his representational world; and character analysis is an elucidation of the nature, developmental vicissitudes, and multiple purposes of the configurations that are its constituents. This conception of character rests on the assumption of a close functional relationship between the structuralization of human experience and the patterning of human conduct. Specifically, we assume that patterns of conduct serve to actualize the nuclear configurations of self and object that constitute a person's character. Such patterns of conduct may include, for example, inducing others to act in a way that replicates key characteristics of object representations. A thematic isomorphism is thus created between the ordering of the subjective and the interpersonal fields.

While "personality" and "character" are extremely broad concepts pertaining to the overall structure of a subjective universe, "self" is a more delimited and specific term referring to the structure of a person's experience of himself. The self, from the vantage point of psychoanalytic phenomenology, is a psychological structure through which self experience acquires cohesion and continuity and by virtue of which self experience assumes its characteristic shape and enduring organization. We believe that this conception of the self as psychological structure illuminates and clarifies Heinz Kohut's unique contributions to psychoanalytic thought. His most central contributions to our understanding of psychopathology and treatment, for example, concern those states in which the psychological structure that organizes the experience of self is missing or defective and in which archaic ties to "selfobjects" are required to restore or sustain a subjective sense of self-cohesion, self-continuity, and self-esteem (Kohut, 1971, 1977).

Motivation

Psychoanalytic phenomenology does not postulate a theory of the nature of personality as an "objective entity." Instead, it consists in a methodological system of interpretive principles to guide the study of meaning in human experience and conduct. Its explanatory concepts thus emphasize not "psychic determinism" and a natural science view of causality, but rather a *subjective contextualism* which brings to focus the nexus of personal meanings in which a person's experience and conduct are embedded (Atwood and Stolorow, 1980). Rather than formulating impersonal motivational prime movers of a mental apparatus, psychoanalytic phenomenology seeks to illuminate the multiple conscious and unconscious purposes (Klein, 1976) or personal reasons (Schafer, 1976) that lead a person to strive to actualize the constituents of his representational world. The configurations that a person strives to actualize may, in varying degrees, fulfill cherished wishes and urgent desires, provide moral guidance and self-punishment, aid adaptation to difficult realities, or repair or restore damaged or lost self and object imagos; they also may serve a defensive purpose in preventing other dreaded configurations from crystallizing in awareness. It is extremely important in conceptualizing a personality structure to determine the relative motivational salience or priority of these multiple purposes in the organization of experience and conduct.

The significance of personal motives such as these has been verified by the clinical work of generations of analysts, beginning with Freud, and need not be belabored here. The evolution of our own framework, however, has led us to propose an additional, more general, supraordinate motivational principle: that the *need to maintain the organization of experience* is a central motive in the patterning of human conduct. This motivational principle can be understood to apply in two senses. On the one hand, a pattern of conduct may serve to maintain a *particular* organization of experience, in which specific required configurations of self and object are actualized, and other dreaded ones are precluded. On the other hand, a pattern of conduct may serve to maintain psychological organization per se, as when concrete enactments are required to sustain the structural cohesion and continuity of a fragmenting sense of self or other. An understanding of this fundamental functional relationship between experience and conduct, whereby certain courses of action are required to maintain the structural integrity and stability of the subjective world, is enormously helpful in guiding the analytic approach to both primitive destructiveness and sexual perversions, as Kohut (1971, 1972, 1977) and others (Goldberg, 1975; Stolorow and Lachmann, 1980) have shown. So-called sexual and aggressive acting out is conceptualized not in terms of a defective "mental apparatus" lacking in "impulse control," but rather in terms of the need for behavioral enactments to shore up an imperiled subjective world.

The Unconscious

In psychoanalytic phenomenology, repression is understood as a process whereby particular configurations of self and object are prevented from crystallizing in awareness. Repression may thus be viewed as a *negative organizing principle* (Atwood and Stolorow, 1980) operating alongside the positive organizing principles underlying the configurations that do repeatedly materialize in conscious experience. The "dynamic unconscious," from this point of view, consists in that set of configurations that consciousness is not permitted to assume, because of their negative affective coloring and/or association with subjective danger. Particular memories, fantasies, feelings, and other experiential contents are repressed because they threaten to actualize these dreaded configurations. Other defenses are conceptualized as further transformations of the subjective world that prevent dreaded configurations from emerging by radically altering and restricting the person's experience of self and other (Stolorow and Atwood, 1979).

In addition to the "dynamic unconscious," viewed as a system of negative organizing principles, another form of unconsciousness has increasingly assumed a position of importance in our framework. The organizing principles of a person's representational world, whether operating positively (giving rise to certain configurations in awareness), or negatively (preventing certain configurations from arising), are themselves unconscious. A person's experiences are shaped by his representational configurations without this shaping becoming the focus of awareness and reflection. We have therefore characterized the structure of a representational world as *prereflectively unconscious* (Atwood and Stolorow, 1980). This form of unconsciousness is not the product of defensive activity, even though great effort is required to overcome it. In fact, the defenses themselves, when operating outside a person's awareness, can be seen as merely a special instance of structuring activity that is prereflectively unconscious.

In the absence of reflection, a person is unaware of his role as a constitutive subject in elaborating his personal reality. The world in which he lives and moves presents itself as though it were something independently and objectively real. The patterning and thematizing of events that uniquely characterize his personal reality are thus seen as if they were properties of those events rather than products of his own subjective interpretations and constructions. As will be discussed in a later section, psychoanalytic therapy can be viewed as a procedure through which a patient acquires reflective knowledge of how his experiences are structured by his representational world. He becomes able to step back from what heretofore had seemed to be the sheer factuality of existence and hence to recognize his world as partially constituted by the structures of his own subjectivity.

An understanding of the form of unconsciousness that we have designated as "prereflective" sheds light on the unique importance of dreams in the evolution of psychoanalytic theory and practice. The particular psychoanalytic utility of dreams derives from the circumstance that the structure of a person's representational world is most readily discernible in his relatively unfettered, spontaneous productions. Hence, dreams constitute one "royal road" to the prereflective unconscious—to the organizing principles and dominant leitmotivs that unconsciously thematize a person's subjective life (Stolorow, 1978b).

Personality Development

In psychoanalytic phenomenology, personality development refers to the *structuralization of personal experience*. Efforts to construct a psychoanalytic developmental psychology of the representational world are still in their infancy. They have been significantly hampered, we feel, by the persistent psychological tradition of artificially dividing human subjectivity into cognitive and affective domains—a fragmentation of psychic reality that has tended to preclude an integration of psychoanalytic knowledge with the wealth of research findings on the perceptual and cognitive development of children. A psychoanalytic developmental psychology concerned with the structuralization of experience would be especially enriched by articulations with the developmental-structural psychology of Piaget (see Basch, 1977). Such an integration has recently been attempted by Greenspan (1979). While he perpetuates the unfortunate theoretical schism between so-called cognitive and affective domains, he nevertheless proposes a model of development in which a series of phase-specific organizing principles shape the child's experiences in *both* of these domains in successive developmental eras. We suggest that with a mending of the rift between cognition and affect, and a focusing on the ontogenesis of unitary configurations of (cognitive-affective) experience, Piagetian concepts such as the principles of structural assimilation and accommodation become even more germane for conceptualizing the course of personality development.

Two ubiquitous psychological processes—differentiation and integration—play a pivotal role in the evolution of the representational world. A brief description of these developmental processes as they have been presumed to operate in early childhood will serve to illustrate our conception of personality development as the structuralization of experience.

In the earliest phase of infancy, self and object are experientially undifferentiated. Gradually, the neonate acquires the capacity to discriminate between his own sensations and the objects from which they are derived (Jacobson, 1964). Thus, perhaps the first developmental task to face the infant, central to the beginning structuralization of his representational world, is the subjective differentiation of self from primary objects—the rudimentary establishment of self-object boundaries (Mahler, Pine, and Bergman, 1975). The small child's incomplete attainment of self-object boundaries makes it both necessary and possible for him to rely on parental figures as "selfobjects" whose idealized attributes and mirror functions provide him with the self-cohesion and self-continuity that he cannot yet maintain on his own (Kohut, 1971, 1977). The child's growing capacity for self-object differentiation develops in concert with the emergence of symbolization and the ability to distinguish his own symbolizing activity from the objects being symbolized—important milestones in the evolution of his subjectivity.

Another characteristic of the very young infant's world is his inability to integrate experiences with contrasting affective colorations. Thus, a second developmental task, coincident with that of self-object differentiation, is the synthesis of object experiences colored with positive affect and object experiences colored with negative affect into an integrated perception of a whole object with both positive and negative qualities, coupled with a similar synthesis of affectively contrasting self experiences into an integrated perception of the whole self (Kernberg, 1976).

From the standpoint of the object world, the attainment of differentiation and integration is reflected in the achievement of "object constancy"—the capacity to sustain an enduring image of another person who is valued for his positive and negative qualities and is recognized as a separate individual with needs and feelings of his own. From the standpoint of the self, the attainment of differentiation and integration is reflected in the establishment of a cohesive image of the self that is temporally stable and has an affective coloration more or less independent of immediate environmental support. Such "self constancy" has been described in terms of the subjective sense of identity (Erikson, 1956) and the continuity of self-esteem (Jacobson, 1964; Kohut, 1971, 1977).

The particular thematic structure of the child's representational world will evolve organically from the critical formative experiences that mark his unique early history and the individualized array of personal motivations that develops as their result. Once the child has established a relatively constant and stable representational world, it will serve as a prereflective frame of reference into whose structure he will unconsciously assimilate his subsequent experiences. Developmental change will occur when this structure is altered and expanded to accommodate new constellations of experience.

From this phenomenological and developmental-structural perspective, Kohut's (1971, 1977) central contribution to our knowledge of personality development has been his conceptualization of the structuralization of self experience. Two concepts pivotal to his formulation of the evolution of self structure are "selfobject" and "transmuting internalization." A selfobject may be described phenomenologically as an object that a person experiences as incompletely separated from himself and that serves to maintain his sense of self. Transmuting internalization, described phenomenologically, is an enduring reorganization of the subjective field in which experienced qualities of a selfobject are translocated and assimilated into the child's own self structure (Atwood and Stolorow, 1980). These two developmental concepts—selfobject and transmuting internalization—are singularly important contributions to a psychoanalytic developmental psychology emphasizing the structuralization of experience.

An aspect of personality development of particular interest to analysts is the relationship between psychosexual development and the evolution of the representational world. We see these developmental lines as complementary features of a unitary ontogenetic progression (see Stolorow and Lachmann, 1980, chap. 8). On the one hand, the sensual experiences, fantasies, and enactments that occur in concert with the epigenetic unfolding of psychosexual modes (Erikson, 1950) in the course of development serve as *psychic organizers* (Spitz, 1959) that contribute significantly to the consolidation of self and object representations. On the other hand, such structuralization in turn makes possible new modes of psychosexual experience, so that the occurrence of particular psychosexual imagery may be seen as an *indicator* of developmental steps in the consolidation of the representational world. We are suggesting that the psychosexual phases can best be understood in terms of this organic inseparability of sensual and representational development. This conception of the vital developmental importance of psychosexual experience helps us understand the damaging effects that traumatic overstimulations, deprivations, and other early distortions in the sphere of sensual experience can have in interfering with the normal consolidation of self and object representations. An appreciation of the role of psychosexuality in normal representational development also sheds light on the meaning of adult sexual pathology in which the early infantile function of erotic experience in restoring and maintaining precarious or fragmenting psychological structure is retained and regressively relied upon (Stolorow and Lachmann, 1980, Chap. 8).

In this section we have shown that important issues pertaining to personality development can be clarified by a strict focus on the child's evolving subjectivity. We shall next attempt to demonstrate that similar clarifications can be achieved when issues pertaining to the nature of psychological health, pathology, and therapy are viewed from our phenomenological perspective.

Psychological Health, Pathology, and Therapy

A theory of personality development centering on the structuralization of experience will seek a conception of psychological health in some formulation of *optimal structuralization*. This ideal can be conceptualized in terms of the healthy person's ability to achieve an optimal balance between the maintenance of his psychological organization on the one hand and his openness to new forms of experience on the other. On the one hand, his self and object representations have become sufficiently consolidated so that they can assimilate into their structure a wide range of experiences of self and other and still retain their integrity and stability. His subjective world, in other words, is not unduly vulnerable to disintegration or dissolution. On the other hand, his representational structures are sufficiently flexible to accommodate new configurations of experience of self and other, so that the organization of his subjective life can continue to expand in both complexity and scope.

Correspondingly, we can conceptualize two broad classes of psychopathology reflecting the two types of failure to attain this optimal balance. On the one hand, there are psychological disorders that reflect the consolidation of *pathological structures* that operate rigidly to restrict the person's subjective field. Examples are found in those persons whose lives are severely constricted by defensive structures that inflexibly order their experiences to prevent the emergence of emotional conflict and subjective danger. On the other hand, there are psychological disturbances that reflect *insufficient or faulty structuralization*—developmental deficiencies and arrests in the formation and consolidation of the representational world (Stolorow and Lachmann, 1980). Examples are found in the persons described by Kohut (1971, 1977) who are prone to self fragmentation and require immersion in archaic ties to selfobjects to sustain the cohesion and continuity of their precarious self experiences.

From the perspective of psychoanalytic phenomenology, the psychoanalytic situation and the technical precepts that govern it may be viewed as a set of facilitating conditions that permit the structure of a patient's subjective world to unfold maximally and find illumination in relatively pure culture in the analytic transference (Stolorow, Atwood, and Ross, 1978). The transference is actually a microcosm of the patient's total life, and the analysis of the transference provides a focal point around which the patterns dominating the patient's existence as a whole can be clarified, understood, and changed. The mode of therapeutic action of this analysis will differ, however, depending on the extent to which pathological structures or remnants of insufficient structuralization predominate in the treatment at any particular juncture.

When pathological structures predominate in the transference, the working-through phase and its therapeutic action can be conceptualized as a gradual process of *structural transformation:* The repeated interpretive clarification of the nature, origins, and purposes of the representational configurations into which the analyst is assimilated, together with the repeated juxtaposition of these structures with experiences of the analyst as a new object to which they must accommodate, both establish reflective knowledge of how the patient's perception of the analytic relationship is being shaped by his representational world, and at the same time invite the synthesis of alternative modes of experiencing self and object. As the ossified, pathological forms that have heretofore structured the patient's experiences are progressively broken up and reorganized, a new and enriched personal reality opens up before him, made possible by the newly expanded and reflectively conscious structures of his representational world (Atwood and Stolorow, 1980; Stolorow, Atwood, and Ross, 1978).

When remnants of faulty structuralization predominate in the transference, a different conceptualization of the working-through phase and its therapeutic action is required. In such instances, the analysis aims not for the breaking up and reorganization of existing pathological structures, but rather for the growth of representational structure that is missing or deficient as a consequence of developmental voids and interferences (Kohut, 1971, 1977; Stolorow and Lachmann, 1980). The patient is permitted to establish an archaic bond with the analyst as a selfobject and hence to revive with the analyst those early phases at which his psychological development had been arrested. When protected from traumatic disruptions, this selfobject tie serves as a facilitating medium reinstating the developmental processes of differentiation and integration that had been aborted during the patient's formative years. Further structuralization is achieved through the repeated analysis of the patient's reactions to tolerable disturbances in this selfobject tie, which fosters its eventual transmuting internalization (Kohut, 1971, 1977).

From the standpoint of a theory of personality that takes the structure of a person's experiencing as its central focus, the often-heard question of whether the treatment of emotional conflicts (pathological structures) and of developmental arrests (failures of structuralization) require two entirely separate psychoanalytic systems is moot. Psychoanalytic phenomenology, conceived as a depth psychology of human subjectivity, can encompass and guide the treatment of both emotional conflict and developmental arrest.

Conclusion

This paper has been a progress report on our efforts to construct the foundation for a theory of personality—a psychoanalytic phenomenology devoted to the illumination of meaning in personal experience and conduct. We have attempted to demonstrate that a framework focusing consistently on the structure and development of personal experience holds great promise in providing a coherent perspective from which to view the array of issues that have been the traditional domain of personality theory. This focus on the organization of experience, drawing on the rich intellectual heritage of modern structuralism, defines the unique place of psychoanalysis among the sciences of man.

References

Atwood, G., & Stolorow, R. (1980), Psychoanalytic concepts and the representational world. *Psychoanal. Contemp. Thought,* 3:267–290.

Basch, M.F. (1977), Developmental psychology and explanatory theory in psycho-analysis. *The Annual of Psychoanalysis*, 5:229-263. New York: International Universities Press.

Erikson, E. (1950), *Childhood and Society*. New York: Norton.

——— (1956), The problem of ego identity. In: *Identity and the Life Cycle*. [*Psychological Issues*, Monogr. 1.] New York: International Universities Press, 1959, pp. 101–171.

Goldberg, A. (1975), A fresh look at perverse behavior. *Internat. J. Psycho-Anal.*, 56:335–342.

Greenspan, S. (1979), *Intelligence and Adaptation*. New York: International Universities Press.

Jacobson, E. (1964), *The Self and the Object World*. New York: International Universities Press.

Kernberg, O. (1976), *Object Relations Theory and Clinical Psychoanalysis*. New York: Jason Aronson.

Klein, G. (1976), *Psychoanalytic Theory: An Exploration of Essentials*. New York: International Universities Press.

Kohut, H. (1959), Introspection, empathy, and psychoanalysis: An examination of the relationship between mode of observation and theory. In: *The Search for the Self*, ed. P.H. Ornstein. New York: International Universities Press, 1978, pp. 205–232.

——— (1971), *The Analysis of the Self*. New York: International Universities Press.

——— (1972), Thoughts on narcissism and narcissistic rage. In: *The Search for the Self*, ed. P.H. Ornstein. New York: International Universities Press, 1978, pp. 615–658.

——— (1977), *The Restoration of the Self*. New York: International Universities Press.

Mahler, M., Pine, F., & Bergman, A. (1975), *The Psychological Birth of the Human Infant*. New York: Basic Books.

Piaget, J. (1970), *Structuralism*. New York: Basic Books.

Polanyi, M. (1958), *Personal Knowledge*. Chicago: University of Chicago Press.

Sandler, J., & Rosenblatt, B. (1962), The concept of the representational world. *The Psychoanalytic Study of the Child*, 17:128–145. New York: International Universities Press.

Schafer, R. (1976), *A New Language for Psychoanalysis*. New Haven: Yale University Press.

Spitz, R. (1959), *A Genetic Field Theory of Ego Formation*. New York: International Universities Press.

Stolorow, R. (1978a), The concept of psychic structure: Its metapsychological and clinical psychoanalytic meanings. *Internat. Rev. Psycho-Anal.*, 5:313–320.

——— (1978b), Themes in dreams: A brief contribution to therapeutic technique. *Internat. J. Psycho-Anal.*, 59: 473–475.

——— & Atwood, G. (1979), *Faces in a Cloud: Subjectivity in Personality Theory*. New York: Jason Aronson.

——— ——— & Ross, J. (1978), The representational world in psychoanalytic therapy. *Internat. Rev. Psycho-Anal.*, 5:247–256.

——— & Lachmann, F. (1980), *Psychoanalysis of Developmental Arrests: Theory and Treatment*. New York: International Universities Press.

Comments on the Rise of Narcissism

ARNOLD H. MODELL

In this Festschrift honoring the contributions of Heinz Kohut, we have been asked to cast our minds forward to imagine the future of psychoanalysis. I have taken this as an invitation to bypass the usual restraints on presenting our views unless we can accompany them with a modicum of proof. Thus, this paper is in the nature of a conjecture—a conjecture that is based on clinical experience, but cannot be tested by clinical experience alone, for it crosses into the domains of psychohistory and sociology.

I shall propose that the ever-changing nosology of the neuroses is the most direct indication of the impact of historical processes on the ego (Modell, 1975a)—that the neuroses are, in effect, a social barometer. It is agreed that the manifest forms of the neuroses are continually evolving. The symptomatic neuroses have been replaced by character neuroses and, although the character neuroses are still very much with us, they have been displaced by a relative increase in what has been labeled the narcissistic neurosis or the narcissistic personality. The relationship between culture and character formation is a large subject indeed, and I will not attempt to summarize the existing literature here. Nevertheless, what I am suggesting is that this shift in the ecology of neuroses is a response to historical change.

Portions of this paper were presented at Commencement, Smith College School for Social Work, Northampton, Massachusetts, August 19, 1981.

Waelder (1962) writes: "The psychoneuroses seem to have changed since the early days of psychoanalysis, with simple and rather transparent cases of *grande hystérie* retreating from sophisticated urban quarters and being reported from backwaters only; and in general with repression, the simple form of defense, giving way to more complicated mechanisms." Gitelson (1954) also has no doubt that the neuroses were continually evolving. He notes the increase in narcissism, but understands this to occur within the context of the character neuroses. He suggests that with the changes in moral and ethical outlooks the boundaries between license and deprivation has become blurred, and the personality itself has become the carrier of the symptom. He stresses the adaptive aspects of narcissism, in that narcissistic character defenses hide behind a facade of normality. This same observation is developed by Tartakoff (1966). She describes an infantile grandiosity that is supported and given the cachet of normalcy, being congruent with certain values of American culture. And we know that Kohut (1977) has expressed the similar view that the increase in the numbers of narcissistic personalities is the result of what he terms psychotropic social factors.

The assertion that narcissistic personality types are on the increase usually elicits the skeptical question, Are you proposing that the narcissistic neurosis is something new? Contemporary life has not produced a new form of neurosis, but there is reason to believe that something—what it is we shall examine further—has increased the numbers of this particular type. The skeptic will perhaps grant that there has been an increase in narcissistic personalities, but would claim that this is merely an epiphenomenon; human nature remains essentially unchanged and the influence of society produces merely a change in style, in what appears on the surface. Comparing the unfolding of the analytic process in the so-called classical case and in that of the narcissistic personality easily demonstrates that the differences are no epiphenomenon. The uniform transferences of the narcissistic personality, based as they are on a relative failure of self-object differentiation, point to a developmental disorder. In contrast, the transference neurosis, infinitely more varied and idiosyncratic, is based not on the externalization and repetition of a developmental disorder, but on a unique experience—the internal elaboration of the individual's early history (Modell, 1976, 1978, 1981a).

Heinz Kohut more than any other contemporary writer, has focused and dramatized this difference. There is now a growing literature both supporting and rebutting his views. As we know, this had led to an unfortunate polarization, perhaps the fate of all controversies. A Festschrift is not the place to underscore our differences with the man whom we have come to honor. But it does not diminish his contribution to acknowledge that there are areas of his work with which I remain in disagreement (see Modell, 1975b, 1976, 1978, 1980, 1981b).

I agree with Kohut that many aspects of the narcissistic personality can be understood as the defensive response to developmental trauma. I have focused particularly on the response of nonrelatedness and noncommunication (Modell, 1980, 1981a). If one attempts to engage certain narcissistic individuals in psychoanalysis, one is first struck by what may be described as a continued state of nonrelatedness—the sense that there are not two people in the consulting room. When a patient is relating to the analyst, the analyst experiences a sense of engagement. This feeling is the consequence of the communication of genuine feeling and interest in the analyst as a separate person. The early countertransference response of the analyst to a narcissistic person is one of boredom, indifference, or even sleepiness—the human response to the fact that the other person does not seem to be interested in oneself, that feelings are not being communicated, and that words are being used simply to fill up empty spaces.

The patient's endopsychic experience corresponding to this state of nonrelatedness is that of being encased in a plastic bubble, cocoon, or bell jar; the patient feels walled off and not entirely in the world. This state of being walled off may be comfortable at times, but at other times leads to a desperate sense of isolation and abandonment. There are exceptions to this description—some narcissistic personalities, at the beginning of psychoanalysis, express a considerable degree of Sturm und Drang. But after some time the sound and fury appears to be empty, signifying nothing. That is, the heightened affectivity is essentially a screen to hide the patient's fundamental sense of emptiness and deadness of the self. This affective distancing unfortunately also occurs in relationship to the self—these individuals lose contact with any affective center—they feel empty and dead. Estrangement from the self is exquisitely painful and may provide the motive that leads them to seek psychoanalysis. These people lack authenticity, both in relation to others and in relation to the self. This description comes very close to Winnicott's (1960a) concept of the true and false self—the false self based on compliance, masking a true, authentic self from which the individual may be completely cut off. We are all familiar with the types and forms of human suffering that this state of affairs produces. The absence of affective authenticity leads to relationships in which there is no sense of commitment. Two people may be living together, apparently sharing a life, but suffering from an extreme sense of loneliness; that is, they are unable to affectively touch each other. Sexuality in this kind of relationship is used to restore a sense of aliveness and offset the feeling that the individuals are psychically dead.

Like Kohut and Winnicott, I believe the trauma that leads to this form of narcissistic defensiveness is a miscarriage in the process of mirroring. Mirroring occurs through the medium of affective communication between mother and child. This communication must be authentic, for the child's cohesive sense of self is forged through the affective bond that is formed when the mother gazes at the child's face, reflecting the child's affects. In this fashion, the mother provides the child with knowledge of his or her own affective state. The child, in turn, learns of the mother's affective state through her facial expression. This process is the foundation of empathy. Since the mother's affective response provides a validation for the child, it is little wonder that children become connoisseurs of authenticity. The vulnerability of the self also arises from this process, and the sense of self is, in this fashion, held hostage by the other. I agree with Kohut that preservation of the self and a sense of self are vital, analogous to the maintenance of vital physiological functions.

In previous analyses (Modell, 1975b, 1976, 1980, 1981a) I have reconstructed characteristic disturbances in the interactions between patients and their parents. Different authors may emphasize different aspects of this process, use different terminology, or be influenced by different theoretical preconceptions, but the fundamental clinical observations are essentially uncontroversial. The parental failures[2] usually

---

[1] This is not to "blame" the parents for the child's neurosis. The etiology of the neurosis is still elusive and still consists of Freud's complementary series of internal and environmental determinants. Environmental trauma may need to be combined with certain internal events to produce neurosis, but it also flies in the face of clinical evidence to ignore the effect of failures in the parental holding environment.

consist of emotional unresponsiveness or an excessive degree of psychological or physical intrusion. Affective absence and intrusion may occur alternately in the same parent or may be characteristic of one parent and not the other. Overall, we may describe these responses as Kohut (1977) has, as a failure of empathy; or, as Winnicott (1960b) has, as disturbances in the holding environment.

In addition to these specific disturbances in the affective area, a child may correctly perceive in an overall sense that there is something wrong with his or her parents or their judgment—that in some way they are "off." This disturbance may vary from frank but unacknowledged psychosis to a certain silliness or fatuousness that makes the parent an unreliable communicator of social reality. In all instances this results in the child's being unable to entrust him- or herself to the parents' judgment. Thus, the parents cannot serve as a protective holding environment. This task creates a real sense of helplessness in the child, which reinforces omnipotent and grandiose fantasies. This induces a pseudomaturation: the child prematurely internalizes parental holding functions on the basis of an illusion of omnipotence. But to varying degrees, the child cuts off from and gives up on his or her real parental environment. The child is turned off, but plays the game of compliance. He or she becomes essentially uncommunicative, for the child learns that his or her fragile sense of self can easily be destroyed by an unempathic or intrusive parental response. Some families simply do not communicate what they feel. Children in such homes are disoriented by mothers who claim that everything is always wonderful. As a result, the children find these parents all but useless as sources of information concerning the real world.

The reader will by now have noted an apparent paradox: I asserted earlier that the changing nosology of the neuroses is perhaps the most direct indication of the impact of historical processes on the ego. Yet, along with Kohut and others, I have confirmed that narcissistic defenses result in part from inauthentic mirroring. If the increase in narcissism is, in part, secondary to cultural change, then how does culture influence development? There are two general but not incompatible hypotheses, as Kohut (1977) implies. The first, that cultural change is transmitted through the personality of the parents, could be described as "indirect cultural transmission." Another hypothesis, to which this author subscribes, is that the individual experiences directly the impact of culture during adolescence, and this impact may accentuate existing character traits. This second theory can be termed "direct cultural transmission."

What I am essentially saying in describing parents as increasingly emotionally unavailable to their children or unempathic and intrusive, is that parents themselves are becoming more narcissistic; so we then have the further problem of accounting for the increase in parental narcissism. Let us assume that the increase of narcissistic personalities has occurred during the last ten to fifteen years.[3] If this observation is correct, I am describing young adults who were adolescents in the late 1950s and 1960s and went through infancy and childhood in the years following World War II. Their parents, therefore, would for the most part have been children in the mid-1920s. Why would this group of parents have become increasingly narcissistic? The end of the twenties marked the beginning of the Great Depression, of course, but the previous years were ones of relative stability compared to our own era.

An alternative hypothesis that does not require positing an increase in parental narcissism is that the *effect* of the parents' neurosis has become magnified because of the loss of the extended family. This is in part the result of the increased mobility of families, which causes them to leave behind supportive aunts and grandparents who lived with them and who might have mitigated the pathogenic effect of the parents' narcissism. An added factor, in this argument, is that as lifestyles changed, the middle class has also given up the nanny and the resident maid. This is a plausible, but essentially unproven, hypothesis. I do not find it fully convincing, for I suspect that there is a more profound relationship between society and character formation.

Kohut (1977) has proposed that the loss of the extended family plus a changing pattern of work activity may contribute to a state of affairs where children are understimulated by the parents' lack of emotional involvement. In modern life, Kohut says, children do not

---

[3] I have the impression from participating in selection committees that there has been a change in the ecology of candidates that is different from the change previously reported by Knight (1953). We are, I believe, selecting an increasing number of candidates who describe many difficulties in the area of relating and commitment, which are characteristic of narcissistic personalities.

have the same opportunities as in the past to observe their parents at work (as opposed to leisure activities); and this failure to observe their parents' competence directly contributes to a certain diminution of the nuclear self.

In his celebrated essay, *Sincerity and Authenticity*, the critic Lionel Trilling (1971), grappled with the same problem. Since he was a literary critic and not a clinician, he examined literature and not patients. He believed that in the late sixteenth or early seventeenth century something like a mutation of human nature took place, with the formation of a new type of personality centered on the virtue of sincerity. Trilling defined sincerity as the degree of congruence between feeling and avowal, and judged it to be a virtue because it supports the working of society. Social institutions require a degree of trust in order to function, and sincerity is in turn a measure of truthfulness. Trilling believed that there was a time when the concept of society did not exist and that this mutation of personality coincided with the emergence of the idea of society as we now conceive it. Given Trilling's definition of sincerity as the congruence between feeling and avowal, the breakdown of sincerity corresponds to what we have described as states of nonrelatedness and noncommunication.

The shaping of character is biphasic. The first phase is the familiar one of early development. The second phase consists of a certain selective reinforcing or reorganization of the personality, which occurs during adolescence when the individual begins to interact with and perceive directly the social environment in which he or she will become a full member. Our contemporary world confronts the adolescent with failures in the protective environment analogous to those experienced earlier in relationship to the parental environment, and this second disillusionment involves similar coping strategies.

There is little doubt that during the last twenty years we have experienced an accelerating disillusionment with our social institutions, based in part on the fact that in public life there is no longer any congruence between what people believe and what they say. Not very long ago, this nation was shocked to learn that President Eisenhower had lied to us concerning the U-2 spy mission. It was during President Johnson's administration that the press coined the euphemism "credibility gap" instead of saying outright that the president was lying.

Today we are no longer shocked—we take the credibility gap for granted and expect to be lied to. As Lionel Trilling observed, sincerity was rightly considered to be a moral virtue, as it supported the notion of society. Thus, spurious or counterfeit communication by the leaders of our society may reinforce the same response that individuals learned earlier in relationship to the affective falseness of their parents: a reflexive reinforcement of the privacy and secrecy of the self, which is hidden behind a facade of compliance, "playing the game." The authenticity of the self remains private. The tragedy of the people who present themselves to us as patients is that they are cut off from this private authenticity of the self. *foresight*

In 1950, a remarkably prescient book, *The Lonely Crowd* (Riesman, Glazer, and Denney, 1950), described a change in the American character. This was a shift from an "inner directed" to an "other directed" character—a change in the direction of compliance, turning off, and playing the game. This finding suggests that a certain degree of counterfeiting of affects is socially adaptive. Pathology ensues when the counterfeiting of affects extends from the outer, public sphere to the inner, private sphere. Thus, preservation of the private authenticity of the self is perhaps the paradigm of the normal narcissistic personality of our time; the failure to maintain this private authenticity defines narcissistic illness.

Additional analogies may be seen between contemporary social institutions and the early parental environment. Defensive narcissism in the child is frequently a reaction to actual helplessness. The child correctly perceives that parents cannot, in fact, protect him or her from the dangers of the real world. This is, of course, the present condition of humanity, as well. The individual has always experienced a certain helplessness regarding his or her own fate. Human beings have always been at the mercy of uncontrolled social eruptions that can inescapably change their lives. Pasternak's Dr. Zhivago is perhaps the clearest example of this. But even after revolutions there is hope for the future. We all know that the spread of atomic weapons gives rise to a real possibility that civilization may be entirely destroyed, that is, that there will be absolutely no hope. We are made aware daily, through television and other media, that events anywhere in the world may threaten the permanence of our culture, and there is really nothing we can do about it.

The response of the individual has been a search for hopefulness, not in relationship to the world, but in relationship to the self (Morgenthau and Person, 1978). One cannot master one's fate, but at least one can master the self. Of course, this too is an illusion. Today the options for self-determination appear to be limitless—one even has the option of changing one's sex. The adolescent's search for consciousness-altering drugs and the adult's quest for some quick psychological technique that will alter the self are, I believe, in part a reflexive turning back to the self because of the recognition that society's institutions are hopeless as sources of protection.

There is another analogy between the situation of the child and that of our contemporary world. We all have a need for privacy and secrecy. We need to keep a part of ourselves isolated from others, a part that cannot be found. Ironically, the social revolution resulting from Freud's discoveries may have inadvertently contributed to intrusions on this privacy. This is true, for example, for the unfortunate child whose psychoanalytically oriented parents interpret the unconscious meaning of his or her behavior. With the spread of psychological sophistication throughout our society, almost anyone can be an amateur psychoanalyst, which in turn has increased the need for us to remain hidden and unfound. Public inauthenticity has combined with a certain psychological intrusiveness, resulting in noncommunication.

If these conjectures are true, we would expect that art as well as the nosology of the neuroses would reflect the impact of this inauthenticity in the contemporary world. In fact, a case can be made for the existence of noncommunication in certain forms of contemporary art. The art historian Meyer Schapiro (1978) in his essay on recent abstract painting, has expressed a view very similar to my own:

> This art is deeply rooted in the self in its relation to the surrounding world. The pathos of the reduction or fragility of the self within a culture that becomes increasingly organized through industry, economy and the State . . . intensifies the desire of the artist to create forms that will manifest his liberty [p. 222].

Schapiro suggests that the rigid, controlled, and impersonal messages of the mass media lead the artist to create works that are not obviously communicating to the audience but need to be found. He says:

What makes painting and sculpture so interesting in our time is their high degree of non-communication. You cannot extract a message from painting by ordinary means; the usual rules of communication do not hold, there is no clear code or fixed vocabulary. Painting, by becoming abstract and giving up its representational function, has achieved a state in which communication seems to be deliberately prevented [p. 223].

From this I conclude that the rise of narcissism is a response to our present troubled times, or, as the Chinese prefer to put it, "our too interesting" times. It is a mistake to believe, as some popular commentators (Lasch, 1979) have asserted, that the rise of narcissism is a sign of our national moral decay. It is not a moral issue at all—it is an issue of adaptation and survival.

References

Gitelson, M. (1954), Therapeutic problems in the analysis of the "normal" candidate. In: *Psychoanalysis: Science and Profession*. New York: International Universities Press, 1973, pp. 211–238.

Kohut, H. (1977), *The Restoration of the Self*. New York, International Universities Press.

Knight, R. (1953), The present state of organized psychoanalysis in the United States. *J. Amer. Psychoanal. Assn.*, 1:197–221.

Lasch, C. (1979), *The Culture of Narcissism*. New York: Norton.

Modell, A. (1975a), The ego and the id: Fifty years later. *Internat. J. Psycho-Anal.*, 56:57–68.

———— (1975b), A narcissistic defense against affects and the illusion of self-sufficiency. *Internat. J. Psycho-Anal.*, 56:275–282.

———— (1976), "The holding environment" and the therapeutic action of psychoanalysis. *J. Amer. Psychoanal. Assn.*, 24:285–307.

———— (1978), The conceptualization of the therapeutic action of psychoanalysis. *Bull. Menn. Clin.*, 42:493–504.

———— (1980), Affects and their non-communication. *Internat. J. Psycho-Anal.*, 61:259–267.

———— (1981a), The narcissistic character and disturbances in the "holding environment." In: *The Course of Life*, Vol. 3, ed. S. Greenspan & G. Pollock. Washington, D.C.: U.S. Department of Health and Human Services, pp. 367–379.

———— (1981b), Self psychology as a psychology of conflict: Comments on the psychoanalysis of the narcissistic personality. Unpublished paper.

Morgenthau, H., and Person, E. (1978), The roots of narcissism. *Partisan Rev.*, 45:337–347.

Riesman, D., Glazer, N., & Denney, R. (1950), *The Lonely Crowd: A Study of the Changing American Character*. New York: Doubleday.

Schapiro, M. (1978), *Modern Art—19th and 20th Centuries*. New York: George Braziller.

Tartakoff, H. (1966), The normal personality in our culture and the Nobel Prize complex. In: *Psychoanalysis: A General Psychology*, ed. R. Loewenstein, L. Newman, M. Schur, & A. Solnit. New York: International Universities Press, pp. 222–252.

Trilling, L. (1971), *Sincerity and Authenticity: Six Lectures*. Cambridge, Mass.: Harvard University Press.

Waelder, R. (1962), Review of psychoanalysis, scientific method, and philosophy. J. Amer. Psychoanal. Assoc., 10:617–637.

Winnicott, D. (1960a), Ego distortion in terms of true and false self. In: *The Maturational Processes and the Facilitating Environment*. New York: International Universities Press, 1965, pp. 140–152.

——— (1960b), The Theory of the parent-infant relationship. In: *The Maturational Processes and the Facilitating Environment*. New York: International Universities Press, 1965, pp. 37–55.

PART II

THEORY

The Scientific and Clinical Functions of Psychoanalytic Theory

ROBERT MICHELS

Psychoanalysts treat patients. They also carry on other activities relevant to psychoanalysis: they read and study; they teach and supervise; and they think about their experiences with patients as well as their other experiences and knowledge. Many of them formulate their thoughts, give talks, write books and articles, and communicate with their colleagues and with others outside of the profession. Frequently, this writing and communicating involves the development and description of theories that relate to psychoanalysis. As many have noted, in spite of the central role of clinical practice in their professional lives, psychoanalysts seem to devote an inordinate amount of time to theory in their writing. In this paper I shall discuss the nature of these theories and their role in both the scientific and the clinical aspects of psychoanalysis.

Psychoanalysts draw on several sources in constructing their theories. First, they draw on their clinical experience. They often emphasize this source of theory far more than a careful study of their theory-building would support. This is, of course, true of other scientists as well. Scientists prefer to think of their theories as growing out of their data, and tend to minimize those aspects of theory that exist prior to the data and help to create them. They are far more aware of their subject matter and their data, while the other elements that contribute to the construction of theory function as preconscious structures to which scientists pay little attention. The clinical data of psychoanalysis consist of the things that patients tell their psychoanalysts, the ways in which they tell them, and the patterns or regularities in patients' accounts of their lives as well as in their behavior during their analyses. Clinical data also consist of the psychoanalysts' responses to their patients and patients' responses to their psychoanalysts, the interpretations and constructions and responses to interpretations that occur in psychoanalyses, and the relationship between what patients say and how they say it, and what interpretations are used and what effect they have. These are the core data of psychoanalysis, and familiarity with and understanding of these data are the core knowledge base of psychoanalytic practice.

Theories in psychoanalysis, like theories in other areas of inquiry, are based on more than the data they organize. They are constructed in accordance with rules and principles stemming from the intellectual traditions that guide the theory builder. Thus, early psychoanalytic theory was patterned after a theory-building tradition that was dominant in nineteenth century natural sciences. Some more recent theories have been constructed after the pattern of theoretical constructions in the humanistic disciplines or the more recent sciences of information processing. Every theory must be constructed in accordance with some model or principle of theory-building—a model or principle that exists apart from the data that it encompasses. These models are often more closely related to the dominant intellectual interests of the culture or the historic period of the theory builder than to the nature of the subject matter that the theory addresses. Principles of theory-building are neither true nor false, although they may be more or less well suited to specific tasks of theory construction. Some of the contemporary discussion about psychoanalytic theory has revolved around such questions as whether the principles that have been brought to bear in constructing the theory were good principles in some absolute sense, whether they are now outdated and should be replaced by new principles, and whether they are well suited for the task of theory-building in psychoanalysis.

Theories in psychoanalysis are also influenced by findings from other disciplines. Freud's early theorizing was heavily influenced by his understanding of contemporary neurobiology, evolutionary biology, and cultural anthropology, and he struggled to make his psychoanalytic formulations consistent with these fields (Sulloway, 1979). In recent years, psychoanalysts have been particularly interested in the findings of developmental psychology and, at times, psycholinguistics. Knowledge developed in other disciplines exists independently of psychoanalysis, and contributes to construction of psychoanalytic theory in a similar way to the general intellectual style of theory-building mentioned above. However, unlike a general style of theorizing, knowledge in other fields may come to be disproven (as have some notions of the inheritance of acquired characteristics that were included in Freud's knowledge of biology). Furthermore, it is possible to construct psychoanalytic theories without any regard for the knowledge developed in other disciplines, although every theory must follow some principle of theorizing. Avoiding knowledge from outside psychoanalysis offers some advantages; it protects theories from one form of obsolescence and it makes possible a clarity of boundaries and a purity of language and principle, a value advocated by some major contemporary theorists (Schafer, 1976). However, a heavy price is paid in return. Some of the most exciting advances in knowledge come from the convergence or at least congruence of separate avenues of inquiry. For example, psychoanalysis has been enriched by the interaction between the study of reconstructed personal histories in the psychoanalytic situation and the observations of psychological development in infants and children. Similarly, many believe that our new understanding of neurobiology promises advances in our knowledge of affect and motivation that will contribute to our psychoanalytic models in these areas, as Freud had hoped.

There are several major goals in constructing psychoanalytic theories. The first is the familiar goal of theories in science: to advance the science, to organize knowledge, to lead to new discoveries and insights, to correct or improve previous ignorance, and to advance the method. Most of the discussion about psychoanalytic theory has considered these goals, questioning whether psychoanalysis is a science or some other form of inquiry, whether its theories are well constructed, whether they are testable or falsifiable, and so on (Hartmann, Kris, and Loewenstein, 1953).

⌐   Psychoanalysis is more than a *gnosis,* however, it is also a *praxis,*
a way of doing something. Most consumers of psychoanalytic theory
are not theory builders, they are not likely to contribute to the science.
They are practitioners of psychoanalysis, and they suggest another goal
of theorizing: to facilitate practice. This is not a subclass of the first
goal. It is easy to imagine a theory that would represent an important
contribution to psychoanalytic knowledge, but would be of little value
to a psychoanalyst analyzing patients. Perhaps more important, it is
possible to imagine theories that would be valuable to the practicing
analyst, but would have little to do with advancing the science. This
second class of theory is common in all the applied sciences, whether
engineering, agriculture, politics, or medicine. In fact, many claim
that virtually all psychoanalytic theory today falls into one of these two
categories—scientifically interesting and practically irrelevant, or practically valuable but scientifically of little interest. Some even add a
third category of theorizing—practically irrelevant and scientifically
worthless!
    There is also a third goal in constructing psychoanalytic theories:
to facilitate the teaching and learning of psychoanalysis. Lewin (1965)
has suggested that this is one of the major sources of theorizing.
However, we generally think of teaching as supporting the other goals,
as educating psychoanalytic practitioners or psychoanalytic investigators. Most psychoanalysts believe that the first step in education
should revolve around developing the ability to practice psychoanalysis, and that the teaching of scientific or research skills should follow.
One of the problems in some psychoanalytic curricula is that the early
teaching of theory fails to emphasize the clinical function of theory,
and is thus strangely disconnected from the immediate goals of the
student. This no doubt reflects the way that much psychoanalytic theory
is written, as well as the social status of "science" as opposed to
"practice."
    Psychoanalytic theories provide the psychoanalyst with perceptual
and cognitive structures with which to apprehend and organize clinical
experience. Transference, conflict, resistance, or unconscious fantasy
are all created in the psychoanalytic situation by the interaction between
the patient and the psychoanalyst on the one hand, and by the psychoanalyst's capacity to perceive and organize his or her awareness

of that interaction on the other. Like the phenomena of other sciences—waves or particles or cells or pathways—these psychoanalytic phenomena require both the event in the world and the prepared mind that organizes the experience that stems from that event. This view of science should be a comfortable one for psychoanalysts, for it is similar to the view of psychological functioning that has been central to psychoanalytic thinking since the abandonment of the seduction model and its replacement with the model of the active organizing of the inner world by the child's mind. Freud alludes to the contribution of theory to the construction of data in the *New Introductory Lectures* (1933) in his discussion of revisions in the theory of anxiety. He states, "It is truly a matter of conceptions—that is to say, of introducing the right abstract ideas, whose application to the raw material of observation will produce order and clarity in it" (p. 81).

Of course, theories in psychoanalysis, like other scientific theories, do more than organize perception; they organize action as well, and provide categories and psychological structures that mediate the psychoanalyst's interventions as well as understanding. Interpretation, like transference and resistance, has meaning only in the context of a theoretically informed analyst as well as a participating patient and analyst. This means that a psychoanalyst who is theoretically informed not only listens, hears, and experiences the analytic material differently, and does so without conscious attention to theory, but the analyst also acts differently, although nonetheless spontaneously. These actions are not deduced from theory, but stem from mental predispositions that have developed as one aspect of the learning of theory. Knowledge changes our perceptions and our responses; indeed, this is a central tenet of the theory of psychoanalytic treatment.

Theories are constructions and have many similarities to works of art. They can be appreciated and evaluated aesthetically as well as scientifically. Moreover, like works of art, exposure to them can enrich a psychoanalyst's network of potential associations to clinical stimuli. Instructions to analysts suggest a state of mind that is "free floating" or "evenly hovering," that is open to empathic perception, trial identification, adaptive regression. This is not the state of mind of someone applying a complex scientific theory to a body of data. It is, however, the state of mind of someone using theory as a work of art, alongside

other works of art, in order to extend and enrich his or her network
of associations. The psychoanalyst who knows and uses psychoanalytic
theories in this way listens to the patient with an associative context
that includes the shared experiences of the entire community of psychoanalysis, past and present, as well as the psychoanalyst's own
clinical and personal experience and the understanding of man that has
been crystallized in great works of art (Cooper and Michels, 1977).
Viewed from this perspective, there is little difference between psychoanalytic case histories and psychoanalytic theories, or between psychoanalytic theories and other theories, or for that matter between
science and art. The only question would be: How does the theory
enrich the experience of the analyst with the patient? Further, there
is little concern about compatibility or contradiction among theories,
just as there is little concern about the compatibility or contradiction
concerning the view of man embodied in works of art. Finally, we
would not ask whether psychoanalytic theories were true or false; just
as critics do not ask whether works of art are true or false, philosophers
do not ask whether scientific theories are true or false, and psychoanalysts do not ask whether interpretations are true or false. The critic
wants to know what impact the work of art has on the audience and
on the culture. The philosopher of science wants to know whether the
theory furthers scientific inquiry, generates hypotheses, or suggests
experiments. The psychoanalyst wants to know whether the interpretation stimulates new material and leads to therapeutic progress. We
want to know whether the psychoanalytic theory helps psychoanalysts
to analyze, whether it guides them to new insights and understanding.
In each case the test is not one of truth or falsity, but of the nature of
the impact on a process.

In addition to providing structures for perceiving and understanding clinical data, and to enriching the psychoanalyst's network of
associations, theories provide systems for classifying and organizing
the clinical material. The psychoanalyst's capacity to understand and
to resonate to the immediate clinical experience is necessary for psychoanalysis, but it is not sufficient. Without further knowledge, every
psychoanalyst would have to start at the very beginning of psychoanalytic history, and few would progress very far. Most psychoanalysts
have some inner cognitive map that leads them to look for certain kinds

of material, and to search when it is not immediately apparent. One impact of specific psychoanalytic theories on the analytic process lies not in the way they order the material that is present, but rather in the way the theories lead the analyst to search for that which is not apparent. This, of course, also leads to one of the methodological problems in the science of psychoanalysis. For reasons that are well known to clinicians, such searches tend to be fruitful; and, therefore, different psychoanalysts with different theories can construct quite different analysands out of what began as the same patient, confirming their own theories in the process.

Probably the most important impact of theory on psychoanalytic practice has a quite different mechanism from those discussed, so far. Psychoanalysis is a difficult profession, and psychoanalysts spend much of their time uncertain, perhaps confused or bewildered, attempting to comprehend amorphous or chaotic experiences that do not always fit into place. The work is also lonely, and psychoanalysts crave reassurance, support, and company. Theory can provide that support. A theory can be seen as a kind of transitional object: it links the psychoanalyst to a teacher or mentor; it provides a sense of security, a reassurance that someone knows and understands; and it gives refuge when the going is difficult. Moreover, like some transitional objects, one may cling to a theory all the more when others ridicule it or try to take it away and replace it with a cleaner, more modern substitute. Old theories, like old teddy bears, are not less beloved because they are torn or perhaps smell a little. This function of theory is particularly important for students or novices—it provides a partially illusory safety and reassurance that functions until accumulating personal clinical experience diminishes both its power and the need for its supportive function. When this process goes smoothly, all is well. However, at times the deidealization of theory precedes the development of personal experience, and the student is exposed prematurely without adequate support. Many such students become critical of psychoanalysis and turn against it. At other times students elevate the theory above clinical experience, and it is never deidealized. These students become followers of psychoanalysis, rather than independent professionals, and tend to be the favorite targets for the attacks of the first group.

This nonspecific function of theory for psychoanalysts again reminds us of the functions that interpretations play for psychoanalytic patients. Interpretations comfort and reassure, whether or not the patient understands and uses them. We have already discussed how interpretations, like theories, are evaluated in terms of their impact on the process, and how it is of little interest to question whether they are true or false. Both interpretations and theories serve to clarify what is confusing, to stimulate associations, and to provide links between surface phenomena that are easily observed and deeper structures that are hidden from direct view; by doing so, both help to bring those deeper structures into awareness.

This calls attention to one more important similarity between psychoanalytic theory and psychoanalytic interpretation. Interpretations are effective only within the context of a specific kind of relationship, what is called by some a therapeutic alliance. Correct timing and dosage is important; they must be "tuned in" to the ongoing psychoanalytic process. Similarly, theories have little value in the development of psychoanalysis as a profession unless they are communicated within an intellectual alliance. Like a therapeutic alliance, this does not imply agreement or acceptance, but rather a readiness to listen, a benevolent skepticism. It means that there is a shared community involving the theoretician and the audience as professional and scientific colleagues. There are many examples in the history of psychoanalysis (as in the history of the various sciences) of theories that had rich potential but little effect because they were poorly timed or poorly phrased, or fell upon unreceptive ears.

Theories in psychoanalysis vary along several dimensions. Some are "experience-near," formulated close to the primary clinical data of the psychoanalytic situation. They may be in the form of generalizations of clinical phenomena or descriptions of patterns or themes that have been observed repeatedly in similar patients or similar situations. Other theories are "experience-distant," relatively further from the data, and more like theories in the natural sciences. These theories are often useful in suggesting potential application of psychoanalytic findings to other areas of psychoanalytic or scientific interest. Experience-near theory is usually focal, that is, it is about some specific type of phenomenon or clinical experience, while experience-distant theory tends to be more comprehensive, about man or the "mind" or a major sector of mental life. Experience-near theories are sometimes criticized for being no more than a restatement of the data, summaries rather than scientific formulations, while experience-distant theories may be considered so abstract as to be independent of the data and, therefore, irrelevant to them, to be no more than general rules for formulating tautologic statements that cannot be falsified and do not add to our knowledge.

These two types of theory both have potential clinical as well as scientific significance; they can both be theories as forms of art, as well as theories as statements in science. Experience-near theories borrow their terms and concepts from the consultation room, and can easily lend these back in the form of interpretations and the criteria for employing them. Experience-distant theories help the psychoanalyst to orient his or her stance with regard to the patient, the analytic situation, and the world. They suggest possibilities that might otherwise be overlooked or ignored, and prevent analyses that are overly deter-mined by the immediate content of the moment rather than the sig-nificance of that content in a larger, although not always apparent, frame.

There is a common course to the history of many theories in psychoanalysis. They begin as focal experience-near formulations, stemming from scientific or artistic inspirations that provide categories and models that seem to fit the clinical experience and enrich its meaning. These stimuli may arise from other areas of psychoanalytic thought, from biology or psychology or observations in child devel-opment or art or literature, but they become psychoanalytic formula-tions when they order the data of clinical psychoanalysis and are tested in the clinical situation.

Following this initial stage, there are often attempts to generalize the formulation, to make it more powerful, more comprehensive, more abstract, more scientific, and more experience-distant. Two forces tend to stimulate these attempts. First is the desire to increase the value of a good idea by exploring its potential, and the universal cognitive desire to link ideas and find common bonds that bridge and unify them. The second is the status associated with "science," and the view of many psychoanalysts that "good" theories must have the form of experience-distant general rules. This shift ruins many good clinical formulations, converting them into bad science. It also tends to cloud the distinction between the clinical and scientific goals of theory construction, implying that the former are preliminary or subsidiary to the latter.

Psychoanalysis profits by having both types of theories, and by exploiting its theories both clinically and scientifically. Theories may shift in either direction, and theories that serve one goal may well be borrowed for the other. However, there is no reason to force a good theory into a style or function that does not suit it. If we attempt to do so we may discover (or perhaps confirm) a Parkinson's Law of Theories, in which each new theory is pushed further and further from its origins until it becomes clinically sterile or scientifically useless or both.

In summary, psychoanalysts treat patients and construct theories. Their theories grow out of their clinical experience, but are also shaped by their intellectual traditions and by other sources of knowledge. Theories are crucial for the advance of knowledge, and they also play an important role in enhancing psychoanalytic practice. They provide the structures that organize the analyst's perceptions and actions; they enrich his associations; they provide cognitive structures that classify and order analytic data; and they are important sources of emotional support. In many regards they are to the psychoanalyst what interpretations are to the analysand. Like interpretations, they are only effective within the appropriate relationship, and the effective theoretician must attend to that relationship as well as to the content of his theory. Various types of theories in psychoanalysis, and the natural history of psychoanalytic theories, can both be viewed in the light of this distinction between the scientific and clinical functions of theory.

References

Cooper, A., & Michels, R. (1977), The impact of theory on psychoanalytic practice. Presented at the Regional Council of Psychoanalytic Societies of Greater New York.

Freud, S. (1933), New introductory lectures on psycho-analysis. *Standard Edition,* 22:5–182. London: Hogarth Press, 1964.

Hartmann, H., Kris, E., & Loewenstein, R. (1953), The function of theory in psychoanalysis. In: *Drives, Affects, Behavior,* ed. R. Loewenstein, New York: International Universities Press, pp. 13–37.

Lewin, B. (1965), Teaching and the beginnings of theory. *Internat. J. Psycho-Anal.*, 46:137–139.

Schafer, R. (1976), *A New Language for Psychoanalysis*. New Haven: Yale University Press.

Sulloway, F. (1979), *Freud, Biologist of the Mind: Beyond the Psychoanalytic Legend*. New York: Basic Books.

Seeing Something New in Something Old

LAWRENCE FRIEDMAN

Narcissism used to be the enemy of the analyst. Kohut (1971, 1977) revealed a new potential in it. His respectful approach depicts narcissism more objectively, and his attention to its natural history illuminates its complexity. But Kohut makes us most vividly aware of the potential of narcissism by pointing to what happens when analysts facilitate a certain sort of striving. Although narcissism originally figured in Freud's writings as a transformational concept, it quickly became anathema as an obstacle to change. Kohut revived its transformational significance by showing what it could build with the analyst's help.

Kohut displays a familiar retardant in such a way that we newly see it as a potential for development. We should pay attention to this procedure because it is so similar to what happens in the construction of theory in general, as well as in the very practice of psychoanalysis. Although a great many things go on in a psychoanalysis, in one sense all the analyst ever does is to see something (in the patient) *as* something—that is, as a certain sort of something, as a manifestation of something, as a participating figure in a larger something, or as something of a certain form. Accordingly, therapists seek help from theoretical viewpoints that reveal potentials they had not seen. Few perceptive activities are as constantly intent as this, but needless to say, the activity is not found only in psychoanalysis. Everybody's every perception does the same thing. We are always seeing things as a this or as a that. The procedure is that of abstracting, ordering, putting *A* in relation to *B,* phenomena in relation to concepts. It is, in short, the general weaving of awareness.

Most Western philosophy has been an effort to describe this process of changing predication. Nowadays the project gets attention mostly from students of science, language, and historiography. They share a concern about the relationship of new meaning to old meaning and to constant truth. They ask how a new scientific theory is introduced; how a word can be given powers beyond its definition; how a sequence involving human aspiration can be objectively described, and moreover, truly described differently after a further sequence of events. Since these disciplines all ask how we can learn to see something as something else, they are all germane to theory innovation (as well as to the process of psychotherapy). My impression is that their proposals converge on a general answer, while Kohut's work suggests ways in which that answer can be specialized for psychoanalytic purposes. I will illustrate this thesis by referring to a few writers who are representative of recent trends.

Philosophy of Science

Current fashions in philosophy are not necessarily more authoritative than earlier ones. But some peculiarities of recent philosophy of science seem especially pertinent to the work of the psychoanalyst. Consider the well-known symposium edited by Lakatos and Musgrave (1970), which calls into question the older, positivist distinction between observation and theory. In that symposium, Popper is closest to the older view, insisting that the progress of science requires it to submit to a nontheoretical challenge. But even he does not expect such a nontheoretical challenge to consist of collectible truths that might be assembled into a better theory. Although Popper's views have grown out of the empiricist tradition, he holds theory to be an imaginative construct that stakes its claim on surviving tests, rather than a doctrine compelled by indifferent facts. With Popper at one end of the spectrum, and Thomas Kuhn at the other, the argument has moved from the older debate about whether theory is compounded out of theory-free descriptions to the last-ditch question of whether there is even such a thing as a theory-free test to which a theory can be submitted.

Kuhn (1970) argues that if one examines the actual evolution of science, one does not find that theories are automatically jettisoned when they run into difficulty. Up to a point, practitioners ignore such difficulties while they are busy exploring a theory's strengths. Indeed, little scientific progress would be made if each first failure felled a theory. It may later turn out that a theory's failure was due to a relatively unimportant appendage or an inessential way of formulating it. Successors to Kuhn and Popper, such as Lakatos, have carried these considerations into a much-needed analysis of what exactly a "theory" is, and Kuhn has been doing the same thing in a different fashion. But Kuhn also has a more radical explanation for scientific conservatism: The puzzles that the theory solves are themselves delineated by the theory. A scientific theory is, in effect, a *way* of both formulating and solving puzzles, learned by practice on exemplars. As such, it constitutes on-the-job training in seeing the world a certain way. The fine detail of science depends on the diligence of this effort, and that in turn requires a standard of competence set up by a scientific community. Historical and sociological forces affect these agreements, but the more advanced the science, the greater the insulation of its practitioners, and the less it cares whether laymen understand it or find it relevant. The specialty community has, in effect, become riveted to the challenge of widening and specifying its special way of analyzing reality.

There comes a day, according to Kuhn, when the theory's difficulties (puzzles that it frames but cannot solve) accumulate, and those deviant scientists who have been focusing their attention on the "anomalies" win over the community to a new way of approaching reality. A storm of debate attends Kuhn's description of change in theory. There is certainly no agreement on this phenomenon either among historians or theoreticians, and Kuhn himself has not settled on a dogma. But he has continued to affirm these principles: that nature does not come already divided into categories; that only theory can introduce a thinkable reality to a scientist; that it does so by offering authoritative examples of how to question nature—examples that train the scientist to ask and answer questions; and that a major change in theory involves something like a switch in gestalt, because the most elementary terms of the old theory already suppose a view that is incompatible with the new. Fundamental to Kuhn's position is the fact that, while you can point to an individual, such as John or Mary, you cannot point to a natural class, such as ducks or swans. Neither the concepts nor the examples of *duck* and *swan* come with instructions telling which instance goes with which label. We learn divisions of nature by example—examples that may come to exemplify something different as we obtain new information. Someone points to one animal and then another, calling them both ducks, and eventually we learn to distinguish ducks from swans—though we may wish to change our groupings if we find some unforeseen type of beast. In the same way, scientists use models as demonstrations, without knowing exactly how much of them applies; these models are practical aids to attention, not abstract definitions. (See also Hesse [1980] on the interchangeable roles of fact and hypothesis in a scientific theory.)

Something like a model, therefore, can never be dispensed with by science. It can never be melted down to a literal, unequivocal, binding, abstract formula. And it follows that a model cannot be exactly translated into another formula (see Kuhn, 1979, p. 415). An outdated scientific theory can be referred to by a new theory, but cannot be exactly translated into it. The replacement of an old scientific model by a new one will appear as a switch in metaphor—''metaphor'' *not* being used here to mean simple substitution of a comparable term or the selection of some aspect of the original meaning, like a simile, but rather a new way of seeing. The metaphor is a new model, redistributing individuals among natural families.

Rhetoric

In this respect, change of theory shares a problem with change of linguistic meaning. Contrary to what some have suggested, the interesting linguistic subject is not transformational grammar, for despite its name and diagrams, that is a theory of language invariants, not change of meaning. The study of how something comes to be seen as something else is an older discipline—rhetoric—invested with new popularity. The renewed interest in rhetoric is shown by an inclination to treat the classic figures of speech as cognitive options, not just oratorical ornaments. All psychoanalysts should read Kenneth Burke (1950) for a spirited evocation of a world saturated in inescapably appetitive language. Burke does for the common world of society what Kuhn does for science. In effect, both say that suggestive models are fundamental to knowing and learning. These are the kind of models that function as metaphors rather than as blueprints. Physics uses the solar system as a model for the atom. The model is metaphorical, since its resemblance to an atom is not fully specifiable. Analogously, the student of rhetoric cites the image of a river god as a way a society can sum itself up without explicitly declaring its principles.

Burke says that *all* predication (he calls it identification, that is, identification of something with something else) is rhetoric; it has a tendentious gist. A special case of the function of bias as a cognitive tool is the account of human happenings. Some historians and students of narrative believe that tendentious organization is necessary for the creation of a meaningful story. Hayden White (1980) refers to the historian as a relentless moralizer. I will consider this special case shortly.

The line of argument followed so far suggests that science replaces theories by offering new exemplars that function as suggestive models. A suggestive model might be a type of problem together with its solution, as well as a type of visualized structure. Furthermore, this approach suggests that the meaning of ordinary experience may shift as it is clothed in changing figures of speech. The figures of speech have a metaphorical effect insofar as they present something in a certain light without argument.

Metaphor and Model

The relationship between metaphor and model has been the subject of much interest lately. Whereas for Kuhn, its metaphorical function explains the usefulness of a scientific model, for Max Black (1979), the modeling function explains the action of a metaphor. But since Black believes that metaphor may transform a subject matter, even his view of metaphor makes modeling something of an open, Kuhnian

operation. Black must be alluding to a model that is open for interpretation, because a closed, literal model, fabricated out of materials
at hand, could not transform the field to which it is applied. Henle
(1958) suggested that a metaphor is a direction for mentally building
a new model which imitates features of the subject. It has even been
suggested, as an escape from the incommensurability of scientific
theories alleged by Kuhn, that metaphor allows one to peek around
the corners of a man-made theory and visualize the natural joints of
the universe (Boyd, 1979).

This kind of speculation is in marked contrast to the idea that
metaphor is poetic synonymy—a mere substitution of an uncommon
word for a more ordinary one—an approach that was encouraged by
the influential theory of Roman Jakobson (1956, 1959, 1960). Neurological deficit shows that people have separately destructible powers,
on the one hand, to combine words into meaningful, purposeful sentences and, on the other hand, to summon up equivalent words when
desired. Noting this, Jakobson suggested that language draws elements
together either on the basis of their connectedness or on the basis of
their equivalence—that is, by metonymy or metaphor (as Jakobson
uses those terms).

Some psychotherapists (for example, Lacan, 1957) have written
as though the mechanism of meaning change is finally illuminated by
Jakobson's discovery that language operates on the axes of substitution
and contiguity: meanings are made either by substituting equivalent
terms (metaphor), or by connecting apposite functions and details
(metonymy). Some writers, implicitly trading on the more creative
nuances of the term "metaphor," have gone so far as to suppose that
treatment consists in converting a predominance of the one language
function into a predominance of the other (see Levenson, 1978, p. 13;
Watzlawick, 1978).

Jakobson uses this linguistic polarity as a grand archetype for *all*
distinctions between category recognition and synthetic invention,
whether those distinctions are involved in stringing sounds into a simple
morpheme, words into a sentence, or sentences into a poem. The brain
does seem to have separate centers for accessing units and for arranging
them in sequences. But if we are concerned with *meaning,* we shall
probably have to take the product of these two activities as our initial

subject. Potential "contiguities" are part of a word's meaning and type, and therefore the meaning and type of a word must involve both metaphor and metonymy. To say that metaphor is the selection of a word with a fixed, categorical relationship to alternative words usable in the same position, does not tell us much about its role in the elaboration of meaning. Jakobson's metaphoric pole is a formal function of every possible *code*, not specifically an aspect of a *concept*, and it may not be as useful for psychoanalytic purposes as that of Ricoeur (1977a, 1978).

After a painstaking survey of the various views of metaphor, Ricoeur concludes that metaphor is not word substitution but a bridge to perceptual discovery. According to him, metaphor makes use of a more general function of imaginative schematism that permits the expansion of knowledge. While psychoanalysts are turning to linguistics to understand meaning change, Ricoeur (1978) gently cautions that linguistics has not gone far in this regard, and psychoanalysis may have more to teach than to learn about this matter.

Ricoeur's theory suggests a Piagetian function for metaphor: the structured language may be thought of as a preexisting schema; metaphorical anomaly ("live" metaphor) represents the challenge of novelty; what happens to a language as the metaphor "dies" into a standard colloquialism, amounts to an assimilation consequent to an accommodation to the live metaphor.

If one regards metaphor as Ricoeur does, it serves language the way that a new disciplinary matrix, in Kuhn's sense, serves science. A live metaphor and a new matrix are open-ended models that orient the mind toward a new kind of abstraction. They both inspire one to slice up the universe differently, promising that the slicing will happen in a systematic and realistic, though unfamiliar way, and they do that without mapping the characterization (or marking the slices) ahead of time. Both the scientific practice and the metaphoric identification *support* a new exploration without actually *specifying* it. They are both models, in that we are introduced to them ostensively rather than discursively. (See Harré [1970] on the need for nondiscursive supplements in science.) And they are both metaphors in that they are not equivalent to anything in the preexisting framework.

The use of metaphor and open-ended model as indispensable ways of picturing the world, is now a frequent subject of discussion. Goodman (1976) proposes that a metaphor makes a familiar method of analysis work toward "the sorting and organizing of an alien realm." Lakoff and Johnson (1980) suggest that the unexplored but tangible structure of metaphor helps to understand more amorphous aspects of reality, such as the realm of feelings. Their book argues that metaphors are grounded in body orientation, and are thus ultimately shaped by reality. Ricoeur (1977a) contends that metaphor is not carried by a single word, but is a product of at least a full sentence. Lakoff and Johnson go further: they draw attention to the endless web of hierarchical and overlapping metaphorical *systems* that structure experience. One may conclude that this systematic quality distinguishes epistemological metaphor from the specialized poetic variety that catches our attention.

Harré (1970) argues that science aims to discover underlying substantial reality, and that (some) models are provisional nominees for substantial things, which can therefore be further investigated in the workings of the model. "Live" metaphor can be found in Harré's work in two guises: One is the kind of model that has only partially known applicability. The other is a seemingly nominal classification that has begun to look as though it might separate natural kinds.[1]

In live metaphor and open-ended models, one thing is understood through another thing, while the logic of the lesson is still unknown. That is quite different from an understanding achieved by abstract concepts that formally and explicitly declare the nature of their lesson to begin with. Indeed, the authors we have looked at imply that abstract concepts are never rich enough to explain anything but formal systems. It is a plausible position, but it does bring difficulties: An abstract concept, although it selects certain features of reality, specifies those features in an objective and universally accessible fashion. But the comparison of as-yet-incompletely-related subjects depends on a point of view, a way of looking. We are trying to understand *A* by seeing

[1] I am indebted to Dr. Arnold Goldberg for calling my attention to the work of Rom Harré, who sums up the exploratory use of models most satisfactorily to my taste. The example of Harré shows that acknowledging perspective bias does not militate against ontological reality and, indeed, as he and I and Immanuel Kant would argue, the bias actually presupposes the objective reality (See Friedman, 1976b).

it in some sort of *B*-ish fashion (as opposed to *knowing* that *A* shares just features 1 and 2 with *B*). Problems associated with relativism and bias are introduced with metaphor and model.

History

Historians and philosophers of history have had a head start of several centuries in trying to accommodate biased perspectives to objective truth. They were forced to this early because history is seen in a changing light—and yet the light in which it is seen seems to be its very meaning. (For a summary of attempts to find a universal vantage point, see Gadamer, 1975; Mandelbaum, 1971.)

Psychoanalysts have been shielded from this trouble by the finitude of the lives they study. Psychoanalysis places itself among the biological rather than the social sciences partly because the short history of an individual has a more constant pattern and limited outcome than the long history of the human race. No one knows how Man will end, but everyone knows how each man will. We do not consider it unreasonable to talk about what it is that childhood prepares for. But if someone talks the same way about the species, we take him for a cryptotheologian or a crackpot.

Out of place in sociology, history, and the evolution of language, the concept of maturity helps to make psychoanalysis a biological study. Since maturity brings limited possibilities, it provides a natural schema for selecting and describing earlier meanings. We arrange the schemas into a theory of the mind.

It might seem, then, that psychoanalysis can evade the problems of history because the drama of development is given by nature, rather than being imposed by artful narrative. That is true, however, only to the extent that maturity is measured in nonvolitional terms. For example, we do not need a specifically historical model of human development to account for the perpetuation of the gene or senescence. But if by "maturity" we mean an integration of purposes, then it will not be described without a history of desire that isolates and combines wishes, and shows their interaction. (Besides Kohut, Loewald [1978] and Schafer [1970, 1980] contribute to this discussion.) The "point of the story" has to be ferreted out of the sequence, just as the historian must find a "logic" in history. So, after all, the psychoanalyst is faced with the same problem as the historian in giving coherence to a sequence of aims.

That means that the theory of the mind has itself a dramatic structure, insofar as it deals with the individual's path to maturity. Various psychotherapies can be distinguished by the morality play implied in their theories of the mind. One can almost always find in them forces cast as evil or reactionary, and these connotations may be one of the major determinants of differential psychotherapeutic effects. On the subject of the implicitly dramatic configuration of people's lives and treatment, Schafer (1980) has been the most eloquent.

Freud attempted to embrace both the historical and biological descriptions of the mind within the core of his theory, and so his theory runs the gamut from supra-individual forces to personal family dramas—from mechanisms of action to nested and evolving meanings. Understandably, many theoreticians would like to deal with these aspects separately, or to banish one or another of the heterogeneous models of explanation. But efforts to purify the theory of the mind do not look promising. I have elsewhere (Friedman, 1971, 1972, 1976a, 1977, 1980a, 1980b) tried to show why that might be expected.[2]

---

[2] Schafer (1980) sees two metaphors in Freud's theory: a mechanistic one and a dramatic one, the former outdated by the march of science. Schafer favors heterogeneity of perspectives, but his attitude toward metaphor is in some respects equivocal. He could have chosen to argue that some metaphors are simply better than others at fostering opportunity and personal responsibility. That would be consistent with his stylistic relativism. But he seems to want to argue that these favored metaphors are more realistic, and that to adulterate them with old-fashioned or fantastic metaphors causes psychic reality to be misperceived. Although Schafer allows a patient's experience of metaphor to be a unique and untranslatable experience, theoretical metaphors that he does not like are reduced to simple, testable similes. For example, one part of Freud's theory is said to describe the mind as a nineteenth century machine. Schafer does not seem to realize that when he calls Freud's theory "mechanistic," *he* is employing a metaphor to understand a *theory,* just as someone else might choose to say that Schafer's action language theory is spiritualistic theory, or a theory of the soul rather than of the mind. If a theory is a complex metaphor, then these descriptions are metaphors for metaphors, and the usefulness of the description must be assessed before it can determine our attitude toward the theory it describes. In my opinion, the description of Freud's theory as a mechanical or hydraulic model or metaphor captures little of importance. The vital workings of the theory are more consistently involved with causation and with the interplay of force and meaning than with any particular image of equipment (Friedman, 1976b, 1977). It is not at all uncommon for process theorists to view any cause and effect theory as "mechanistic" (Meyerson, 1930). Ironic relativism is hard to live with: If every tale we tell is just a more or less

The kinship of history and psychoanalysis is illustrated by the problem of empathy. Philosophers of history such as Herder, Dilthey, and Collingwood have noted that history requires a primary capacity for representing the meanings of more or less remote people; if that representation had to come from contemporary historical theory, then historical explanation would be circular. In his plea for renewed psychoanalytic curiosity, Kohut, too, has emphasized the reliable capacity of the human being to make sense out of another human being's meanings, untutored by sophisticated theory. He does not say that we ever approach a subject with a blank mind. But he holds that interpersonal recognition is not completely dependent on disposable conceptual constructs.

Some theoreticians have reacted as though Kohut had urged the cause of extrasensory perception. It is occasionally forgotten that part of Kohut's teaching has to do with the *impact* of empathy on its recipient, not just its formation within the analyst. But we are interested in the cognitive question, and it should be pointed out that, as far as we know, even simple perception of objects requires a preestablished capacity (no one yet having shown how to construct an inductive logic); yet we hear no complaint that this faculty implies an extra sense. Nor is an extra sense required for empathy. As Cassirer (1929) pointed out, if we did not possess the capacity to read something *into* our sensations—to see them as signs of what lies beyond them—nothing could teach it to us. Accordingly, if we did not have (or find unfolded within us) an initial capacity to project perceived stimuli into forms of human meaning and intention, no data would ever take that shape. (I do not speak of the genetic development of this capacity in the infant, though it is beginning to appear that it is accomplished very early.[3]) The issue

convenient narrative, and if the theory we advance is just another tale we tell, then so is the description it pleases us to make of the other fellow's story.

[3] In considering this problem, it might be useful to reflect on Hesse's (1980) idea that within our theories there are no completely fixed "observation sentences," but just more or less tenacious ones—the more tenacious ones playing the role of observations, and the less tenacious ones of hypotheses. The roles can be modified and reversed, and theoretical constructs can take on the quality of primitive observations. If this is true, "theory" might change "empathy." Schafer (e.g. 1980) evidently shares this view. On the other side of the argument, Lakoff and Johnson (1980) "ground" basic metaphor in brute physical facts of experience, implying a fixed order of explanation in our understanding. Trevarthen (1980) argues from observation of children that some understanding of intention is biologically determined, but this leaves open the possibility that even these basics are conceptually rearranged with expanding experience.

is not whether we possess a special capacity for empathy, but rather what manifestations of it involve learning. A paradigm of this sort of debate, on the issue of the capacity for language, may be found in the Chomsky-Piaget conference (Piatelli-Palmerini, 1980). We do not need to subscribe to a formal theory to be aware of the world, and by the same token, one might suppose that we can listen to patients "atheoretically." Nevertheless, just as physics, for example, puts no warrant on any single awareness of objects, so no single hearing of a patient can claim to arbitrate the analyst's perception of him. Whether this view leads to unqualified relativism will be considered below. In any case, Kohut's plea has been not that his own empathic researches are conclusive, but that analysts should touch base with—and allow some freedom to—their empathic registrations of meaningful configurations and not rely exclusively on learned patterns.

Thus, many psychoanalysts are now willing to share the methods and dilemmas of history. It is no accident that items of current psychoanalytic interest, such as empathy, the self, and validation of reconstructions, are old agenda for history. (Nor is it encouraging to see how little consensus their longevity has brought.) Comparisons of the psychoanalytic enterprise with the historian's have been made for some time. (See Novey [1968] for an earlier discussion, and Leavy [1980] for a more recent one. Schafer's "The Psychoanalytic Vision of Reality" [1970] is exemplary.) Kenneth Burke (1954) writes: "Human conduct, being in the realm of action and end (as contrasted with the physicist's realm of motion and position) is most directly discussable in dramatistic terms" (p. 274). White (1973) suggests that narratives connect events involving human aims by arranging them according to grammatical tropes and dramatic forms. Speaking philosophically, one might say that while comprehension of the objective world requires one to think in terms of entities, comprehension of human desire requires, in addition, models of narrative art. (Langer [1953] describes memory as a kind of protofiction, which is what makes a ragged chain of mental events into experience.)

Following the line of our (admittedly selective) review, we might say that, just as the advance of science requires a biasing model, and just as new perception is conditioned by metaphorical suasion, so history, and that large part of psychoanalysis that is history, employs rhetorical figures to train the observer to spot organization that can then be studied.[4]

Psychoanalysis

Psychoanalysis has, however, more specialized requirements than have history and literary criticism. For instance, as is implicit in most of Schafer's writings (1959, 1970, 1979, 1980), psychoanalysts study a subject that is partly of their own making. It is the psychoanalytic *relationship* to which historical, dramatic, and appreciative interest is especially turned. This situation is not without parallel in literature and history. Many versions of history are themselves influential historical

---

[4] At the same time, however, we must be careful to note that neither science nor history is entirely composed of a single mode of thought. Harré (1970) makes that quite evident in the case of science. Kuhn does far more justice to the variety of cognitive activities in science than is sometimes appreciated (see, for example, Kuhn, 1976). In the case of history, attention should be paid to Mandelbaum's (1980) criticism of Hayden White. In effect, Mandelbaum points to the various categories of objects and projects that the practicing historian actually deals with before even getting to the choice of narrative style or interpretive principle. White is the chief advocate in the field of historiography of the doctrine that an arbitrary, preliminary narrative configuration puts together the primary field of study. But even White admits that narrative begins only after we form the idea of some entity (in the case of history, the State) for the narrative to be about. Even this supreme tropologist tells us that not all is tropes. Almost all philosophers of science (including Kuhn) accept science's claim to be *ruled* by reality, though they may disagree about where and how the authority is exercised. And historians, for all their philosophical speculation, do not regard the past as an absolute invention. Schafer makes passing reference to familiar cognitive criteria of coherence, consistency, comprehensiveness, and nondisconfirmation. The casualness with which he sprinkles these binding formal criteria over the heavily stressed optional perspectives tilts his work toward an unnecessary relativism. If the philosophy of science chose to dwell on what was common to Bohr and Democritus, and left the formal criteria of theoretical sufficiency to a footnote, even physics could be made to look like one of the fine arts. (I believe that Schafer has been led into this disrespect for the interrelation and implications of cognitive criteria by the shallowness of the English school of language analysis [Friedman, 1976b].) We should not say, therefore, that either science or history is defined simply by views of the world, but rather that we can be introduced to the world only in specific ways, and that when we deal with human strivings, those ways of being introduced have dramatic form.

forces. And there are critics, such as Gadamer (1975) and Barthes (1979), who, if I understand them, feel that literary meaning can only be a joint product of reader and text.

But the participant observation of psychoanalysts is of an altogether different order. Neither the historical figure nor the man of letters inscribes his message directly on the scholar. A patient, in contrast, works partly *in the medium* of his analyst's feelings and attitudes. That is the patient's intention. (Lacan [1977] has elaborated this theme.) Thus, rather than studying a *work* influenced by previous purposes, the analyst surveys a field of *effort,* since he is himself (partly) the canvas and pigments it uses. It is about that field that the analyst develops his firmest convictions, and a model that discriminates aims within such a field is the one that will help him the most.[5]

What, then, according to our line of argument, might we expect a psychoanalyst to look for in a theory? As a scientist, he will look for a practice that makes him see new articulations among true, enduring substrates of the patient's appearance. As an historian of sorts, he will tend to use those articulations that foster stories as well as structures, and he will hope that these stories have the truth that is appropriate to history. But since he is a psychoanalyst, he will want this training, or biasing, to orient his experience of the patient's appeal in a way that ultimately picks out of the appeal what the patient can refine and use. The first two objectives are shared by purely academic enterprises, but the third is not; and it is to Kohut's innovations that we turn for a hint about what such theories will look like.

How Psychoanalytic Theory Introduces Novelty

In Kohut's theory we find models and metaphors of an academic type. For example, there is the model of internalization of slightly

---

[5] Schafer's (1973) tortured, ingenious action language probably derives some plausibility from the fact that the paramount datum in psychoanalysis is the patient's effort, rather than the kind of perfected structure other disciplines study. It does not seem to me, however, that any one "language" or level of abstraction, is adequate to the simplest experience. How much less adequate, I should think, would be a language unable to cope with a characterizable subject, yet forced to describe a synoptic, multilayered psychoanalytic event! Just to apprehend even appetitive pressure on the analyst, one must structure it into discrete wishes, aims, and purposes by models of substance. I have elsewhere (Friedman, 1976a) tried to show why the action language, which I regard as the least important part of Schafer's important project, cannot succeed.

failed parental duties; there is the metaphor of the mirror transference; there is the dramatic figure of Tragic Man. These are aspects of a detailed, clinically oriented conceptual system. His theory, however, has an additional persuasiveness, and I suggest that what lies beyond illustrates the special nature of psychotherapy models.

Any tenable conceptualization is useful to the extent that it situates the patient in the analyst's thought. British object relations theory, represented, for instance, by Guntrip (1969), offers academic ideas somewhat similar to Kohut's. Both characterize certain needs and the signs of their frustration. But Kohut, in addition, groups together as manifestations of an aspiration various actions in which patients involve their analysts. One recognizes these actions as forms of the aspiration because when they are regarded this way during treatment they can be paired with a corresponding group of resulting accomplishments. Thus Kohut equips the analyst with a reactive pattern that abstracts newly postulated aims or desires from the general influence exerted by the patient. He does not just name aims: he makes those aims appear before the analyst's eye. Loewald (1960) has also described how growth might come about when a yet-to-be-built virtual object within the patient is responded to by a therapist. What I wish to call attention to is the cognitive usefulness to the analyst of this sort of reaction, and the peculiar type of model it requires. I suggest that what happens here is that an abstract theory is supplemented by a *performable model or metaphor,* that is, a way of reacting *as though* the personal interaction signifies the structure of wishes, the structure of perceptions—in short, the structure of the patient's mind.

By itself, a simple conceptual map can only tell what categories to look for and how to connect them. It cannot identify the things these categories designate embedded in the flux of life. No map says, "Here it is!" It is up to the reader of the map to discern the corresponding configurations of reality. One can use conceptual maps without learning much about the world. People sometimes imitate a communal speech pattern in order to affiliate with a group. Fortunately, theoretical maps are usually used to learn a communal *language,* and that involves classification and perceptual sharpening.

If an altogether new kind of map is introduced, it is used first as a suggestive model for discovering divisions in nature. Correspondences between a new kind of map and reality are empirical discoveries. The process is a lower-level version of Kuhn's "normal science," which employs an open model, together with exercises in feeling out its applicability.

After a map is established as a formal diagram of certain delimited aspects of reality (and that is what we usually mean by a map), it has become something different. Like an exploratory map, this mastered map might be called a model, but it is not an open model. It is the kind of model whose applicability is exactly known, just as it is exactly known how a miniature automobile does and does not correspond to a passenger car, or a blueprint to a building. It is a product, not a part, of the scientific process of discovery.[6]

The relationship between a new type of map (or open-ended model) and a standard map (or completely specified model) is comparable to the relationship between a new, "live" metaphor, on the one hand, and a simile or "dead" metaphor on the other hand. By a performable model or metaphor, I mean first of all a live metaphor or a model whose use is incompletely known; one that is therefore a new framework for exploring as yet invisible divisions in nature. And, second, I am suggesting that this open-ended model or live metaphor is embodied in, or evoked by, a personal relationship.

To be sure, a model is typically something that can be pointed to, and, literally, metaphor is a linguistic term. But there is a sort of model that can only be enacted—for example, a dramatic play (see Gadamer, 1975). And if metaphor extends propositional meaning to new areas, then surely its function is frequently served by action. Indeed, action is by far the most common way that people develop new categories. For instance, it has been argued (Ranum, 1980) that the system of slights and courtesies that Richelieu evolved around Louis XIII gradually altered the nature of French royalty. In ordinary interaction, we do not usually interpret other people's motives conceptually; we conspire with them in action to build a virtual model.

[6] For a more technical discussion of what I have here oversimplified, see Harré (1970). Harré argues that we suppose a model to correspond vaguely to an underlying reality, and we work toward a model that depicts reality exactly. Goodman (1976) makes a more precise distinction than I between diagram, model, and metaphor. But my point can be followed into Goodman's discussion if we suppose that the newly introduced map has taken its form from a distant terrain where it is already established.

(An anthropologist may then identify the model and interpret it conceptually.) We treat other people's treatment of us as illustrating one thing or another. Indeed, one of the peculiarities of psychoanalytic treatment is that therapist and patient are encouraged to go beyond implicit attribution and supplement their actions with conceptual abstractions. That we ordinarily interpret other people's meanings by reciprocal attitudes rather than by theories does not mean that attitudinal interpretations or actions have philosophical priority over conceptual ones, or that conceptualizations are artificial reifications. They are all simply different ways of registering abstractions made from concrete experience. My point is just that attitudes are present and frequent among these ways.

Is Performable Metaphor Suggestion?

But, it will be objected, are not psychoanalysts supposed to keep their gestural input to a minimum? To begin with, theoreticians have recognized that the minimum is not nil. Many features of the analyst's role qualify his neutrality. The relationship of physician to patient, for example, is a model or metaphor with its own schematism, as Stone (1961, 1981) points out. From the time of Wilhelm Reich (1933, p. 49) and Waelder (1936), theorists have acknowledged that each comment of the analyst betrays a selective perspective. Nothing human can be exhaustively or univocally described, and the analyst's choice is a function of himself as well as of the patient. Kohut (1975) says, in effect, that the baseline of human sociability renders silence a stronger rather than a lesser gesture. Loewald (1960) describes a special forward-looking, structuring attitude of the analyst. Schafer characterizes the analyst's coloring attitudes in detail (making it clear that they should be multiple and flexible). And, after all, training analysis was never intended simply to treat interfering illness, but also to make a full repertoire of attitudes accessible to the analyst.

Nevertheless, not everyone feels that the analyst's perspective is a paramount definer of his behavior. And when such "sets" are acknowledged, it is often because they are regarded as unavoidable, uniform, nonspecific, and personally unexpressive elements built into the analytic situation. What worries analysts most is an *individualized* signifying attitude. It is precisely this aspect of Kohut's theory that has raised some theoretical eyebrows. An individualized, metaphorical interaction with a patient might be called suggestion, and suggestion is feared as meddling with the patient's autonomous reshuffling of his own meanings.

In particular, the example of Franz Alexander (1956), with his "corrective emotional experience," is often held up as a warning to theorists who talk about nonconceptual, discursive, noninterpretational elements in psychoanalysis. Ironically, that aspect of treatment, though noted by him, was not Alexander's prime concern. Basically, he used an enlightenment model. He believed (pp. 78–102) that good analysts, knowing that their countertransferences were "set up" by patients to confirm a false picture of reality, had always intuitively taken steps to adopt an attitude that would avoid entrapment. Sometimes bare neutrality was the artificial attitude adopted, but the patient might subvert this, or see it as a repetition and confirmation of a childhood environment. And Alexander would ask us to admit that, despite all precautions, neutrality might not be achieved: the analyst might be a poor illustration of reality because of his own character. Therefore, Alexander argued, although exceptional analysts might work intuitively, it would be far better for analysts to know what they are trying to do, and to do it more deliberately. They should consciously judge what attitudes need to be avoided, and then deliberately avoid them. The purpose of the emphasized attitude was not to give patients what they craved, but the reverse: It was to thrust on them against their will an experience that would destroy their illusions. It was not a matter of making the patient feel good. Still less was it a way of making up to the patient for previous deprivations. For Alexander it was *a lesson about reality* that counted. Alexander was a "realist." The patient was misperceiving reality, and Alexander was resolved to demonstrate reality to him: "At the same time recognizing and experiencing this discrepancy between the transference situation and the actual patient-therapist relationship is what I call the 'corrective emotional experience' " (1956, p. 41). The "corrective emotional experience" is not a paradigm of a nonrational, influencing therapy. It is the unfortunate isolation of a rationalistic component in psychoanalytic treatment.

Admittedly, Alexander was an avowed influencer as well as a

promoter of reality. He regarded regression as defensive, and distrusted it. That led him to campaign purposefully against the wish for dependence. But even such a frankly controlling strategy was related to his paramount concern for the patient's "reality testing." (Anyone who doubts the impact of Alexander's "realism" on his activism should compare Alexander's attitude toward regression with that of Loewald [1978].) If Alexander is a bad example of something, that something is not manipulation but naiveté. He thought that a pathogenic issue might be simple enough and wrong enough to be symbolized by the analyst in a single contrary attitude.

Alexander used himself as a model of reality, and he therefore set about regulating his reactive selection of the patient's pressures with an eye to the resulting image of Alexander. His posing was required because he wished to interfere with the patient's model of external reality. (He endorsed conventional analytic neutrality if it would shake up the patient's preconceptions.) Nothing could contrast more sharply with Kohut's theory. Kohut is not interested in correcting the patient's errors. He does not wish to instruct him in the reality of the world. He does not try to stop the patient from doing one thing or force him to another. He is interested, as we all know, in nurturing primitive strivings out of respect for their potential power to construct reliable and permanent internal states. Therefore, we may say that what is created by his response to the patient is neither a vision of Heinz Kohut, nor any other structure of external "reality," but an open-ended model of a relationship that allows a new exploration of motives and feelings. The analyst colludes with the patient in modeling this, much as one would participate with a child who is playing an adult role. (I regret the patronizing connotations of this analogy, and use it simply because it is easier to picture play with children than among adults. Play may be regarded as a performable model [see Vygotsky, 1933].)

It is important to note that Kohut's mission is *not* to make the patient see his analyst as an empathic person (though that is bound to happen to some degree), but to make the patient feel how his wishes combine with the analyst's attitudes to attain a new significance. (In all fairness, it should be said that Alexander hoped his reality training would accomplish this objective; that line of thought is more evident in the work of French [1958].)

Learning Performable Models

Every psychoanalysis enacts a meeting with a hidden self (Fried-man, 1976b). That enactment is explored differently by the participants and has different meanings to each of them. The patient may experience the search as a path to gratification. He explores it according to his personal and tacit inclination. But by his responses, the analyst insures that it is the model of a hidden self which is explored.

The psychoanalytic relationship is an open-ended model because it is a concrete structure of events that shows how new meaning can be assigned to strivings, thoughts, and feelings, even though it is not known to begin with exactly how it will shed that light (see Schafer, 1977). (By contrast, an ordinary relationship is more like a simile or a closed model, since its fixed roles and customary relationships pick out fixed features of the parties' constitutions and give them implicit meaning ahead of time.) Likewise, one can view the psychoanalytic situation as an action metaphor, in that the analyst treats the patient's actions *as though* they were manifestations of something central and essential. The patient experiences himself differently *through* the new relationship. Such perceptions of an interaction are metaphorical.

I use these terms only to connect change of meaning, theory revision, and psychoanalysis, in order to bring together work on shared problems such as those related to learning, ostension, change, and distortion of perspective. Simply calling a psychoanalytic relationship an open-ended model or a live metaphor says no more—indeed says much less—than, for example, Loewald (1960) does in terms proper to psychoanalysis.

The psychoanalyst learns to construct the fundamental model by acquiring a taste for conflict and especially for incompatible wishes directed toward himself. By gravitating toward these situations, he dissects real particulars of the patient and draws them into an action model of a therapist communicating with a hidden, essential mental constitution. Because the analyst builds the model with the bricks and mortar of the patient's effort, the patient finds himself exploring this same conflicted mental entity, though in a spirit often different from the analyst's, and usually accompanied by transference distress. The patient sees his efforts in the light of what he takes to be the analyst's attitudes, and from that structured interaction, senses a metaphorical truth about himself.

What gives Kohut's procedure its power to discover something we had not previously seen in the patient? What makes this kind of model so useful for discovering potential?

Many therapists have been helped by British object relations theory when it says to them: "This person before you has a false self and feels weak. You must get him to meet you with his true neediness or else you will not be able to help him build something better." Though this theory fails to say what precisely will happen when the patient reveals himself as needy and unguarded (growth being an undissectable given in this theory), even such a simple diagram will help to discriminate some aims by giving them a form that ties them to known theory.

It is quite another thing, however, when we are told by Kohut (as I understand him): "This person is doing something to you (in a representative act, that is, in a kind of play that we are always engaged in with other people) which is an outcome of a lifelong motive that will, if you respond to it in a specified way, tend to build specific, evident structures."

Both instructions say, "See the patient's behavior as an illustration of this or that." What Kohut's message does that the other does not is to prescribe an attitude that collates a patient's varying impact on the analyst as though the analyst were face to face with a hidden germ of internal strength.

I noted earlier that analysts appreciate a model or metaphor that not only gives them new thoughts, but also teaches them how to react to pressure in a way that makes new categories appear. For instance, Kohut's theoretical model instructs the analyst to feel a pressure as an effort toward independent security, although it used to be felt as a dead-end claim. The analyst is instructed to feel it as though it were a stage in the consolidation of the self. He practices visualizing himself being handled by the patient to achieve that goal. His specific *sense* of how he can be manipulated in this way is a template that registers the aspect of the patient's pressure that Kohut wants him to perceive. The analyst's cultivated *readiness* to be used for that particular kind of "play" (a deadly serious kind of play) translates the theoretical or discursive model into an action model that allows him to discover a new aim in his particular patient.

This is learning to abstract—to ''see-as''—by developing a sense of personal manipulability, all in the context of a historical (genetic) drama, and a theory of the mind.

This historical, personal drama and theory of the mind are extremely important in preparing the analyst to observe new configurations. And so is the drama of treatment that unites these two. But to say that these structures help the analyst find new configurations means that they match similar models and metaphors which the *patient* experiences with an analyst who is working that way. The analyst's truth is dependent on the consequent truth found by the patient. (I think this is the point Ricoeur [1977b] makes in his article on the truth claim in psychoanalysis; see also Habermas [1968].) What guides the practicing analyst is some perception of an answering construction on the part of his patient. Unfortunately, it is not at all clear what we should mean by ''answering,'' or what that perception is like. Yet without such constant signals of confirmation, we could not long track a seamless clinical happening faithfully and coherently.

There are, of course, the familiar objective confirmations of psychoanalytic understandings: dreams, associations, and change in symptoms and personality. Unfortunately, association is not the answer: it is a name for the continuity whose postulated orientation is just what needs confirmation. The other indices are not the sort of things that can act as a continuous monitor, nor are they sufficiently microscopic to guide flowing attention from minute to minute. They cannot serve as a *perceptual* homing device. They are intermittent checks and reassurances.

Assuming the general sort of success that it can hardly miss, it is unlikely that Kohut's theory will find its crucial test in the type and thoroughness of the cures obtained with it. Rarely is such theory discarded or adopted on the basis of comparative end-points. The analyst's understanding will tend to be guided momentarily by signals that the patient has found some truth comparable to his own. He listens for announcements that he is collaborating with a fruitful exploration. In whatever form it arrives, that announcement from his patient will probably be what keeps him veering toward a given model or metaphor in his listening, understanding, and behavior.

What prompts the patient's announcement of a converging meaning? Perhaps he sees an opportunity in his analyst's receptivity (see French, 1958, p. 40), and betrays some special "èlan," from which the analyst senses how much play his attitudes afford the patient's strivings. (On this point, see Gendlin, 1964.) If the analyst can never know for sure exactly what an interpretation meant to a patient, he may nevertheless learn that it meant a great deal or very little.

Reasoning along these lines, we would expect analysts to be grateful for a theory that gives them an appetite for states of unstable meaning and uncertainty of aim. An appetite is the sort of orientation that selects continuously, minutely, and without deliberation, because its reward is not distant and theoretical. A theory that trains an appetite for situations marking nodes of change has provided its own ostensive definitions. The therapist will find concrete examples of theoretical references like a radar-guided missile finds its target.

What in general is this appetite an appetite *for?* It is for a pressure from the patient, which will be felt as a manifestation of some other evocable liveliness or expressiveness already present *in statu nascendi,* as postulated by the analyst's model of mental growth, and experienced by him with gratification. Classical appetites include the taste for conflict, especially when directed toward the analyst. (There are many other examples in clinical theory.)

Can we find a special appetite in Kohut's theory? Is it the tuning of the analyst's interest to reactions of disappointment? Kohut describes disappointment in terms of the structure that the patient wants to build. Here, disappointment is not the frustration of a completed need. Nor is it a manifestation of a complete but unfortunate mental state. The poignant and primitive sense of disappointment is a sign to the analyst of how the patient can profitably use him. The analyst consequently develops a taste for disappointment reactions. The sight and sound of them are sought for and welcome. They stand out readily from the scene because they are fundamentally wanted by the analyst: they carry natural highlights. At the same time, the patient often indicates that the analyst's reaction to his disappointment has allowed him to make something new and complex out of that state. The theory has given the practitioner both a natural analyzer of phenomena (in the form of a professional desire), and a built-in receiver for signals of metaphorical relevance. With these, Kohut provides a single model that can be explored by the analyst (with his theoretical appetites) and patient (with his aspirations), and both can find a useful metaphor in it.

Summary

Those who inquire into the process of knowledge acquisition have lately been telling us that we must first structure a field in accordance with some comprehensive, preliminary, patterned allusion to fruitful but unspecified saliencies and entities, which exploration can thereafter discover. Models, metaphors, and dramatic tropes are among the ways that this requirement is met, in science, descriptive language, and history. Psychoanalysis partakes in all these activities, and therefore employs similar devices for structuring its field. Kohut's novel vision naturally uses such cognitive tools. But I suggest that change in psychoanalytic perception requires, beyond these academic forms, something else of the sort that gives Kohut's psychoanalytic reorientation its particular power: something that teaches the analyst to develop an affinity for features of the patient's pressure on him, from which a model or metaphor arises, susceptible to fruitful exploration by both analyst and patient. This model or metaphor is not something said by the analyst, or a set of propositions in his head (although they contribute to it). Nor is it a charade designed to teach a lesson (which would actually model something quite different). It is constituted by the structure of the action between the analyst and his patient, and can be explored in different ways by each.

References

Alexander, F. (1956), *Psychoanalysis and Psychotherapy: Developments in Theory, Technique and Training.* New York: Norton.

Barthes, R. (1979), From work to text. In: *Textual Strategies: Perspectives in Post-Structuralist Criticism,* ed. J.V. Harari. Ithaca, N.Y.: Cornell University Press, pp. 73–81.

Black, M. (1979), More about metaphor. In: *Metaphor and Thought,* ed. A. Ortony. Cambridge: Cambridge University Press, pp. 19–43.

Boyd, R. (1979), Metaphor and theory change: What is "metaphor" a "metaphor" for? In: *Metaphor and Thought,* ed. A. Ortony. Cambridge: Cambridge University Press, pp. 356–408.

Burke, K. (1950), *A Rhetoric of Motives*. Berkeley: University of California Press.
——— (1954), *Permanence and Change: An Anatomy of Purpose*. Indianapolis: Bobbs-Merrill.
Cassirer, E. (1929), *The Phenomenology of Knowledge. The Philosophy of Symbolic Forms*, Vol. 3. New Haven: Yale University Press, 1957.
French, T. (1958), *The Reintegrative Process in a Psychoanalytic Treatment. The Integration of Behavior*, Vol. 3. Chicago: University of Chicago Press.
Friedman, L. (1971), A criticism of Gendlin's theory of therapy. *Psychother.: Theory, Res. Practice*, 8:256–258.
——— (1972), Difficulties of a computer model of the mind: A critical review of Emanuel Peterfreund's book *Information, Systems and Psychoanalysis*. *Int. J. Psycho-Anal.*, 53:547–554.
——— (1976a), Problems of an action theory of the mind. *Internat. Rev. Psycho-Anal.*, 3:129–138.
——— (1976b), Cognitive and therapeutic tasks of a theory of the mind. *Internat. Rev. Psycho-Anal.*, 3:259–275.
——— (1977), Conflict and synthesis in Freud's theory of the mind. *Internat. Rev. Psycho-Anal.*, 4:155–170.
——— (1980a), George Klein's *Psychoanalytic Theory* in perspective. *Psychoanal. Rev.*, 67:195–216.
——— (1980b), The barren prospect of a representational world. *Psychoanal. Quart.*, 49:215–233.
Gadamer, H.-G. (1975), *Truth and Method*. New York: Seabury Press.
Gendlin, E. (1964), A theory of personality change. In: *Creative Developments in Psychotherapy*, ed. A. R. Mahrer & L. Pearson. Cleveland: Case Western Reserve University Press, 1971, pp. 439–489.
Goodman, N. (1976), *Languages of Art: An Approach to a Theory of Symbols*. Indianapolis: Hackett.
Guntrip, H. (1969), *Schizoid Phenomena, Object Relations, and the Self*. New York: International Universities Press.
Habermas, J. (1968), *Knowledge and Human Interests*. Boston: Beacon Press, 1971.
Harré, R. (1970), *The Principles of Scientific Thinking*. Chicago: University of Chicago Press.
Henle, P. (1958), Metaphor. In: *Language, Thought and Culture*. Ann Arbor: University of Michigan Press, 1965, pp. 173–195.
Hesse, M. (1980), *Revolutions and Reconstructions in the Philosophy of Science*. Bloomington: Indiana University Press.
Jakobson, R. (1956), The metaphoric and metonymic poles. In: *Critical Theory Since Plato*, ed. H. Adams. New York: Harcourt Brace & Jovanovich, 1971.
——— (1959), Sign and system of language: a reassessment of Saussure's doctrine. *Poetics Today*, 2:33–38, 1980.
——— (1960), Closing statement: Linguistics and poetics. In: *Style in Language*, ed. T.A. Sebeok. Cambridge, Mass.: M.I.T. Press.
Kohut, H. (1971), *The Analysis of the Self*. New York: International Universities Press.
——— (1975), Letter, April 10, 1975. In: *The Search for the Self*, ed. P.H. Ornstein. New York: International Universities Press, 1978, pp. 899–900.

———— (1977), *The Restoration of the Self.* New York: International Universities Press.

Kuhn, T. (1970), Logic of discovery or psychology of research, and Reflections on my critics. In: *Criticism and the Growth of Knowledge,* ed. I. Lakatos & A. Musgrave. Cambridge: Cambridge University Press, pp. 1–23 and 231–278.

———— (1976), Mathematical versus experimental traditions in the development of physical science. In: *The Essential Tension: Selected studies in scientific tradition and change.* Chicago: The University of Chicago Press, 1977, pp. 31–65.

———— (1979), Metaphor in science. In: *Metaphor and Thought,* ed. A. Ortony. Cambridge: Cambridge University Press, pp. 409–419.

Lacan, J. (1957), The agency of the letter in the unconscious or reason since Freud. In: *Écrits: A Selection,* trans. A. Sheridan. New York: Norton, 1977.

———— (1977), *The Four Fundamental Concepts of Psycho-Analysis,* trans. A. Sheridan. London: Hogarth Press.

Lakatos, I. & Musgrave, A., eds. (1970), *Criticism and the Growth of Knowledge.* Cambridge: Cambridge University Press.

Lakoff, G. & Johnson, M. (1980), *Metaphors We Live By.* Chicago: University of Chicago Press.

Langer, S.K. (1953), *Feeling and Form: A Theory of Art.* New York: Scribner's.

Leavy, S.A. (1980), *The Psychoanalytic Dialogue.* New Haven: Yale University Press.

Levenson, E. (1978), Two essays in psychoanalytic psychology. *Contemp. Psychoanal.,* 14:1–30.

Loewald, H. (1960), On the therapeutic action of psychoanalysis. *Internat. J. Psycho-Anal.,* 41:16–33.

———— (1978), *Psychoanalysis and the History of the Individual.* New Haven: Yale University Press.

Mandelbaum, M. (1971), *History, Man, and Reason: A Study in Nineteenth Century Thought.* Baltimore: Johns Hopkins University Press.

———— (1980), The presuppositions of *metahistory. History and Theory,* 19(4):39–54.

Meyerson, E. (1930), *Identity and Reality.* London: Allen & Unwin.

Novey, S. (1968), *The Second Look: The reconstruction of personal history in psychiatry and psychoanalysis.* Baltimore: Johns Hopkins University Press.

Piatelli-Palmerini, M., ed. (1980), *Language and Learning: The Debate between Jean Piaget and Noam Chomsky.* Cambridge: Harvard University Press.

Ranum, O. (1980), Courtesy, absolutism, and the rise of the French state, 1630–1660. *J. Modern History,* 52:426–451.

Reich, W. (1933), *Character Analysis.* New York: Orgone Institute Press, 1945.

Ricoeur, P.(1977a), *The Rule of Metaphor: Multi-disciplinary Studies of the Creation of Meaning in Language.* Toronto: University of Toronto Press.

———— (1977b), The question of proof in Freud's psychoanalytic writings. *J. Amer. Psychoanal. Assn.,* 25:835–871.

———— (1978), The metaphorical process as cognition, imagination, and feeling. *Critical Inquiry,* 5:143–159.

Schafer, R. (1959), Generative empathy in the treatment situation. *Psychoanal. Quart.,* 28:342–373.

———— (1970), The psychoanalytic vision of reality. *Internat. J. Psycho-Anal.,* 51:279–297.

———— (1973), Action: Its place in psychoanalytic interpretation and theory. *Ann. Psychoanal.*, 1:159–196.

———— (1977), The interpretation of transference and the conditions for loving. *J. Amer. Psychoanal. Assn.*, 25:335–362.

———— (1979), The appreciative analytic attitude and the construction of multiple histories. *Psychoanal. Contemp. Thought*, 2:3–24.

———— (1980), Narration in the psychoanalytic dialogue. *Critical Inquiry*, 7:29–53.

Stone, L. (1961), *The Psychoanalytic Situation*. New York: International Universities Press.

———— (1981), Notes on the noninterpretive elements in the psychoanalytic situation and process. *J. Amer. Psychoanal. Assn.*, 29:89–118.

Trevarthen, C. (1980), The foundations of intersubjectivity: development of interpersonal and cooperative understanding in infants. In: *The Social Foundations of Language and Thought: Essays in Honor of Jerome S. Bruner*, ed. D.R. Oldson. New York: Norton, pp. 316–342.

Vygotsky, L.S. (1933), The role of play in development. In: *Mind in Society: The Development of Higher Psychological Processes*, ed. M. Cole et al. Cambridge, Mass.: Harvard University Press, 1978, pp. 92–104.

Waelder, R. (1936), The principle of multiple function: Observations on overdetermination. *Psychoanal. Quart.*, 5:45–62.

Watzlawick, P. (1978), *The Language of Change: Elements of Therapeutic Communication*. New York: Basic Books.

White, H. (1973), *Metahistory: The historical imagination in Nineteenth-Century Europe*. Baltimore: Johns Hopkins University Press.

———— (1980), The value of narrativity in the representation of reality. *Critical Inquiry*, 7:5–27.

Some Perspectives on Self Psychology

JAMES S. GROTSTEIN

In the span of just a few years the school of self psychology has emerged as representing perhaps the most important paradigmatic shift in psychoanalytic theory and practice in decades. Its deceptive simplicity belies its conceptual sweep as a major *systematized* alternative to classical theory. Its appearance follows on two major trends within psychoanalytic thinking: on one hand, the ego psychology of Hartmann, Rapaport, and their followers, including the variations introduced by Jacobson, Erikson, and Mahler; on the other hand, the object relations schools of Melanie Klein and of Fairbairn, Winnicott, Balint, and Bowlby.

The school of ego psychology seemed to proceed in the direction of greater distance from primitive emotional life and more approximation to mechanization of experience. In Kohut's new pragmatic terminology this trend might be called "experience-distant." In contrast, the British Object Relations School focused on the primitive "experience-near" phenomenology of infantile mental life in relation to maternal bonding. At the time there was only one other trend of

Dr. Grotstein is Associate Clinical Professor of Psychiatry at UCLA, Training and Supervising Analyst at the Los Angeles Psychoanalytic Institute and Society, Attending Staff Physician at Cedars-Sinai Medical Center, and Director of the Interdisciplinary Group for Advanced Studies in Psychotic, Borderline, and Narcissistic Disorders.

importance in psychoanalytic thinking in the English-speaking world, but one not in the mainstream of official psychoanalysis—the school of William Alanson White. One of the founders of this school, Harry Stack Sullivan (1956), coined the phrases "participant observation" and "consensual validation," which presage Kohut's insistence on empathic or vicariously introspective observation.

A careful reading of the contributions of Kohut and his followers suggests many congruences with these antecedents, but also at least one important difference in conceptualization. Classical theory, ego psychology, Kleinian theory, and object relations theories all utilize what might be called the paradigm of *detached observation;*[1] that is, their theories and their avowed techniques emphasize the objective deduction of mechanisms, processes, and fantasies alleged to be taking place within the patient's (or infant's) mind on different levels of consciousness. While the observations spawned by ego psychology seemed to come from a more mechanistic, experience-distant vantage point, the British school, especially Klein, did try to zero in on ex-perience-near phenomenology. Nevertheless, the phenomena Klein discerned were unconscious fantasies, which had to be reconstructed by inference; consequently, her observations still qualify as experience distant. As I understand it, detached or "scientific" observation de-notes neutrality and independence on the part of the observer, who is distanced from the observed. Empathic observation, on the other hand, denotes vicarious participation by the observer in the observed's sub-jective experiences, implying a specific connection at that moment. The latter form of observation is more immediately phenomenological; therein lies its difference.

---

[1] I use the term detached observation to designate a mode of analytic observation from the point of view of the *subject* of observation who detaches himself from the object of observation in order to designate what had formerly been called "objective," by which was meant a neutrality "uncontaminated" by empathy, sympathy, or prej-udice; its counterpart today would be empathic observation, which now implies a vicarious connection with the object of observation. The object of observation is the patient's recitation of his experiences, which, to the patient, may be either experience-near or experience-distant. The analyst may use detached or empathic techniques in order to observe the experience-nearness or the experience-distance of the patient's feelings.

The Empathic Point of View

Kohut (1975) summarizes his view of the application of empathy as follows:

> (1) Empathy, the recognition of the self in the other, is an indispensable tool of observation, without which vast areas of human life, including man's behavior in the social field, remain unintelligible. (2) Empathy, the expansion of the self to include the other, constitutes a powerful psychological bond between individuals which—more perhaps even than love, the expression and sublimation of the sexual drive—counteracts man's destructiveness against his fellows. And (3), empathy, the accepting, confirming, and understanding human echo evoked by the self, is a psychological nutriment without which human life as we know and cherish it could not be sustained [p. 705].

Kohut's conception of empathy, elementary at first glance, constitutes a major shift in scientific theory. Actually it is one that Freud adumbrated long ago when he discovered that other area of the mind—the unconscious. Kohut has refocused attention on what might be seen as the missing link in psychoanalytic observation. In my opinion, his contribution allows us to conceive of a dual-track model for psychoanalysis, combining experience-near (empathic) and experience-distant (detached) observations, as well as our own subjective and objective perspectives.

To begin with, however, I should like to reflect for a moment on the *object* of observation by an empathic observer as distinguished from that of a detached observer and consider the consequences of these two modes of observation. The development of psychoanalysis itself may well have rested on this distinction insofar as the body of psychoanalytic theory seems to have been the product of detached speculation.

When Breuer and Freud (1893–1895) initiated psychoanalysis in the last decade of the nineteenth century, they had at their disposal not only their own observations of hysterical patients who clearly demonstrated *double consciousness* (''double conscience'' in the original text), but also the observations of numerous novelists on both sides of the Atlantic who seemed to have been obsessed by the phenomenon of the "double." These novelists had already discovered our dual nature and were exploring it through vicarious introspection. Examples are Dostoevsky's *The Double,* Mary Shelley's *Frankenstein,* Robert Louis Stevenson's *The Strange Case of Dr. Jekyll and Mr. Hyde,* Edgar Allan Poe's "The Story of William Wilson," and others.[2]

Breuer and Freud were quite impressed by this phenomenon of duality and launched the field of psychoanalysis attempting to explain it. Freud (1905) was later to depersonalize and abstract one of the components of the duality—the id. He explained the existence of this duality in terms of incompatibilities that, at bottom, arose from conflicts over passion, the irreducible component of which was the libidinal instinct. The vicissitudes of libido were then used to explain even more complex aspects of human nature, a complexity augmented by Freud's later attention (1920) to the passion of hate.

The "id" which Freud had discovered became opposed to the ego, and Freud assigned perceptual consciousness to the ego but not to the id. The id, therefore, became, amongst other things, an object of observation by the ego. What Freud seemed to have missed was the fact that the id is also an observer in its own right. My dual-track theory is a plea to allow for co-subjectivity so that the id can be an observer much like the ego, and it observes empathically—that is, via empathic introspection, whereas the ego may be the agency of detached observation.

Perhaps another way of talking about this would be primary process observation as opposed to secondary process observation. The self psychologist must use primary process, in this new sense, in order to projectively identify himself into the patient's experience. The abstract observational capacity of secondary process, strictly speaking, does not allow for this. It must borrow from primary process in order to do this, I believe. Freud, in distancing the id from the ego and placing perceptual consciousness—and therefore the seat of observation—in the ego, created a linearity of observation based upon sec-

---

[2] For an engaging survey of this fascinating sidelight, see Rogers (1970), Guerard, (1967), particularly Rosenfield's contribution "The Shadow Within: The Conscious and Unconscious Use of the Double," and Gilbert and Gubar (1979).

ondary process, neglecting primary process, and precipitated a psychoanalytic theory which was based upon the Newtonian observational paradigm, that is, of a detachment between the subject and the object. Had he gone a step further, he would have realized that his prime discovery, the unconscious, and particularly its principal component, the id, was the seat not merely of impulses alone, but also was a subjectively observing "I" which "sees" the data of experience personally, whereas the so-called "ego" tries to see things "objectively," by which is meant abstractly or conceptually. The duality of consciousness which Breuer and Freud had uncovered was to be eclipsed, therefore, by Freud's topographical model which pushed the unconscious into the cellar of the mind and deprived it of co-equal perceptual consciousness. Only recently have brain laterality studies revealed that duality of consciousness is a neurological fact (Gazzaniga and Le Doux, 1978).

Freud's theorizing on the dual nature of the individual, arrived at by detached rather than empathic observation, fed into the psychoanalytic conception of the individual as a mental apparatus consisting of conflicting components: biological instincts in the id (experience-distant conception of self as baser object), an administrative agency or series of functions known as the ego (experience-distant conception of sense of "I"-ness), and moralizing representations in the superego (experience-distant conception of spiritual self).

"Dual consciousness" denotes two separate, simultaneous modes of observation, one of which is personal, subjective, analogic, and vicarious, whereas the other is logical, sequential, and abstract. These roughly correspond to the id and to the ego. The superego would be a unique combination of elements from each. Kohut himself once stated to Klaus Hoppe, an analyst in Los Angeles who is interested in brain laterality research, that empathy is a right-brain phenomenon (Hoppe, personal communication). That is what I am trying to establish—that empathy is a right-brain consciousness, whereas detached observation is the method of consciousness and of observation pertinent to the left brain—roughly.

Freud's theorizing on our dual nature imposed a cosmic view of human beings as guilt-laden because of our split instinctual inheritance, and this view came to dominate much of psychoanalytic thinking.

Klein (1933), for instance, took Freud's concept of conflict between life and death instincts a step further. She posited a paranoid-schizoid position in early infancy as this conflict's primordial acme, with a subsequent depressive position, in which there is an attempt to reconcile the aims of the instincts and the objects that are their targets. Others used the framework of the dual-instinct theory but modified the impact of passion through the idea of adaptation to an average expectable environment (Hartmann, 1939), or the cogwheeling of a sense of identity with the simultaneously evolving environment (Erikson, 1959).

Still other psychoanalysts, in attempting to explain the duality of human nature, sought to make passion secondary to bonding. These contributions include Winnicott's (1958) maternal concern, Bion's (1959) container and contained, Bowlby's (1969) ethological instincts based on innate behavior coordinators, and Balint's (1968) basic fault. Yet Freud's "Guilty Man" had to await Fairbairn's (1940) rescue of him as "Schizoid Man" and later Kohut's (1971) "Tragic Man." Fairbairn's and Kohut's depictions of our duality are more existential, less moralistic, closer to the phenomenological experience of dual subjectivity within the self.[3]

What would have happened had Freud relied more fully on empathic or vicarious observation? My hypothesis is that he would have recognized the relation of dual consciousness to dual *being,* i.e., dual subjectivity or co-subjectivity. Instead of setting up the unconscious, in particular the id, as an antagonist to the ego, he would have made it a co-subject with the ego—a different agency simultaneously judging the data of internal and external experience. In Freud's (1914) conception of narcissism, for instance, the id chooses the ego as its object. What I would now say is that each communicates to the other as its partner.

Indeed, I would argue that in some ways Freud sidestepped the implications of his discovery of the unconscious and the laws governing its functioning (primary process). He postulated a realm of peremptory *subjectivity,* of the personal, affective aspects of our being, existing side by side with the rational, abstractive ones (secondary process).

---

[3] Kernberg (1975), on the other hand, follows Freud and Klein in explaining splitting morally (as a defense against "good" and "bad" internalized self and object representations).

Today, we might roughly equate the former with nondominant hemispheric functioning and the latter with dominant hemispheric functioning (McLaughlin, 1978). The research on brain laterality suggests that each hemisphere reflects a different mode of information processing, with the nondominant hemisphere employing visuospatial, holistic perceptions of data and the dominant one, sequential, verbal reasoning.[4]

What has not been fully appreciated, in my opinion, is that Freud's own scientific discovery challenged the very notion of science that began with Descartes and reached its apogee with Newton—the idea of a subject-object dichotomy, in which the subject was separate from the object, and could observe the object without participating in what was observed. This idea predicated a science of *unemotional or detached objectivity,* in which the phenomena observed were believed to be totally independent of the observer. In contrast, Freud's discovery might be seen within the series of scientific advances that culminated in the superordination of the Cartesian-Newtonian model by quantum mechanics. To take this a step further, we can see such concepts as the general theory of relativity, Heisenberg's uncertainty principle, the wave-quantum disparity, and the "phenomenology" of subatomic particles as offering a perspective analogous to Kohut's empathic point of view. This perspective holds that (1) the subject changes the object by the very act of observation, and (2) the subject is always linked in some way with the object it is observing. Detached objectivity is not possible. Kohut's concept of empathy underlines this interrelationship of subject and object within the field of psychoanalytic observations.[5] Moreover, he points to what I believe is already implicit in Freud's discovery of two mental principles—the idea of *co-subjectivity* within the framework of individual psychology.

By "internal sociology," I am using the term offered by Gazzaniga and Le Doux which they concluded from their bilaterality brain

---

[4] Gazzaniga and Le Doux (1978) have also shown through experimental techniques that normal people possess simultaneous dual consciousness, but appear to have single consciousness for perceptual simplicity. They state that the concept of individuality must be altered to encompass a new conception of the individual as "an internal sociology."

[5] Stolorow and Atwood (1979) speak of "intersubjectivity" in human affairs—thus underlining the subject-subject linkage between individuals.

research in which they established the stimultaneous duality of consciousness. Each human being, they believe, is composed of many discrete selves—at least two—and probably more. We are normally more dissociated than we have imagined. This multiplicity or dissociation of selves is not apparent, thanks to the normal cohesion of the self, but, when this cohesion fails and we become fragmented, our separate subselves begin to emerge.

It is true that the concept of empathy has been discussed by analysts before Kohut, but only in a narrower sense. Sullivan's (1956) idea of participant observation, for instance, focuses on the use of empathy within the analytic situation. Although Melanie Klein (1940) did look at the developmental vicissitudes of empathy, her infant, like Freud's, is significantly more disingenuous than Kohut's. Her infant is separate from the very beginning and already has the inchoate, omnipotent power of the life and death instincts in its armamentarium. Empathy for her resides in the infant's renouncement of or transformation from the paranoid-schizoid position of persecutory anxiety, with its consequent abandonment of omnipotence and acceptance of its dependence on a mother. Thus, Klein described the infant's development of empathic concern for its object, but she did not emphasize the reverse. She was phenomenological insofar as she paid attention to the infant's feelings and fantasies, as Cohler (1980) has pointed out. One might say that her conceptualizations about the infant constitute inferred phenomenology and are therefore inferentially experience-near phenomena but are made from the perspective of detached (experience-distant) observation.

Winnicott (1954) went a step further than Klein in emphasizing the complementarity of the infant-mother relationship. He spoke of the infant's *ruth* for the mother and the mother's *concern* for the infant. What emerges from Klein's depressive position and Winnicott's writings is a picture of the mother as a person in her own right, like the infant. She is not merely an *object* for the infant's narcissistic needs, but also a *subject,* with a separate agenda and individual vulnerabilities. She has a life of her own, which interfaces now with the infant and at other times with other objects. What is lacking, however, is a systematized view of the function of empathy. It is here that Kohut makes a major contribution.

Instead of a single line of development from narcissism to object love, Kohut (1971, 1977, 1980) has proposed separate lines for the development of the self and of the self's relationship to objects, with the former as the superordinate principle. These separate tracks are considered by Kohut to be natural bifurcations, not emergences from primordial conflict. In other words, the development of the self takes place in its own right. Narcissism is no longer simply the pathological result of a disappointment in a relationship to an external object or of the irruptive impact of the instincts with subsequent withdrawal of cathexis from the object, as Freud (1911) stated. Kohut posits that the organizing principle for the evolution of this separated (but not divided) self and object lies in the vicissitudes of *empathy*. In thus focusing on empathy, he has made comprehensible a vast realm of normal and abnormal development that was not explainable by conflict theory and has organized the experience of psychic deficiency into a metapsychological framework. As an added bonus, he has reclaimed the all but lost personalness of the self for psychoanalysis.

Kohut (1980) goes to great lengths to distinguish between empathy and compassion. For him, the analyst's empathic point of view may lead to compassion, but is itself a form of scientific inquiry into the patient's state of mind. Kohut equates empathy with vicarious introspection, a mode parallel to the scientist's vicarious extrospection of data in the external world. He thus distinguishes, I believe, between objective empathy, obtained by vicarious introspection, and subjective empathy, which may be closer to compassion and similar to sympathy.

As a consequence of empathic observation, self psychology has developed many conceptual "instruments" that are worthy of note. These include the concept of the selfobject with its implication of an inherent duality in human nature, the idea of a unique bipolar development of the experience of self, the emphasis on self regulation, the distinction between self libido and object libido, the metapsychological view of psychic deficiency, the perspective on normal infantile omnipotence and the sense of entitlement, and the ongoing scenario of the selfobject in adult mental life. I shall now turn to these concepts more specifically, with an eye to their implications for a dual-track theory.

As I have already noted, Kohut's empathic point of view suggests

174

dual tracks of experience-near and experience-distant observation. On
another level, the dual nature of the individual is implied in his concept
of a bipolar self, which is organized originally around a grandiose self
image on one axis and an idealized object imago on the other. Further,
these dual aspects of the development of a nuclear self comprise yet
another track, which complements the track of object love. Kohut's
concept of the individual thus seems to me a versatile one. It allows
one to envision the boundaries of the self both as transcending the
boundaries of the body and as shrinking within, as a partial unit—yet
another instance of dual tracks.

Developmental Concepts

Kohut and his followers have taken great pains to differentiate
their own concepts of development from those of Mahler, Spitz, and
Erikson, as well as from other psychoanalytic contributors. Behind
this insistence is their belief that the other schemes do not do justice
to the development of the self as a separate entity and instead view
the development of the self only in terms of the vicissitudes of instinctual drives in relation to an object. Yet I believe it is useful to compare
and integrate various authors' developmental concepts in the attempt
to formulate a dual-track theory.

As a beginning step, I have already (1980, 1982) tried to reconcile
Mahler's views on development with those of Klein and her followers.

Mahler's developmental scheme, like that of Freud and Klein,
follows an epigenetic sequence. The dual-track allows us to postulate
the simultaneity of these phases all occurring at once but seemingly
occurring sequentially as times of succession or of prominence. The
autistic phase of Mahler may yet turn out to be (a) an artifact and (b)
merely a designation for the earliest development of self both in the
sense of its inchoate separateness and in the sense of its continuing at-
one-ment with the primal object (primary selfobject). If there be an
autistic stage at all, I believe that it is the earliest stage, both of
symbiosis and of separation-individuation (from one point of view on
the dual-track) and, from another point of view on the dual-track, I
believe it to be the progenitor of Kohut's independently developing
self. Applying the dual-track notion to this combined schema, I also

posited that while individual phases may *seem* to succeed one another in the calendar sense, they might better be thought of as being separate but overlapping from the very beginning. That is, the paranoid-schizoid position of the symbiotic stage and the depressive position of separation-individuation begin at the same time as the adhesive identification of the autistic stage. The latter only *seems* definitive. All stages are present all along, but they have different times of dominance. ⟶ *positica notta*

A dual-track developmental framework suggests a number of other possibilities. For instance, one can conceive of the infant's having two different mental experiences from the very beginning—the experience of separateness and the experience of nonseparateness. These two tracks may overlap in simultaneous montage or they may alternate. As another aspect of dual-track development, one might envision the mother's relationship to the infant undergoing a metamorphosis in synchrony, or in dissynchrony, with the child's development.

Further, I believe that one might place Klein's theory of reparations by the infant self in relation to its object on one track and Kohut's theory of parental empathy toward the infant on another track. A dual-track notion would thus embrace the concepts of reciprocity and mutuality in self-selfobject development and in analysis. True intersubjectivity in infant development would encompass empathic (and compassionate) relatedness by the infant self to the subjectivity of its own mother as well as the reverse. The mystery of good and bad relationships exists in the nature of the bond between the self and its selfobject as well as the other way around. Winnicott (1951) conceives of this as the transitional space between the infant and mother. Winnicott (1960) observed that ''there is no such thing as an infant; there is only an infant and its mother''—a statement that would seem to anticipate Kohut's selfobject concept. Basch (1977), Cohler (1980), and Wolf (1980) all underline the reciprocal importance of the infant and mother in the formation of early self-selfobject relationships. Hypothetically difficulties can develop either from the infant's side or from the mother's, culminating in pathological states, in a dysrhythmia between them.

There seems to be a field of mutual empathy between child and mother, in which each is encouraged and mirrored by the other. That imparts a feeling of self-satisfaction to the infant. Good ''mirroring'' by a maternal selfobject is probably not enough to make an infant self feel good about itself. The infant must also develop the sense of reciprocity and responsibility—the capacity for care and concern for mother and the desire to mirror her as well.

Perhaps a crucial difference between Klein's approach to the infant and Kohut's is that Kohut seems to suggest more responsibility on the part of the selfobject in the genesis of infantile experience, whereas Klein emphasizes the responsibility of the infant for the occurrence of breaks in the bonding and minimizes the responsibility of the mother. Moreover, in Kohut's concept of the drives (which resembles the much earlier ideas of Fairbairn, 1941), instinctual pain is felt as a break in cohesion, one for which the selfobject is responsible. In Klein's theory, the object is not responsible for the pain, although Klein acknowledges that the pain is consequent upon the object's pulling away its support and thereby disrupting primary identification. The result is the experience of separation, with the instinctual pain this brings. The difference between the two theories may seem small, but is nonetheless crucial.

An important consideration here is that Kohut eschews the traditional notion of the increasing independence of the self from its objects. Fairbairn also rejected the classical notion of a development from dependence to independence. He suggested instead that the infant grows from infantile dependence into mature dependence. Indeed, he believed independence to be a myth—as does Kohut. Both Fairbairn and Kohut (and also Bion, Winnicott, and Balint), therefore, propose the concept of a lifetime of mature dependence in connection with an object. One feels autonomous as long as one is properly dependent—connected to someone who provides selfobject support. In other words, the selfobject *function* never disappears; it only undergoes transformation and maturation. In this regard, the concept of *transmuting internalization* is noteworthy. Kohut believes that the idealized and mirroring aspects of selfobjects become normally and abnormally compromised as the infant inevitably finds chinks in the armor of its selfobjects and their functioning as time goes on. The healthy infant (or child) is able to utilize the good selfobject functioning it has already experienced and is able to internalize those functions into its own psychic structure.

Following Fairbairn, however, I would ask: Does the infant (child) take in aspects of the selfobject and internalize these as its own self-regulating function, as Kohut indicates? Or is this self-regulating function always there potentially from the beginning, and is it more a maturation and development that takes place under the auspices of the interpersonal other? Perhaps what one internalizes is not so much the object and its functions, as one's *experience* with the object. If we take Fairbairn's and Bion's point of view, we might rephrase Kohut's idea of transmuting internalizations as transmuting *realizations* or *transformations* of undeveloped functions that exist in the infant from the very beginning. The selfobject experience then "shepherds" the development of these rudimentary functions.

I suggest this latter concept as a substitute for that of the internalization of an object, since it seems unlikely that there is a "little homunculus" existing within the normal human being. What we internalize are experiences with objects, not objects per se. The experience of the internalization of objects constitutes fantasies of internal objects, which have not yet been released to become object representations. In this regard I should like to state parenthetically that Kohut seems at times to be more empirical, like Locke and his tabula rasa, than rationalistic in the tradition of Plato, Descartes, and Kant, the latter of whom underlie the theories of earlier Freud, Klein, and particularly Bion.

Self Regulation

Self psychology emphasizes the function of self regulation and in this way suggests that the selfobject's principal function is to decrease the infant's tensions. Classical psychoanalysts referred to erotogenicity, to the instinctual excitement that emerged from the autoerotic zones and was then organized and integrated by the genital zone in the oedipal stage. Klein, on the other hand, shifted the emphasis from the genital zone to the oral zone and from the genitals of the object to the breast. This nurturing paradigm subordinated the erotic-cathectic manifestations to states of defense against frustrations with the nurturing object. Kohut's notion of "breakdown products" seems congruent with Klein's ideas in this regard.

Klein's (1952) view, however, focuses on the reactions to the object in unconscious fantasy. She believed that under the impact of frustration excessive libido turns into greed and a desire to scoop out mother's breasts and possess their contents for oneself. In this process, the inner perception of the object changes from (1) a scooped-out, deformed object, which is taken in and identified with in the ego, to (2) a scooping-out or demanding object (an object transformed by the projective identification of the greedy infant), which is internalized and identified with as a demanding, insatiable superego object. Thus, according to Klein, objects are internalized in two phases as a gradient in the ego. This corresponds to Freud's (1917) melancholic paradigm.

In my understanding, what Kohut emphasizes is the *reality* of the disappointment or failure of selfobject support, rather than the infant's *unconscious fantasies* about the object. This real experience is then registered as (1) a failure in the development of self-regulating functions under the sponsorship of the selfobject, and (2) the re-identification with a bad internal object from the real world who cannot be trusted. In short, in both Klein's and Kohut's formulations, the importance of genital sex is diminished and caretaking of the infant is emphasized. Libidinal or aggressive attacks against the object follow disappointment or frustration, according to Klein. Her concept of envy of the good breast presents a seeming exception to this view and seems to confirm her belief in primary destructiveness. One could alternatively view envy as the infant's perception of a state of danger consequent upon its acknowledgement of the goodness of the breast because of the danger inherent in its absence. Klein's notion of the paranoid-schizoid position is a way of talking about the institution and organization by conflict in order to give differentiation to the infant's objects—good and bad, inside and outside, etc. Similarly, McDougall's concept of the infantile neurosis and of autoerotism is that the data of emotional experience is organized around zonal experiences in order to allow them to be symbolized, displaced, and condensed so as to become phantasies, dreams, and emotions. Otherwise, they become nameless dread.

McDougall (1980) offers a novel argument for the importance of primary autoerotism. She has found that, in alexithymic patients, there seems to be a foreclosure of the instinctual, autoerotic "touchplates" of receptivity to the corresponding organs of the object. These patients, having thus foreclosed on their instinctual life and autoerotic zones, exist by default in a state of autistic pseudo autonomy, which disallows intimacy with objects on deep emotional levels. The technical innovation McDougall offers is the introduction of a newly begotten *infantile neurosis* to the patients to reintroduce them to their foreclosed autoerotic zones.

Pao's (1979) concept of "the best possible solution" to describe the defensive mechanism in schizophrenic patients is in line with these ideas of Klein and Kohut. Pao believes that the schizophrenic deteriorates, not so much through will or conflict alone, but because withdrawal and disorganization seem the best possible solution under the circumstances, given the individual's inner and external resources at that moment. In my opinion, Pao's concept transcends the dichotomy between deficiency and conflict, an issue I shall now consider in more detail.

Psychic Conflict and Psychic Deficiency

A thread running through Kohut's innovative contributions is the insistence that the psychology of the self is distinct from the conflict model, instinctual model, or object relations model of classical psychoanalysis and is to be treated as a separate entity. Yet I wish to emphasize that while self psychology *seems* to have split off from some of the main tenets of classical psychoanalysis, it has *not* disavowed them. My doubts at this juncture are not about the validity of self psychology, but about the validity of the "mother country" and her tenets. Kohut seems not to have divorced himself completely from classical theory. He still allows for a conflict theory in addition to a deficiency theory; and his conflict hypothesis is still based on a conflict of drives. At issue here, in my opinion, is the validity of the very concepts of instinctual drives. Drive psychology and the discharge model emanating from it seem not only experience distant but even "reason distant" by today's standards.

I am in accord with Fairbairn's desire to eschew the separate status of the id and to unite it with the ego (self). (I think this is also in accord with Kohut's newer concepts.) Moreover, I believe that the drive concept should be abandoned altogether since it is mechanistic

and poorly describes the intrapsychic situation. Rather, the id, as I
stated earlier, should be seen as an agency of mental functioning that
is co-subjective with and parallel to the ego.

I envision a dual-track arrangement corresponding to the simultaneous functioning of the two cerebral hemispheres. Cross-cuing takes
places not only between the two hemispheres and the two separate
consciousnesses that characterize them (Gazzaniga and Le Doux,
1978), but also between the logical functions of the self and the emotional and fantasied aspects of the self. In other words, the id and the
ego are separate data-processing agencies, which work harmoniously
in tandem. They are oppositional primarily when there is a breakdown.
(I believe this, too, is in accord with Kohut's views.)

Information theory (Pierce, 1960; Chomsky, 1968; Peterfreund,
1971, 1978) serves as a useful alternative to the drive model in this
regard. We can view information coming from the ''id'' as a message
of urgent personal significance that must be translated by the primary
process (alpha function [Bion, 1965]) for *meaning* to become apparent. ''Translated'' would be a better term than translated without the
quotes. The id speaks a language, and that language is *not* impulse.
I totally disavow the impulse theory and replace it with a semiotic
theory. In other words, we are a bunch of meanings looking to be
''translated,'' understood, etc. The ''id'' and the ''ego'' are different
data processing systems. They process the data of internal and external
experience separately and then cross-cue. The language of each must
be transformed as it reaches the other. This transformation I am calling
''translation.'' Thus, I do not believe that the id needs the ego to
express it. I believe that is correct as far as it goes but is inadequate.
Self psychologists do not go nearly so far as I do in disavowing the
biological notion of the unconscious personality.

The ''id'' is trying to help, not to hinder. Its messages must be
attended to, empathically *and* objectively, not ignored or disavowed.
What is important here is that if we employ a semiotic paradigm as
opposed to an obsolete drive paradigm, psychic conflict takes on a
different meaning.[6]

---

[6] Within this semiotic paradigm, I would also include ''inherent preconceptions''
(Bion, 1970), which denote the genetic code that enables the infant to be prepared
for experience it has not yet confronted. Hartmann (1964) alluded to this phenomenon
under the rubric of primary autonomy prior to conflict. This concept will have great
relevance for my later discussion of the background selfobject of primary identification.

(1) presented phenomena would involve self-selfobj.
relationships rather than object relationships
PERSPECTIVES ON SELF PSYCHOLOGY   181

In my view, psychic conflict normally emerges from the ambivalent relationships of the ''I'' to its self (as its first object) and to
interpersonal objects (the legacy of attaining Klein's depressive position). Fairbairn (1952), too, saw psychic conflict as occurring between the experience of primary identification and the experience of
differentiation. I would describe this conflict as a difficulty in being
in touch with inner feelings that warn us of significant aspects of our
inner and outer life which might put us temporarily or permanently in
jeopardy if we accepted them. In other words, we are in conflict about
accepting the data of our own inner personal resources. Thus, psychic
conflict is ultimately semiotic conflict, a conflict in the evaluation of
states of relative or absolute danger. In this light, we can depict conflict
in borderline and psychotic cases in terms of splits in the personality;
that is, separate subselves have set up ''light housekeeping'' within
the self, with separate, conflicting agendas.

Self psychologists are, as a rule, reconstructed classical Freudians
and therefore have not had access to the Kleinian conception of the
oedipal phase. They assume that the oedipal phase is something which
develops in the phallic-genital stage at approximately two to four years
of life. The Kleinian point of view has the oedipal phase beginning
during the depressive position of the late oral stage and is simultaneous   (1)
with the symbiotic relationship of the infant with its mother. I consider
the oedipal phase as a staging area for the development of object
relations based upon a separateness between the self and its objects,
whereas the symbiotic relationship is one which describes the bonding
between the infant and its mother corresponding to what Kohut and
self psychologists call the self-selfobject relationship. Thus, I believe
there is a dual-track between the development of the bonding (symbiotic) relationship and the relationship based upon separation inherent
to the oedipal phase. Thus, the oedipal phase really describes interpersonal theory, whereas the symbiotic relationship (self-selfobject
relationship) describes the biography of the development of the self
in its own right.

To my mind, the most important aspect of conflict concerns the
will of the infant (and of the patient in analysis). If the infant or patient
has a will, then he or she is the author of the scenario which engenders
the fantasies and actions which develop into guilt. Kohut's infant seems

not to be plagued by will, and suffers helplessly instead, like a character in a novel written by Fate—Fate being the selfobject. Again, I would apply the dual-track principle to suggest that the infant (or the patient) experiences *both*—being a character in the selfobject's novel on one track, and being the author of his or her own scenario on another. Ultimately, psychic conflict is not only the conflict over the fantasied or actual use or misuse of one's experience of will, but also the existential conflict between having a will and being helpless.

I believe that this dual point of view is necessary to describe the human condition under normal and clinical circumstances. Human beings are predisposed to experience their experiences in individual ways. How and with what subjective equipment the experience is experienced differs. Not all people with similar selfobject experiences, for instance, turn out the same. Each individual tends to choose from the "cafeteria" of selfobject experiences those that promote his or her optimum welfare. Ultimately, I believe there is an epigenesis in the experiencing of experience. *To be or not to be* is followed by *to do or not to do*. Alongside these are *to become or not to become* and *to allow or not to allow*. All of this takes place within the framework of intersubjectivity and the toleration of dualities implicit within that framework.

Also important to the conception of conflict is the question of unconscious fantasy (as opposed to fantasy that is conscious or preconscious). Unconscious fantasy is perhaps that aspect of psychoanalysis with which self psychology deals least. Yet no discussion of conflict or of phenomenology is complete without considering that imaginative vehicle of primitive accountability in which the *shadow of the self falls upon its object* (a reversal of Freud's [1917] injunction that identification is the shadow of the object upon the ego). Unconscious fantasies are personifications of experiences before the advent of secondary process (they coexist with secondary process as well). They operate on different developmental levels, with "built-in" incompatibilities, inconsistencies, and discrepancies, thus making for conflict as the levels begin to coalesce. In my opinion, then, Klein made a major contribution in positing a system of psychology based largely on the vicissitudes of unconscious fantasies and their transformations. By contrast, Kohut's innovation lies in his focus on the reality experience of the infant in terms of appropriate versus inappropriate selfobject support. His theory, therefore, like Fairbairn's and Winnicott's (to say nothing of Hartmann's) is largely a reality-based one. Here again, I believe that a dual-track model is necessary to account for the impact on psychic organization of unconscious fantasies on the one hand and of reality on the other. Experience is not limited to a single noun.

The Question of Normal Omnipotence

Kohut's focus on the transformations of the "grandiose self" and the "idealized parent imago" suggests that he is dealing with the failure or sucess of real interpersonal objects to bestow a sense of normal omnipotence on the infant. One of the serious defects in the classical and the Kleinian points of view is their failure to discriminate between normal and abnormal omnipotence. These paradigms emphasize the achievement of independence from fusion, and omnipotence is seen as detrimental to this separation. An alternative perspective comes from Winnicott (1958) and Balint (1968), who have called attention to the need for normal omnipotent protection. Winnicott's (1952) concept of the *true* and the *false* self, in which the true self goes into a state of hibernating sanctuary, is an example of this trend.

In another paper (Grotstein, 1980), I have described normal omnipotence as a "frontier" of psychic immunity that protects the infant until its self has matured sufficiently to deal with its experiences more realistically. Using Kleinian terminology, I would suggest that the so-called paranoid-schizoid position, rather than being earlier than and counterposed to the depressive position, is parallel to it, offering an alternative from a primary depressive position and thus helping to protect the infant from a premature precipitation of the depressive position. In line with this idea, Tustin (1981), a Kleinian who has worked with autistic infants and schizophrenic children, points out that these illnesses may result from a premature abruption of primary oneness into a precocious twoness. The infants become realistic too quickly and lose the omnipotent "magic blanket" they need for reassurance and survival.

I believe that Kohut is right in indicating that the selfobject must facilitate the infant's acquisition of a sense of normal grandiosity and exhibitionism as well as of appropriate idealizations. Availing myself of Winnicott's (1963a) valuable distinction between *being* and *doing,* I would go a step further and say that there is an even earlier stage when the selfobject must guarantee the *safety* and *privacy* of the *being* self before the development of the exhibitionistic *doing* self. In other words, the passive or "being" self, must first be protected through omnipotent fantasy to allow it to mature to the stage of active exhibitionistic grandiosity and self affirmation. Thus, an early selfobject function is the silent mirroring of the passive self in the phase of normal autism (a fateful battleground in the development of the capacity to be or not to be).

Kohut's concepts of narcissistic rage and the sense of entitlement are intimately linked to omnipotence. An implication of these ideas is that the infant has the "right" to expect a restoration of the lost state of primary narcissism. We might think of primary narcissism as a state of blissful symmetry, of primary at-oneness between the self and the background selfobject of primary identification. This state of total symmetry might be compared to what is mathematically known as the zero dimension—a field where no delineation of differences can be ascertained (Grotstein, 1978). The first breach in this stage of symmetry is birth itself, which inaugurates the experiences of being in the world. Primal symmetry, then, can be thought of as the stage of infantile and childhood innocence, whereas assymetry constitutes what William Blake calls the "journey through the forest of experience." Whether or not this journey will result in a higher innocence or in despair depends on the sense of normal omnipotence engendered by the selfobject relationship.

The Nature of Selfobject Functioning

Kohut and his followers have conceived of at least two different lines of selfobject functioning—the mirroring of an archaic grandiose self and the idealizing of the parental object. The mirroring aspect is associated with merger and twinship transferences (although the twinship transference seems to have become an independent focus of increasing importance to self psychologists). Taking my cue from

Kohut's (1980) remarks, in which he suggests the need for further exploration of selfobject functioning, I should like to offer some ideas of my own on different kinds of selfobjects.

To begin with, I will cite a particular case example that illustrates the existence of diverse selfobjects. The patient, a 42-year-old female attorney, is married and has four children. She entered analysis because she was depressed. She complained particularly about not being loved by her husband, which reminded her of a lifelong absence of warmth. I advanced the tentative formulation that she felt she did not have a good "background" figure behind her. I realized afterwards that I had used my own theoretical formulation and indeed had been too theoretical (as opposed to experiential) in my language. Her reply was the following:

> No, you're wrong. I do have good background people behind me. I have very good heredity. Many of my relatives are famous and illustrious. I certainly come from good stock. It is my parents who did not give me enough love. I suppose, however, that I am just like them insofar as I don't love myself either. My father and mother were always worried about people who were enemies. They never had peace of mind and they did not impart peace of mind to me. I never had anything to look forward to, never any sense of ambition. I drifted into law because there was nothing else to do.

Here I am trying to use an elementary case example briefly to demonstrate that there is a considerable difference phenomenologically between background objects and interpersonal objects which are impressed into service as selfobjects. The concept of selfobject, I strongly maintain, transcends far more than just simply the mother or father. It includes tradition, heredity, the mother country, the neighborhood, etc., etc., etc. The case example, which may not be the best one, demonstrates that the patient experienced a strong sense of a background object but did not have a good sense of a selfobject relationship with her mother or her father—and, by identification with them, does not have a good empathic relationship with herself. Moreover, because of their fears and their difficulty in dealing with their fears, they seem to enhance the power of the enemy selfobject—the hereditary predator of the group—and consequently offered no security or protection to their daughter.

The Interpersonal Selfobject

The idea of the interpersonal selfobject emphasizes that the prototype for the ''object'' aspect of the selfobject is a person with whom the self also has an interpersonal relationship as well as one of ''placental bonding,'' metaphorically speaking. It is obviously interchangeable with and the orchestrator of all the other selfobject functions.

Despite the innovative claims of self psychology, the subject of selfobjects has a long history, and I intend to draw on this history. Freud himself hinted at the concept when he talked about the dissolution of primary identification, the development of object love, and the return by the ego to a state of secondary identification, as a consequence of object loss. This idea of secondary identification clearly implied the selfobject. Indeed, Giovacchini (1967) first coined the term in that context. In my opinion, the most important foreshadowings of the selfobject concept lie in the work of Fairbairn and Klein. Fairbairn depicted multiple egos (by which he meant selves) in intimate union with repressed objects, making for repressed ''selfobject'' endopsychic structures in dynamic relationship to each other. I would argue that both Fairbairn and Klein took what are essentially selfobjects into the psyche and gave them a dynamic interrelationship, an internal phenomenology that has yet to appear in Kohut's self psychology.

I will now describe a variety of selfobjects. These are categories of experiences that I believe are worthy of differentiation. At the same time, however, they constitute the composite experience of selfobjecthood in its primary, primitive essence, and at any moment they may be indistinguishably isomorphic. Each one, moreover, seems to alternate between mirroring and idealizing functions.

The Background Selfobject of Primary Identification

A dual-track concept offers the possibility that the infant is born with two different experiences simultaneously and/or alternately: (1)

a sense of separateness and (2) a continuation of the state of primary at-oneness. This view leads to the idea that Kohut's selfobject may be a composite, comprising a primary selfobject—what I call the background selfobject of primary identification—and an interpersonal object that is given selfobject status by the infant through projective identification (regression). The background selfobject, which supports the infant from birth onward, includes the infant's hereditary givens and therefore would be responsible for the infant's ability to reciprocate with the interpersonal object—the mother. Whatever difficulties arise from the infant's constitution, genetics, or prenatal (intrauterine) environment would be located in this background selfobject. Thus, the background selfobject, would account for the failure of certain infants to thrive, even with potentially good selfobjects, as it allows for individual variability in the infant's interaction with the interpersonal object.

Perhaps the major function of the background selfobject of primary identification is the promotion in the infant of a sense of *being* and of *safety,* to be followed later by the achievement of selfaffirmation. It corresponds to Winnicott's (1963) concept of the environmental mother, Sandler's (1960) concept of the background of safety, and Freud's (1909) concept of the idealized parents of the family romance. Ultimately this background selfobject of primary identification becomes the inspiring source of imagination and fantasy. I have referred to it in another paper as the ''dreamer who dreams the dream and the dreamer who understands it'' (Grotstein, 1981b). We avail ourselves of it in every analytic hour as the mysterious, uncanny author of free associations, the one who *knows* the agenda which we can only ignorantly anticipate.

The background selfobject of primary identification includes, within its broad sweep, the mystique of temperament, that indefinable but distinctly inherent propensity for individual personality that is mysteriously bequeathed to us. Another exceedingly important aspect of the background selfobject of primary identification is seen in patients who report having moved from one home to another when they were infants or children. One patient, for instance, moved here with her family from Germany when she was three years old in order to escape the Nazis. She still regards Germany as her ''Ur Mutter'' and has a passionate sentimentality for it, even though she is Jewish. I believe that the environment is of enormous significance as a background selfobject.

The background selfobject of primary identification, then, gives us a sense of "I"-ness which is united with our genetic and prenatal background. It includes Bion's inherent preconceptions and our individual temperament prior to experience. In its ultimate evolution, the background selfobject of primary identification normally leads to an ongoing sense of separate self cohesiveness on the one hand and the sense of a divine being in the spiritual sense, on the other. The latter aspect is coextensive with the spiritual aspects of what has generally been called the superego, but which I prefer to call the selfobject of destiny.

To summarize thus far, I believe that the infant experiences a postnatal continuation of primary at-oneness with a background self-object of primary identification and also a sense of separateness from it. Yet these two experiences are ultimately inseparable—like Siamese twins. In other words, ultimate "I"-ness is the unique amalgam of the separateness of the developing "I" and its intimate bonding with the background selfobject of primary identification. The latter functions as a backer, protector, inspirer, prime resource and partner, and perhaps godhead. To explain further the essential role of this background selfobject, I would like, for a moment, to employ a Cartesian artifice to describe an internal conversation between "I" and "self," with "I" as subject related to "self" as object, or other. The subject(ive) "I" here connotes oneness and thus encompasses the initial background selfobject of primary identification. Put another way, the subjective "I" is mysterious and multifaceted. It reflects a oneness of many.

The Body Self Object

As Tausk (1919) long ago suggested, one of the infant's first experiences is the discovery of its body self, which at first seems indistinguishable from the body of the mother. The acceptance of its body self as its own self object (self as object), distinguished from mother's body, is a major achievement for the infant. This empathic function is performed by classical and Kleinian analysts in particular when they introduce the patient's "I" to the body self to facilitate the patient's acceptance of body instincts, autoerotic zones, and feelings.

The Selfobject of Destiny

I believe the superego and the ego ideal constitute a selfobject unit insofar as they represent a tie between some aspects of the self and aspects of the background selfobject of primary identification as well as the interpersonal selfobject. I prefer to call this the selfobject of destiny in order to deemphasize the aspects of it associated with guilt and shame (although they have tremendous importance in moralizing boundary maintenance). I believe this selfobject to be the repository of the future agenda of the growing self, the house of its ideals and ambitions. Lederer (1964) also refers to the future aspects of the superego. In addition to being a guardian of the future, the selfobject of destiny (or superego) constitutes an internalized or quasi-internalized aspect of an older (and therefore future) aspect of the self, which can help guide the individual, much like an older sibling or parent. It represents a barrier or border that helps to define and limit the nascent self. The object of destiny, in short, is the guarantor of ambition.

The selfobject of destiny also functions as the container of the repressed. That is, it holds all that has been experienced and then disavowed; (2) all that never can be experienced and so remains as undigested components of feelings and thoughts (Bion's "beta elements," which the alpha function would not or could not accept for "alpha-betization" as mental elements suitable for experience); and (3) aspects of the primary unconscious that are yet to be realized in realistic (external) form and thus have not yet been summoned into being (these correspond to Bion's [1962] notion of inherent preconceptions). Thus, the selfobject of destiny serves a containing function as a "memoir of the future," to use Bion's (1975, 1977, 1979) ambiguous but poetic term. It is responsible for the "return of the repressed."

Ultimately, the whole phenomenon of idealization may come to rest within the province of the selfobject of destiny insofar as this function has to do with reverence, whether between a disciple and a guru or between a person and a god. Reverence, otherwise known as the religious function, is an inherent faculty of each human being, and idealization is its quintessence. In this connection, I would like to touch briefly on the theme of the messiah. In *Experience in Groups,* Bion (1959b) cryptically observed that one of the resistant subgroups that develops within the fabric of a group is a pairing subgroup (the others being fight-or-flight and dependency subgroups). This subgroup develops a "folie à deux" fantasy that a messiah will be born from their pairing and will save the group. In everyday life we see how infants idealize one or both of their parents as they surrender their own omnipotence and discover reality. In a sense, this idealization of the parent makes the parent something of a messiah who will save the child, since the child no longer feels able to save itself. At the same time the parents may idealize the infant and make it into a messiah. This usually happens when the parents have, to one degree or another, given up their own sense of purpose in the world, have foresworn their ambitions, and feel depressed and inadequate. The desire for a younger messiah develops and becomes fixed on the emerging generation. In other words, there is an interchanging of messiah-dom between one generation and the next, a strange link with a mystic thirdness. The messiah theme thus suggests a special spiritual aspect of what I have called the selfobject of destiny, although it is difficult indeed to separate it out from the background selfobject of primary identification.

The Mysterious Stranger or Predator Selfobject

I have borrowed this concept from Bowlby, who suggests in a personal communication that there is an inherent fear of the predator. My idea also corresponds to Bion's (1970) notion of inherent preconceptions and to Benjamin's (1965) remarks on stranger anxiety. I believe that the infant is born with the capacity to divine both the objects it needs to guarantee its safety and survival and the objects that present a danger to its survival. The infant has the capacity to know that strangers can harm it and that even the objects on which it depends can become predators. I see this selfobject as corresponding in one sense to Klein's concept of a bad internal object. However, it differs in that it is not so much created by the projection of the child's destructiveness onto the object as by the projection onto reality of the infant's inherent preconception of dangerous objects.

From another point of view one can see the mysterious stranger or predator selfobject as a way of talking about the personification of danger itself, combining the real enemy on the outside with our inherent preconceptions of it. From analytic reconstructions it appears to me that what patients seem most often to complain of, at bottom, is that their own parents were afraid of life and betrayed their own failures to deal with persecutors *and* enemies. They could consequently bequeath to their child only a legacy of fear, not of courage. It is of utmost importance in psychoanalytic treatment to help the patient to differentiate between a persecutor and an enemy, as well as to see that his or her significant objects can be benevolent, persecutory, and dangerous—separately and collectively. I believe the phenomenology of real danger has been underemphasized in psychoanalytic theory; my designation of this selfobject is an attempt to rectify this omission.

The Environmental Selfobject

This selfobject refers to the cultural environment aside from and beyond the parental selfobjects. In ancient days it would have corresponded to the clan or horde. Today, it encompasses culture, neighborhood, etc. An example of the failure of this kind of selfobject support, and an attempt to compensate for it, might be seen in the gangs of inner city youths who band together for protection, paradoxically, against rival groups. This banding together appears to give these youths a sense of safety that environmental selfobjects no longer afford. If anything characterizes the inner being of these youths, it is their sense of being orphans of fortune. They no longer feel protected by their established culture and therefore seek safety by reverting to more primitive techniques. The phenomenon of the environmental selfobject—of the twinship type ("alter ego") can be demonstrated in a ubiquitous form in the case of troops in combat who seem to huddle together as different heads upon a collective body, a response which seems to deny the terror of individual death.

Self Objects and Internal Objects

In a recent publication I tried to examine the relationship between Klein's internal objects and Kohut's selfobjects (Grotstein, 1982). Both

seem to connote archaic relationships by the self to its objects antecedent to the development of object constancy and the attainment of
the object representational world which is its consequence. Perhaps
the greatest major difference between the two concepts, aside from the
spatial location assigned to them (internal for internalized objects and
external for selfobjects), is the way in which the self allegedly feels
about them. Klein's internal objects are inherently bad ones and are
dreaded by the self which must ally itself with idealized objects (also
internalized secondarily) in order to deal with these feared objects.
Thus, these internal objects correspond to Klein's concept of inferred
phenomenology. Kohut's selfobjects seem to be external and to provide
functions for the self which the self does not yet have at its disposal.
Kohut does not seem to emphasize the formation of internal objects
of a destructive or a malevolent character. The only aspect of internalization he seems to deal with is that of transmuting internalization
which is the internalization of a function formally belonging to a
selfobject and which now belongs to the self. He dimly implies internalization of malevolent objects when he discusses empathic failures
and the resultant reversion to archaic selfobject merger (Kohut, 1971,
1977).
    When one surveys the vast literature on object relations theory
since Freud first introduced it (1914, 1917) one finds that the word
"objects" has different meanings to different psychoanalytic scholars.
My own impression is that Klein's internal objects correspond to Kohut's selfobjects. Both suggest the internal view of the object at a point
where the self has not yet achieved complete separation. Object representations, on the other hand, are the "souls of departed objects,"
which can be conjured up symbolically in their absence. An object
representation, in other words, is where an object used to be but no
longer is and yet can still be thought to be. Klein's internal objects do
suggest homunculi occupying space within the mind of the infant,
although Kohut may fall into this same reductionism when he talks of
transmuting internalization.
    In my opinion, Klein gets into trouble with her formulation that
an object is identified with (externally) through projective identification
by the infant, modified by the nature of the projective identification,
internalized according to the transformation, and then identified with

internally (see Grotstein, 1982). It is difficult to understand how an object with which the self is fused via projective identification can at the same time be internalized since ego boundaries disappear in such merger fantasies (and therefore there is no inside or outside and consequently no way of taking in). My own way around this seeming contradiction is, once again, to utilize the dual-track notion. On one level, one might postulate that a separate self (not participating in the fusion) experiences another aspect of itself undergoing this merger, with the image of this experience being internalized. On another level, one might say that the subject experiences itself as fused to one degree or another with an external object *without* internalization so that the boundaries of the psyche extend beyond the boundaries of the subject's body. It is to Kohut's credit that he has introduced the latter idea into psychoanalytic thinking.

Thus, we can envision two different experiences occurring simultaneously and/or alternately: an internalization of the experience of fusion and the experience itself of fusion with an object external to the self, with the result that subjective ''I''-ness becomes a composite experience of self and object. This dual-track conception might be pictured as a kind of Siamese twin, with the infant and the mother possessing separate heads but a continuous body. That, I think, is the basic paradigm for the symbiotic experience of the selfobject. On another level of abstraction, we might use this image to designate the different experiences of the object as internal on one level and as coextensive on another level. A correlated dual-track idea is my belief that all selfobject functions arise from the vicissitudes of projective identification, on the one hand, and a continuation of primary identification, on the other.

The Fate of the Unconscious in Self Psychology

Central to a true dual-track model is an accounting of the unconscious. Kohut and his followers have maintained the tenets of classical psychoanalysis generally and still hold and maintain an allegiance to the importance of the unconscious. Yet there may be a danger. Let me clarify what I mean with a parallel example. Although Klein maintained that she took cognizance of the external environment, in actual fact her theory made little allowance for it. It was not until Bion's conception of the container and the contained that the external environment found its way into Kleinian metapsychology. Something similar may become true for self psychology in regard to the unconscious. Certainly self psychologists do analyze the unconscious elements of dreams, etc., yet the unconscious seems to be submerged as an experience-distant inference about the self within the self's frontier.

In the classical and Kleinian models, the unconscious is positioned as a separate area with its own scenario but one which touches the data of conscious experience. With self psychology, a question arises about the ultimate relationship between the experience-near interpretation of empathic failures and the experience-distant inference of unconscious conflict. Might self psychology prepare a narcissistically impaired patient for the insights offered by conflict analysis? In other words, would Mr. Z. have benefited if he had been analyzed by Kohut in the reverse order? I would argue that one aspect of the unconscious, the secondarily repressed, is necessarily an affectation of experience. Thus, classical and Kleinian interpretations work, when they work, because they bring to light this aspect of the unconscious, *which has been experienced.* Without a cohesive self, however, it may not be possible to touch on these aspects of the unconscious for fear of fragmentation being too great. Proper selfobject support is necessary.

Does the self have a primary unconscious, above and beyond—or below and beyond—that of its relationship to Kohut's selfobject? In this instance, I am specifically thinking of the background selfobject of primary identification, an experience I allege to be behind ultimate ''I''-ness and encompassing the vast expanse of our inner creativity beyond and/or before our first contact with an interpersonal object. I am referring to the capacity for imagination and inspiration, to our inherent preconceptions, to all the instrumentalities of creativity itself—the will of ''I'' to *be,* like Michelangelo's *Prisoners* or Wordsworth's immortal babies.

Psychoanalytic Treatment as a Consequence of the Aforementioned

Psychoanalytic therapy can be seen from one point of view to have been effective because of its capacity to foster the weaning of the patient from infantile and childhood bondages as fixations (Freud) to internal objects (Fairbairn and Klein). Thus, interpretations allowed the patient to differentiate as he was released from these earlier strictures. Self psychology, which addresses itself to empathic failures and states of deficiency, seems to call attention to defects in the infant's bonding to its mother (and father). I suggest, therefore, that the analytic therapy proposed by self psychology complements the techniques earlier proposed by classical and Kleinian analysis. Every infant needs to be adequately bonded to its care-taking object (selfobject) before it can be properly weaned into its maturity. Failure to realize this has imposed dire tasks on patients whose analyzability may have been more in question than analysts have realized. An analysis based upon addressing itself empathically to selfobject deficiencies allows for the reconstruction of a bonding which, in turn, can allow more easily for subsequent weaning. If bonding and weaning are the underlying common denominators of psychoanalytic technique, then we should be able to observe them in every analysis. From another point of view it can be stated that self psychology seeks to address the defects in the establishment in the patient's sense of uniqueness and specialness, whereas classical and Kleinian analyses seek to introduce the patient to his ordinary human neediness. Both sides of the self need to be dealt with—on a dual-track. From both emerges *realness*—in depth.

It may be that certain analyses, particularly those where states of self-deficiency are prominent, would be characterized, especially early in the analysis, by the need for bonding and, therefore, of empathic observation. These patients may benefit later in the analysis by a greater emphasis on detached observation when they are better able to achieve weaning. Detached observation may be necessary, furthermore, in those patients who have developed a sense of pathological dissociation in which each subordinate self has developed such an autonomy that it seeks to obstruct the effect of empathic observation on the authentic, helpless self, which seems to be a prisoner within its own beleaguered personality.—This is analogous to the Japanese soldier from World War II who just recently surfaced in Bataan, not realizing that the war he was still fighting had ended thirty or forty years earlier—I believe that there are many patients who must first ''be made safe for empathy'' so that the latter is not considered collusive weakness. On the other hand, it may very well be that empathic observation is sufficient, and that weaning will take care of itself if there be sufficient empathic bonding in the analysis. Time will tell.

Conclusion

In but a few years' time, self psychology has established itself as both an extension of classical analysis and a body of thought distinct from it. It has added new conceptions of early mental life and of transference phenomena in psychoanalysis. Narcissistic disorders have been rescued from neglect and brought into the limelight. At long last the concept of psychic deficiency has been given a metapsychological base. What Kohut has in effect done is to herald a major philosophical shift, not only in the psychoanalytic treatment of patients, but also in our understanding of child-rearing and life-styles. Kohut's recognition of the infant's sense of entitlement reminds one of Plato's theory of the Memory of Justice, which we can think of as an inalienable contract between the self and the selfobject to restore one's lost safety and emotional security. We live forever in the shadow of the need for selfobject support, if I can summarize Kohut succinctly. What remains is to consider how self psychology can interface with classical analysis and whether the latter itself can undergo a metamorphosis so as better to interface with self psychology.

I have already suggested that a Cyclopian view tends to idealize one aspect and demonize another. In order for Freud to establish the importance of the ego, he had to demonize the id. Klein's conception of unconscious fantasy ended up demonizing the infant's instinctual unconscious and inadvertently idealizing the parents. Kohut's self psychology may be in danger of inadvertently demonizing the parental environment at the expense of idealizing the infant's experience. Yet the dual-track elements in his theory might, if employed more fully, safeguard against that possibility. My plea is for the use of a dual-track perspective on every level of psychoanalytic consideration.

I believe the infant is born with a dual consciousness and utilizes the instruments of this dual consciousness through the remainder of his life. That consciousness which is the servant of the secondary process of reality will register the realistic pain of parental-environmental intrusion much more realistically and painfully than has ever been recognized. The other consciousness, the servant of primary process, seeks to abet the agony of inner and outer experience by transforming the painful data of experience into fantasies and dreams so as to mitigate the effect of the experience and to allow the infant to survive. The infant thus develops two (at least) different views of experience. Self psychology, in its use of the empathic principle of observation, beautifully addresses itself to the realistic experience of pain, of deprivation, and of empathic failures and seeks furthermore to redress these defects as best it can by a retrospective vouchsafement of the infant's sense of entitlement. Classical and Kleinian analyses (although not, strictly speaking, ego psychology) seek to put the patient in contact with his sense of responsibility for the experiencing of his experiences. The dual-track allows for the infant—and the patient—to be Kohut's tragic victim and also Freud's (and Klein's) guilty victim. We cannot help what happens to us, but we do believe we are responsible for the acceptance of our lot. Beyond entitlement there is fate!

References

Abraham, K. (1924), A short study of the development of the personality. In: *Selected Papers*. New York: Basic Books, 1953, pp. 418–501.

Atwood, G. & Stolorow, R. (1978), *Faces in the Cloud*. New York: Aronson.

Balint, M. (1968), *The Basic Fault: Therapeutic Aspects of Regression*. London: Tavistock.

Basch, M. (1977), Developmental psychology and explanatory theory in psychoanalysis. *The Annual of Psychoanalysis*, 5:229–263. New York: International Universities Press.

Benjamin, J. (1965), Developmental biology and psychoanalysis. In: *Psychoanalysis and Current Biological Thoughts*, ed. N.S. Greenfield & W.C. Lewis. Madison: University of Wisconsin Press, pp. 57–80.

Bion, W.R. (1959a), *Attacks on Linking in Second Thoughts*. London: Heinemann, 1967.

——— (1959b), *Experiences in Groups*. London: Tavistock.

——— (1962), *Learning from Experience*. London: Heinemann.

——— (1963), *Elements of Psychoanalysis*. London: Heinemann.

——— (1965), *Transformations*. London: Heinemann.

——— (1970), *Attention and Interpretation*. London: Tavistock.

——— (1975), *A Memoir of the Future. Book One: The Dream*. Rio de Janeiro: Imago Editora.

———— (1977), *A Memoir of the Future. Book Two: The Past Presented.* Rio de Janeiro. Imago Editora.

———— (1979), *A Memoir of the Future. Book Three: The Dawn of Oblivion.* Perthshire: Clunie Press.

Bowlby, J. (1969), *Attachment and Loss,* Vol. 1. New York: Basic Books.

Brazelton, T.B. (1980), The current status of neonatal research. Presented at 69th Annual Meeting of the American Psychoanalytic Association, San Francisco, May 3.

Breuer, J. & Freud, S. (1893–1895), Studies on hysteria. *Standard Edition,* 2. London: Hogarth Press, 1955.

Chomsky, N. (1968), *Language and the Mind.* New York: Harcourt, Brace & World.

Cohler, B.J. (1980), Developmental perspectives on the psychology of the self in early childhood. In: *Advances in Self Psychology.* New York: International Universities Press, pp. 117–132.

Emde, R.N. (1981), Changing models of infancy and the nature of early development: Remodeling the foundation. *J. Amer. Psychoanal. Assn.,* 29:179–220.

Epstein, J. & Feiner, A.H., eds. (1980), *Countertransference: The Therapist's Contributions to Treatment.* New York: Aronson.

Erikson, E. (1959), *Identity and the Life Cycle [Psychological Issues,* Monogr. 1]. New York: International Universities Press.

Fairbairn, W.R.D. (1940), Schizoid factors in the personality. In: *Psychoanalytic Studies of the Personality.* London: Routledge & Kegan Paul, 1952.

———— (1941), A revised psycho-pathology of the psychoses and psychoneuroses. *Int. J. Psycho-Anal.,* 22:250–279.

———— (1943), Repression and the return of bad objects (with special reference to the 'war neuroses'). In: *Psychoanalytic Studies of the Personality.* London: Routledge & Kegan Paul, 1952.

———— (1946), Object-relationship and dynamic structure. In: *Psychoanalytic Studies of the Personality.* London: Routledge & Kegan Paul, 1952.

———— (1952), *Psychoanalytic Studies of the Personality.* London: Routledge & Kegan Paul.

———— (1958), On the nature and aims of psychoanalytic treatment. *Internat. J. Psycho-Anal.,* 39:374–385.

Freud, S. (1905), Three essays on the theory of sexuality. Standard Edition, 7:125–243. London: Hogarth Press, 1953.

———— (1909), Family romances. *Standard Edition,* 9:235–244. London: Hogarth Press, 1959.

———— (1911), Psycho-analytic notes on an autobiographical account of a case of paranoia (dementia paranoides). *Standard Edition,* 12:3–84. London: Hogarth Press, 1958.

———— (1914), On narcissism: An introduction. *Standard Edition,* 14:67–104. London: Hogarth Press, 1957.

———— (1917), Mourning and melancholia. *Standard Edition,* 14:237–258. London: Hogarth Press, 1957.

———— (1920), Beyond the pleasure principle. *Standard Edition,* 18:3–66. London: Hogarth Press, 1955.

Gazzaniga, M.S. & Le Doux, J.E. (1978), *The Integrated Mind.* New York: Plenum Press.

Gilbert S.M. & Gubar, S. (1979), *The Madwoman in the Attic: The Woman Writer and the Nineteenth Century Literary Imagination.* New Haven: Yale University Press.

Giovacchini, P. (1967). Some elements of the therapeutic action in the treatment of character disorders. In: *Psychoanalytic Treatment of Characterological and Schizophrenic Disorders,* by L. Bryce Boyer and Peter L. Giovacchini. New York: Science House, pp. 235–271.

Goldberg, A. (1981), Self psychology and alternative perspectives in internalization. Unpublished manuscript.

Grinberg, L. (1980), Projective counteridentification and countertransference. In: *Countertransference: The Therapist's Contributions to Treatment,* ed. L. Epstein & A.H. Feiner. New York: Aronson.

Grotstein, J.S. (1978), Inner space: Its dimensions and its coordinates. *Internat. J. Psycho-Anal.,* 59:55–61.

——— (1980), A proposed revision of the psychoanalytic concept of primitive mental states: Part I. Introduction to a newer psychoanalytic metapsychology. *Contemp. Psychoanal.,* 16:479–546.

——— (1981a), *Splitting and Projective Identification.* New York: Aronson.

——— (1981b), Who is the dreamer who dreams the dream and who is the dreamer who understands it: Extended version. In: *Do I Dare Disturb the Universe? A Memorial to Wilfred R. Bion.* Beverly Hills: Caesura Press, pp. 357–416.

——— (1982), Newer perspectives in the object relations theory. *Contemp. Psa.* 18:43–91.

Guerard, A.J. (1967), *Stories of the Double.* New York: Lippincott.

Hartmann, H. (1939), *Ego Psychology and the Problem of Adaptation.* New York: International Universities Press, 1958.

——— (1964), *Essays on Ego Psychology.* New York: International Universities Press.

Kernberg, O. (1975), *Borderline Conditions and Pathological Narcissism.* New York: Aronson.

Klein, M. (1933), The early development of conscience in the child. In: *Contributions to Psycho-Analysis 1921–1945,* pp. 267–277.

——— (1935), A contribution to the psychogenesis of manic-depressive states. In: *Contributions to Psycho-Analysis, 1921–1945.* London: Hogarth Press, pp. 282–310.

——— (1940), Mourning and its relation to manic-depressive states. In: *Contributions to Psycho-Analysis, 1921–1945.* London: Hogarth Press, pp. 311–338.

——— (1952), Notes on some schizoid mechanisms. In: *Developments in Psycho-Analysis,* by M. Klein, P. Heimann, S. Isaacs, & J. Riviere. London: Hogarth Press, pp. 292–320.

Kohut, H. (1971), *The Analysis of the Self.* New York: International Universities Press.

——— (1975), The psychoanalyst in the community of scholars. In: *The Search for the Self,* ed. P.H. Ornstein. New York: International Universities Press, 1978, pp. 685–724.

——— (1977), *The Restoration of the Self.* New York: International Universities Press.

——— (1979), Two analyses of Mr. Z. *Internat. J. Psycho-Anal.,* 60:3–27.

———— (1980), Two letters: From a letter to one of the participants at the Chicago conference on the psychology of the self [and] From a letter to a colleague. In: *Advances in Self Psychology*, ed. A. Goldberg. New York: International Universities Press, pp. 449–472.

Langs, R.J. (1976), *The Bipersonal Field*. New York: Aronson.

Lederer, W. (1964), *Dragons, Delinquents, and Destiny: An Essay on Positive Superego Function* [*Psychological Issues*, Monogr. 15]. New York: International Universities Press.

Lévi-Strauss, C. (1968), *The Origin of Table Manners*, trans. J. Weightman & D. Weightman. New York: Harper & Row, 1978.

———— (1980), *The Naked Man*, trans. J. Weightman & D. Weightman. New York: Harper and Row.

McDougall, J. (1980), *Plea for a Measure of Abnormality*. New York: International Universities Press.

McLaughlin, J.T. (1978), Primary and secondary process in the context of cerebral hemispheric specialization. *Psychoanal. Quart.*, 47:237–266.

Pao, P.-N. (1979), *Schizophrenic Disorders*. New York: International Universities Press.

Pierce, C. (1960), *Collected Papers*. Vol. 1–6. Cambridge: Harvard University Press.

Peterfreund, E. (1971), *Information, Systems and Psychoanalysis* [*Psychological Issues*, Monogr. 25/26]. New York: International Universities Press.

———— (1978), Some critical comments on psychoanalytic conceptualizations of infancy. *Internat. J. Psycho-Anal.*, 59:427–441.

Rogers, R. (1970), *A Psychoanalytic Study of the Double in Literature*. Detroit: Wayne State University Press.

Rosenfield, C. (1967), The shadow within: The conscious and the unconscious use of the double. In: *Stories of the Double*, ed. A. J. Guerard. New York:Lippincott.

Schafer, R. (1968), *Aspects of Internalization*. New York: International Universities Press.

Sandler, J. (1960), The background of safety. *Internat. J. Psycho-Anal.*, 41:352–356.

Searles, H. (1958), The schizophrenic's vulnerability to the therapist's unconscious processes. *J. Nerv. Ment. Dis.*, 127:247–262.

Stern, D. (1977), *The First Relationship: Infant and Mother*. Cambridge: Harvard University Press.

Stolorow, R. & Atwood, G.E. (1979), *Faces in a Cloud: Subjectivity in Personality Theory*. New York: Aronson.

Sullivan, H.S. (1953), *The Interpersonal Theory of Psychiatry*. New York: Norton.

———— (1956), *Clinical Studies in Psychiatry*. New York: Norton.

Tausk, V. (1919), On the origin of the 'influencing machine' in schizophrenia. In: *Psychoanalytic Reader*, ed. R. Fleiss. New York: International Universities Press, 1948, pp. 52–85.

Tustin, F. (1981), Psychological birth and psychological catastrophy. In: *Do I Dare Disturb the Universe? A Memorial to Wilfred R. Bion*. ed. J.S. Grotstein. Beverly Hills: Caesura Press.

Winnicott, D.W. (1951), Transitional objects and transitional phenomena. In: *Collected Papers*. New York: Basic Books, 1958, pp. 229–242.

———— (1952), Psychoses and child care. In: *Collected Papers*. New York: Basic Books, 1958, pp. 219–228.

———— (1954), The depressive position in normal emotional development. In: *Collected Papers*. New York: Basic Books, 1958, pp. 262–277.

———— (1958), *Collected Papers: Through Paediatrics to Psycho-Analysis*. New York: Basic Books.

———— (1960), The theory of the parent-infant relationship. In: *The Maturational Processes and the Facilitating Environment*. New York: International Universities Press, 1965, pp. 37–55.

———— (1962), A personal view of the Kleinian contribution. In: *The Maturational Processes and the Facilitating Environment*. New York: International Universities Press, 1965, pp. 171–178.

———— (1963a), Communicating and noncommunicating leading to a study of certain opposites. In: *The Maturational Processes and the Facilitating Environment*. New York: International Universities Press, pp. 179–192.

———— (1963b), The development of the capacity for concern. In: *The Maturational Processes and the Facilitating Environment*. New York: International Universities Press, pp. 73–82.

———— (1965). *The Maturational Processes and the Facilitating Environment*. New York: International Universities Press.

Wolf, E. (1980), On the developmental line of selfobject relations. In: *Advances in Self Psychology*, ed. A. Goldberg. New York: International Universities Press, pp. 117-132.

Is There a Weltanschauung to be Developed from Psychoanalysis?

JOSEPH D. LICHTENBERG

Freud: Truth and Reason

"I must confess that I am not at all partial to the fabrication of *Weltanschauungen,*" Freud wrote (1926a, p. 96). "Psycho-analysis, in my opinion, is incapable of creating a *Weltanschauung* of its own. It does not need one; it is a part of science and can adhere to the scientific *Weltanschauung*" (Freud, 1933a, p. 181). Freud thus developed his case against a Weltanschauung for psychoanalysis in two of his major late works: "Inhibitions, Symptoms and Anxiety," where the discussion plays a small but "philosophically" pivotal role, and The *New Introductory Lectures on Psycho-Analysis,* where Freud devotes the entire concluding lecture to it.

In this lecture (1933a), Freud takes the opportunity to define the term, and to discuss religion, politics, and culture and their relationship to science. While, as Strachey points out in an accompanying footnote (p. 158, n. 1), Weltanschauung could be translated simply as "a view of the universe," Freud explains its meaning in terms that convey a strong value judgment: "In my opinion, . . . a *Weltanschauung* is an intellectual construction which solves all the problems of our existence uniformly on the basis of one overriding hypothesis, which, accordingly, leaves no question unanswered and in which everything that interests us finds its fixed place. . . . Believing in it one can feel secure in life, one can know what to strive for, and how one can deal most expediently with one's emotions and interests'' (p. 158). Having defined ''a view of the universe'' in this way, Freud acknowledges that ''the answer as regards psycho-analysis is made easy . . . —it is quite unfit to construct a *Weltanschauung* of its own'' (p. 158).

But while Freud may introduce a straw-man argument, only to knock it down easily, he would never leave the issue in so simplistic a form. He proceeds to explore in depth the ways science contains and constructs a uniform explanation of the universe as the long-range program of its research. Psychoanalysis, he asserts, is that part of science that aims to explain the human mind. Interestingly, Freud's objection is not so much to the rigidity of Weltanschauung as he defined it. In fact, he argues for a similar rigidity for science: ''It is simply a fact that the truth cannot be tolerant, that it admits of no compromises or limitations, that research regards every sphere of human activity as belonging to it and that it must be relentlessly critical if any other power tries to take over any part of it'' (p. 160). The critical difference is that science pursues the truth, recognizing its limitations at the moment, but aiming to conquer through research the dominion of truth for humanity in the future. ''Our best hope for the future is that intellect—the scientific spirit, reason—may in process of time establish a dictatorship in the mental life of man.'' Unlike religious dogma, the ''nature of reason is a guarantee that afterwards it will not fail to give man's emotional impulses and what is determined by them the position they deserve. But the common compulsion exercised by such a dominance of reason will prove to be the strongest uniting bond among men and lead the way to further union'' (p. 171). Freud mounts his major attack against religion. ''Religion is an attempt to master the sensory world in which we are situated by means of the wishful world which we have developed within us as a result of biological and psychological necessities. But religion cannot achieve this. Its doctrines bear the imprint of the times in which they arose, . . . the childhood of humanity. Its consolations deserve no trust. Experience teaches us that the world is no nursery'' (p. 168).

Freud notes other enemies of science. One that he dismisses rather easily is the Weltanschauung of intellectual nihilists, who argue that "scientific truth is only the product of our own needs as they are bound to find utterance under changing external conditions" (p. 175). About these anarchists, Freud remarks wittily, "Just now the relativity theory of modern physics seems to have gone to their head" (p. 175). (I shall return to this issue later, since I believe this to be an instance in which Freud's usual sagacity failed him.) The last Weltanschauung, Marxism, Freud regarded as an enemy far more serious than the "nihilists." "The newly achieved discovery of the far-reaching importance of economic relations brought with it a temptation not to leave alterations in them to the course of historical development but to put them into effect oneself by revolutionary action. Theoretical Marxism, as realized in Russian Bolshevism, has acquired the energy and the self-contained and exclusive character of a *Weltanschauung,* but at the same time an uncanny likeness to what it is fighting against" (pp. 179–180). Any critical explanation is forbidden, doubts of its correctness are punished as heresy. Its promulgators "are men of action, unshakeable in their convictions, inaccessible to doubt, without feelings for the sufferings of others if they stand in the way of their intentions" (p. 181).

Freud concludes this brilliant philosophical survey by stating "A *Weltanschauung* erected upon science has, apart from its emphasis on the real external world, mainly negative traits, such as submission to the truth and rejection of illusions" (p. 182). Momentary consolations, Freud counsels, must be found elsewhere—although there is hope in the long view of history for a "process of cultural development" (p. 179).

In this lecture Freud pits the Weltanschauung of science, including psychoanalysis, against enemies from without. It is instructive, therefore, to pay particular attention to Freud's earlier (1926a) brief comment on the subject since it refers to a Weltanschauung developing *within* psychoanalysis or, at least, as a direct outgrowth of psychoanalytic theory. In this work, Freud carries forward the revolutionary ideas put forth in *The Ego and the Id* (1923), especially as they called for a revision in his theory of anxiety and other affects. He states: "we may legitimately hold firmly to the idea that the ego is the actual seat of anxiety and give up our earlier view that the cathectic energy of the repressed impulse is automatically turned into anxiety" (1926a,

p. 93). He then proceeds to develop the concept of the power of the ego to control instinctual impulses, their psychical representatives, the path to action, and the access to consciousness. Then, as is typical in Freud's writing, he interrupts his narrative to deal with the resistance he anticipates from his reader:

> At this point it is relevant to ask how I can reconcile this acknowledgement of the might of the ego with the description of its position which I gave in *The Ego and the Id*, . . . its dependent relationship to the id and to the super-ego . . . and . . . how powerless and apprehensive it was. . . . Many writers have laid much stress on the weakness of the ego in relation to the id and of our rational elements in the face of the daemonic forces within us; and they display a strong tendency to make what I have said into a corner-stone of a psychoanalytic *Weltanschauung*. Yet surely the psycho-analyst, with his knowledge of the way in which repression works, should, of all people, be restrained from adopting such an extreme and one-sided view [p. 95].

What had aroused Freud to admonish his psychoanalytic colleagues? He seems to be saying that they had taken an earlier view of his and turned it into a "Baedeker" for their conceptual journey, a "Handbook to Life," a "Catechism" (p. 96). Their adherence to one theoretical position and embellishment of it now stood in the way of the progress Freud continually attempted to make by revising his concepts in accordance with new information and his awareness of internal contradictions. Freud was ready at the time he wrote this to make a significant leap forward into a more fully articulated structural hypothesis by resolving the problem of anxiety—as a signal of danger utilized by an autonomously functioning ego. Freud's impatience to make progress shows in the intensity of his annoyance with those analysts who would insist on using the prior discoveries about the id as a blinder to the new explorations. Freud's metaphor expresses his feelings when he ends his comments on their Weltanschauung in this way: "The benighted traveller may sing aloud in the dark to deny his own fears; but, for all that, he will not see an inch further beyond his nose" (p. 96).

What then is Freud attacking in his critique of Weltanschauungen? In his later, extended attack, he is decrying the timidity of humankind in general that leads people to seek false certitude by adhering to doctrines outside of science. In his earlier, brief attack, he is decrying the timidity of some psychoanalysts that leads them to seek a false certitude by adhering to a particular theory *within* psychoanalysis. It is this earlier concern I believe that cut deeper. What Freud said then applies equally now or in the future. When the psychoanalyst "of all people" adopts "an extreme and one-sided view" then progress and discovery will cease.

What is Freud advocating? He makes a rather vigorous plea for the replacement of illusion with truth and a softer plea for the replacement of consolation and exaltation with reason. Truth and reason are to Freud the essential spirit of science; illusion and consolation are its enemy. But in the name of science Freud used some of the rhetoric of its political and religious enemies: "the truth cannot be tolerant," "no compromises or limitations," "relentlessly critical," "a dictatorship in the mental life." Freud resolves this seeming paradox by his conviction that the dictatorship of truth and reason irrevocably commits itself to being open-minded—each element in the individual—impulses, ego, and superego will therefore receive the position it deserves. Freud's advocacy of this "program" provided later psychoanalysts with a foundation for the development of what has become in effect a psychoanalytic Weltanschauung—one that I believe has much to recommend it. I shall return to this later.

At this point I would like to return to Freud's attack on the so-called intellectual nihilists who argue that "scientific truth is only the product of our own needs" (1933a, p. 175). Freud's arguments are irrefutable; the sophist who would deny experimental evidence because of the limitations on what is knowable is, as Freud says, a fool who "might build bridges just as well out of cardboard as out of stone" (p. 176). My question is not about Freud's logic; it is about the discovery he failed to make: that the observer's point of view *is* a factor in the experiment. By having his opponents say "we find *only* what we need and see *only* what we want to see" (pp. 175–176, italics mine), Freud missed making a connection between the relativity theory of modern physics and psychoanalysis. Each science discovered in its own sphere that the proper interpretation of the data, no matter how carefully collected, requires a consideration of the positioning of the experimenter-observer. In decrying the popularized misconception that "everything is relative," Freud failed to appreciate that what he had discovered about countertransference represented a remarkable confirmation in one sphere of science of a discovery in the other. Broadly speaking, the parallel is the following: To properly appreciate measurements of space and time, to resolve issues of whether light is straight or bent, the physicist must take into account the positioning or the point of view of the observer recording the data. To insist that space and time are categories independent of observation leads to inexplicable contradictions, not only philosophical, but practical as well. To properly appreciate the data of psychoanalysis, the analyst must take into account his perspective as a listener, his needs as excited by the patient, his defenses against awareness of those needs in his patient and in himself, and the influence of his responses—verbal or unstated.

It can be argued that this is a false parallel. The observer of the physical phenomena is free to observe what is there to observe. The observer of the analytic data would be free to observe what is there to observe were he free of his countertransference bias—hence the need for personal analysis to rid him of his neurosis. This argument defines countertransference as the result of a specific disturbance in the analyst—a definition with which I would agree. Does this not eliminate the parallel and my suggestion that Freud missed making an important discovery? I think not, because Freud's discovery of specific biases—blind spots on the part of the analytic observer—might have led him to extend the question of biases beyond the extreme instances of countertransferences to all instances of observer involvement. At the least, he might have acknowledged that when the observer looks for evidence of specific trauma, he is more apt to find it; or conversely, if he looks for evidence of conflicts based on fantasy elaboration of "ordinary" events, he is more apt to find that. This might be extended a step further, that when the observer is finding trauma, he might be in danger of overlooking the fantasy elaboration, or in finding fantasy sources, he might overlook trauma—especially of the undramatic continual type. Furthermore, when the occurrences within an analytic hour are examined, the activities of the analyst biased by his countertransferences are recognized as affecting the immediate and longer-term responses of the analysand. This too might be extended to include other or even all choices made by the analyst. The experience of supervision repeatedly confirms that the analysis as observed by the supervisor constitutes a contextual exchange between analyst and analysand, and, in addition, the situation of supervision constitutes a contextual exchange between supervisor and supervisee. To eliminate from consideration the activity—mental, verbal, and nonverbal—of the "observer" for any of these traditional psychoanalytic situations is to restrict the explanatory potential inherent in the "experiment."

This extension of Freud's discovery of countertransference on the part of the analyst and its effect on the analytic encounter is one he easily could have made—but did not, I suggest, because he regarded it as scientifically unnecessary. Freud worked from the conceptual base that a rational ego existed in the adult that operated on the basis of the reality principle. This was the source of the scientific observer's capacity to seek truth and reason. Distortions of truth abound, of course, but their origin lies in the effect of the instinctual impulses and the repressions used by the defensive ego to tame them. In all of Freud's theorizing, he assumed indirectly that in one sector of the personality—the dominant mass of ideas, consciousness, the rational ego—an unimpaired capacity for reasoning reigned. Even in psychosis, he believed, a little remainder of this rational ego survived to make realistic observations. Thus for Freud, in the world of illness—neurosis (childhood remnants) and psychosis—psychic reality is decisive in creating distortions outside that realm. Material reality and objectivity (the reality principle) would coincide if the individual would adopt the scientific Weltanschauung.

This is an instance, I believe, where Freud's adherence to the scientific Weltanschauung of his teachers—the positivist position—interfered with his usual discernment and his openness to new ideas. If as psychoanalysts we follow Freud's advice and utilize the Weltanschauung of science, we must consider that scientific opinion has changed considerably with regard to the notion of relative subjectivity of all knowledge. We must begin our studies with questions about the intersubjectivity of the infant-caregiver experience. We must follow this thread of intersubjectivity throughout each phase of life. We must assume that truth and reason cannot stand outside this intersubjectivity, as though independent of the human experience of them, any more than scientists can now assume that space and time follow a course of existence independent of observation. In fact, by accepting the contemporary Weltanschauung of science, psychoanalysis can become the best laboratory humanity has yet devised for studying the effect of the observer on the field observed, when that field is the psychological state of a fellow human being. I shall return to this issue later.

Before proceeding further, I should like to address the problem of the definition of the term "Weltanschauung." Freud never agreed to an English translation of Weltanschauung, preferring to retain the German word with its linkages to philosophy and its ambiguity of meaning. Although he defined it as a false construction to live by, thereby giving it a precise but negative connotation, when he spoke of it in respect to science, he broadened the usage considerably. The general usage of Weltanschauung by Freud and others, and any of its English translations, indicates that it is an "envelope" word, the very flexibility of which is useful for discourse. In my discussion, "Weltanschauung" refers to a set of assumptions or beliefs that make up a general philosophical position about how the world or some important aspect of it is constituted. The paramaters of this philosophical position range from a loosely constructed personal image of the way the world or people function, to a more strictly constructed set of guides for conducting scientific investigations. A psychoanalyst's Weltanschauung, then, might encompass both the personal values with which he imbues the world and the personal values that guide his approach to the discoveries inherent in analysis.

Waelder, A. Freud, Hartmann: Balance, Comprehensiveness, and Flexibility

When Freud decried the making of a psychoanalytic Weltanschauung in 1926, he directed his criticism against "an extreme and one-sided view." I suggest that implicitly he was arguing for a psychoanalytic "view of the universe" of human mental life that was *balanced, comprehensive,* and *flexible,* and that this view was made explicit by three of his most brilliant followers, Robert Waelder, Anna Freud, and Heinz Hartmann.

Anna Freud begins her pivotal study by also denouncing the position Freud decried:

> There have been periods in the development of psychoanalytic science when the theoretical study of the individual ego was distinctly unpopular . . . Whenever . . . research was deflected from the id to the ego—it was felt that here was a beginning of apostasy from psychoanalysis as a whole. The view held was that the term *psychoanalysis* should be reserved for the new discoveries relating to the unconscious psychic life. . . .
>
> When the writings of Freud . . . took a fresh direction, the odium of analytic unorthodoxy no longer attached to the study of the ego [1936, pp. 3–4].

Of the three authors, Anna Freud's approach is the most directly clinical and her proposal the least complex: the analyst "takes his stand at a point equidistant from the id, the ego and the superego" (p. 28).

Waelder begins his famous paper on "The Principle of Multiple Function" (1936) with a direct reference to its impetus: "The immediate occasion for the observations which follow is the new framing of the theory of anxiety which Freud has given in his work, 'Inhibition, Symptoms and Anxiety' " (p. 45). Waelder does not deal directly with the controversy about "the odium of analytic unorthodoxy" or "apostasy," but takes up the challenge he sees inherent in Freud's suggestion of looking at the same phenomenon from two sides "both from the angle of the id and from that of the ego. This two-sided consideration gives rise to the presumption that the same method might be adopted and fundamentally applied to all psychic phenomena" (p. 45). In Waelder's analysis, the number of viewing angles quickly multiplies to a remarkably complex balancing of valences and forces. He sees the ego responding to concrete problems from the outside world, the compulsion to repeat, the id, and the superego and assigning to itself the problems of joining or overcoming these other agencies. Thus, there are, eight groups of problems.

Waelder's aim is to define a general principle, *the principle of multiple function,* according to which "no attempted solution of a problem is possible which is not of such a type that it does not at the

same time . . . represent an attempted solution of other problems"
(p. 49). Waelder rescues his proposal from an unbalanced one-sided
vector-force conception by his assertion that a multiple *meaning* corresponds to a multiple function. Furthermore, he attempts to avoid the
atomizing or fractionating effect of his vector analyses: by speaking
of a "collective function of the total organism" (p. 51).

But Waelder, whose thinking was of a strongly philosophical
bent, could not resist an attempt at a psychoanalytic Weltanschauung.
To Waelder "psychoanalysis is a kind of polyphonic theory of the
psychic life in which each act is a chord, and in which there is consonance and dissonance" (pp. 53–54). At the very end of his paper,
Waelder brings up Freud's warning about exaggerating the weakness
of the ego and accepting a demonological theory of life. He rejects the
macro-structure approach that was to become so popular. Rather than
using id, ego, and superego as sharply distinguished parts of the personality, he sees in each action and fantasy an ego, id, and superego
phase, as well as a phase conforming to the compulsion to repeat.
Waelder moves to the broadest anthropological scale to suggest his
"view of the universe." The id represents the most basic element of
organic existence. The ego represents the central steering in the organism, perhaps only attainable with the appearance of the central
nervous system.

> The superego is the domain of the human being: it is that element
> through which man in his experience steps beyond himself and
> looks at himself as the object. . . .
> Here belongs the ability . . . to recognize that the individual
> is independent of his own ego and that this independence outlives
> his own ego. . . . There is always the possibility of transcending
> the instinct and interest foundation in a given situation, of stepping
> beyond thinking, experiencing, acting, in short of placing one's
> self in the realm of the superego. If this be true, it would seem
> that by Freud's choice of elements we have found the stages of
> everything organic: organic life itself, the central steering of the
> organism after the individuation of organic life, and finally man's
> reaching beyond himself [pp. 61–62].

Hartmann reacted to Freud's challenging remarks about Weltanschauung with two papers and a monograph: "Psychoanalysis and Weltanschauung" (1933), "Psychoanalysis and the Concept of Health" (1939a), and *Ego Psychology and the Problem of Adaptation* (1939b).

The least well known of the three, "Psychoanalysis and Weltanschauung," begins with a supportive reference to the ideas Freud advanced in his *New Introductory Lectures.* Hartmann concurs that psychoanalysis is unsuited to building its own Weltanschauung and that it has a special relation to the Weltanschauung of science. But, he argues, the fact that science is based on empiricism does not do away with the problem of presuppositions based on a personal Weltanschauung or *Weltbilt* (image of the world). For example, when science is conceived as representing the highest value, this judgment is itself an expression of a personal Weltanschauung. In this sense, an empiricism without presupposition is, strictly spreaking, impossible. Although this can lead to error, it does not have to. Freud's Weltanschauung aims for the increase of well-being and the decrease of suffering, and, even more important, values reason as the tool to achieve the goal. The psychoanalytic profession places its supraordinate value on insight and knowledge. Hartmann asserts that the primacy of Logos, of intelligence, of truth about the self offers the best assurance for morality. Psychoanalysis thus can be a decisive force for the realization of ethical and education goals and, in this way, affects the actual shaping of Weltanschauungen. But to the question of what people should do, psychoanalysis cannot give an answer. Once a personal goal or an ethical social aim is selected by presupposition, psychoanalysis can say what the individual has to do to reach it. Whether the goal itself is good or bad, progress or not, can neither be proved nor disproved by empirical means. Therefore, the question of what presuppositions might be incorporated in a Weltanschauung for psychoanalysis cannot be answered in the same way for all epochs. Psychoanalysis may mean something new in terms of values for each generation and each cultural-historical cross section. Today, Hartmann states, despite the fact that its subject matter is the irrational, psychoanalysis has a position among all those streams that have as a goal the influencing of people by reason. The stream of psychoanalysis, he concludes, is longer and stronger than those of all the psychological rivers and rivulets that would deny the psychoanalytic heritage.

"Psychoanalysis and the Concept of Health" (1939a) addresses the problem Freud described from a different angle: "The concepts of 'health' and 'illness' always exert a 'latent' influence . . . on our analytic habits of thought, and it cannot but serve a useful purpose to clarify the implications of these terms" (p. 308). Hartmann notes how simple it was to define mental health and illness in earlier times when the conflicts present in neuroses appeared to signify pathogenesis. This view proved to be overly restrictive and false—the same conflicts appear in healthy people. Once this simplistic view was abandoned, however, the focus shifted to an investigation of "health"; and that led, in Hartmann's view, to the opposition Freud decried from those writers who made the strength of the "daemonic forces" into a Weltanschauung. But Hartmann spells out the issue in richer detail. A study of health reveals that development proceeds in the two directions of rational behavior and instinctual life.

> This twofold orientation already commands our interest because it reflects the twofold origin of psychoanalysis in the history of thought—the rationalism of the age of enlightenment and the irrationalism of the romantics. . . . Now the analytic conceptions of health . . . often proceed to assign undue prominence to one of these standpoints at the expense of the other.
>   When . . . all biological values are acknowledged as supreme, one has approached dangerously near to that malady of the times whose nature it is to worship instinct and pour scorn on reason. To be sure, these tendencies, which lead to a glorification of instinctual man and which at the present time have widely assumed a highly aggressive and political complexion, play a less conspicuous part in the literature pertaining to psychoanalysis. . . .
>   At the other end of the scale, we find the ideal of a rational attitude and the 'perfectly rational' man. . . . The most rational attitude does not necessarily constitute an optimum for the purpose of adaptation. . . . A healthy ego should be able to make use of the system of rational control and at the same time take into account the fact of the irrational nature of other mental activities [pp. 9–10].

In his famous monograph, in which the focus shifts from ''health'' to ''adaptation,'' Hartmann (1939b) refers in a subtly humorous way to the controversy over the analytic Weltanschauung of the id and the reluctance ''to broaden to a more general view of psychic structure.'' ''Even the objections against psychoanalytic ego psychology differ from those leveled against id psychology; they are . . . less hostile and less categorical. To some psychoanalysts this is evidence that the findings of ego psychology are invalid or unimportant'' (p. 6). After this sardonic reference to the psychoanalysts who regarded Freud's going forward with a study of the ego as apostasy, Hartmann makes his personal statement about the place of Weltanschauung. ''Even though Freud rightly declined to regard psychoanalysis as a 'system,' it is nevertheless a cohesive organization of propositions, and any attempt to isolate parts of it not only destroys its over-all unity, but also changes and invalidates its parts'' (p. 6). Without considering psychoanalysis as a Weltanschauung such as a religious or political system, Hartmann had a great deal to say, about the cohesive organization of propositions that he believed psychoanalysis constituted: the conflict-free ego sphere, the undifferentiated state, change of function, neutralization, preconscious automatisms, autonomous ego development, the organizing function, and numerous others.

Hartmann's proposals do not stop at these intrapsychic delineations of apparatuses and the principles by which they function. He ranges into a much broader cohesive organization of propositions, so that the boundary between proposals about the mental apparatus and a psychoanalytic Weltanschauung becomes indistinct. ''The observation underlying the concept 'adaptation' is that living organisms patently 'fit' into their environment'' (pp. 23–24). ''Man not only adapts to the community but also actively participates in creating the conditions to which he must adapt. . . . Thus the crucial adaptation man has to make is to the social structure, and his collaboration in building it'' (p. 31). ''Both flexibility and automatization are necessary to and characteristic of the ego; purposive achievements depend on some functions taking a flexible, others an automatized form, and still others combining these two forms in various proportions'' (p. 92). ''The normal ego must be *able* to control, but it must also be *able to must*. . . .'' Thus, ''the healthy ego thinks and acts flexibly, but not exclusively so; furthermore, . . . in the healthy human being certain superordinate ego functions determine when the ego can make purposive use of automatisms; and finally . . . in the service of ego regulations even highly developed ego achievements must be temporarily suspended'' (pp. 94–95).

It is generally agreed that Anna Freud's *The Ego and the Mechanisms of Defense,* Waelder's ''Principle of Multiple Function'' and Hartmann's *Ego Psychology and the Problem of Adaptation* ushered in the full development of ego psychology or, as I prefer to call it, structural psychology. I suggest that these works, beginning with the challenge to follow Freud by repudiating one Weltanschauung and opening the way for new discoveries, have become in time the foundation for another Weltanschauung. The properties of this new psychoanalytic view of the universe are very appealing to an educated professional of the atomic age. They include the following:

balance—three structures whose energies and functions (aggression and libido within the id; defenses and nondefensive functions or conflict-determined or conflict-free functions within the ego; prohibitions, benign guides, and ideals within the superego) can each be balanced against each other, with the analyst hovering in between.

comprehensiveness—id (drive, biological factors, motivational source), ego (executive functions, defensive functions, hierarchical arrangements, biological and experiential factors internalized and transand transformed), superego (moral and ethical values, ideals, experiential factors internalized and transformed), external reality.

flexibility—focus and importance can shift back and forth between oedipal and preoedipal factors; between biological, ontogenic psychological, and cultural factors; between autoplastic and alloplastic approaches to change, and so on.

Thus, while Waelder and Hartmann explicitly and Anna Freud implicitly profess their adherence to Freud's assignment of the highest values to truth and reason, each one's fashion of following Freud's continual efforts to systematize his discoveries gives rise to a new set of specific internal values: balance, comprehensiveness, and flexibility. Within this grouping, each can comfortably differ with the other. Anna Freud can indicate that it is best to remain close to clinical problems, especially those of the neuroses, and to investigate external reality as it impinges on the individual's defensive activities. Later, she can suggest a completely different systematizing effort—a focus on separate lines of development. Waelder can give greater weight to the repetition compulsion; assign lesser weight to id, ego, and superego as macrostructures; and emphasize throughout dynamic considerations as opposed to structural. Hartmann can attempt to provide order throughout the whole range of normal and pathological structure-building, evolving a metapsychology of remarkable internal consistency and comprehensiveness—the general psychology he hoped to achieve. To these three authors whose seminal works appeared so close together can be added a distinguished group of others: Fenichel's textbook (1945) and book on technique (1941), Glover's writings on technique (1955), Jacobson's work on the self and the object world (1964), Schur's reclassification of anxiety (1958) and the regulatory principles (1966), and many, many others. The work of this group has come to be regarded, at least in the United States, as constituting the "mainstream" of psychoanalysis, a metaphor that recalls Hartmann's concluding remarks in "Psychoanalysis and Weltanschauung" (1933).

The "Mainstream" as a New Weltanschauung

The metaphor of the mainstream has become, I suggest, a way to conceptualize a set of values that on the one hand represents extremely valuable and appealing scientific ideals and on the other hand "an intellectual construction which solves all . . . problems" (Freud, 1933a, p. 158)—a Weltanschauung in the negative sense in which Freud used the term. The Weltanschauung within science can be easily supported. Since the "mainstream" can trace its lineage back to Freud, it can regard its source to be truth and reason—the supremacy of cognition, knowledge, and reason over emotion, ignorance, and instinct—without neglecting the study of these "daemonic" elements that it has replaced. Likewise, it can vigorously substantiate a claim that its theory, its methods of research, and its therapeutic practices evidence balance, comprehensiveness, and flexibility. Furthermore, it can claim that "the common compulsion exercised by such a dominance of reason" has proved to be "the strongest uniting bond" among psychoanalysts, to paraphrase Freud (1933a, p. 171). Even in nature a mainstream does not exist—it is a matter of a judgment by a beholder. Similarly in psychoanalysis, the mainstream is a judgment about one or another trend in theory, research, and practice, changing over time. Some things are in it now that may not have been before—the theory of separation-individuation, the utilization of direct observation, and the widening scope of cases treated. Some things remain outside—Kleinian postulates of a developmental timetable, observations claimed to have been made by "thought transference" (although Freud himself included them in), and Alexander's role-playing in the transference. In time, rivulets and tributaries connect concepts outside with those in the mainstream: For example, important Kleinian formulations about aggression and splitting appear in the mainstream concepts of Kernberg and Mahler; Alexander's corrective emotional experience in altered form corresponds to ideas at least talked about inside the mainstream in response to Kohut's challenges about transmuting internalizations as the curative agent; and someday, in some altered form, issues of deep empathic thought transferences and even extrasensory perception may find their way into the mainstream through the studies of Lacan. The metaphor of the mainstream works well for this process, since it involves absorption, dilution, and an inexorable flowing together of the elements.

Some groups of psychoanalysts resist this flow. They may question whether a mainstream exists at all. They may insist on maintaining ideas of theory and practice in sharp distinction to the balance existing in what others claim to be the mainstream. The mainstream's conceptual framework and methods of research and practice probably could encompass the ideas of these proponents if they were more compliant. They may refuse to make the necessary modifications, preferring what to the mainstream adherents may appear to be unbalanced insistence on, for example, a specific theory of object relations, or a particular concept of the self, or the recasting of the whole theory in another framework—information theory, general systems theory, a linguistic model, and so on. They may aver that their theories are comprehensive enough in themselves, however incomplete they may appear to the definers of the mainstream. The result is that other tributaries or even rivers (considering the number of Kleinian analysts) compete with the mainstream. It is here that the scientific Weltanschauung of psychoanalysis and the ''system'' Weltanschauung part ways. The scientific Weltanschauung can proudly claim a high standard of ethics in Freud's tradition. Old truths are protected and new truths sought. Reason is a decisive factor in determining the place of a concept, a research method, and a technical procedure. Balance, comprehensiveness, and flexibility provide a basis for consistency without rigidity and for necessary elaboration without loss of appropriate parsimony. A particular high water mark of the mainstream was Rapaport and Gill's (1959) parsimonious systematization of the whole development of psychoanalysis as comprising five metapsychological points of view—dynamic, economic, structural, genetic, and adaptive—leaving room in the mainstream for debate on whether to reinclude the topographies.

I contend that the success of this group of concepts and the appeal of the values that they represent is the source of their possible misapplication as a Weltanschauung—in Freud's negative sense of a handbook to adhere to, providing comfort to those who, in following its rules and rituals, believe that no further challenge need be faced.[1] This may seem to be illogical and contradictory. If the scientific Weltanschauung is balanced, comprehensive, and flexible, absorbing new ideas all the time, how can it become debased into one-sidedness, a form of resistance to possible progress? The answer is, when its balance of the moment is perceived as truth, its comprehensiveness is mistaken for completion, and its flexibility operates as a pose for reductionist diminishing and dissecting of alternative conceptions. To state this differently, the success of the synthetic and organizing capacity of Freud, Anna Freud, Hartmann, Waelder, and the others of the mainstream has been so impressive that it has perhaps created in a group of sincere psychoanalytic scientists a belief that they had achieved the

---

[1] As Kohut notes:

Once theories have been with us for a long time . . . and we have adjusted to living with them, we are prone to close our eyes not only to internal inconsistencies but also, and especially, to lack of correspondence with the data we gather. Theoretical systems tend to become rigid, take on the quality of dogma, become imbued with moral qualities, and, instead of being the helpmates of the observer, stand more and more in his way, interfering with his ability to perceive formerly unrecognized configurations in the aspect of the world under investigation, or to alter his understanding of configurations that were formerly misunderstood [Kohut, 1980, p. 492].

truth about the human mind through a basically completed theory, capable of holding whatever bits and pieces of new data present themselves.

To whatever degree this has happened with ego psychology, it constitutes a repetition (a group repetition compulsion?) of the first Weltanschauung created *within* psychoanalysis. A difference is immediately apparent. Freud stated that the system Weltanschauung based on id psychology was created by those who wished to remain adherents of the "daemonic" because they were caught up in an extra-analytic Weltanschauung—the romantic movement and its downgrading of Logos. I have explained the development of a nonscientific Weltanschauung out of ego psychology as a possible result of its scientific success. This indeed may have been true of the adherents of id psychology too. They may have been too dazzled by the power of the explanatory tool at their disposal to want to begin again as relative neophytes in an entirely new area of exploration. These were psychoanalysts who had learned to navigate in the unconscious. They could explain symptoms, they could interpret dreams, they could elicit and interpret transferences—and all in the course of two or three months! The same concepts could explain myths, slips, and jokes and could unravel biographies of geniuses (Leonardo) and psychotics (Schreber). Of course Freud did not say to give all this up—he said to add to it (as has the proponent of each contending psychoanalytic proposal since). But from a position presumed to be in the mainstream, adding can only be done a bit at a time, and Freud's new ego psychology was too revolutionary for that kind of competing perception. Few men share with Freud and his alter egos, Leonardo and Goethe, a Faustian "insatiable and indefatigable thirst for knowledge" (Freud, 1910, p. 75; Lichtenberg, 1978). For the group of analytic pioneers that followed Freud, Anna Freud, Waelder, and Hartmann into the new ego psychology, and the generation that knew only what I call structural psychology, the new discovery indeed added much to the old. Success in theory-making was accompanied by success in opening up child analysis as a technique and research method. Success in child analytic observation enhanced reconstruction in adult analysis, which in turn reconfirmed the theory.

If religion is the opiate of the masses, is success the opiate of the psychoanalyst? Religion is the Baedeker of the unscientific because it provides consolation and exaltation so successfully that it saps the urge of all but the passionate searcher for knowledge. If knowledge is likewise the Baedeker of the scientific, it is because it provides explanations and interpretations so successfully that it saps the urge of all but the passionate searcher for uncertainty. On the face of it, we can easily understand the man who searches through miles of uncharted land and water to find the true source of the Nile, but can we understand the same prodigious effort to discover uncertainty? Yet I believe this is the point at which we have arrived in psychoanalysis and at which we must remain if we are to stay within the Weltanschauung of science as Freud wished.

Uncertainty in the Analyst's Weltanschauung

The first argument for uncertainty is that psychoanalysis does not have available a satisfactory means to disprove a proposition or postulate. The inability to prove that a particular construction is wrong is especially serious when clinical activity is involved because this is in essence our data base. Moreover, this problem has been with us for so long that the difficulty has become largely ignored, and pertinent questions about validation are rarely raised. For example, if an analyst conjectures that hysterical symptoms contain a core of oral fantasies or wishes, does he ask how could it be proved that they do not?

An experiment reported by Spence (1977) is very telling. Spence recounts a dream that was experimentally induced by presenting a film designed to elicit castration concerns. He then takes two dreams chosen at random from a book on technique, and illustrates convincingly that when approached with the same presupposition that they will be castration dreams, the random dreams "fit" as well as the experimental one. He concludes that since specific parts of one sequence can all too easily be matched to parts of another, the way is constantly open to adventitious matches molded by the analyst's preunderstanding. "When," Spence asks, "has it been possible to say this dream and this event are *not* related?" (1977, p. 377).

An analyst may argue that no conclusion can be drawn from this experiment about psychoanalytic practice. In analysis, we do not analyze a dream, we analyze the dream of a particular patient immersed in a process in which the patient reveals through associations the verbal products of the symbolic process—of primary and secondary process—which tell us the correct meaning. For example, if a male analysand reported a dream in which he picked up his small son as an indistinctly perceived person approached, the analyst might be led by this patient's associations to conclude that this dream was built around the analysand's underlying fantasy of rescuing his son from the danger threatened by his wife's sarcastic disparagement (castration) of men. Even if the analyst felt convinced of this interpretation as dominant at that moment, could the analyst eliminate the idea that the analysand might be defending against his inclination to exploit his son for his own protective ends by placing the son between himself and his wife, as he often seemed to do? Would the analyst wonder if the patient's momentary altruism had its origins in a sadistic impulse, for example, toward his own younger sibling as a rival? or conjecture that the child the patient was saving might represent himself, perceived to be in a highly vulnerable state? This sequence is nothing more than a familiar statement of multiple determination. Each of these proposals may indeed be correct, and any one might be dominant at any given moment—but can we say for certain that one is wrong? Could we not, with enough material, find an indication to support each of these and more besides (homosexual inclinations, transference representations, etc.)?

I believe that Spence's experiment and this example lead us to another conclusion. The possibility of mismatches in clinical constructions is not the main problem that results from the inability to disprove our hypotheses. The basic problem rests in the fact that each of the major competing psychoanalytic theories organizes clinical data *too* effectively. It is commonplace for a group of experienced analysts, all sharing the traditional point of view of a conflict theory based on libidinal phase development and defensive operations of the ego, to listen to clinical material convinced that the presenting analyst's formulation has been arrived at sensitively and intelligently. Nonetheless, one of the listeners is then apt to present what may sound to himself and to others as an equally or more valid interpretation. And then yet another listener may order the material still differently and make a convincing fit. For example, the infinite ambiguity of the imagery of primal scene experiences have been convincingly portrayed as contributing to a series of worldwide and personal myths, to a specific patient's crucifixion fantasies, to the imagery in machine fantasies, and even, by regressive variants, to banquet fantasies. Similar universality has been claimed for beating fantasies, impregnation fantasies, etc.

Classical conflict theory integrated into ego psychology is not the only convincing way to organize data available to the psychoanalytic practitioner. These include theories based on a concept of lines of development, diverse object relations theories, and theories based on the concepts of identity and of self. Each of these differing ways to organize data obtained by the psychoanalytic method into clinical formulations and into specific and general theories is remarkably serviceable therapeutically and internally consistent. By stating that these theories are too powerful, I mean that while each is hypothetically more accurate for certain aspects of the human experience, each also works well beyond its area of maximum explanatory utility, so that its adherents, however inclined to open-mindedness, find difficulty in defining reservations they may have. Now, if we add that we have no way to disprove many or most of our proposals, we can see the dilemma we face.

It might be reasonable to assert that I have just placed myself in the Weltanschauung of the nihilists Freud decried. If nothing is provable, and many things are right, or more or less right, then all is relative and open to doubt. Thus, one would appear to be forced either into the anarchist view or into illusory belief, the religionist form of escape from nihilist anxiety. I shall categorically state that this is not the Weltanschauung I believe can be derived from psychoanalysis. I also believe that, without going all the way to nihilism, the path toward relativism is a salutary intellectual journey for those psychoanalysts who would take comfort in defining the "mainstream" as the full achievement of Freud's truth and reason. This applies to those who would define the "mainstream," whether they claim their heritage from Freud's id psychology, from Freud's ego psychology, from Freud's death instinct, or from Freud's thought transference. The journey on the path toward nihilistic anarchy should stop at the way station of uncertainty to look for ways of resolving doubt to a relative degree. This is, so to speak, a regression from reason to the service of rationality—the kind of flexible rationality that Hartmann prized.

Empathy and Uncertainty

What besides reason is available to the analyst in choosing a specific formulation or a general theory? I believe the answer is the analyst's empathic feel for the closeness of the specific formulation to the state of mind of the analysand at that moment, and the closeness of the general theory to the state of mind of human beings, including the analyst, as he knows them. This answer may arouse derision from two sources.

One group might react as men were wont to do some years ago to claims of woman's intuition—that is, empathy is a fuzzy-minded claim to knowing something by a person who cannot or does not reason, and yet wants to be regarded as insightful. This argument establishes what I believe to be a false dichotomy between logic and empathy. Psychoanalysis is a science and a practice based on the deepest and fullest understanding of one human being by another, and this argument dismisses the mode of perception by which this communication is made. This group might argue that even if reason does lead to uncertainty at times, this is only temporary and no cause to replace hard-minded logic with soft-minded empathy. I would respond that it can never be a matter of replacement but of a hard-minded attempt to study how empathy functions in the moment-to-moment exchange between analyst and analysand to help us resolve doubts to a relative degree.

Another group might base its derision on just this point, saying that empathy is nothing new—Freud assumed it from the beginning. It is at the basis of the very career choice, of good analysts. It is generally something to be taken for granted. This group might add that giving it more careful attention might be helpful with narcissistic or other difficult patients. This argument would place empathy in the mainstream, as a routine part of the general functioning of the competent analyst, hardly worth singling out for special mention. I am in sympathy with the first part of this argument because I agree that empathy has always been a mainstream concept. But I strongly disagree that it need not be singled out for special consideration. I have elsewhere argued this from the merit of its impact on clinical practice (Lichtenberg, 1981, in press), but here I wish to assert that empathy would be worth special study in any case—precisely because it provides us with a means of deciding how to respond to alternative formulations of equal internal logic.

Empathy, analysts would agree, allows us to enter into the state of mind of a particular individual in an analytic setting. Drawing *general* conclusions from such immersion in a series of analytic patients is made not by empathy, but by the unique cognitive integrative ability of the discoverer, who, through a creative synthesis, arrives at a new organization of the data. The discoverer comes up with something new to listen for by means that do not derive immediately from empathy, and then, as an analyst, uses empathy to test its fit—to adjust the level of uncertainty. But empathy is not the only means available to make this adjustment; there are also the means used in deriving relationships from the study of sequencing—for example, when the analysand's associations are treated as a text and analyzed using rules of logic applied to form. Similarly, issues of levels of uncertainty are negotiated productively within the dialectic of debate. But these methods of *arriving* at new formulations and *assessing* their worth still leave analysts with the task of deciding how to respond to alternative formulations that are equally internally logical. I suggest that the analyst's empathy has been undervalued as a primary means of reducing uncertainty in the clinical situation.

The term "empathy" has been used in many ways, both generally and in psychoanalysis; for the purpose of this discussion, I am using it as a technical term referring to a specific mode of perceiving utilized by the analyst in the psychoanalytic situation. The empathic mode of perception is a method used by the analyst to gain information, in which the analyst orients his listening stance from within the perspective or the state of mind of the analysand. Listening from within the analysand's perspective means perceiving and conceptualizing, in its entire context, how the analysand is sensing himself, how he senses others, how he senses the source of his affective-cognitive state, and what he believes to be the range of his potential active and passive responses to his state. Through the vantage point of the empathic mode of perception, the analyst attempts to be in touch, as closely as possible, with the analysand's entire experiential state—the manner in which he senses himself and others (animate or inanimate, separate or with distinctions blurred), as well as his sense of time, causality, values, affect and mood states, and the trends of his conscious, preconscious, and (as far as possible) unconscious associative patterns.

The reader may object that this extends the usual definition of empathy, that is, to understand vicariously another's feelings by placing oneself in the other's mind through a temporary trial identification. Even if we acknowledge that the usual definition is overly restrictive, the objector may continue, and that it should include the context in which the emotions occur—the other's anguish about something, his happiness in reference to something else—we would still be stretching "empathy" to say it could accomplish being in touch with the analysand's entire experiential state. The empathic mode of perception, as I mean the term, comprises intuition and an even more labored form of cognitive reasoning. The key distinction is that the analyst systematically and consistently takes his listening stance from within the state of mind of the analysand; empathy thus furnishes the *leading* edge to the analyst's listening. As in the usual definition of empathy, the analyst's listening is a sensing from within the analysand's emotional life. The analyst is not an observer from "outside," an onlooker as one might be in observing a scientific experiment; he is a listener, a sensor, from "within." And having taken his stance within the patient's subjective reality, the analysand utilizes his intuition. This is generally automatic—intuition being one of the learned tools of the profession—a form of preconscious automatized cognitive sharing. Still as much from "within" as possible, the analyst may also recognize the need to utilize conscious rational cognition in a problem-solving mode. Thus, the key element of the mode of perception I am calling empathic is that, as in conventionally defined empathy, the *placement* of the analyst's listening and sensing and organizing stance is *from within* the analysand's state of mind. (A more detailed discussion of these issues can be found in Schwaber, 1981a, 1981b; and Lichtenberg, 1981, in press).

This excursion into empathy leads us back to the issue of uncertainty in general and the attempt, to a relative degree, to resolve doubts about competing theories. Indeed, uncertainty leaps out at the reader from these proposals. Any attempt to place oneself into the state of mind of any other person is approximate at best. When we consider that the person in question is in analysis, where his communication is marked by resistance, and his associations generally disguise by defensive means his "true" inner state, our uncertainty is still greater. Although for analysts to position themselves as though they were "outside" observers looking on at the workings of the patient's mental functioning may provide them with a greater sense of certainty, from the standpoint of technique alone, analysts' uncertainty stimulates their acuity for the in-depth inquiry that constitutes analysis at its best. Feeling empathically attuned to the patient's state of mind one minute, and uncertain where the analysand is the next, generates a focus on shifting states that requires the understanding, the precise insight that the patient seeks.

How then does the impact of competing theories enter the process? As the analyst positions himself the best he can (that is, uncertainly) within the analysand's state of mind, he automatically, largely pre-consciously, attempts to organize what he hears. One or another of the many powerful theoretical constructs he has learned will serve best to reduce the unknown aspect of the mental terra incognita he is attempting to explore at that moment. One or another of these formulations will illuminate the analysand's subjective reality of the moment in such a way as to enlighten the analyst about some emotion-laden where or how or when or why. The shared vista from within the analysand's state of mind, his subjective reality, expands in some form that the analyst can sense and—in a timely, tactful manner—interpret. Thus, the selection of the theoretical means of ordering data is made on a moment-to-moment basis as it fits the needs of the analyst to organize the uncertainty he experiences as he attempts to keep himself maximally attuned to the patient's inner world. At some later time, the analyst may conclude that a particular general theory seems quite frequently to expand his sensitivity to sensing the patient's inner state of mind. In this way, then, he may come to reduce his general uncertainty.

A serious objection to this solution of the problem must be raised, however. Each competing theory is exceedingly complex—it has various components that range from clinically distant abstractions to more clinically near formulations. To "learn" a theory, in the sense of having it available for an intuitive grasp of material as it unfolds in the clinical situation, is an arduous task involving long immersion in the interplay between cognitive appreciation and clinical application. How can analysts, in the midst of a given hour with an analysand, determine the relative worth of a formulation derived from ego psychology or from object relations theory or from self psychology, if they have not mastered their many subtle nuances—many of which thoroughly contradict each other? Regretfully, I have no answer to this objection. To reiterate that considering the internal logic of the theories does not make the choice more certain, or that even to attempt to choose by internal logic would require the same immersion, does not help. This becomes an issue of education and curriculum, not of Weltanschauung. So I can only conclude that the choice is a matter of preference. I would prefer that analysts focus their primary effort on immersing themselves in the inner state of the analysand and have their grasp of whatever therein they have mastered aid them as much as possible. I believe that relative mastery by analysts of the empathic mode of perception will enable them to more readily absorb and use different formulations to organize the data of their immersion into the patient's state of mind. This suggestion is in line with Freud's technical precept that the analyst suspend any prior judgment and instead give "impartial attention to everything that there is to observe" (1909, p. 23). While Freud was speaking of the analysis of symptoms that can be observed from the viewpoint of an "outside" observer, I am referring to the analysis of the patient's total experiential state, which only can be observed through an "inside," empathically centered mode of perception.

The Influence of the Observer on What is Observed

One remaining factor requires consideration in this appraisal of a psychoanalytic Weltanschauung—the neglect of the effect of the observer on what is observed. When Freud spoke of the analyst remaining neutral, he was recommending that the analyst not superimpose his values on the patient, that is, not use his authority to suggest, maneuver, or manipulate the patient to the ends the analyst thought best. This precept is today as valuable as ever. But like Freud's truth and reason, neutrality can serve either as an ideal and a variable to be studied or as a banner—a system Weltanschauung—to limit disquieting questions.

To imply that psychoanalysis has not examined the problem of neutrality would be incorrect. The investigation of the analyst's countertransference—the unconscious conflictual reactions to the patient—is the hallmark of the analyst's commitment to truth and personal honesty, regardless of the personal cost in painful, even potentially humiliating, self-exploration. "Know thyself" is a precept of the analyst, beginning with his personal analysis and continuing with his self-analysis as he conducts his inevitable struggles with countertransference. Possibly because of analysts' justified pride in their introspective search for unresolved conflicts affecting their work, they may become less assiduous in the exploration of their nonconflictual attitudes and activities. Analysts would like to assume that when conflictual interferences are not present, by following such technical principles as remaining equidistant from id, ego, and superego, they can be a "neutral" but beneficial factor. They need not carefully study the way in which they, as observers, affect the field they observe. The point is, however, that by their clinical theory, analysts affect the moment-by-moment conduct of the analysis; by their general theory, they affect their clinical theory; and by their personal Weltanschauung, they are moved to adhere to or oppose particular clinical and general theories.

I shall approach the problem of the clinical observer's influence on what he observes by referring to an issue with great potential for misunderstanding: the use of suggestion in ordinary psychoanalytic practice. Freud saw the danger in his earliest discovery period. First he attempted and then abandoned the direct use of suggestion by hypnosis. Then he attempted its use by his hand pressure method to recover specific memories, often with remarkably good results. Finally he abandoned it as a method and as a principle, exploring instead the method of free association. In fact, the new method was to be the precise, scientific opposite of suggestion. The documentation of the patient's memories and conflicts as revealed by his "free" associations would emerge uncontaminated from within his psyche—just as the sterile technique of the surgeon allows him to discover what infection or pathology is in the patient's abdomen without introducing any into the field.

But can suggestion so easily be eliminated? Does it not conform more to experience that the patient enters analysis with a set of pre-suppositions about what matters, and then continuously scans the analyst's responses for confirmation or contradiction of them? For example, the patient believes dreams are important, and the (for him) all too silent analyst asks a "neutral" question or two about his dreams when he reports them—a confirmation. Or, the patient believes that talking about his sexual feelings is important, and the analyst picks up instead on the anger, hostility, envy, or greediness in his hetero-sexual relations—a disconfirmation. Or, the patient wants to talk about his past, his parents, his upbringing, his outside life, and the analyst listens carefully, asking few questions or offering few clarifications; then the patient makes one or two references to the treatment or to something assumed to be a reference to the analyst, and the analyst displays an active interest—a puzzlement. The patient concludes that the analyst confirms that dreams are important, thinks negative feelings are more significant than sexual ones in problems with heterosexual relations, and emphasizes recognizing disguised attitudes and feelings toward the analyst. What the patient does with these "suggestions" will of course depend on the patient, but the field is never thereafter uncontaminated. The point here is not to devalue analysis for not living up to an idealized neutrality. Rather, my position is that we should study the influence of suggestion rather than abhor it and refuse to recognize it. I would speculate that the limited amount of suggestion that occurs in analysis, with its effect of focusing on what the analyst believes is important, would prove under careful evaluation to be a minimal prerequisite for the development of a working analytic relationship. The analysis will flourish better if the analysand feels he is receiving workable, effective suggestions about what would be helpful for him to notice and relate than if he were to feel completely unguided.

But again, does this relativist view return us to the problem of the individual system Weltanschauungen? Let us say that a Kleinian analyst suggests to the patient that his free associations indicate problems of the paranoid position or the depressive position; and the patient picks up on these suggestions—his associations confirming the analyst, directly or in defended (disguised) forms. Or, a traditional ego psychology analyst works systematically with a patient's defenses, noting that these defenses appear in conjunction with material indicating derivations of sexual wishes and attendant fears of castration or of penis envy; and the patient picks up on these suggestions, and his associations confirm the analyst in increasingly less disguised forms. Or, an analyst of the object relations group interprets to the patient the disguised manifestations of his belittling and devaluing of the analyst, his occasional or frequent regressive splitting of his relationship into all-good and all-bad groupings, and the origin of these disturbances in his oedipal but largely preoedipal separation-individuation experiences; and the analysand responds angrily to these suggestions but confirms them by a gradual acceptance of his broadly ambivalent approaches to relationships. Or, an analyst trained in self psychology notes the analysand's states of self depletion, his grandiose expectations of the analyst, or his idealization of the analyst and glowing, happy responsiveness; the analyst explains to the analysand that his sense of need is a result of deficiencies from unempathic parenting at different developmental stages; and the analysand accepts these suggestions and provides associations that deepen his awareness of his feelings and attitudes in respect to his changing self states.

Would this series of impressive sequences be proof that analysis works by suggestion? I don't think so. Rather it indicates another source of uncertainty, but one to which the approach, if not the solution, is clear. We must include in our inquiry about the observed data (the patient's associations over the course of the analysis) the continuous effects of the observer. While retaining an ideal of evenly hovering attentiveness, we must investigate the analyst's listening stance as it is in actuality. We must consider how he orients his listening and how he organizes what he hears. We must consider how this translates itself into what he does—his interventions: silent, nonverbal, and verbal. Special importance must be given to assessing whether, if the analyst includes himself as a subject for observation, he is accurate in his self-observation. Does he believe himself, for example, to be more "abstinent" than he actually is? Does he offer to the patient more personal or supportive or mirroring comments than he philosophically believes in, or than he thinks he does? Or, if in his general theory, he believes that idealization of the analyst is inherently defensive, is he less confrontative about some idealizing statements of the patient than he might himself recognize?

These conjectures about the role of the observer raise the question of whether the importance placed on the dissimilarities among the approaches has been overstated and the significance of similarities underestimated. Is it possible that in correctly appraising key distinctions at the level of general theory, we fail to recognize equally key similarities at the level of clinical interaction common to all these psychoanalytic experiences? Although general and even clinical theories tend to be atomistic, might actual relationships between analyst and analysand, observer and observed, be conducted by each on a sufficiently holistic level to transcend the presumed differences? Perhaps even if the observer-analyst who perceives himself as doing something quite differently from another analyst is found, on examination, to be correct, another level of abstraction might reveal similarities—such as a still undiscovered aspect of the symbolic process that reduces the delineating discursiveness of secondary process to a more holistic, generalized reverberating psychic effect resulting from any of the analytic processes developed from any of the methods discussed. Such a finding would not be entirely surprising in the light of recent neurophysiological studies that emphasize diffuse integrations where previously only differentiations had been seen.

The Observer's Vision of Reality

Hartmann (1933) stated that once an individual selects the Weltanschauung of science, he commits himself to empiricism, but his choice of science is an outcome of his personal Weltanschauung or image of the world *(Weltbilt)*. Could it be that the choice by a psychoanalyst of a general theory and the clinical approach derived from it is an outcome of his personal world image? Such an image might be related to the four "visions of reality"—the comic, romantic, tragic, and ironic—described by Schafer (1970), each of which derives from a classical literary tradition and can be found in psychoanalytic thinking. Roughly speaking, the "comic" vision is one of optimism that humanity's problems can be overcome, obstructions removed, and "a new and legitimate sense of secure self" (Schafer, 1970, p. 282) achieved. The analyst with this vision might perceive his task as restoring "a healthier narcissism" by moving the analysand "to the center of his inner society . . . by his sense of being more at one with his body and his heritage, more alive in his senses and sensuality, more worth his own attentions, and freer to pursue and enjoy success and security" (p. 283). "In the romantic vision . . . life is a great quest" (p. 283). The seeker is an adventurous hero, and his quest ends, after crucial struggles, with the dragon slain. The analyst might see himself as valiantly confronting and overcoming challenges posed by unruly instincts and dangerous introjects. The "tragic" vision is alert to inescapable dangers, terrors, and mysteries. It requires one to recognize elements of defeat in victory and victory in defeat, of pain in pleasure and pleasure in pain. It sees time passing, with its inevitable losses and the omnipresent burden of unanswerable questions and incomprehensible afflictions. The analyst with this vision sees himself as deeply involved in a remorseless search, while being fully aware of the limitations of what he can achieve in the way of "gaining complete and stable insight into the mastery over the mysterious unconscious" (p. 286). Like the tragic, the "ironic" individual seeks out internal contradictions, ambiguities, and paradoxes; the ironic vision "aims at detachment, keeping things in perspective, taking nothing for granted, and readily spotting the antithesis to any thesis so as to reduce the claim of that thesis" (p. 293). The ironic vision, when applied to the self, is self-deprecatory and appeals to that aspect of an analyst that tries not to take any one aspect of himself or his activities too seriously. Schafer points out that each vision has its place in psychoanalytic thought: the ironic and tragic in the relative emphasis each places on reflective thought and an inner articulation of feeling, "while the comic and romantic have more to do with its healing and emancipating aspects" (p. 294). Schafer's arguments suggest that he stresses the tragic along with the ironic, and plays down the comic and romantic.

Might each vision, or some combination of them, constitute the *Weltbilt* of each prospective analyst as he selects within analytic theory the "visions" that most appeal to him? At some later date, out of maturity on the one hand or disillusion on the other, might he shift his personal vision and with it his analytic allegiance? Or conversely, might he reform his analytic vision and with it his personal allegiance? If so, then we have discovered another way to explore the influence of the observer (analyst) on what is observed (the analysand, his goals, and the criteria for measuring his progress in analysis).

What was Freud's inclination? He stated that he owed his "clear consciousness of inner identity" (1926b, p. 274) to his Jewish heritage and pointed specifically to two indispensable characteristics that he derived from it: to be "free from many prejudices which restricted others in the use of their intellect" and to be "prepared . . . to do without agreement with the 'compact majority' " (p. 274). Freud's testament that he is free from prejudice is an ironic reference to the victimization of the Jew by prejudice, while his statement that he was prepared to do without majority agreement ironically expresses the improbability that any member of the Jewish minority would be able to attain a leadership position with a broad following. In his choice of expression, Freud is illustrating a predominately tragic-ironic view of life that he derived from the Jewish experience. The full irony, however, is that Freud turns what he must endure passively as a Jew into the assets of being creatively unrestricted and able to bear the loneliness of the discoverer. In his more philosophic theoretical writings, Freud commonly struck a note of high tragedy: the inevitable discontents of the civilizing process, the inescapable pull of the death instinct against Eros. In his personal statements, he regularly expressed himself in self-deprecatory terms of irony, but in writing about his alter egos—Leonardo, Goethe, Faust, Hannibal, and Moses—his tone is both heroic and tragic. His own reverence for truth and reason assumes, at least to me, a heroic note. In his writings about clinical matters and technique he was completely responsive to the contradictory and paradoxical, but chose terms of personal detachment to deal with them. As for Freud the researcher, he is persevering, but he progresses very slowly. In his quest, as is true of all mankind, his note is somber: "The benighted traveller may sing aloud in the dark to deny his own fears; but, for all that, he will not see an inch further beyond his nose" (1926a, p. 96). Freud was known for his generally pessimistic attitude about mankind: "we shall . . . have to struggle for an incalculable time with the difficulties which the untameable character of human nature presents to every kind of social community" (1933a, p. 181). But Freud did find a circuitous route to express the optimistic side of his nature. "The process of cultural development—of civilization" (p. 179) produces, despite inevitable discontents in the area of sexuality, a positive, long-range change with respect to aggression. In some individuals, such as himself and Einstein, Freud believed, this produced "a *constitutional* intolerance of war" (1933b, p. 215).

Conclusions

To conclude, I shall return to the original question: Is there a Weltanschauung to be developed from psychoanalysis? This question can now be phrased more precisely as a group of related questions: Is it possible to develop a Weltanschauung within the field that assists psychoanalysts in their clinical and theoretical pursuits? If so, can we safeguard this Weltanschauung from becoming a "system," a Baedeker, a closed-ended resort of security and consolation? How would this Weltanschauung coincide with, oppose, or replace, the psychoanalyst's general Weltanschauung as a member of the community at large?

For myself, I conclude that the relativist position allows psychoanalysts to imbue the world with values compatible with their profession and to evolve a mode of investigation appropriate to their search. The values of the pursuit of truth and reason that seemed absolute, unchanging foundations of science to the positivists would be regarded as ideals, the attainment of which is an illusion. This does not lessen their importance, however, since the ideals of science, however illusory in their attainment, are powerful sources of motivation for maintaining an investigative spirit. In this sense, one can idealize Freud in his search for truth and reason, without adopting his absolutist position. This does not mean abandoning oneself to falsity and irrationality, as he implied might happen, but being the same kind of "traveler in the dark" as Freud and the early discoverers. While Freud was absolute with respect to truth and reason, he consistently took a health values position that cure was to be regarded in more relative terms. This posed no threat to Freud's firm inclination to work with the greatest discipline for the maximum possible benefit to his patients. Thus, in my relativist view, ideals—even the pursuit of the absolute—occupy a relatively unchanging position. By this I mean that in their personal values and scientific goals, psychoanalysts need and utilize ideals as guides; but the specific contents of these ideals may and will change as general conditions, scientific knowledge, and psychoanalytic knowledge change. For example, I would treat differently Freud's specific choices of truth and reason as ideal values. For the scientist the search for truths remains a strong motivating factor, but how a scientist in a given era would define a specific truth is subject to reformulation. The definitions of truths would then introduce the factor of the observer's values as a means to guide the scientist's choices. Reason becomes less an ideal and more one of a group of methods available to negotiate the uncertainties of competing conceptualizations. Within the clinical setting, empathy would provide the leading mode of listening and of perceiving data. With respect to appraising a theory, whether clinical or general psychoanalytic, its balance, comprehensiveness, and flexibility remain valid principles. These principles are essentially relativist precepts—although in some instances, the remarkable systematizing effort of ego psychology's discovery period, which used these guides, led some adherents to treat their clinical and theoretical successes as proof that an absolute in the science of psychoanalysis had been reached.

Thus, to the precepts of balance, comprehensiveness, and flexibility must be added a healthy respect for and acceptance of uncertainty in order to prevent the history of the first "system" Weltanschauung from repeating itself. But this viewpoint can be accompanied by an equally healthy search for means to reduce uncertainty's scope. New discoveries will continue to be made, requiring new means to test their usefulness. On the one hand, they will draw on the analyst's empathic mode of perceiving the data to assess their fit with the clinical problem under consideration. On the other hand, preconceptions by the analyst about the discovery (new or old) will inevitably influence the observer's response to the field of study.

Our capacity to evaluate the influence of the observer on what he believes himself to observe may increase in time if this source of variance in appraisal is studied in more detail. Such a study might begin with the presuppositions of an analyst's personal Weltanschauung and its influence on what the analyst is drawn to in psychoanalysis. It might end with the influence of his analytic Weltanschauung on his general view of the universe. The details of an analyst's professional and personal Weltanschauung can and should change with the exigencies of life. Moreover, the main factors we now see as constituting the parameters of this discussion will probably, in time, seem as bound to our century as the absolutist view seems to the nineteenth century. This accords with the relativist position.

Kohut's (1980) unique contribution to this discussion is to set forth in clear terms a changing view of humanity that derives from psychoanalysis and encompasses a personal Weltanschauung as well:

> Man's self, once it has been established, is, in its essence, an energized pattern for the future that, lying in the area of free will and initiative, has a significance all of its own, independent of the genetic factors that—in the area of cause-and-effect determinism—had originally laid down its contents and had given it its shape. It is this aspect of man, man's self struggling to fulfill its creative-productive destiny, failing or succeeding, hurt and raging or fulfilled and generous, which has been neglected by analysis heretofore [p. 540].

References

Fenichel, O. (1941), *Problems of Psychoanalytic Technique*. Albany, N.Y.: Psychoanalytic Quarterly.

——— (1945), *The Psychoanalytic Theory of Neurosis*. New York: Norton.

Freud, A. (1936), The Ego and the Mechanisms of Defense. *The Writings of Anna Freud*, 2. New York: International Universities Press, 1966.

Freud, S. (1909), Analysis of a phobia in a five-year-old boy. *Standard Edition*, 10:3–149. London: Hogarth Press, 1955.

——— (1910), Leonardo da Vinci and a memory of his childhood. *Standard Edition*, 11:57–137. London: Hogarth Press, 1957.

——— (1923), The ego and the id. *Standard Edition*, 19:3–66. London: Hogarth Press, 1961.

——— (1926a), Inhibitions, symptoms and anxiety. *Standard Edition*, 20:77–178. London: Hogarth Press, 1959.

——— (1926b), Address to the society of B'nai B'rith. *Standard Edition*, 20:271–274. London: Hogarth Press, 1959.

———— (1933a), New introductory lectures on Psychoanalysis. *Standard Edition,* 22:3–182. London: Hogarth Press, 1964.

———— (1933b), Why war? *Standard Edition,* 22:203–215. London: Hogarth Press, 1964.

Glover, E. (1955), *The Technique of Psycho-Analysis.* New York: International Universities Press.

Hartmann, H. (1933), Psychoanalyse und Weltanschauung. *Psychoanal. Bewegung,* 5:416–429.

———— (1939a), Psychoanalysis and the concept of health. In: *Essays on Ego Psychology.* New York: International Universities Press, pp. 3–18.

———— (1939b), *Ego Psychology and the problem of adaptation.* New York: International Universities Press, 1958.

Jacobson, E. (1964), *The Self and the Object World.* New York: International Universities Press.

Kohut, H. (1980), Summarizing reflections. In: *Advances in Self Psychology,* ed. A. Goldberg. New York: International Universities Press, pp. 473–554.

Lichtenberg, J. (1978), Freud's Leonardo: Psychobiography and autobiography of genius. *J. Amer. Psychoanal. Assn.,* 26:863–880.

———— (1981), The empathic mode of perception and alternative vantage points for psychoanalytic work. *Psychoanal. Inquiry,* 1:329–355.

———— (in press), An application of the self psychological viewpoint to psychoanalytic technique. *Reflections on Self Psychology,* ed. J. Lichtenberg & S. Kaplan. Hillsdale, N.J.: Analytic Press.

Rapaport, D., & Gill, M.M. (1959), The points of view and assumptions of metapsychology. In: *The Collected Papers of David Rapaport,* ed. M.M. Gill. New York: Basic Books, 1967, pp. 795–811.

Schafer, R. (1970), The psychoanalytic vision of reality. *Internat. J. Psycho-anal.,* 51:279–298.

Schur, M. (1958), The ego and id in anxiety. *The Psychoanalytic Study of the Child,* 13:190–220. New York: International Universities Press.

———— (1966), *The Id and the Regulatory Principles of Mental Functioning.* New York: International Universities Press.

Schwaber, E. (1981a), Narcissism, self psychology and the listening perspective. *The Annual of Psychoanalysis,* 9:115–132. New York: International Universities Press.

———— (1981b), Empathy: A mode of analytic listening. *Psychoanal. Inquiry,* 1:357–392.

Spence, D. (1977), Clinical interpretation: Some comments on the nature of evidence. *Psychoanalysis and Contemporary Science,* 5:367–388. New York: International Universities Press.

Waelder, R. (1936), The principle of multiple function: Observations on overdetermination. *Psychoanal. Quart.,* 5:42–62.

Part III

DREAMS, TECHNIQUE AND CLINICAL THEORY

Freud's "Specimen Dream" in a Widening Context

MARK KANZER

It is by no means a coincidence that Heinz Kohut's (1976) stimulating essay, "Creativeness, Charisma, Group Psychology," began with comments on Max Schur's (1966) paper on the "specimen dream" (Irma's injection), which revealed to Freud (1900) the "secret of dreams" on the morning of July 24, 1895 (p. 121). Kohut shifts our attention from the writer of *The Interpretation of Dreams* to the reader—particularly when the reader is a budding analyst who is likewise being initiated into the meaning of dreams and finds the autobiographical "specimen dream" lying across the pathway like a sphinx at his own initiation into the secrets of practice as a psychoanalyst.

As Kohut points out, the student's initiation takes place on two levels—personal (and influenced by his own immediate transferences) and as a candidate on trial for membership in the analytic community, hoping to gain entry into this profession for a lifetime. Freud's more limited experience in 1895 becomes a living part of the student's experience—both as an individual and as part of a group, instilled with the collective impressions of the community. The student is directing his own ideals to a legendary figure and absorbing (or rejecting) the group hero of psychoanalysts.

In the course of time, each individual student, as well as the

241

community, will experience changes in response to this ambivalently perceived father figure. The attitude toward the specimen dream, therefore, becomes part of an ongoing reanalysis of Freud's original self-analysis, in which student, teacher, and the broad analytic community all participate. Consequently, the figure of Freud and the idealizations that cluster about him are subjected to reality testing, which contributes to the science of applying psychoanalysis to history.

A spontaneous ritualization of such reanalysis may be discerned in the series of commemorative volumes that included studies of the Irma dream: Schur's (1966) contribution to a volume in honor of Heinz Hartmann, a subsequent commemorative volume to honor Schur (Kanzer, 1971), and now one dedicated to Kohut. The insights in the successive studies derive from new material from without and new perspectives from within, as history and psychoanalysis complement each other. Inevitably, the resistances and traditions that fortify the old and oppose the new outlook are also invoked.

The additional material that Schur was able to contribute to Freud's legendary presentation of the Irma dream, admittedly incomplete, would have been impossible without the belated discovery of Freud's (1887–1902) correspondence with Fliess, the publication of which Freud opposed. Without the special permission granted Schur to utilize unpublished portions of the letters, we would know nothing even today of important aspects of secrets revealed to Freud nearly a century ago! Certainly, as with all dreams, nebulous areas still remain. Free association, we must recognize, derives part of its usefulness through provisions that force the revelation of secrets.

My own ambitions in forcing my way further into the secrets of the Irma dream are strictly limited but perhaps not unimportant. I shall follow Schur, and for that matter Freud, in emphasizing material that deals essentially with day residues. I shall also consider the creative process in the formation of the dream and in Freud's recognition (only partly communicated to us, as he acknowledged) of its meaning—a landmark in the achievements of the human intellect.

The appellation of "genius" has suggested itself over and over again for this event, but there is little to be learned from genius—except perhaps that it is not in us! It leaves the analytic instructor with little to impart to candidates about how to acquire and apply genius themselves. But I do find myself wondering with Schur how the element of genius operated in the succession of ideas and experiences that Freud reported to us. The answer is not found in the additional material now available.

I shall briefly review the pertinent facts and assume that the interested reader is already in possession of Freud's (1900) account. In the preamble, Freud describes Irma as a young widow whom he had been treating for hysteria. At the time treatment was interrupted for the summer vacation, he considered that the analysis had done its work—such symptoms as remained were probably somatic. It seems likely (though he is not explicit) that he had suggested, in accordance with his views at the time, that the patient was suffering from sexual deprivation and required measures he was not in a position to offer. Irma rejected this solution, and whether treatment would resume later had not been settled.

On the day before the dream, Freud encountered a mutual friend, Otto, also a physician, who indicated that the young woman was not faring too well. He seemed to be hinting that this was a reflection on Freud himself. Upset at this thought, Freud sat down that evening and drew up a case history to submit to Dr. M., described as the dominant figure in Freud's circle (Joseph Breuer), in the hope of obtaining reassurance from this colleague. "That night (or more probably the next morning)," Freud wrote, "I had the following dream, which I noted down immediately after waking" (p. 106). (This is of particular importance, for Freud was not to publish the dream for more than four years.)

The dream itself followed Freud's chain of ideas based on this experience. It involved a visit from Irma, whom he found looking more ill than he anticipated. He conducted a medical examination with Dr. M. and Otto as consultants. Dr. M. made a nonsensical diagnosis; but the dream dealt even more severely with Otto. It was he who was responsible for Irma's condition, having given her a dangerous injection and perhaps even using a dirty needle in the process. Generations of readers have learned the message that Freud received from this sequence: dreams provide wish fulfillments, and the unpleasant Otto, who had so disturbed Freud's peace of mind that the worries carried over into sleep, was symbolically punished when it was made apparent that he, not Freud, was making Irma ill. A child's retort, no doubt, but then dreams arise from the area of childish thought.

Freud invites us to accompany him along the path to the clearing in the wilderness where the secret of dreams was hidden: "I must ask the reader to make my interests his own for quite a while, and to plunge along with me, into the minutest details of my life; for a transference of this kind is peremptorily demanded by our interest in the hidden meaning of dreams" (pp. 105–106). This meaning did not "pounce" on Freud; he was hunting for it. Erikson (1954) asserts that all history converged on this moment—that the dream was dreamed to be interpreted.

Freud seems to have been unaware of this burden of historical responsibility. He had "no notion" of the dream's meaning. However, he did have a method for discovering the meaning. He had been applying systematic investigation to patients for some time, discovering thereby that their dreams, symptoms, and behavior had unconscious meanings. As early as May 1889, he had discovered, by systematically writing down his own dreams in the morning, that they continued to work on ideas that he had not completed during the day and that they linked together ideas that were present in the same state of consciousness (Breuer and Freud, 1893–95, p. 69). Freud had set his friends to observing their own dreams and reporting them to him. Recently a young physician and nephew of Breuer (Dr. M.), had described a wish-fulfilling convenience dream. This observation also applied to the convenience of consulting with Dr. M. without having to send off the letter to him. The extra step in the woods that Freud had to take on this occasion was to subject every part of the dream to his associations; he had recently written that apparently insignificant ideas can turn out to be the most important and were a particular sign of resistance (Breuer and Freud, 1893–95, p. 279).

The conditions were ripe, if not overripe, for Freud to put these discoveries together. Why did it happen on this morning? To be somewhat unanalytic, could it be because he was on vacation and did not have to dismiss the dream in order to plunge ahead with his regular schedule? Perhaps there were other motives. Freud does not tell us, but with information provided by Schur, we can be reasonably definite about them.

Perhaps the least important character in the Irma dream was Freud's friend Fliess, who is represented only indirectly by a formula for a sexual chemical. In the associations, he comes out positively as Freud's honored friend and supporter, in contrast to the inimical Otto and to Breuer, who was sceptical of Freud's sex theories. (It would have been quite a humiliation for Freud to consult Breuer about the treatment of a case of hysteria, since they had recently quarreled vigorously about differing conceptions of the disorder. Freud's intense discouragement is hardly to be explained by the ambiguous words and tones of Otto, one of his closest friends.)

The state of his relationship with Fliess at the moment hardly reflected the mutual confidence that emerges from the dream associations. Schur (1966) reveals a shocking story. In recent months, Freud had summoned Fliess, an ear, nose, and throat specialist, from Berlin to operate on Irma's sinuses. He had been impressed by certain of his friend's theories linking the nose and female sexuality, and had brought him down for similar purposes in the past. The operation was routine, but Irma nearly died later. A second operation by another physician revealed a gauze ribbon that had been left in the wound—a flagrant bit of malpractice with similarities to the dirty and dangerous injection given by Otto in the dream. Freud tried with the utmost tact to exculpate his friend from any blame and to assuage his hurt feelings, which were unjustly turned against Freud himself.

The intense friendship between the two men (in which Freud's dependence was suggestive of the transference of an unconscious analytic relationship) had dwindled, and Fliess had taken to ignoring the letters of his erstwhile friend. It was in the depths of this crisis that Freud became so exaggeratedly guilty about the harm he might have done Irma. When he set down her case history for Breuer, it was at the desk and at the time of night that he was accustomed to writing Fliess in communications that were apparent equivalents of analytic sessions (Freud, 1887–1902, p. 120).

Schur points out the apparent superimposition of the Irma dream on the antecedent operation scene, with the guilt displaced to Otto (who, ironically would become Fliess's brother-in-law in later years) and only warm appreciation left for Fliess. In a sense, the dream undid the operation and removed the shadow that had fallen between the two men. If a still deeper wish fulfillment was discernible, it was to proceed from that point to make up with Fliess; and this is precisely what Freud did on July 24, following his discovery of the "secret" revealed by this dream. That same day he wrote a letter to Fliess, into which the unlikely letter to Breuer had now turned.

We will assume that the thoughts that followed Freud into sleep and would not let him rest dwelled on the likelihood that Breuer would make his typical ridiculous diagnosis that eliminated sex, while Fliess would support Freud's own. The dream, with its strong anchorage of convenience in both the present and future, was the medium to speed and make known to the dreamer a decision that was already all but made. Simultaneously, it brought him into the clearing on the subject of dreams as well. These mental processes had their roots in the day residue and were important aspects of decision-making. Does not *The Interpretation of Dreams* prove the adage that decisions should not be made until we have had a chance to sleep on them to insure that all facets of our attitude will enter into the decision? The ancients, after all, brought their dreams to the temples of their gods, inhaled vapors to make them dream, or left it to the empathic and ecstatic pythoness of Delphi to dream for them and then from those dreams to extract the decisions they wished to hear.[1] Wish fulfillment is modified intention—even the infant who "hallucinates" (dreams of) the image of the breast is intending to have dinner and makes the demand known in no uncertain terms.

To return to the letter to Fliess on July 24, it was as cordial as in the old days. Freud bypassed any reference to clouds existing between them and promised to come to Berlin soon to visit his friend. (A significant aspect of the latter resolve was agreement thereby to undergo a sinus operation by Fliess, just as Irma had—a visible demonstration of his confidence in Fliess—at which Freud had been balking. This aspect of identification of Freud with Irma may be discerned in the dream, when the physical examination of the patient turns into one of himself. The decision to go to Berlin for such an operation was presumably another settlement of a conflict mediated by the dream.)

But the letter to Fliess does *not* mention the dream that Freud

---

[1] Kohut (1977, pp. 251–252) depicts the drawing forth of the patients' archaic fantasies by the empathic analyst in a comparable process.

would later declare deserved a marble plaque to commemorate its significance. At this point I must part company with Schur, whose sharp mind seems to have been deflected from considering certain issues. With respect to Freud's withholding of the critical dream, in contrast to his usual habit of eagerly sharing new ideas with his friend, Schur offers explanations that seem to me unlikely. (1) Schur (1966, p. 73) suggests that Freud, on the day of the greatest insight in his life and admittedly refraining from giving all the data, failed to connect the dream with the operation in his own mind due to repression. Yet Schur himself assumes the reader will see the connections as "self-evident" (p. 67). (2) Schur elaborates on this thesis by suggesting that Freud's lack of insight was due to the fact that he had not yet recognized the influence of transference on dream formation, especially negative transference. Aside from the self-evident factors, I find the dream replete with positive and negative transferences (Breuer, Otto, Irma) that Freud correctly interprets for us. (3) Schur further postulates that "He was saving the news for their 'congress,' hoping that Fliess's treatment of his nose would leave him with enough energy to talk about it all" (Schur, 1972, p. 89). We can find no reason to assume that Freud was devoid of energy before the operation; it was only after the operation that he complained he did not feel well.

There was, however, a more obvious motive for not divulging the dream to Fliess. Just because the connection with the operation was so obvious, it was predictable that Fliess would be more offended than ever, whereas it was Freud's purpose in writing him to resume their friendship, which had all but broken up over this matter.

Schur assumes that in Berlin Freud told Fliess about the dream. Indeed, Freud told him something about it, for after returning to Vienna he included a single line on dreams in a letter of September 23 otherwise devoted to the Project which at that time absorbed his interest. "A dream the night before last provided the most amusing confirmation that the motivation of dreams is wish-fulfillment" (Freud, 1887–1902, p. 125). But would he have had to tell Fliess the Irma dream, at least in unexpurgated form, to convey the idea of wish fulfillment in dreams? The answer to this possibility is contained in the Project itself (1895a, p. 403), where Freud (in a truncated form that puzzles Kris and other commentators) explains wish fulfillment without any reference to the illness of the girl. Freud also places Fliess in a prominent role in this account that he actually assumed only in Freud's associations in connection with the unabridged dream! We shall return to this second version later.

In tracing the relationship of Freud and Fliess during the years of reconciliation that followed, Schur shows convincingly how the resentment and distrust displaced to Otto continued to seethe beneath the surface and displayed itself in dreams (see especially Schur, 1972) as well as in needling references to Irma. Here we must remark that (1) the girl's name figured as "Emma" in the correspondence between the two men (actually, I am inclined to think that this too was a pseudonym to protect her identity from the reader, and I will have more to say about this later); and (2) Irma-Emma was in fact taken back into treatment after the summer vacation and continued in treatment until at least 1897. From the references to her in the correspondence between Freud and Fliess, she may have been one of his most important cases, but was not destined to be preserved in the literature after the Irma dream, as far as Freud was concerned. However, the resumption of treatment, along with the renewal of the ambivalent relationship with Fliess, may well figure as realistic solutions mediated by the specimen dream!

The allusions to Irma in these letters during the latter phase of her treatment show Freud preoccupied with bleeding and operations, as Schur points out; and quite justifiably Schur regards the references to these matters as intended to make Fliess feel uncomfortable. In analyzing the famous dreams about Goethe and *"non vixit"* as viewed from the perspective of transferences to Fliess, which could no longer be regarded as "unconsciously negative," Fliess is made to appear as a ridiculous theorist and the object of flagrant death wishes that Freud apparently enjoyed pointing out to him (Schur, 1972, pp. 153–191).

If, then, Freud avoided directly linking Emma with the Irma dream, as I am indicating, when did Fliess finally recognize the connection, and what were the consequences? Surely this would have had to occur when the specimen dream was presented to him—for Freud insisted, despite obviously dwindling positive feelings, on making Fliess his "supervisor" during the writing of the dream book, which began in May 1897.

From Strachey's introduction to the latter, we learn that Fliess required him to remove a "completely analyzed sample dream." The resulting gap left Freud so despondent that he laid aside his work in October 1898 and did not take it up again until May 1899 (1900, p. xix). We find Schur (1966, p. 76) arguing vigorously that the "completely analyzed sample dream" could not have been that of Irma's injection, for the latter was merely subjected to a "thorough" analysis, and since then Freud had discovered the Oedipus complex, necessary for a "complete" analysis.

Freud first mentioned the Oedipus complex on October 15, 1897 (1887–1902, p. 223), and could hardly have thoroughly analyzed a case based on this concept within a year, especially as he reported on February 9, 1898 that his "hysterical cases are doing rather badly. I shall not finish any this year either; next year I shall have no patients to work on" (p. 245). Schur also points to the obvious fact that the specimen dream is, after all, included in the dream book, but it is possible that as Freud's self-analysis continued to progress, he dropped the need to submit to Fliess.

Still other considerations dispose me to accept Schur's hypothesis. For on June 12, 1900, nearly six months after the dream book had been published and with it Freud's dependency on Fliess had been diminished, symbolically and perhaps in fact, Freud sent a remarkable letter to Fliess in which he inquired "playfully": "Do you suppose that some day a marble tablet will be placed on the house inscribed with these words: 'In this house on July 24, 1895 the secret of dreams was revealed to Sigmund Freud?' " (1887–1902, p. 302).

Schur (1966) raises the question, rightly I believe, of whether this was not a triumphant challenge on Freud's part that "unconsciously" (and on this point I do not agree) conveys the message: "One . . . part of me already knew at the time of the Irma dream who had committed an error and whom I really had to protect because the other part was not yet as strong, sure, and *steady* as it is now" (p. 69).

Schur still insists, "in view of Freud's superb honesty," that "any connection between the Irma dream and the Emma episode had been even more thoroughly repressed than before" (1966, p. 73). This hardly comports with the message he himself sees Freud sending Fliess on June 12, 1900, albeit he supposes the message was "unconscious."

Still, he does assume that it testifies to greater self-reliance and an advanced state of self-analysis that could dispose at last with the need to overestimate the virtues of a colleague who had not only shown himself guilty of malpractice but would not tolerate any recognition of it.

Schur does not tell us about the severe reaction of Fliess to the dating of the revelation, but this we learn from Ernest Jones (1953). Fliess at once wrote Freud requesting that he verify the date of the dream. He received a speedy answer in which Freud declared that he had done so with the aid of a diary he had kept at the time, apparently without ever communicating the "secret" to his friend before. The apparent shock to Fliess and another severe reaction that followed tend to substantiate the impression that it was Fliess who, up to this time, had not sensed the connection of the Irma dream with his unfortunate operation on Emma.

One may well ask how *he* could have failed to make the connection. At least two years had gone by between the operation and the time he saw the specimen dream. None of the figures in it were identified by name. The manifest content emphasized Freud's problem in evading a feeling of guilt for the plight of the girl. Only Fliess himself emerges as the steadfast friend whom Freud honored. If a comparison is to be made with Freud's own supposed failure to connect dream and operation, we must recall that all associations were available to him but not to Fliess.

The intensity of Fliess's reaction, I believe, may have been responsible for the irreparable break between the two men when they met for one of their vacation congresses a few weeks later. There is a wide discrepancy in the accounts both men subsequently gave. Freud attributed their misunderstanding to a disagreement over the importance of psychic determinism as compared to the laws of periodicity (Schur, 1972, p. 209). This is surely too intellectual an issue—and not a new one at that—to bring about the collapse of an old friendship! Fliess, in his explanation, at least invoked strong feelings between them, declaring that Freud had attacked him personally and without provocation (1887–1902, p. 324, n. 1). In this footnote recording Fliess's rendition of the break, Kris adds: "This was the last meeting before the *latent* estrangement between the two men became *manifest*" (italics added). The metaphors of "latent" and "manifest" point to dream formation and unwittingly suggest that the long, latent hostility that engendered the Irma dream had found a manifest outlet at last.

Blum (1981), in a study on the superego and insight, appropriately picks the Irma dream to illustrate his thesis. He recognizes in the manifest content (for example with respect to the disguise of Joseph Breuer as Dr. M., who makes fatuous remarks when consulted about a diagnosis), the dethronement of old idols who proved to be ignorant and no longer sources of insight. I would suggest that a dichotomy was brought into being in which M. screened the scorn for Fliess, while associations still extolled the unique insights of the latter. The Irma dream marked the birth of insight into the meaning of dreams for Freud, but the oedipal accompaniment, the triumph over the ignorant father, had to wait for another occasion!

My last comments will be directed to the third member of the oedipal triangle involved in the acquisition of insight into the meaning of dreams—Irma, or more accurately Emma. Most likely her identity is still concealed from us in that guise also. Even in the dream book, there is the hint of a still more deeply concealed name for the mystery figure when Freud comments, in a footnote, that "the sound of the word 'Ananas' [pineapple, which figures in the dream], bears a remarkable resemblance to that of my patient Irma's family name" (1900, p. 115, n. 1). Physicianly discretion was not sacrificed in the interest of abstract and unnecessary scientific honesty. Therefore it seems likely that Freud was protecting the girl's identity by invoking her family name, for comparison of "Ananas" with her first name could only have suggested "Anna."

Some evidence has surfaced in recent years, however, to identify "Irma" with Anna Hammerschlag, daughter of Freud's respected teacher Professor Samuel Hammerschlag, who taught Freud Hebrew and the scriptures (Knoepfmacher, 1979). Jones (1953) quotes Freud as saying, "He [Hammerschlag] always regards me as his son." Jones adds, "Years later Freud named his youngest daughter after a daughter of Hammerschlag's who in 1885 was married to Rudolf Lichtheim of Breslau, a man who died within a year" (p. 163) (the rosy widow!). Freud named yet another daughter, Sophie, after a niece of Hammerschlag. The interrelations of this close-knit circle also made Anna a sister of Breuer's daughter-in-law; so that Freud's need to consult Breuer about "Irma" would have been reinforced by that circumstances. The specimen dream further links "Irma" to another of Freud's daughters, Mathilde (Freud, 1900, pp. 111–112). Thus the need to protect her as a member of the family would have been quite understandable.

There may well be much about Irma-Emma-Anna that still has not been divulged and may emerge from the fuller disclosure of the Fliess letters or otherwise. How much Schur himself learned one may question from an observation in which he laments the "loss of so many of Freud's early case histories—for example, that of Emma" (1966, p. 84). Perhaps there is another clue. In the "Project," besides the patient's disguise in the truncated specimen dream, there is only one other clinical fragment. This describes the childhood origin of a hysterical symptom in a patient named—Emma! We do not know if this refers to the same Emma, but oddly enough, Strachey remarks in a footnote on this case that "Freud seems not to have mentioned this case elsewhere" (1895b, p. 353, n. 2).

Insofar as we have been able to follow hitherto undisclosed aspects of the Irma-Emma case as disclosed by Schur, it is my impression also that she may have offered data that would have made her one of Freud's great case histories in the very exciting period between the cathartic stage of his insights and their transition into self-analysis and the dream book. The ongoing analysis of the Irma dream is indeed testimony to the process that translates personal into group and scientific history!

Summary

1. Heinz Kohut has made the point that the reanalysis of Freud by each generation of analysts carries Freud's self-analysis further as well as contributing to the reality testing of the individual and the community of analysts and to the application of psychoanalysis to the science of history.

2. Various strands of psychoanalysis and history continue to focus on the "specimen dream" (Irma's injection), which Freud declared had revealed to him the secret of dreams. The dramatic element of this revelation likewise raises interest in the connections between creativity,

genius, and self-analysis—to which Erikson has added historical convergence as a related factor.

3. The belated discovery of Freud's letters to Fliess, and the special permission granted Max Schur to publish hitherto undisclosed portions, have added considerably to our understanding of the Irma dream and its significance in relation to Freud's unique experience and the circumstances that surrounded it. It is now more possible to place the dream in a context of real events, both earlier and later, just as in the course of a regular analysis.

4. Schur has shown the part played in the dream and its aftermath by a crisis between Freud and Fliess over their mutual patient Irma; and the dream still seems to have played an important part in the final break between them that occurred in 1900.

5. The present review parts with Schur in an obscure area: the question of whether Freud told Fliess the full dream or its relation to their mutual patient before 1900. Freud did present a much truncated version in 1895 in "the Project" some weeks after he had dreamed it, which has puzzled commentators because it shows so much less grasp of the meaning of dreams than Freud was later to show. Yet Freud declared that the essentials of the dream were understood by him at that time.

6. Various aspects of creative insight, the function of the Irma dream in Freud's immediate and later problem-solving, and Irma's identity are discussed. These issues are related to the author's view of Freud's need to conceal from Fliess the accusations against him, which the dream contains at a deeper layer of wish fulfillment than Freud describes in his official version.

References

Blum, H. (1981), The forbidden quest and the analytic ideal: The superego and insight. *Psychoanal. Quart.*, 50:535–556.

Breuer, J., & Freud, S. (1893–95), *Studies on Hysteria. Standard Edition,* 2. London: Hogarth Press, 1955.

Erikson, E. (1954), The dream specimen of psychoanalysis. *J. Amer. Psychoanal. Assn.,* 2:5–56.

Freud, S. (1887–1902), *The Origins of Psychoanalysis: Letters to Wilhelm Fliess, Drafts, and Notes,* ed. M. Bonaparte, A. Freud, & E. Kris. New York: Basic Books, 1954.

——— (1895a), Project for a scientific psychology. In: *The Origins of Psychoanalysis: Letters to Wilhelm Fliess, Drafts, and Notes,* ed. M. Bonaparte, A. Freud, & E. Kris. New York: Basic Books, pp. 347–445.

——— (1895b), Project for a scientific psychology. *Standard Edition,* 1. London: Hogarth Press, 1966, pp. 283–397.

——— (1900), The interpretation of dreams. *Standard Edition,* 4. London: Hogarth Press, 1953.

Jones, E. (1953), *The Life and Works of Sigmund Freud,* Vol. 1. New York: Basic Books.

Kanzer, M. (1971), *The Unconscious Today: Essays in Honor of Max Schur.* New York: International Universities Press.

Knoepfmacher, H. (1979), Sigmund Freud in high school. *Amer. Imago,* 36:287–300.

Kohut, H. (1976), Creativeness, charisma, group psychology: Reflections on the self-analysis of Freud. In: *The Search for the Self,* ed. P.H. Ornstein. New York: International Universities Press, 1978, pp. 793–843.

——— (1977), *The Restoration of the Self.* New York: International Universities Press.

Schur, M. (1966), Some additional "day residues" of "the specimen dream of psychoanalysis." In: *Psychoanalysis—A General Psychology,* ed. R. Loewenstein, L. Newman, M. Schur, & A. Solnit. New York: International Universities Press, pp. 48–85.

——— (1972), *Freud Living and Dying.* New York: International Universities Press.

Self Psychology and the Interpretation of Dreams

PAUL TOLPIN

A misunderstanding about the interpretation of dreams according to self psychological principles has developed in the minds of some readers of the literature of the psychology of the self. The problem seems to have arisen from Kohut's having called attention to a specific kind of dream—the "self-state dream"—in his two major expositions of the psychology of the self, *The Analysis of the Self* (1971) and *The Restoration of the Self* (1977). Self-state dreams are those in which the manifest content, without *much* further associative information, reveals the essential meaning of the dream. Kohut's writings contain many examples of the analysis of dreams that are not typically or strictly self-state dreams (see, for example, 1971, pp. 87, 149, 159-160, 173-174, 261; 1977, pp. 126–220). Yet explication of the self-state dream in these two works has apparently misled some readers to believe that *all* dreams interpreted from the point of view of the self-psychological framework are self-state dreams—as Kohut originally described them.

In this brief note I would like to clarify this misunderstanding by (1) reviewing its possible origins in Kohut's initial presentation of self-state dreams; (2) making some general remarks on the formation and types of dreams found in disorders of the self and on the role of theory in the interpretation of dreams; and (3) presenting two specimen dreams to illustrate how they can be interpreted according to a self-psychological conceptual framework.

To review the possible origin of the misunderstanding: In *The Restoration of the Self* (1977), Kohut describes two types of dreams: "those expressing verbalizable latent contents (drive, wishes, conflicts, and attempted conflict solutions), and those attempting, with the aid of verbalizable dream-imagery, to bind the nonverbal tensions of traumatic states (the dread of overstimulation, or of the disintegration of the self [psychosis])" (pp. 108–109). The latter, which Kohut calls self-state dreams, "attempt to deal with the psychological danger by covering nameless processes with namable visual imagery." In the first type of dream the analyst follows "the patient's free associations into the depths of the psyche until the formerly unconscious meaning has been uncovered. In the second type of dream, . . . free associations . . . at best provide us with further imagery which remains on the same level as the manifest content of the dream" (p. 109). Examinations of these associative elaborations provide clues to the fact that "the healthy sectors of the patient's psyche are reacting with anxiety to a disturbing change in the condition of the self" ranging from manic stimulation to a depressive drop in self esteem to a threat of dissolution of the self. Kohut also describes transitional and mixed forms of dreams, in which aspects of the archaic self are present (perhaps at times as the total setting or background atmosphere of the dream), while other elements are the consequence of and represent varieties of structural conflict. These self-state dreams are "similar to dreams of children . . . to the dreams of traumatic neuroses . . . and to hallucinatory dreams occurring with toxic states or high fever" (p. 109). Self-state dreams are not necessarily limited, however, to what in Kohut's description may sound like rather extreme states of self disturbance. This will be discussed shortly. (For Kohut's examples of self-state dreams see *The Analysis of the Self*, 1971, pp. 4–5, 149.)

Kohut's original description of self-state dreams focused the understanding to which he had recently come of a specific experience of the self that was expressed in manifest dream imagery. The confusion came about because other types of dreams about the trials of the self and its experiences with selfobjects, although scattered in the case material were not explicitly mentioned or provided with a descriptive name or explicit dynamic. It was therefore incorrectly assumed by some that (except perhaps for transitional and mixed dream forms) the dreams of patients with disturbances of the self were all to be understood as depictions of the observing self, observing an endangered, traumatized, or "potentially crumbling" experiencing self. Empirically, however, that is clearly not the case. Dreams about the self or dreams of patients whose core pathology is best understood by the use of the conceptual framework of self psychology are frequently both different from and more complex than the self-state dream emphasized by Kohut.

Patients with disturbances of the self do not dream in a way that is operationally different from patients whose dreams are dominated by drives, defenses against drives, and all the structural elaborations of those interactions. Dreams understood with the use of a self-psychological framework have the usual manifest contents of the related dream, beyond which—through the patient's free associations, aided by the analyst's prolonged immersion into the patient's psychological life and an understanding of the transference—the latent dream thoughts may be recognized. In addition, as in the "structural conflict" dream, one can find the usual psychological devices of the dream work: symbolization, condensation, displacement, and secondary revision, to name a few. What *is* different, however, is the guiding theoretical framework that the observer imposes on the dream. In the classical dream of structural psychology, to put it simply, the interacting forces of the id, ego, and superego orient the analyst's investigation of the latent dream thoughts. In self psychology, the vicissitudes of the self are the orienting principle that leads the analyst to an understanding of the meaning of the dream. This theoretical framework, more precisely, is the organization of the bipolar self in the midst of change and in relation to its selfobject experiences. It is this orienting framework that causes the dream to be understood in a different way from a dream whose contents are examined within the conceptual framework of drive-conflict psychology.

At one point on the spectrum of dreams about the self are what Kohut has called self-state dreams. These are not dissimilar from dreams of childhood, of the traumatic neuroses, and so on. Associations do not lead much beyond the metaphorically understood manifest content. Further dream thoughts are not prominently at issue. The state of the self as it is constituted at the moment is observed by an observing sector of the self, and that observation is represented in the dream. "And if that self is in pain, is injured, is having difficulty holding itself together, is depleted, or, to the contrary, if it is in an unusually good state of organization with a sense of success and heightened well-being, our dreams can hardly fail to depict these various states" (P. Tolpin, 1980, p. 6). At another point on the spectrum are dreams about the self in relation to its selfobjects. These dreams usually cannot be understood from their manifest content alone. Only a combination of present-day associations, clues from day residue, and an in-depth understanding of the patient's transference, dynamics, genetics, character, and defensive tendencies, grasped empathically all together, leads to an appreciation of the meaning of the dream, both in the present and in relation to its roots in the childhood past. In these dreams, unlike self-state or traumatic dreams, the manifest content alone is insufficient for an adequate comprehension of what they represent.[1]

To illustrate this point, I shall present two dreams from two different patients, both of whom were considered to be suffering from self pathology. The first patient's dream illustrates a self-state dream, while that of the second patient illustrates a dream about the self in relation to its (transference) selfobjects. Both dreams are understood from within the conceptual framework of the psychology of the self.

Mr. G., a married man in his mid-forties, had been in therapy with me for about six years. He began treatment following the onset of a rather severe, agitated depression, which developed when he was

[1] Of course, in dreams about the self, as in any other kind of dream, depending on the particular state of mind of the dreamer at the time the dream is being dreamt, some elements will be more dominated by thoughts "from above" than "from below" (Freud, 1923, p. 111; see also Freud, 1900, p. 561, and 1929, p. 203). There is such a complemental balance in all dreams. Dreams about the self are not any different in this regard than dreams dominated by drives and their vicissitudes. And in those dreams "from above," the metaphorically understood manifest content may be more clearly grasped. And there are "mixed" dreams whose interpretation is arrived at from a grasp of self-state elements as well as more concealed metaphorical and symbolic elements.

not awarded the significant promotion at work that he had expected. Within a few weeks, his initial disappointment had turned into an increasingly agitated depressive state accompanied by a terrible feeling of hopelessness about his future. He experienced a revival of the dreadful isolation and loneliness he had felt repeatedly as a child when he was castigated by his erratically enraged and at times sanctimoniously humiliating mother. For example, she would punish him for relatively minor infractions of her strict rules of behavior with mortifying punishments. Sometimes, enraged beyond endurance by her critical attacks, he would hide in the closet and make violent "fuck you" signs at her with his finger. A dream that occurred early in treatment (not the self-state dream to be discussed later), following an interruption for a three-day weekend and a spat with his wife, is indicative of his depressive tendencies. In the dream, he was riding his bicycle through a deep forest searching for the small rustic cabin where he was to meet his wife. With some difficulty he found his way to the cabin clearing, only to discover that she was gone. No one was there. He felt overwhelmed by despair and was not sure if he could find his way out of the woods.

In fact, Mr. G. was a brilliant man with creative talents. Sometimes his positive feelings about his abilities became exaggerated and took on a grandiose-manic coloration. That state of mind was usually transient and unstable, however, and was replaced, as it had been regularly in childhood and adolescence, by a chronic sense of worthlessness, which he could barely conceal from his peers. They nevertheless regarded him as a model of conservatism, creativity, business acumen and sought his opinions and judgments. Within a few years after leaving the company that had not promoted him rapidly enough, he had made a small fortune for himself.

Mr. G. recovered from his presenting depression within a few months, and despite less severe recurrences of the same depressive symptoms three times in the next several years, did quite well in treatment. The dream that is presented as an illustration of a self-state dream occurred during a recent revival of some depressed feelings, accompanied as usual by a sense of utter worthlessness and bitter self-deprecation. In the midst of this, as was his tendency, the patient had days of feeling appreciably better, more self-confident, and more capable of managing his business affairs. This sense of well-being usually occurred when some feared confrontation in his working life turned out favorably for him, and he could see that his business expertise and ability to function was still intact. He would be briefly released from the grasp of his pervasive depressed mood. Following just such a development, he began his session by saying that he had done better with some negotiations the day before than he thought he'd be able to. They hadn't gotten the best of him after all. He'd been able to hold his own. That night he had the following dream, which foreshadowed the return of his depression:

> I am in a city somewhere. I become aware that someone had committed a crime and they are escaping via a helicopter. The police didn't have one. I get into a plane and start to chase them. D. [his wife] is with me and we go after them. At first I was doing okay, but the plane gets more and more difficult to operate, to control. It seems to have no power. I begin to wonder if I know how to fly a plane at all. I'm not sure. The plane struggles along. I don't give up but I am battling this problem. I go past an airport. The control tower says that I'd better come down, that I'm not flying well, that I'm tired. I don't feel it but I know it's true. So I touch down nearby. I think to myself that I'll rest and go up after the thieves again later on.

Along with what I had learned about the patient during the course of his analysis, his present sparse associations to the dream and his past associations to similar kinds of dreams suggested the following: The initial sequence of the dream is a portrayal of a brief sense of heightened well-being (modeled after some expansive childhood day-dreams). These also double as a defense against the already sublimi-nally experienced growing sense of depletion that was about to occur. The patient then begins to succumb to his still dominating depression. He struggles briefly against it and then, vanquished, slumps into the apathetic mood in which he had lived frequently throughout his adult life. What I want to highlight, however, is the gradual shift in the second portion of the dream from his initial energetic activity to a gradual feeling of loss of power, with increasing difficulty in managing

depletion verges toward a renewal

the plane—that is, himself. He wonders again if he is at all capable of operating it. Though he doesn't quite give up, he finally accedes to an externalized representation of his own (partially denied) self-awareness. The controller (his inner self-observing voice) tells him that he is not flying well, that he is tired. He salvages his pride to some extent and retains some hope by planning to take to the skies again after a rest to catch the thieves.

To offset doubts that I have overlooked the more usual approaches to the understanding of this dream—for example, remobilized castration anxiety, a negative therapeutic reaction, a sense of guilt over his success, or the consequences of other issues inherent in the structural model of the mental apparatus—I want to indicate that I was, of course, aware of the possible applicability of those ideas. However, in light of my overall understanding of the patient's core pathology as I had come to see it in the course of several years of analytic work with him, I did not feel that those ''classical'' clinical theories and models offered the most useful framework by which to plumb the depths of the patient's *primary* needs and fears.

The dream as I saw it was about a patient with a highly vulnerable self organization. It represented the fluctuation in that self's integration or sense of fullness and firmness—even though that could be experienced at a secondary level as a problem of phallic oedipal drives and fears in relation to them. In my view, that formulation would be incorrect because it does not describe the underlying primary pathology of the depletion-prone self. Instead, it describes crystallization points around which a primary depleted self state took a specific (secondary) verbalizable or pictorializable form (see Kohut, 1977, p. 225 regarding pseudo-transference neuroses).

While the dream was not the kind of self-state dream described by Kohut, I believe it nonetheless qualifies as a type of self-state dream. Throughout almost the entire dream, the dreamer is directly or indirectly observing himself and ''commenting'' about the state of his self—whether it is expansive and action-oriented or in a process of partially denied collapse into powerless exhaustion, which is accepted and yet ameliorated by plans for the future.

I want to emphasize that I am presenting a less ominous, less extreme self-state dream than that originally described by Kohut. I am

expanding the use of his terminology to include dreams in which a
significant threat to the integrity of the core self is not at issue. (I am
suggesting that one can conceive of a continuum of self-state dreams,
from those that at one pole represent the self at a point of near disintegration (or even in the process of disintegration) to those that at
the other extreme represent, for example, an experienced and observed
change of mood in the self.)

The second dream I want to present is not a self-state dream either
in Kohut's original sense of the term or in the expanded sense I have
just proposed. Rather, it is a dream that depicts the state of the patient's
self in its struggle to maintain a decidedly increased but still vulnerable
sense of independence and self-confidence. Self-selfobject experiences
are clearly depicted in this dream.

A man in his early thirties, who had been in treatment for several
years, had the following dream on the night after a Monday morning
session:

> I was standing on Michigan Avenue on the east side of the street
> thinking of how I might get to my office. It was early morning
> and the street was relatively empty. I decided to hitch a ride. A
> late middle-aged man in a sporty looking car came by and offered
> to drive me to my office. He was going that way, south from
> where we were. I noticed that although he was a bit formal look-
> ing, he was wearing an unbuttoned, tweed sport coat. He had a
> full head of dark hair. He was no one I knew and we didn't talk
> much, but he seemed to be likable somehow—a solid, self-con-
> fident person. I indicated to him that my office was just across
> the street, a hundred yards or so from where we were, and that
> he would have to cut across the street at almost a forty-five-degree
> angle to drop me off at my building. He didn't seem to mind that,
> nor did he question why I wanted such a short ride. Expertly
> edging in front of and in back of several other cars, he easily
> made it across the street and let me out at the curb. (I realized
> either in the dream or after I woke up and began to think about
> it that I must have made Michigan Avenue a one-way street going
> south or he wouldn't have been going south on the east side of

the street, but that didn't seem important in the dream itself.) I thanked him and he drove off.

At that moment I realized I had left my briefcase in his car on the back seat. I turned to a policeman standing on the sidewalk nearby and thought of asking him to help me but he was looking the other way or didn't seem to be interested or aware of what was going on. I then panicked and began to run after the car as it picked up speed going toward the river. Almost desperately I yelled to the man to stop his car but he didn't hear me. I kept running and yelling and then I realized that I'd better stop being so anxious and disorganized, that I'd better collect my wits and try to identify the car and the license plate so I could trace it and the man if he got away from me. I tried to read the license number, but couldn't see it clearly. I searched for some other identification. I saw that it was a green Mustang—it had the galloping horse insignia on the trunk. I began to feel somewhat relieved. I was getting some clues so that I could find him again if he got out of sight. South of the bridge, near here where your office is, he pulled across the sidewalk to drive into a parking lot. (It couldn't have been Michigan Avenue, then, it was more like Lake Street, where the lot is.) I caught up with him and told him about the briefcase. He reached into the back seat and handed it to me. I don't think he said anything. He didn't seem upset. He looked like a hard worker, like someone who enjoys his work. He liked getting to work early. I think he was a businessman, or he owned a business, or he was in business for himself—not really wealthy, more down-to-earth, not like me but like someone I could rely on. Then I woke up.

The patient's associations were, briefly, as follows: He had been feeling somewhat better than he usually did over the three-day weekend but had come to his hour on Monday in one of his characteristic self-deprecating moods, bordering on self-hate, which were part and parcel of his chronic feeling of inadequacy and low self-esteem. No one, he thought, would ever find him as competent as A., a friend, whom he sometimes admired and at other times despised. No woman would ever respond to him with anything but grudging acceptance, and even then only because of his social and economic position—certainly not out of attraction to him as a prepossessing, manly man. Still, he recalled that on Monday, after a discussion that connected the weekend letdown with some relevant current and childhood issues, he had left his session feeling less morose. As the day went on he began to feel less inadequate, surer of himself, more competent in his work. Monday night he had fallen asleep easily (an accomplishment for this man who sometimes had to read late into the night or watch television mindlessly until his feelings of tension and emptiness subsided and he could drift off into an uneasy slumber). He *had* been given a lift by the Monday session, something, he reminded himself, that often happened on Mondays. Oh yes, the man in the green Mustang had given him a "lift," too. Yes, it probably was the analyst—something about his youthfulness despite his age. The Mustang—actually it looked more like a friend's Triumph convertible in which he had been given a ride a few weeks before. Why was the street one-way going south? He didn't know. That was confusing, but his office was indeed north of the river and the analyst's was south of it, and so on. Still, he did need the analyst—his aliveness, his quiet strength, his expertise at maneuvering his vehicle, the sense of admiration he felt as the man in the dream deftly angled the car across the street. He really had felt better on Monday; he *was* given a lift.

The patient's thoughts began to run out at this point. He wasn't sure about the rest of the dream. Then he picked up again and continued. The man's relative silence wasn't like the analyst, who spoke quite a bit. In fact the analyst's very talk, his involvement with the patient by way of his responsive talk, was helpful—sometimes more than the content was, although the content was helpful also, or was at least the vehicle for the connectedness. There was the car again—the vehicle, the place where the connectedness took place. The analyst's words, the deftness with which he put things together sometimes, he admired those things, too. Why had he left his briefcase in the car? He couldn't understand that. He had just forgotten it and then panicked when he saw the car driving off and realized what had happened. He couldn't get along without his briefcase. It had everything he needed for the day's work. Losing it would be as though he lost part of his mind. It was a part of himself that he couldn't do without. He became silent again.

I began to comment on what I had understood the dream to mean in the context of the patient's past and present associations, the transference that had been activated in the last few months, and my understanding of the pathogenic experiences of his childhood. I said that he was replaying in his mind the experience of the Monday session with me (or anticipating the next session) and reviewing his feelings about it. I suggested that, along with feeling revived after the Monday session, he might have recognized as he had before how important his experiences with me were for him. During the day he had begun to feel stronger than he usually did—and it surfaced in the dream—but he must have also felt that it lasted only as long as he was with me, as long as he was given a lift by me. When he left the session, he felt as though he had left a part of himself behind—an essential part of himself that was not yet fixed within him. It was outside of him, like his indispensable briefcase, whose presence gave him a sense of structure and substance. He felt stronger by virtue of his involvement with me during the session, but he began to fear—as graphically portrayed in the dream—that once he and I separated even temporarily, the good feeling would be lost, he would lose the recently acquired strength and be left with his old, chronic sense of impotence and inadequacy.

But, I added, this time he did something different, despite the panic that welled up in him as it had over and over again in his childhood when he had felt bereft of the supporting presence of his father. He faced the imminent collapse of the sense of well-being, integration, and expansiveness that he had experienced by a transient identification with the vigorous, sporty, skillfully maneuvering analyst; but this time, instead of feeling helpless, he was able to pull himself together on his own. The nearby policeman—an old childhood symbol of strength and reliability—did not rush to his aid, but that did not lead to further disorganization. Instead, he found that he could begin to collect his wits. He was able to use his recently developed feelings of strength and self-reliance, his self-integrating capacities in the form of rational thoughts, to slay the rearoused dragons of inner catastrophe which always beset him when he felt deserted by those he depended on for support. He began to take care of himself. He looked for the license number, he noted the color of the car; but he had begun to feel better even before that—when he began to run after the car.

The patient interrupted me. He recalled an incident from the previous winter. He'd gotten out of a taxi with his girlfriend and had begun to walk away, when he suddenly realized that he'd left his gloves in the cab. His heart sank, he felt helpless. Then, without thinking, he took off down the street after the cab. As luck would have it, the taxi was slowed enough by traffic that he was able to catch up with it. The driver heard him shouting and stopped, and the patient was able to retrieve his gloves. He had felt elated by his unaccustomed assertiveness and his success. He had thought then, too, as in the dream, that he'd never catch the cab; so he had tried to note its license number as he ran. In the dream, he caught up with the man who had given him a lift, the man who knew how to get around in the world and take care of himself, an admirable self-made man, the kind the patient idealized. Instead of his usual passivity, he was able to find the wherewithal to turn to action, and he found that it accomplished something. Was he scared of his success, would he now be too much on his own and have to face a ruthless, uncaring world as an adult? Well, he knew where the man worked, where his place of business was. He could find him again. He could return to therapy the next day and go a bit farther along the road to increased self-confidence and strength.

The patient's next associations concerned the policeman on the street to whom he turned for help, who had been interested but un-helpful. The policeman did not rush to assist him as his father would have done. His father, although in many ways admirable, usually lived in an emotional atmosphere far removed from the patient. The patient admired his father, but was unable to feel involved with him. He felt his father was preoccupied and was indifferent to his son except when he could take care of the son's childhood physical needs. That behavior was heartfelt, but it did not acknowledge or encourage the patient's independent growth as a boy or a young man. Rather, his father had done for his son what had not been done for the father as a child: he took care of him in a motherly way. In the dream, however, the policeman to whom the patient looked for help seemed to indicate that he should do whatever was necessary for himself; and surprisingly, he had found within himself the power to act on his own behalf.

As with the first dream, I shall not attempt to be thorough about the understanding of this dream. Clearly much has been omitted. I have not presented a summary of the patient's history, the early transference clues that led to the tentative formulations of his central pathology, and so on. I have not, to cite one example, clarified the detail of Michigan Avenue as a one-way street going south. That aspect of the dream remained problematic. Rather, I have presented the dream as an example of how, using the framework of self psychology, the meaning of a dream may be investigated and understood.

The dream of the second patient is clearly operating on a different psychic level from the self-state dream of the first patient. True, in his dream the second patient was threatened with danger and for a moment he was frantic and almost panicked, but the coherence of his self was not at stake or on the verge of fragmentation. His self was buttressed by a far more reliable structure than that. More in evidence in the dream of this second patient was a particular configuration of his self development, one that had been the subject of a year or more of analytic work. It was represented by his use of an idealizing transference in the process of its being transformed into a more reliable part of his functioning self. He was suffering from the fear that he had not yet made the idealized father-analyst's strengths part of him. He turned alternately to the idealized policeman, to himself, and again to the idealized father-analyst in a fascinating display of oscillating self-confidence. He wanted to be the man he perceived the analyst to be—and to an extent he *had* developed some of that self-reliance in the course of treatment. In this dream he was able to make use of that stability in a limited way, but he was still not sure enough of himself. He left the businessman-analyst reassured that he could see the man again for continuing help and for a further consolidation of developmental needs.

This is not the dream of a patient whose core self and basic cohesiveness are on the verge of disintegration, nor is it a dream in which the state of the self is focal in Kohut's original sense. Moreover, the full meaning of the dream is not a relatively simple elaboration of the manifest content, beyond which further investigation offers few additional clues. Free association *does* supply additional thought imagery that is not on the same level as the manifest content of the dream. In fact, it leads to an understanding not just of the state of the patient's self in a broad sense, but also of his current dominant selfobject transferences, and beyond those to their origins in his experienced childhood relationship with his father. Thus, although it is not a self-state dream, it is a dream about self-selfobject experiences and about the overall functioning of the patient's self at a moment in time. In short, it is a dream that has been interpreted within the guiding framework of self psychology.

As noted earlier, the purpose of this paper is to make explicit an understanding about the interpretations of dreams from a self-psychological point of view. I hope to put to rest the erroneous idea that all dreams about the self are self-state dreams that describe relatively simply the self observing the state of the self, which can be discerned mostly from the manifest content of the dream. I believe that in the course of that effort I have also demonstrated that the fortunes of the self are as richly and complexly displayed in dreams as are the fortunes of the Oedipus complex, of regressed or fixated preoedipal disturbances, of drives and conflict psychology (as modified by ego psychology)—in sum, as in dreams organized along and understood by more traditional theoretical lines.

This traditional understanding of dreams—Freud's monumental discovery that dreams have an underlying latent meaning that by way of free association of their manifest content can be logically arrived at through analytic work—was one of Freud's proudest early achievements. The specimen dream that illustrated his discovery, the dream of Irma's injection (Freud, 1900, pp. 108–121), was designated a wish-fulfillment dream. The wish "for expulcation" was not yet seen to be dominated by an infantile drive and the conflicts arising from that, however. The wish for exculpation was present but it was, to use terms that had not been invented at the time, more of an ego wish than a drive wish. Shortly after this, however, Freud postulated that almost all dreams were energized by childhood drives that, when mobilized by often trivial events of the day (residue), gave these events the force to act as a cover for the still surviving and remobilized derivatives of the dreamer's infantile wish (see Freud's analogy of the entrepreneur and the capitalist, 1900, p. 561). Freud modified this notion somewhat in relation to traumatic dreams (1920, pp. 13–14, 32) and dreams from above and dreams from below (1923, p. 111; 1929, p. 203).

As Freud conceived it, all dreams had components of present and childhood concerns amalgamated in varying proportions. In a dream from below, the past disturbances were decisive in the motivation of the dream; and in dreams from above, current disturbances were the decisive motivating factor; but each dream had varying proportions of the other. One could assume the existence of such a complemental series, just as one could assume such an interlocking series in the overlapping influence of constitutional and external factors in the formation of a neurosis (see Freud, 1916–17, pp. 346–347). Freud (1900, pp. 344, 503, 523–524; 1914, p. 97) commented on another type of "anagogic" dream discovered by Silberer; but this might be classified as a rather specialized dream from above with little if any drive motivation (aside from an [ego?] wish to sleep) implied in its formation. These dreams do not significantly alter Freud's conception that, in general, dreams are wishes for drive gratification motivated strongly or weakly by childhood drives.

The psychology of the self as defined by Kohut (1971, 1977) holds that the development, organization, and the maintenance of the stable coherence of the (bipolar) self is the overriding motivating factor in the everyday struggles of the individual's psychic life. This theoretical approach to the mind of course affects how the analyst understands the dreams of a patient whose mental organization is best understood by that theory. In other words, one's theory, whether broad and loose or specific and refined, determines to a great extent how one understands the basic data of observation. As far as dreams are concerned, then, the individual whose psychological organization is understood in terms of self psychology is understood to dream about the fluctuating state and the vicissitudes of the self.[2] In other words, one's bias or what one believes to be a correct, applicable, and overarching theoretical framework generally defines one's approach to understanding the data of observation—in this instance, the dream.[3] With regard to the broad motivational and organizational forces behind

[2] A self-psychological approach to the understanding of dreams does not exclude the recognition of the presence or influence or effect in the dream of drives or conflicts over drives. It does position them, however, within the larger framework of the organization of the self.

[3] To paraphrase myself (Tolpin, 1980), it is not usual and perhaps not possible for one to have "a mind of winter"—that is, to be utterly free of personal reactions or acquired theories regarding scientific, much less everyday, observations.

the dream process, dreams informed by the psychology of the self might be called *self-psychological dreams*, in contrast to dreams informed by the drive-defense model of the mind, which are in essence (drive) wish-fulfillment dreams.[4]

Returning to the issue with which I began this paper—the misunderstanding about self-state dreams and the interpretation of self psychological dreams in general—I believe it has become clear by now that self-state dreams as Kohut originally described them are not the only kind of dream that can be explored by the use of the conceptual framework of the psychology of the self. It has probably also become apparent that self-state dreams constitute only a relatively small portion of those dreams that can be understood by the use of the self-psychological framework. The self-state dream is to self psychology what the dreams of the traumatic neuroses and their like are to structural psychology. There are other types of self-psychological dreams, for example, the idealizing self-selfobject dream of the second patient described here. The difference between the self-state dream and other self-psychological dreams, as noted earlier, is that in the former the self is at the edge of disorganization or is experiencing some less drastic change in its prior state of balance. The observing sectors of the self react to this change with responses ranging from fragmentation panic and energy depletion to relatively mild shifts of mood.

If one were to require a term for self-psychological dreams that would differentiate them from dreams associated with the framework of classical structural analysis, one might designate them *self-selfobject* dreams. That term indicates the crucial role of the "relationship" of the self to the selfobject, regardless of how archaic or mature the self-selfobject experience in the dream is found to be. However, we have put forth the notion that the overriding theoretical framework by way of which the "data of observation" are apperceived determines the understanding of the latent dream thoughts. Self-state dreams and self-selfobject dreams, then, are both part of a theoretical system organized by the guiding framework of the psychology of the self, and both are thus simply varieties of self-psychological dreams.

---

[4] I have not abandoned the idea of the supraordinate position of the self here, but, as Kohut (1977, pp. 96–97) has suggested, if the essential stability of the self is not at issue in a particular instance, it need not be taken into account as a crucial focus of attention in a particular moment of analytic work.

References

Freud, S. (1900), *The Interpretation of Dreams, Standard Edition*, 4 & 5. London: Hogarth Press, 1953.

———— (1914), On narcissism: An introduction, *Standard Edition*, 14:67–102. London: Hogarth Press, 1957.

———— (1916–17), *Introductory Lectures on Psychoanalysis, Standard Edition*, 16. London: Hogarth Press, 1963.

———— (1920), Beyond the pleasure principle, *Standard Edition*, 18:1–64. London: Hogarth Press, 1955.

———— (1923), Remarks on the theory and practice of dream interpretation, *Standard Edition*, 19:107–121. London: Hogarth Press, 1961.

———— (1929), Some dreams of Descartes, *Standard Edition*, 21:197–204. London: Hogarth Press, 1961.

Kohut, H. (1971), *The Analysis of the Self*. New York: International Universities Press.

———— (1977), *The Restoration of the Self*. New York: International Universities Press.

Tolpin, P. (1980), Letter to the editor, *J. Philadelphia Assn. Psychoanal.*, 7:1–12.

Construction, Reconstruction, and the Mode of Clinical Attunement

EVELYNE SCHWABER

John Archibald Wheeler, the eminent physicist and colleague of Einstein, describing the impact of the era of relativity on our thinking, has written: "What is so hard is to give up thinking of nature as a machine that goes on independent of the observer. What we conceive of as reality is a few iron posts of observation with papier-mâché construction between them that is but the elaborate work of our imagination. . . . For our picture of the world, this is the most revolutionary thing discovered. . . . We still have not come to terms with it" (quoted in Begley, 1979).

Louis Sander, the eminent infant researcher and psychoanalyst, has described the impact of modern-day biology and systems research as follows: "A major difficulty in conceptualizing at the psychological level [has arisen] from a tendency to view the organization of behavior as the property of the individual rather than as the property of the more inclusive system of which the individual is a part." He notes a shift toward the perspective that "the concept of the 'unity of the organism' relates to an organism functioning in its proper environment" (1975,

This paper was presented at panel of the American Psychoanalytic Association on "Construction and Reconstruction: Clinical Aspects," San Francisco, May 4, 1980. The issues discussed here are further considered in Schwaber, 1981.

273

p. 147). This represents "a major turning point in developmental research" (personal communication).

This shifting perspective on the observation of phenomena in modern biology, physics, and developmental research represents the point of view I would like to offer for the gathering of psychoanalytic data. This perspective views the organization of behavior and intrapsychic experience not as the "property of the individual," but rather as the "property of the more inclusive system" of which the individual is a part. It holds that we do not know things in themselves—we can only know in a patient's inner world that which *we* perceive. The world we perceive must include ourselves as perceiver. So, too, the patient's perceptual world must be understood in the context of his or her perception of us; we can only know that perception insofar as it includes us, rather than as a phenomenon "that goes on independent" of us. What are the implications of this idea for analytic listening?

If, as analysts we were to assume the position of the "outside" observer, we would define some objective reality against which we might then judge the patient's perceptions, taking them to represent some other, an intrapsychic reality. Thus, we might consider the patient's perceptions (expressed as transference) "distorted," perhaps through the input of instinctual and affect-laden wishes and the defenses against them. The analyst who takes the position of the observer from "within," however, holds that phenomena may only be ascertained within the subjective view of that observer. This view would consider spurious the attempt to divide an inner reality from a "real" reality and the notion that we can ultimately disengage our "real" selves from the patient's psychic view of us. The transference, as the expression of the patient's reality, is the only reality that is our task to ascertain. Rather than being viewed as a distortion to be modified, it is seen as a perception to be recognized and articulated, in the hope that it may facilitate a deeper entry into the patient's inner world. Although the psychological impact of this perception and the meaning and response assigned to it will be a reflection of the analytic moment and may shift in accordance with that moment, this does not mean we must question the validity of the perception. We will, to be sure, still need to check the patient's perceptions and view of reality against our own, but this is primarily to maintain vigilance against the superimposition of our view, which often may be conveniently rationalized as our theoretical stance.

The emphasis here conveyed, then, is that the organization of the patient's immediate experience, whatever the intrapsychic stirrings within him or her, will be influenced, perhaps to a profound degree, by the patient's perception of the analyst and the surround, and by the meanings assigned to those perceptions.[1] Understood in this way, the analytic focus on the emergence of some affect state, presenting fantasy or other content, or on a defensive stance may be seen as a vital clue to a silent or as yet undefined perception of the analyst and to the relationship between that perception and the nature of the patient's response. Thus, accepting the perceptual validity of the patient's experience of the analyst or of anyone else in his or her world permits a retracing of the history of the patient's perceptual world and the meanings assigned to it as well as of the patterns of responses and affective impact associated with it. All these relationships are continually shifting, yet maintain an inherent continuity. It is this history of the interplay of the patient's perceptual world and inner experiences (feelings and fantasies)—particularly the *impact* of that perceptual world on the inner experience—that engages our efforts at construction and reconstruction. What is then reconstructed is a view of the past, not as an objectively held reality, but as a subjective experience, whose meaning is to be understood within the momentary context of the presence of the analyst—that is, the patient's experience and perception of the analyst. As this context shifts, so too may the reconstruction.

Utilizing this point of view as a way of listening would lead to a heightened attention to the surround, to the analyst's contribution—whether silent or stated—and to its immediate experiential impact. It implies a sharpened focus on aspects of shifts in affect or state, bringing certain nonverbal phenomenology under heightened illumination. This sharpened look at the context does not

[1] Such a view is consonant with the early writings of Kohut, as in "Introspection, Empathy, and Psychoanalysis" (1959), in which he notes the presence of the empathic or introspective observer as defining, in principle, the psychological field. I have recently expressed my concern about the apparent shift in direction away from Kohut's early emphasis on the mode of depth-psychological data gathering to that on theoretical preference (Schwaber, 1981, 1982).

skew the focus to the "outside"; rather, it deepens what we can see of the experience "inside."

I should like to illustrate this with some clinical material from each of two cases which I have presented at greater length elsewhere (Schwaber, 1979, 1980). I will try to detail some of the patients' words and my own, to facilitate the readers' entry with me into the analytic moment. The readers may then draw their own inferences as to how the patient may have perceived me and how I may have been listening. My focus will be on the listening perspective and its influence on the understanding of the emerging material and on the kinds of data that are highlighted thereby. Based on this, I will also consider the process of construction and reconstruction.

Mr. R., a young man in his early twenties, was referred to me as an exceptionally gifted photographer who was unable to proceed with his work because of somatic symptoms—stomach distress, headaches, and dizziness, for which no organic etiology had been found. He also complained of a feeling of "detachment"—an uncomfortable, sometimes frightening sense of being very far removed from things. He did not complain of any difficulties in relationships. Although he noticed that his symptoms had begun to disturb him at the time of a recent move away from home, the patient later realized that fleeting moments of such symptomatology might have occurred for years—indeed, as far back as he could remember.

Mr. R., a pleasant-looking young man with a golden brown hue to his moderately long hair and full beard, spoke with no visible manifestation of anxiety, or for that matter, any shifting affective response. Though direct, friendly, and thoughtful, he could also be described as "detached"—echoing his own description of his inner experience.

Mr. R. remembered little of the first thirteen years of his life—just vaguely outlined images of housekeepers taking care of him when his parents were away, and of disappointing his father by coming home early from summer camp because he was unhappy there. He began to consider, in the early face-to-face hours, that there had been a shift in his development sometime around age thirteen. From being weak, unathletic, and shy, he had become strikingly more competent, with new-found abilities in gymnastics, film development, and music. He conjectured that he might still have a less confident "self" underneath that he was afraid to discover. Indeed, whenever he attempted to look at pictures or listen to tape recordings of himself before the age of thirteen, he experienced unbearable dizziness and other of his somatic symptoms. In some profound way, he felt no continuity with the part of himself that was a child.

Mr. R. spoke spontaneously of father and of his strong wish to please him. He felt a similarity with him, his easy-going manner, his pursuit of numerous hobbies. His mother, on the other hand, was never mentioned in his early hours, unless I asked about her directly. Then he described her and his relationship with her with one word: "fine," adding that "she's easy to get along with, though tending to be on my father's side in an argument." He literally had nothing more to say about her. When I wondered about this, he said he simply felt, "That's all there is."

Although the absence of the mother in such an early communication may have any number of meanings, the message, "that's all there is" may convey in the present context an experiential absence of the mother. This might have bearing, therefore, on the patient's feeling of detachment. Mr. R.'s comments about his older sister were similarly unspontaneous and seemingly lacking in conflict; so, too, were his descriptions of his girlfriends.

Mr. R. entered analysis seeking help in pursuing his career goal of becoming a filmmaker; however, he had great trepidation about the likelihood of having to return to his childhood years. Once on the couch, his symptoms often proved quite distressing to him—dizziness, a feeling of gastric hyperacidity, or a fear of losing control emerged.

Mr. R. often talked about the importance of photography to him, speaking with vivid imagery and, on this subject, with great affective involvement:

I can remember way back even, having the experience of elation. I can remember it being triggered by how it might look photographically, as in a beautiful scene, or in music. When I see something that looks good, there is a very strong desire to take a picture and kind of freeze it there, as with a beautiful sunset. It's an experience of all of a sudden my sensibilities becoming really heightened, like I'll notice the pores of someone's skin and it looks great, and I want to take a picture and catch it. . . . I know a psychiatrist who became interested in photography and took it up more and more . . . on his vacations . . . finally giving up psychiatry . . .

Since my own vacation was imminent, and Mr. R. had made no reference to it, I said, "I wonder if my vacation may have been stirring such thoughts, of my waning interest in my profession." Mr. R. responded, "I'm not sure how to understand what you mean. I'm thinking of the joke of the two psychiatrists meeting in an elevator. I wonder if you know the joke, and if you do, will you answer." He spoke more slowly. "I think you responded defensively to the idea of a psychiatrist switching to photography . . . I didn't mean to be critical . . ."

Mr. R's train of associations seemed to be derailed; his words came more slowly and haltingly and trailed off. Somehow we had gotten off the track. The session was over then; as he walked out I noticed that he avoided looking at me, and his body seemed strikingly shrunken in its stance.

One might consider that I touched here on an area of anxiety about separation that was profoundly resisted, and that is why the patient responded as he did. But even if this were so, the specific trigger of his response included a perception of me—how it felt to him that I said what I did when I did. Perhaps this was a historically meaningful recreation.

What, then, had he felt about my comment? He saw me as defensive—meaning that, from his vantage point, I seemed to be responding out of my own needs or concerns. He mentioned the joke of the two psychiatrists. There are several such jokes, perhaps with similar messages; I assumed he was referring to the one about the psychiatrist who, being told "Good morning" by a colleague, thinks, "I wonder what he means by that." The idea, as I see it now, is that the first psychiatrist is so caught up in his own work and ideology as to be unable to comprehend the point of view of the person relating to him. But I did not yet understand this.

In subsequent hours, Mr. R. spoke of his girlfriend, complaining that she seemed interested primarily in her own work and hardly at all in his. Only much later, when he began to refer more specifically to his mother, did he begin to recall his sense of her lack of involvement in *his* interest in photography and films—a kind of self-preoccupation that he experienced from her. When I responded to him with the issue of my profession and my vacation, I was recreating this old injury. The shrunken stance, the avoidance of eye contact, the halting speech—all aspects of detachment—lent specificity to his response to his perception of me, made in the context of having to defend against certain feelings stirred within him. These specific responses further indicated how he experienced himself in that early, forgotten, dizzying childhood world.

In one hour, the patient came in complaining that he felt his girlfriend didn't seem to like him, that she wasn't touching him very much, and so he didn't feel talkative. Words came slowly and gradually trailed off. He paused. I said nothing, and then he said he had been hearing music and listening to it silently. I asked him to say more about this, and he reflected, "It seems I heard the music when I was waiting for you to comment and you didn't." What was he waiting for from me, and what did my silence mean to him? As he thought about it now, he had felt "untouched" by me, too; and, feeling that he needed soothing, he chose an old familiar pathway which he now shared with me: listening to music. This was an auditory mode, as my words would have been, albeit on an imaginary level.

I learned then how he had turned to music in childhood to ease his feeling of isolation and insignificance. Again, it may be likely that he was retreating along a familiar course from threatening feelings toward me. But it was my acceptance and elucidation of his perception of me—of my silence as "untouching" at a moment when he felt some heightened need for my responsiveness—that enabled us to reconstruct the contextual sense of the childhood experience and of the pathway that he had found as a way out. Music (like the Brahms to which he was "listening" on the couch) was something his father loved. Listening to music in the hour, then, offered a symbolic representation of a comforting connection to his father, especially sought, perhaps, in the wake of such painful feelings. (Toward the end of his analytic work, I was to learn of the role music had for him when his parents went on trips in the first few years of his life—perhaps a very early tie to mother.)

Much later in the analysis, when Mr. R. began to consider sexual feelings within the transference, we could see that this kind of shift in the direction of his thoughts—often to photography—also occurred when these feelings—particularly the sense of them as unrequited—were stirred up. We also saw a parallel in the sustaining haven his photographic darkroom afforded him, especially in his adolescence.

It seemed then, that we were picking up clues about Mr. R.'s pathological interaction with his mother, often through rather subtle nuances. This might indicate that the patient's difficulty with her was an elusive one that could have been overlooked by the casual observer and perhaps also by the child, particularly as there had been little overt conflict. If so, it could have been all the more insidious in not affording the child opportunity for anger or for differentiation of what was his own experience, leading thereby to a diffuse sense of helplessness.

For example, Mr. R. described the following dream: "I was standing on a street corner . . . Two kids were threatening me, pulling a gun out. It turned out to be just a toy gun. . . . [In his associations] the kids feel like me, that I feel very threatened by my own childhood, . . . my fear of vomiting that I had as a child. . . ." He was by now somewhat more able to tolerate affectively experienced remembering, and he recalled:

> This brings up a sadness about my life again . . . I remember a time I vomited, then I felt better. I was carried upstairs by my mother, and I asked, "Am I going to miss Lassie [on TV]?" The sad feeling seems to be from thinking about my saying that, like I need to reject that I said that, almost that I can't accept that I was once a little kid . . . That question I asked of my mother . . . my sounding so cute . . .

I found myself jarred out of the experience he was evoking, and I interrupted: "Cute? You had conveyed it was sad." "Yes, well," he answered, "the word 'cute' seems appropriate . . . sort of like 'cute' belongs to what a child feels." I responded, "Oh, so this is like the weapons that turn out to be toys, a kind of negation of the validity, of the intensity of the feelings a child may have." Mr. R. interrupted excitedly, as he did whenever it seemed to him that I had recognized something which he felt touched the essence of his experience. "Exactly! Children's feelings are not taken very seriously. . . . I can easily imagine someone's saying, 'Oh, that's cute,' and kind of laughing at the child."

Sander (1975, 1980) has written about children's developmental need to have their perceptions and experiences validated and given credence in order to attain an inner sense of certainty about the centrality of their own experience. Translated to the analytic situation, of course, this does not mean offering external or "objective" corroboration; rather, it is a validation of an internal state. Now, deepening his own attention to the nature of his inner states, Mr. R. began to notice a quality of vagueness, which he felt had perhaps always been with him.

This is what made our transference focus on the nuances of his responses to me so essential—because he could accept my interpretations, even work with them, but only out of his own uncertainty. Had we not elucidated his state of vagueness or uncertainty, Mr. R. could have used my interpretations, like his mother's response of "cute," as offering some definition, but not affirming his own reality.

As he gradually attained a sense of inner conviction about his own feeling states, Mr. R. could look more closely at the painful imagery of his mother and its relation to the more global sense of his childhood; he could also see how his symptomatology appeared with the evocation of such an image. He was, for example, exquisitely sensitive to the "look" on people's faces, on my face—perhaps especially so as a photographer. If he saw a look that seemed to him "kind of neutral, indifferent," or "like, 'are you crazy?' " he would "get a feeling that I would lose something." Later, he was to say, "It is like mother's looks, like when I'd talk of my excitement about movies . . . or, like when you ask about her disapproval, I get a hint of that indescribable feeling I get in thinking of my childhood . . . a kind of sorrow . . . It's sort of like a physical feeling . . . It's kind of like the bottom falls out of everything . . . I get dizzy."

Once he described the following scene:

When I was home recently and my mother was very upset about

my sister, I was thinking of putting both arms around her . . . That seemed too much while my father was watching . . . I eventually put one arm on her shoulder, but even that was hard to do. *She seemed so far away* . . . crying, neither of us moving . . . She was more separate from us than I would have liked . . . That statement seems to have frightened me . . . I can't remember now what I said, as though I haven't said it . . . but I can recreate the detachment . . .

Here we could see more directly the poignant links between the experience of the mother as so distant, the memory lapse, and the detachment. We can see how this occurred at a moment when, perhaps, threatening oedipal strivings were stirred, resulting in a defensive retreat. But it was the sense of the patient's more engaged, much-needed father and of his far-away mother that lent contextual specificity to our reconstruction of the form and imagery of his oedipal constellation.

In the course of our work together, each of Mr. R.'s parents emerged in more complexity. Mr. R. also came to recognize and to tolerate a deepening range of varying affective experiences, relinquishing the somatic expressions, both within and outside the transference. "I see now how detachment is loneliness made physical," he said. "Feeling anger, instead of vagueness or detachment, is new," he said another time. "Loving feelings—toward you . . . I had a dream of feeling your arms around my neck and you kissed me, and I turned around and kissed you . . . I wasn't so self-conscious . . . I didn't need to be so in control . . . I see now how shallow my responses to women had been and how now I am able to be concerned with their feelings . . ."

And so Mr. R. could allow to surface and to feel as his own, many childhood memories and even some dreams, which lent further tangibility to the quality of the experiences he had been conveying: his enuresis, for which an electrical mattress device was used; wetting his pants at school; the hives he had on a train ride to camp; being told not to cry during a separation; being left alone in hotel rooms on family trips; his ambivalent relationship with his sister; and other memories. Looking more closely at those first thirteen years, he described "a feeling of a continuity between my life, myself, then and now."

I shall not detail further the distances we traversed in the course of Mr. R.'s analysis. In the external world, his relationships deepened and became more intimate; he went on to become a successful film-maker; his symptoms abated. But it was the inner shift that he felt which was the most intense for him: "Remembering now that scared little boy at camp, with the lump in his throat," he said, in his last analytic hours. "It feels good to remember, without dizziness, feeling connected to him . . . I feel sad that I'm going to miss this, but I also feel excited . . . There's a pride I have in having feelings . . . The difference in me is incredible between how I was when I first came here and now . . ."

Not having ever in fact experienced it, Mr. R. imagined how it might feel to be taking off a cast. The idea of the cast, a device for healing a broken body part, may be understood on multiple levels of meaning; it seemed to us, it had also to do with his having reunited his first thirteen years together with the rest, reconnecting his inner experience on a continuum—perhaps the ultimate aim and meaning of reconstruction.

Mrs. G. was thirty-eight years old when she first came to see me. Married to a successful lawyer, she was the mother of three children. Mrs. G. centered her work around home and family. She sought help for feelings of worthlessness, shyness, anxiety and inability to study despite wanting to do graduate work. Tall, thin, with dark, long hair, dressed in somewhat Bohemian fashion, Mrs. G. was articulate and soft-spoken; she seemed rather intelligent, though there was something about her appearance and her manner that was not particularly engaging.

She was an only child, born in poverty to immigrant parents to whom she did not feel close. She described her relationship to her grandfather as the best part of her childhood. Although her marriage had had some stormy times, Mrs. G. said that she and her husband had always enjoyed an intense sexual relationship, which was the best and binding part of the marriage. The patient felt quite comfortable and generally pleased with her children, although it was very important to her to be different than her own mother. Space does not permit me to present an overview of her history, but I shall highlight some particular aspects of our work together, to further illustrate certain dimensions of the listening stance I am trying to convey.

From the first sessions, Mrs. G. asked me many questions about myself, and I reflected on her seeming wish to know about me personally. She considered this: "I always felt the need to find someone who had experienced things like me, especially a parental figure. As a child I always felt myself to be an oddball, different from peers and from parents . . . Mother had black hair, was short, heavy. She used to think I was an odd egg . . ."

In contrast to the experience with Mr. R., Mrs. G.'s mother was consistently present in her associations. In the early hours, she emerged as a frightening, alien figure: "Mother envies me, would take from me or spoil what I have—like a dark fungus . . . I always felt she would hex me. She was riddled with anxiety and could never touch with any comfort . . ."

Despite this unfolding imagery, I often had difficulty in understanding the quality that Mrs. G. was trying to convey, of the present-day injuries inflicted by the mother. When she described mother's words, they didn't seem to communicate to me the terrible feelings they evoked in the patient. For example, when the patient learned to drive, her mother remarked, "Isn't it wonderful, you learned to drive a car!" Mrs. G. felt wounded, "shattered" by this. She said it felt as though her mother was again responding to only a part of her, rather than to the *whole* of her, which would have included other feelings, such as the fear and anxiety that go with learning to drive.

Thus, there was a discrepancy between the image she portrayed and the one she experienced—at least, I had some difficulty in understanding her experience. I thought about the possibility that Mrs. G. may have had defensive reasons for insisting on a negative image, and I knew she sought an ally against her mother. But such an explanation did not arise from the experiential immediacy of the data offered in the hour by the patient. It was clear to me that I was making an extra effort to seek an explanation out of my own wish to bridge the gap I felt in my capacity to gain attunement. Perhaps, as with the response evoked by Mr. R.'s phrase, "that's all there is," the very difficulty I was having could be seen as meaningful in its own right. We might then consider that the "injuries" felt to be inflicted by the mother lay in her quality of *being*, rather than in the words she chose. This may suggest that the original pathologic interaction, which is "telescoped" into these latter-day incidents, took place very early developmentally—even going back to preverbal communications. Further, the sense of discrepancy I experienced in listening to the patient's communications may offer a clue about difficulty others might have in following her. This might help us to understand the isolation and aloneness Mrs. G. felt in social interaction, particularly with women, and might tell us why her search for experiential similarity between us seemed so crucial.

There is another dimension to my difficulty in trying to make sense out of the imagery Mrs. G. conveyed. It related to my feeling that I so often seemed to lose her—I had to grope and struggle to find my place in *her* experiential world, while still trying to maintain my own self-reflective vigil; for there was a quality of affectlessness about Mrs. G., a kind of lifelessness, with no manifest warmth. Unfortunately, I often became aware only in retrospect that I had been impatient, fatigued, or bored. Perhaps these were in some way self-protective withdrawals, *out* of the intense immersion in her experience. Often, the clues to such responses on *my* part were subtle shifts in the patient's communications, such as a change in tone, sounding more mechanical, or a shift in the style of her stream of associations. Her intense sensitivity to my responsiveness seemed to indicate that maintaining "connectedness"—part of her search for experiential similarity—was a central issue for Mrs. G. Indeed, her often-stated wish for direct dialogue with me was a further clue to that felt need. For the analytic work to take place in an affectively meaningful way, the vicissitudes of this issue had to become a central focus.

"I'm thinking of this lovely poem in *Ms.* magazine," she said in one session. "Did you read it? Do you know the poem I mean?" There was a seeming urgency to her questions. "Such a strong wish, to have me answer directly," I said to her. "Can we look at what that means?" "There is something to that," she replied. She paused, then noted:

I—feel—now a strangeness about myself—alone—different. That's why I don't write; it's not mutual . . . not mutual makes me feel strange. It's like coming home from school and telling my mother what happened; she'd just sit there and listen, like from another world. Something about asking you if you read that poem is like that. It would have been so nice growing up if mother had said, 'Yes, I had the same experience; I know about that.' My mother never told me things like that . . . like she grew up in a big fishtank different from mine. If you had said something about the poem, I'd have felt better. Otherwise, I get this goldfish-in-the-tank feeling. One looks at it, admires it, feeds it. What I'm saying is I want to get out of the bowl.

Later she was to say, "When I ask you what you've read, what you've seen, it is really, 'Do you experience the same bodily feelings I do?' " Thus, in the patient's response to my not having answered her questions directly, we saw the recreation of an early perception of her mother, who did not communicate a sense of experiential same-ness with her little girl.

Early imagery of mother's intense anxiety about the child's body emerged: "She worried about my hair, got me orthopedic shoes, pad-ded bras . . ." Mrs. G. also told of the enemas she had been given until she was about age seven as a remedy for illness—further adding to her uncertainty about the integrity of her bodily experiences and sensations. She recalled the "seemingly endless," lonely childhood and adolescent masturbation. "Masturbating gave me a clearer sense of myself . . . It was a way to really feel my own body, but it also made me feel shame and terror."

In the course of the analysis, Mrs. G. began to feel more socially outgoing. She spoke with apparent pleasure one day of a project at her children's school in which she was involved. Her thoughts shifted to her fear of being successful, and it was this fear—the shift in her thoughts away from the new step rather than the initial pleasure in her feeling about herself as a woman—to which we then turned our at-tention. Suddenly she saw the walls in my office as further away, the objects in the room as smaller. She experienced a sense of spatial disorientation. She began to recall this symptom as one familiar to her from her childhood and a few occasions since then. She knew the name, micropsia. She could remember experiencing it at around age five or six; she could see the image of her mother standing in the doorway to her room at night in the darkness, sometimes holding an enema bag, sometimes when she was masturbating—a sense of her mother's "hovering, evil presence"—so small and so distant.

Dreams of spatial disorientation or disconnection then came to increased prominence, such as finding herself on a different train from her children, or of being outside a space capsule in outer space. I learned that Mrs. G. was told that her mother did not touch her very much as a baby and propped up her bottle for greater "sterility." We had yet to understand the specific meaning of the recurrence of the micropsia with me.

Sometime after Mrs. G. had begun a new job, she spoke about how successful she felt at work, and then began to compare her work with mine. I wondered, in the context of the emerging material, if she was perhaps thinking about surpassing me and whether that might not stir up a familiar conflict. The micropsia recurred. In accordance with the view that the transference included the *experience* of the meaning of my remarks as an *integral* part of the recreated past,[2] I also wondered how my comments, interwoven with her experience, led to the micropsia. Mrs. G. answered:

> Whenever I shared anything with my mother that I felt good about, she'd say something to take it away, some comment directing me elsewhere, whenever I showed something off to her. What just happened with you happened with mother all the time. I was sharing with you my most *adult* self, and you talked about a conflict; like suddenly in barges my mother and takes it away.

Thus, we could begin to reconstruct how the micropsia became a defensive choice, weaving the little girl's affect-laden competitive and growth-oriented strivings with her perceptions of the responses to them. The symptom recreated the disorienting imagery of the darkened room where it first appeared, the bodily confusion evoked by the enemas and expressed in the patient's masturbation experience, and the sense of spatial disconnectedness from the either "intrusive," or

[2] See Myers (1977), for an alternate view. See also Schwaber, 1981.

"untouching" mother who was felt as somehow negating the child's blossoming feminine strivings. The symptom, then, represented a particular phenomenon to be observed and given *meaning* in the presence of the analyst. More specifically, it was the analyst who was felt to be nonaccepting of Mrs. G.'s wish to share herself and who was felt to have questioned the patient's very sense of her femaleness.

"I used to have the sense," she later said,

> like I wasn't completely female . . . When I got my period, it was like despite the fact that I'm not really a woman . . . Like they were all sitting around waiting for my breasts to develop . . . If Mother discovered an injury, she'd be wildly upset . . . One time [during the course of analysis], after I hurt my foot, I had a dream in which I experienced myself as being like all wire and cardboard. When I woke up I felt all elbows and awkward. . . . Lying next to Alan [her husband] made me feel soft. . . . Love-making makes me feel so good about my whole body grace . . ."

We could then see how Mrs. G.'s earlier anxiety about the integrity of her body became a part of her uncertainty about herself as a woman. As she attained some resolution of her conflictual feelings about her femaleness, she began to express her sexual and competitive strivings with an increasing sense of inner confidence. Her feelings about herself as one woman *to* or *versus* another, with a man in between, emerged in the transference at a point at which she felt more hopeful. Even if she should still perceive a "negating" response, she no longer felt the intense risk of an ensuing disorienting state.

Mrs. G. felt freed from the sense of urgent dependence on her husband's physical presence. She became able to expose and deepen her recollections of her relationships to men in the past and to effect some shifts in the present. New dimensions of the father and grandfather emerged, as affectively rich childhood memories and romantic fantasies came into sharper focus. Other views of the mother also arose; the mother's own life and pain were reconsidered with some empathic grasp. The patient was, in a sense, offering "multiple histories" (Schafer, 1979).

Mrs. G.'s appearance, her manner and dress had been gradually and subtly changing—becoming softer, more graceful, more engaging. She had by now begun her graduate studies, at which she was quite successful.

Again, whatever memories emerged, whatever childhood pieces were reconstructed, they were seen in relation to the shifting view of herself and of me. Following a change I had made in the appointment time, she told me:

I had a dream in which you made a mistake and I held your face closer and it was cute, and we both felt tolerant of your mistake. There was a moment in the dream when I had a realization of how much things were now making more sense . . . how much I was able to change my view of reality from a confused unknown, to one I understand . . . Like the way I changed my view of you—from hostile, mysterious, to uncryptic and comfortable—even when you make a mistake.''

"Now I can see," she said another time, "how I used to pursue anything you commented on, just to stay connected; it wouldn't matter what." (I felt that statement told me that had I not been attentive to the way in which she was perceiving and thereby responding to me—then no matter what we had talked of, it would have lacked specificity and realness.) "Like with my husband," she continued, "I see how I had been so exquisitely tuned into Alan's moods; now I can initiate my own. I can see now what is his reality and what is mine."

"I'm feeling something now that I never did experience in this way," she said in her last analytic hour, ". . . good about you and good about myself . . . I hope you know that I care and have a continuing sense of that—my caring—as something that I would give to you . . . Being touched intimately within my mind, I'll keep that . . . However it was that my parents didn't know me, so I somehow didn't get to know me . . . I'll keep on working on it."

There were, to be sure, many questions and uncertainties in my work with Mrs. G. and Mr. R. that I have not discussed here, for they would take us in other directions. I have chosen these two patients, in whom certain striking similarities were manifest, not as representative of a particular kind of psychopathology, but rather to illustrate a mode of clinical attunement. I believe that the vicissitudes of such phenomena as feelings of connectedness, realness, autonomy, and spatial or temporal orientation, speak to issues and patterns of early development that are ubiquitous—although individually organized. These issues emerge more systematically because of the mode of attunement.

Further, the heightened emphasis on the impact that the context has on the nature of experiencing brings into sharper focus the role of the early milieu, of the early parenting figures and their relationship to the organization of each developmental phase. It is not the personalities of the "actual" parents that we attempt to reconstruct, but the patterns of subjectively experienced relationships and responses, seeking to articulate the perception of the "outer" as it forms an integral part of the experience of the "inner." I believe this highlighting of the immediate, experiential significance of the moment of perception brings to our patients the sense of having gained a more vigorous sense of reality.

In summary, this paper has considered the concepts of construction and reconstruction from the vantage point of the mode of clinical attunement. Drawing on the view that perception is a vital component of intrapsychic reality, the analyst pays particular attention to the impact of perceptual cues on the organization of the patient's immediate experience. Thus, greater emphasis is given to certain aspects of nonverbal phenomenology, such as shifts in affect or state, that offer salient clues to perceptions of the analyst or of the surround. The emergence of some presenting fantasy or other content or a defensive stance—for example, the appearance of a symptom—may also be seen as clues to such a perception. Transference, then, rather than a distortion to be modified, is understood as a perception to be recognized and articulated. The patient's subjective reality is thereby more scrupulously viewed as our sole *psychoanalytic* concern rather than including the perspective of the analyst's own views of "objective" reality, which is implicitly introduced in assessing the "reality" of the patient's perceptions.

The objective of such close attunement to the analytic moment is to serve not as an interactive experience in its own right, but as an avenue for deeper recognition of the patient's intrapsychic world and thus as a pathway for reconstruction. When the patient sharpens his own attunement to inner states and perceptions, he begins to recognize them as familiar and as having historical relevance. The patient is then more likely to initiate the rediscovery of his own history, enriched by the contextual specificity of the perceptual world in which his development unfolded. Thus, there will be less need for inferential leaps on the analyst's part, while the patient feels a deeper conviction of his own sense of reality.

References

Begley, S. (1979), Probing the universe. *Newsweek*, March 12.

Kohut, H. (1959), Introspection, empathy, and psychoanalysis: An examination of the relationship between mode of observation and theory. In: *The Search for the Self*, ed. P. H. Ornstein. New York: International Universities Press, 1978, pp. 205–232.

Myers, W. (1977), Micropsia and testicular retractions. *Psychoanal. Quart.*, 46:580–604.

Sander, L. (1975), Infant and caretaking environment: Investigation and conceptualization of adaptive behavior in a system of increasing complexity. In: *Explorations in Child Psychiatry*, ed. E. J. Anthony. New York: Plenum Press, pp. 129–166.

————, reporter (1980), Panel on New knowledge about the infant from current research: Implications for psychoanalysis. *J. Amer. Psychoanal. Assn.*, 28:181–198.

Schafer, R. (1979), The appreciative analytic attitude and the construction of multiple histories. *Psychoanal. Contemp. Thought*, 2:3–24.

Schwaber, E. (1979), Reflections on the analysis of Mrs. G.: A clinical illustration—In consideration of a particular perspective for analytic listening. Presented at a conference on Narcissism, sponsored by the University of California at Los Angeles Extension Division, October.

———— (1980), Self psychology and the concept of psychopathology: A case presentation, and Reply to Paul Topin. In: *Advances in Self Psychology*, ed. A. Goldberg. New York: International Universities Press, pp. 215–243 and 253–262.

———— (1981), Empathy: A mode of analytic listening. *Psychoanal. Inq.*, 1:357–392.

———— (1982), Psychoanalytic listening and psychic reality. Presented at a conference on Reconsiderations of Psychoanalytic Listening, sponsored by the Southern California Psychoanalytic Society, March.

On The Nature of the "Misfit"

Arnold Goldberg

Introduction

This essay seeks to describe and explain a particular form of character that has not heretofore received attention in the psychoanalytic literature: the misfit. Fenichel (1945) defined character as "the ego's habitual modes of adjustment to the external world, the id, and the superego, and the characteristic type of combining these modes with one another" (p. 467). Kernberg's (1970) addition to the accepted knowledge of character pathology was based on a consideration of "structural and genetic-dynamic [factors] in addition to purely descriptive ones" (p. 820). This paper will offer a developmental perspective, describing the misfit as a person in transition from one developmental stage to another, unable to either forge ahead or adapt successfully through retreat. Being a misfit has a certain universality since everyone has at some time had the experience of being in a situation and feeling he or she simply did not belong. Some individuals, however, have a chronic and pervasive subjective feeling of not being able to fit in; thus, we can examine this as a particular form of character pathology.

In discussing the manifestations of a person's character in analytic treatment, I would echo Freud's (1916) statement that "Peculiarities . . . which [the patient] seemed to possess only to a modest degree

293

are often brought to life in surprisingly increased intensity, or attitudes reveal themselves . . . which had not been betrayed in other relations of life" (p. 311). This emphasizes the fact that a psychoanalytic definition of character is less concerned with overt behavior or a phenomenological nosology and more with the analytic method for developing such a classification. Our focus is thus on the patient's subjective sense—the patient's feeling about himself or herself as it becomes revealed in the transference. One of the dilemmas of character classification is that it attempts to bridge intrapsychic and interpersonal considerations and thus may blur what should remain a primarily psychoanalytic method of organizing clinical material. Just as depression is a diagnosis that concentrates on the subjective sense of sadness rather than merely the objective listing of depressive features, so too, the psychoanalytic definition of the misfit conforms to this focus on the subjective.

Definition of Misfit

When Heinz Hartmann (1939) discussed adaptation as an individual's relation to "a typical average environment" (p. 16), he was emphasizing the coming together of ego and external world; and he underscored this as the basis of the concept of "health." To isolate the misfit as a person with a particular form of character pathology it is necessary at the outset to define the term primarily in its *subjective* sense as a feeling of not belonging, of not fitting in. Of course, this feeling need bear no relationship to how successfully such a person adapts to the environment in reality. Misfits are people who *feel* themselves alien to those around them and who, for a variety of reasons, fail to attain that comforting harmony that Hartmann felt was so essential for a designation of health. Their actual success in functioning is therefore subordinate to their lack of a sense of union and connectedness.

Misfits are defined in terms of their individual relationship to the larger group. As such they merit comparison to another characterological subgroup of Freud's: the "exceptions" (Freud, 1916). These are people who claim privilege over others because of suffering they experienced early in childhood, which they regard as an unjust disadvantage. Freud used the deformity of Richard III as an example of one such person who magnified an early wound or narcissistic injury into a privileged position and thus into exemption from "life's importunities." He likewise noted that women in general regard themselves as having been damaged in infancy and therefore feel continual embitterment and reproach toward their mother.)

My own clinical material deals with patients who have clearly and consistently felt exceptional and different as well as outside of things and apart from others. They did not belong, did not fit in, felt terribly excluded, and longed to lose themselves in the larger group. Although they clearly fit the superficial dynamics of the exception in having sustained a narcissistic injury that set them apart, there is also a distinct disparity in the degree of comfort with which misfits treated their difference. Some misfits relish the feeling of being a bit outside the ordinary. Others periodically experience the longing to belong. This dimension of indifference is one criterion of how one reacts to being different.

Misfits can also be seen as clustering at one end of a continuum of being exceptional and different. The issue of eccentricity or strangeness that partially characterizes the misfit places this individual on the end of the line extending from absolute conformity to the position of the bizarre outsider. One's exceptionality can be treated as a vice or a virtue, either appreciated or condemned by others. The relationship of the outsider to the inner group and its emotional tone further differentiates him or her. Nonbelongers may be talented, strange, freakish, etc., but these are further distinguished by their wish to be less so and by their longing for acceptance. The group that I have chosen to examine is thus characterized by a dual problem of eccentricity and exclusion. On some occasions, members of this group become resigned to this state of affairs, and even treat their exclusion with a "sour grapes" attitude. However, for the most part, this is a protective facade and soon gives way to the more painful longing to belong. In contrast to Freud's group, the feel both exceptional *and* underprivileged.

It would appear most natural or fitting to approach this topic from the positive; that is, to examine how one manages to achieve a feeling of belonging or group membership, rather than how one fails at this task. Such a study would entail an examination of certain functions having to do with the adaptation and modification of one's infantile needs in response to the harshness of reality, much as Hartmann has suggested. It would also concentrate on the development of those capacities that allow one to perform adequately with and among others, as well as upon the ability to control certain obnoxious characteristics and behavior.

This is not the point of view of this paper, however. The feeling of being a misfit has a special meaning for people, and the elucidation of this meaning is the goal here. The feeling of belonging is a positive accomplishment that is part of most people's normal development. The experience of not belonging is an equal partner in many of life's sequences. However, the ever-present sense of being an outsider who knows what to do and yet cannot do it, of being at a loss as to how to perform are states peculiar to the misfit.

Clinical Example

The clinical material that follows will be used to develop a possible generalization about misfits. Even though the misfit's state can rightfully be viewed as a universal phenomenon not peculiar to any sort of familiar diagnostic category, it is hoped that this analysis will reveal some principle or set of relationships particular to this condition. The case to be presented also serves to differentiate the "misfit" from Freud's "exceptions."

This is a case of a homosexual man who despised his sexual orientation, who longed to be heterosexual, and who entered analysis primarily because of his unhappiness over homosexuality. He presented a rather blatant case of someone who did not fit in, because he refused to belong to any sort of homosexual group, yet could not bring himself to an identification with heterosexuality. His sense of being "neither fish nor fowl" had its origin quite early in his life, and it went far beyond his sexual proclivity. Besides being the only son, in between an older and a younger sister, he was also a strikingly unusual child. Born into a family of blue-collar, high school graduates, the patient became a professional with an outstanding college record. He seemed different from his family in almost every conceivable way. His father was a gruff, beer-drinking, television-watching, factory worker. The patient loved music and fought with his parents to get violin lessons. He was bookish and sensitive and totally at odds with the interests of his family. To this day, his mother is never quite certain as to just what he does in his work, and she has an air of not quite comprehending that he is indeed her son.

The mother's difficulty in accepting her maternity seemed to be an issue early in this man's life. His mother seemed chained to her own mother, who seemed overtly psychotic and who was always at their home. The patient's mother had little time for her son. The patient always was fearful of his grandmother, and knew that he was intruding into the relationship between her and his mother whenever he wanted a little time and attention from his mother. He recalled being sent off repeatedly to play, at the early age of about 4 years, when this hardly was his desire or intent. Sometimes he would go upstairs to a neighbor's house to talk or to sit in the kitchen with her. He was a thin boy until about age 7½, when this neighbor moved away, and he began to eat a great deal. Although his sister was 8 years younger than he, he insisted that he felt the eating change was not due to her birth but to his having nowhere to go and no one to talk to. Overall, he recalled being quite anxious all through his childhood and strongly insisted that no one supervised him or paid much attention to him. It was evident in the transference, however, that he felt only certain aspects of him merited attention, while other parts of his personality were best left ignored.

The patient's sexual history seemed to parallel some of the key points of his life. He recalled the age of four years as the time when he looked at and touched little girls; and the age of eight years as when he began homosexual activity of a sort by grabbing and feeling other boys. He described how a classmate in grammar school later involved him in mutual masturbation. He said that he was afraid to tell the teacher and unable to resist the advances of the other child. He masturbated regularly and continually throughout high school. Later in the analysis he revealed that, as an adult, masturbation or going to pornographic movies was an almost daily occurrence. He was shocked to realize the all-consuming nature of his sexual preoccupation.

Apart from the mutual fondling in grammar school, which only lasted a short time, this patient's first homosexual behavior did not

occur until he was approximately twenty years of age. His first experience was not a pleasant one, but he soon became involved with
a young man who was his lover for several years before he started
analysis. Shortly before treatment began, their sexual life became
meager, and they drifted apart soon thereafter. The patient was unable
to attend homosexual bars since he felt horrified at the idea of being
identified as a homosexual. His sexual orientation was unknown to all
save a few close friends.

During the beginning of the analysis, the patient revealed another
form of sporadic sexual behavior that he found particularly distasteful.
This consisted of going to a particular and popular place in the park
where a number of men congregated nightly. Sex there was flagrant,
anonymous, and abbreviated. The people so totally lacked involvement
that no one knew or cared who was doing what to whom. The patient
was a completely passive sexual partner throughout the entire episode,
which filled him with disgust, yet he periodically felt drawn to the
place. This seemed to be a sexual display of his need to remain aloof
and struggle against more meaningful involvement.

He described his family in bitter terms, with the exception of his
older sister, who lived in California and whom he visited periodically.
She was happily married and had a daughter and a son. The patient
had less positive things to say about his younger sister, whom he
described as needy and miserable. Next to his grandmother, his most
negative description was saved for his father, who had died two years
before our first analytic meeting. The father had sustained a heart
attack some sixteen years earlier (when the patient was ten), and had
taken poor care of himself while relentlessly intimidating the family
with his illness and possible death. The patient was extremely angry
when discussing his father and commented that he had ''not yet buried
him.''

The patient's mother was initially described as sweet, passive,
and dependent on her own mother, who had died shortly before the
patient's father. This description of mother did not hold up in the
analysis, since every conversation with her was reported in exasperated
and frustrated words and tones. She had been ill several years previously and could speak only about herself, her operation, and her suffering. There were few visits between the two, but they spoke on the

telephone regularly. The patient did not see his mother as being much different than she was during his childhood, except that his hateful grandmother was no longer in the way—but something else was. On the few occasions when they seemed close it was because he was in the position of mothering her. As the analysis progressed, this relationship changed markedly, and he was able to create a situation in which his mother became more of a parent and even a friend.

This brief overview of the patient's history is intended as an orientation to the major points of the analysis that are pertinent to the consideration of the patient's picture of himself as a misfit. Similarly, the brief summary of the treatment will not be an all-inclusive case presentation, but will only highlight some salient points regarding the patient's character development.

The analysis progressed with relative ease. After a great deal of shame and embarrassment accompanying the exposure of the multitude of his sexual activities, the patient settled into a clear and intense father transference in which idealization played an important part. His relationships with others were passive and masochistic; and he complained bitterly about the mistreatment he felt that he endured from friends and colleagues. In the analysis he showed a deepening idealization of me and a quick change to incredible rage and subsequent sexualization at my failings and lack of concern. Missed appointments or weekend breaks usually resulted in homosexual acting out.

Over time, three phases of the relationship to the father were delineated. The first was that of periodic disruption of the relationship. This was most clearly related to the sexualization, which represented an attempt to harness severe excitement (Goldberg, 1975). Initially a rather common occurrence in analysis, the sexualization gradually diminished. When the patient was able to give up his daily, ritualized masturbation, he recalled for the first time an important experience that centered around the father's working nights and coming home in time to have breakfast with his son. When the father was late, the patient would be unable to wait because he would have to leave for school. At these times he would carefully watch the minute hand of the clock; and he would almost be in pain as the last minute ticked away, and he was forced to miss seeing his father. Often the father would bring home sweet rolls for breakfast and, on occasion, would bring a very special one that only the patient liked. The father did not always do this, but the patient remembered yearning for the special relationship with his father that that sweet roll represented. He also remembered that, for some reason, he never could ask his father to buy that special treat for him.

The second form of the relationship with the father was one of harmony. These recollections connected to increasing, long periods of equilibrium in the analysis. The patient recalled joining father on his many expeditions to sell certain wares, an extra business activity for the father, who wanted to be more than a mere factory worker. Some of the factors contributing to the patient's not fitting in are evident in the father's lack of contentment with his own lot in life.

The third relationship to the father was the most frightening for the patient and had to do with the lost and/or absent father. This issue always was in the air in analysis and was most likely to emerge during longer vacations. The patient likened his feeling about this to a feeling of falling apart and related it to both the father's heart attack and his death. The patient also recalled long periods of waiting quietly outside of father's door while he slept. The patient yearned for his father to awaken but feared his wrath if any noise woke him prematurely. This was the totally lost and then hated father. All of this was reexperienced and repeatedly interpreted in the analysis. After working through this paternal relationship, the analysis turned to the more frustrating one with the neglectful mother.

It may be of interest to try to explain why this man failed to gain a positive response from his mother. The interference offered by the grandmother was only one factor. Later we learned that his grandfather (the husband of this delusional woman) was an unusual person and perhaps even something of a misfit himself. He stayed away from the rest of his family, did his own work of carpentry in a private area of his house, and never seemed to be upset by the rantings of his wife. Her accusations against the grandfather were characteristic ones of jealousy and sexual betrayal; and it is small wonder that the patient's mother behaved in an unusual and apprehensive manner toward her father. She may have had a parallel transference toward her own son, considering him strange, unusual, and frightening. It would be too superficial an explanation, however, to say that the patient identified with the grandfather as a misfit and lived out maternal expectations. There is little doubt that eccentricity can serve to organize a personality, but such postures or "identities" are always social phenomena that need an in-depth psychological explanation. In this case, I concluded that the explanation lay in the fact that the patient was not properly mirrored by his mother, who could not free herself sufficiently from her own neurotic entanglements to do so adequately. Then, of necessity, the patient turned from her to his father, seeking an avenue for self-expression and development.

Coexisting with all of the analytic work relating to the idealizing and disappointing relationship with the father was the patient's ever-present fear that the analysis and the analyst were forcing him toward heterosexuality. He experienced marked improvement in every other area of life, and he repeatedly faced his fear of and revulsion at being heterosexual. Although he had several women friends, he never had any intimate physical contact with them, and he could not manage much more than an occasional kiss.

For this patient, all sex was disgusting; he hated his body and felt ugly and awkward. As the material in the analysis shifted and revealed his secret pleasure in his own specialness, he recalled how his aunt and sister dressed him as a girl when he was quite young. His mother made fun of his penis. He was laughed at whenever he was nude and the small size of his penis was emphasized. Later, everyone seemed to laugh at the possibility of his dating. He spoke about a fantasy in which he announced his marriage to his family; they would be shocked; it would hurt them. They thought of him as an eccentric and a weirdo. He would have especially liked to tell his best friend's mother, who had only contempt for him and who would have been crushed at his happiness. The analysis shifted to an intense feeling of hate toward those persons who might have responded positively to his achievements, his body, his masculinity, but who failed to do so.

At one point he reported a dream in which he felt as much in limbo in relation to his sexuality as he ever had. The dream report followed a session in which he told me how his father always belittled his masculine accomplishments and gloated over his failings. He dreamed of his French-made coffee maker, which has a plunger that separates the coffee grounds from the hot water in order to leave clear coffee floating on the top. He mistakenly added the coffee grounds to the top of the plunger and then stared at what he had done, feeling stupid because of his error, which would not allow the mixture to form. The patient associated to the evening before, when he had dinner with an old homosexual lover and the very attractive girlfriend of another friend. He felt very estranged from both of them and their relationships. The old lover was distant and still a little angry about his failure to revive a homosexual relationship with the patient. The sexually stimulating girl was filled with plans for her new marriage to their mutual friend. The patient felt very much a misfit since neither world seemed open to him, and the dream seemed to signify this inability to reconcile the separate parts of his life. The mix could not take place. Pushing the plunger (heterosexuality) would mix water and grounds, and would be distasteful. Leaving it as it was would be unfulfilling. He felt just as he did when he could not be what he wanted to be for reasons unknown to him, and only appreciated for what he did not especially like about himself. He could not bring his worlds together, nor could he straddle them. The dream seems to graphically illustrate this failure.

From the early focus on sexual issues to the ever-present failure to have recognition and appreciation from his parents, there was an extension to his overall brightness and talents. He recalled his graduation from grammar school and how everyone present seemed to feel that his celebration party was a burden. Every time he won an award in school, he was embarrassed and ashamed. He felt that his family was put out by his successes. As this feeling was examined in the transference, it became clear that his father especially was afraid of losing him and experienced every difference between himself and the patient as a loss. The patient's homosexuality represented the sexualization of a self presentation which could not otherwise evoke a positive response. Briefly, he felt his achievements hurt and angered others who would then be lost to him. His perverse sexual behavior took the form of being the passive partner in fellatio. Symbolically, this acted out his wish to maintain a relationship with his angry, threatened, unresponsive father by a sacrifice to the older man's needs.

In summary, the patient turned primarily to the father for fulfillment of both mirroring and idealizing needs. Although he seemed less traumatized in the idealizing aspect of his personality, he showed the dual problem characteristic of most perverse disorders. What was so telling about this patient's problem was his inability to reconcile these two sectors of his personality. His grandiose, narcissistic self was not responded to by his preoccupied or threatened parents. His need for an idealizing relationship was equally impaired. Each aspect of his self was sexualized separately. As one was repaired and reorganized, the other came more clearly into conflict. A total solution to his problem lay in the analysis of the unresolved grandiose fantasy, which carried the seed of a masculine self that needed further growth through responsiveness. At every point in the transference, the developmental problem of "fitting in" came sharply into view. Neither a comfortable regression nor an easy road of progress was available to this man, for whom a happy union with his selfobjects had not been achieved. His temporary points of rest had to do with a fantasy of being "neuter," but this always was short-lived, and he soon returned to feeling a misfit. No evidence of a twinship transference was seen. His problem was clearly one of fitting in rather than one of finding an alter ego.

Discussion

There is an advantage to using the theory and models of self psychology to examine the phenomenon of the misfit, since it is essentially a very personal experience, albeit one directed toward an interpersonal or social state of affairs. The relationship between the self and others is, at times, less well depicted using the perspective of the self and discrete, separate objects than that of the self and selfobjects. The latter perspective directly expresses the positive experience of fitting in and a concomitant feeling of unity and belonging. Thus, we might fruitfully study the attainment of such a feeling using a developmental approach to the self vis-à-vis its selfobjects. Such an approach would employ the models of the two poles of self development suggested by Kohut—the grandiose self and the idealized parental imago.

In Kohut's (1977) latest discussions of self disorders, he emphasizes the bipolarity of the self. Whereas initially we could follow development along either the grandiose self axis or the idealized parental imago axis, one or the other usually predominated, and this was the focus of the transference in analysis. Next Kohut urged a study of the relations *between* the two poles, concluding that the psychic health of the entire personality could be restored when functioning along one axis was rehabilitated; the archaic layers of the other would then fall away. Kohut emphasizes less the content of one or another of the poles of the bipolar self than the relationship of one pole to the other. He suggests that development can be seen either as a succession of self-selfobject relations along one pole or as movement from one pole to the other. He also states that later experience at one or another pole could compensate for an earlier defect. Psychoanalytic treatment would thereby heal a defect in one but not necessarily in both poles, since unipolar compensation could be wholly efficient in restituting a personality.

When Freud wrote about the "exception," he described the external and social manifestation of one type of disordered internal narcissistic configuration. In the exception, the relationship of the two poles is usually resolved in favor of the grandiose self; the misfit, however, remains in limbo. In terms of a developmental scheme, the misfit may represent a particular typological variation involving repeated incursions into a succeeding stage, which are unsuccessful but are not abandoned. Rather, the child (and later the adult) remains poised on the edge of a new developmental experience but has gone too far to be able to retreat. Successfully traversed, a developmental step allows integration of mastered behavior into one's personality; conversely, failure to participate in such a stage can lead to a lack of integration and mastery and the unique posture of being neither in nor out that is characteristic of borderline phenomena. In terms of later defensive arrangements, such a stance can be used as a strategy for secondary gain, and it can become so gratifying that it serves as a stalwart resistance to analytic work. Primarily, however, the misfit struggles at the door but, gaining neither entrance nor exit, remains unsatisfied.

For example, as my patient became more and more involved and interested in a relationship with a woman, he experienced intense humiliation at being *seen* as a suitor. At the same time, he was intensely jealous of any competitor for the woman of his interest. In this manner he seemed like a child who had had some relevant oedipal experiences but they seemed, for want of a better phrase, to have been truncated ones. He had no fantasies of actual rivalry, and, in a somewhat characteristic manner, immediately associated the idea of change with that of loss. I use this example here only to illustrate what seems to be the salient point about misfits: they do not achieve either successful regression or adequate progression. A recurrent dream had by this patient seemed to reflect this condition. It was about an intricate violin piece, which he practiced but never quite finished. The dream was only of music, but it changed during the analysis to display shading and tones not previously heard. The associations to the dream indicated that the music was a symbol for heterosexuality, and the patient slowly mastered its performance as the analysis proceeded. When eventually his sexual and masculine self emerged, a new dream heralded the appearance of a vigorous male who was looked upon positively by others, i.e., he was seen in context and in a group and with pride.

It is hoped that this general scheme will aid in the better delineation of the misfit. Certainly, every perverse individual does not feel like a misfit, and finding a congenial group allows many homosexuals to gain comfort and support from a feeling of belonging. The comfort of this particular form of ideals and values was unavailable to this patient, however. Perversions that exist in relative isolation from the main sector of the personality are often associated with a great deal of shame and humiliation, but they need not lead to the pervasive feeling of internal dissent that, unfortunately, this patient and misfits in general experience.

The misfit is at odds with himself. This kind of eccentric cannot fit in because he is unable to commit himself to the values and ideals of a larger group. Though he may fit in superficially, he remains unfulfilled much of the time, and he fails to gain sufficient mirroring response from the selfobjects around him. Thus, he demonstrates his internal dilemma in his conflict with the world. In order to adapt or conform, to join the larger group, one either must be compatible with it or one must subordinate oneself to it.

Returning to the ''exceptions'' of Freud, we see that these are narcissistically damaged people who feel ''entitled'' and who remain in conflict with the realities of the world. As Freud (1916) says, they "will submit no longer to any disagreeable necessity" (p. 312). They remain fixated or arrested at the primitive, grandiose levels of development. However, the yearning and longing that is so characteristic of the misfit is relatively lacking in these exceptions. This lends support to the idea that misfits are more aware of their internal dilemma and thus are more motivated to change.

As we examine the case of any misfit, ranging from the universal feeling that Freud attributed to all women, to those few truly outstanding or talented people for whom fitting in would be disastrous, we can observe the crucial relationship between one's picture of oneself and the capacity to give oneself over to a larger entity. The woman who feels damaged or unresponded to, for example, can reconcile herself to her fate by accepting the conventional woman's role, or by embracing an aggrieved set of values. Likewise, she can achieve harmony by modifying her feelings about herself. She takes on the character of a misfit only when such a reconciliation is not possible for her. She cannot change her unhappy state and she cannot lose herself in or belong to a desired group. This combination leads to the chronic outsider.

The extremely talented or unique individual may experience the same dilemma. He or she cannot give up specialness, and yet may not be able to find inner peace by remaining in such an individualistic position. A longing for merger with an idealized other may be expected to result from the childhood of very talented individuals. Any person who is thrust into a new environment may find a period of fitting in to be painful or prolonged. This reflects the universality of developmental processes that are at odds with environmental supports. Such periods of disharmony are part and parcel of every normal growth pattern.

The so-called secondary gains that are to be derived from feeling estranged, injured, or abused are notorious and have been underlined by Freud (1916) in his discussion of the feeling of privilege and/or compensation. The patient discussed above was obsessed with both the experience of self-pity and the complementary one of compassion for the underdog. He alone would befriend and champion the weak underdog. He recalled how in grammar school he befriended an ugly, limping, unfortunate girl and defended her against the jeers and scorn of his classmates. Such a position of specialness in the service of the outcast sometimes takes the form of championing causes and leading separatist movements. These supposed ''gains,'' however, are not easily given up, inasmuch as they offer tremendous support and a necessary definition to a person seeking a place to stand. As my patient moved away from his homosexual orientation, he was met initially by an extraordinary hostility from certain of his friends, both men and women, for whom it was necessary for him to be a sexual deviate. As he wrenched himself free from these very needed others, he felt periods of extreme anxiety at being abandoned and alone, and vividly characterized the options available to him as a child of being alone or being what he did not want to be.

Thus we can see the secondary gains of the characterologic organization as offering further evidence of the needed but essentially more archaic selfobject relationships. The analysis of these gains and this character leads to intense anxiety unless and until the selfobject nature of character is comprehended. However, the developmental path of an individual who feels like a misfit need not always take the form of movement from one pole of self development to the other. By way of generalization, I have said that a misfit has tested a developmental stage and can neither advance into it nor retreat from it; the misfit thus can be seen as on the verge of developmental failure. From the vantage point of selfobjects we can study the movement from one pole to another or along one pole to delineate just where the individual failed to achieve a match with the needed selfobjects, so remaining in a perpetual state of limbo. Misfits thus can be found at every transitional point of development. They characterize a movement from one set of relationships with selfobjects to another, and as such the relationships can be primitive or mature. Thus we can see that their experience is more or less universal. To return to the view of the adaptation of the individual to the demands of the environment, we can again examine the shift in perspective required to move from the interpersonal to the subjective to emphasize that misfits are only to be diagnosed from an analytic vantage point of the personal experience of the patient.

Conclusions

A psychoanalytic examination of the misfit that concentrates on the subjective experience of a person fitting into a group is essentially a contribution to the consideration of psychoanalysis as a social science. The study of adaptation as an extension of psychoanalysis seen as a general psychology (Hartmann, 1939) runs the risk of removing the focus from an intrapsychic experience to an interpersonal examination of adjustment. Just as Freud's contribution to group psychology concerned itself with the experience of the individual in a larger group, so, too, should all psychoanalytic efforts at explicating social phenomena ideally proceed from and confine themselves to the data derived from the analytic process—the intrapsychic state. Misfits, therefore, are defined by the individual experience of feeling alien, and they are studied to determine what developmental issues lead to this complex state of affairs. The utilization of selfobject models is a felicitous conceptual aid to such an investigation. At the same time, such an investigation can also serve as an avenue for developing new insights regarding so-called social phenomena by considering the variety of personal configurations that go under the overall rubric of "relationships." The area between persons is a proper psychoanalytic study with the aid of conceptual models that concentrate on connections rather than on differentiations. Such linkages between persons are core units for a psychoanalytic contribution to the study of the social world of individuals. The investigation of the misfit as a form of character pathology can focus our study on the attainment of these ties.

References

Fenichel, O. (1945), *The Psychoanalytic Theory of Neurosis*. New York: Norton.

Freud, S. (1916), Some character-types met with in psycho-analytic work. *Standard Edition*, 14:309–333. London: Hogarth Press, 1957.

Goldberg, A. (1975), A fresh look at perverse behavior. *Internat. J. Psycho-Anal.*, 56:335–342.

Hartmann, H. (1939), Psychoanalysis and the concept of health. In: *Essays on Ego Psychology*. New York: International Universities Press, 1964, pp. 3–18.

Kernberg, O. (1970), A psychoanalytic classification of character pathology. *J. Amer. Psychoanal. Assn.*, 18:800–822.

Kohut, H. (1977), *The Restoration of the Self*. New York: International Universities Press.

Empathy and Countertransference

Ernest S. Wolf

Empathy

One of the most difficult issues in contemporary psychoanalysis is the precise definition, coherent theoretical conceptualization, and therapeutically effective clinical application of what we commonly call "empathy." These difficulties are not due to neglect of the subject. On the contrary, many of the leading psychoanalysts since Freud have given much thought to these issues, resulting in much discussion and sometimes significant disagreements. I will not review the pertinent literature here, but I will mention some landmarks.

Freud used the term *Einfühlung* (or *einfühlen*) or *Sichhineinversetzen*. *Einfühlung* or *einfühlen*, means, when translated literally, to feel oneself into something or somebody. *Sichhineinversetzen* literally means to place oneself into something or somebody. In psychoanalysis we use the term "empathy," which was introduced in 1903 by Theodore Lipps in the study of humor (p. 194). Freud, who had read Lipps's work, probably learned something about empathy from Lipps because Freud first used the concept in his book on *Jokes and Their Relation to the Unconscious* (1905). Freud's library, now at Hampstead, contains seven books by Lipps. Freud signed some of these and made marginal notes in some, indicating that he read them with interest and used the ideas (Trosman and Simmons, 1973).

309

The word "empathy" is derived from the Greek *pathos*, which means anything that befalls one; one's experience. Empathy was introduced into the English language in 1904 (pp. 45–46) in a translation of Lipps's use of the term in aesthetics. The psychologist E. B. Titchener (1909) originated the psychological meaning when he said: "Not only do I see gravity and modesty and pride but I feel or act them in the mind's muscles. This is, I suppose, a simple case of empathy, if we may coin that term as a rendering of *Einfühlung*" (p. 21). The Oxford English Dictionary defines empathy as the power of projecting one's personality into, and so fully comprehending, the object of contemplation.

Yet, two facts might make us question the significance of empathy for Freud: Freud does not elaborate on the concept of empathy; and in all the English *Standard Edition*, the concept is mentioned only fifteen times. One might easily think that Freud did not consider empathy very important. But Freud himself contradicts this view in one of his papers on technique when he states that in establishing an effective therapeutic transference, "it is certainly possible to forfeit this first success if from the start one takes up any standpoint other than one of empathic understanding such as a moralizing one" (1913, p. 140). The original is *Einfühlung*, which I have here translated as "empathic understanding." (Strachey's translation as "sympathetic understanding" seems to me subtly but significantly in error.) In another statement Freud said: "A path leads from identification by way of imitation to empathy, that is, to the comprehension of the mechanism by means of which we are enabled to express any attitude at all towards another mental life" (1921, p. 110, n. 2). Thus, Freud stated unambiguously that if we moralize instead of empathize, we will forfeit the proper development of transference. Further, he said that empathic comprehension is the only means by which it is possible to have any opinion at all about another's mental life.

I believe these statements to be absolutely correct. What remains for us to do is to explain why and how empathy—feeling oneself into another—is so central to analytic theory and practice.

Before going on to this task, I would like to speculate briefly on Freud's apparent neglect of empathy in not writing a major essay on this central concept. I believe there were two reasons. First, the lexical meaning of the words "to feel or place oneself into another" may have seemed quite clear and straightforward to Freud, without need for elaboration. If we used similar straightforward terms in English—such as "I can feel what you are feeling," or "I can resonate with what is going on inside of you," or, as we sometimes say colloquially, "I am in tune with you"—instead of that fancy Hellenic term "empathy," most of our misunderstandings about the concept of empathy would be avoided. But, alas, using such fancy terms sounds scientific and, I will grant, such terms have a certain usefulness as passports that can convey our ideas into the scientific community. I greatly doubt, however, that the superficial trappings of science actually improve the quality of our thinking.

The second reason for Freud's apparent neglect of empathy stems, I believe, from similar considerations. Freud was committed to the materialist philosophy of science of his day, which had no room for the collection of data that could not be publicly measured and verified. Yet the data that Freud collected in his consulting room—empathic psychoanalytic data—were not measurable and verifiable like the data in the physical sciences and in physiology. This must have been embarrassing for the student of Helmholtz, Brücke, and Meynert. Freud knew that psychoanalytic observations were data—obtained introspectively rather than extrospectively, but still data. To his scientific mentors, however, they were a scandal. I think we are fortunate that Freud was a man of courage and mentioned *Einfühlung* fifteen times.

Let us go back to Freud's statement that only by virtue of empathy can one have any opinion about another's mental life. Does that mean that without empathy we cannot tell whether someone's behavior is hostile or intoxicated or pleasing or annoying? Obviously, we can judge another's behavior without being empathic. The mental life that is accessible only with the help of empathy is the subjective, experiential life of another, not another's behavior; not even a patient's verbal behavior on the analyst's couch. A dictionary can tell us about the lexical meaning of a patient's words but only by being empathically in tune does the analyst know what this patient is saying about his or her mental life. It is this mental life that we study in psychoanalysis. As Kohut (1959) notes: "Only a phenomenon that we can attempt to observe by introspection or by empathy with another's introspection may be called psychological. A phenomenon is 'somatic,' 'behavioristic,' or 'social' if our methods of observation do not predominantly include introspection and empathy'' (p. 209). Kohut links empathy with introspection, and, in fact, he defines empathy as ''vicarious introspection.'' Kohut describes vicarious introspection as thinking oneself into the inner life of another. This is essentially the same as Freud's *Einfühlung*—feeling oneself into another. Furthermore, Kohut states explicitly that empathy defines the field of psychoanalysis, that it is a value-free tool of observation, which can be used in the service of compassion or of inimical purposes.

There has been much confusion about the role of psychoanalytic theory in making empathic observation. Assuming that empathy is a method of collecting data about the mental life of another person, does that mean that these data will depend on the psychoanalytic theory that we prefer? Schaefer (1979), in a recent paper on empathy, declared that Freudian analysts get Freudian material from their analysands, Jungians get other material, and so on. Philosophers generally agree that one cannot make any observations without first having a theory to guide the collection of data, and this philosophical principle seems to support the idea that in psychoanalysis, one's empathic observations depend on one's psychoanalytic theory.

I shall try to demonstrate that this conclusion is not warranted and is the result of confusing psychoanalytic theories with schemata for observation. At the same time, I hope we can dispose of those confusions that come about by referring to our mental life as ''inner'' while referring to the world around us as ''outer.'' The inner-outer dichotomy, as Goldberg (1981) has recently demonstrated in a most convincing manner, misleads us into not being sure whether object relations take place outside us, between people, or inside us, between internal object representations. I propose to distinguish more sharply between two different types of perceptions, namely, subjective perceptions and objective perceptions. We can also term these introspective perceptions and extrospective perceptions.

As an illustration, consider your hand. You can see its contours, color; you can feel its shape, its texture, its position in space. You could enumerate in exquisite detail how this hand appears to you as it is apprehended via your sensory apparatus when these sensory data are organized by *extrospective* schemata into an *objective* description of your hand. This would be the hand as an object along with other objects in an extrospectively observed world, except that this particular object is attached to another object, your body. Now, this very same hand is also perceived *introspectively*, that is, sensory stimuli and memories, some conscious, some unconscious, ideas, expectations, are all organized via an *introspective* schema into a *subjective*, experiential apprehension of the hand. The most important aspect of this subjective experience of the hand is that it is part of one's subjective experience of one's self. If for some reason one was to lose one's hand, one would feel one's self to be defective and incomplete, and it would take much therapeutic work to restore the self to its former sense of wholeness. In this connection it is also noteworthy that not all of one's anatomy is similarly a part of the self. For example, I could lose a significant amount of my hair, or of my fingernails, or of my blood, or even some parts of my internal organs without experiencing my self as diminished at all.

Note that I have made no statements about the specific sensory pathways that are involved, their origin inside or outside the body, or where their central connections may be made. It would probably not be too difficult to determine, or at least to make some well-informed speculation about, the parts of the nervous system involved in these perceptions. I am deliberately setting these biological facts aside so that we will not be distracted from the psychological phenomena that we are interested in. If that seems too radical a dismissal, I would suggest, analogously, that we would not bother with the structures of switchboards if we were trying to study the dynamics of telephone conversations.

To summarize, we live in two worlds, an objective one organized on the basis of extrospective schemata, and a subjective one, organized on the basis of introspective schemata. It makes little sense to quarrel over which of these worlds is more real or more illusionary. Nor does it make much sense to argue over whether something exists in the "inner" world or in the "outer" world. To return to the example of a hand: looked at extrospectively it is an object in the world; experienced introspectively it is part of the self. Hence, Kohut's felicitous term "selfobject" describes the large class of people, things, and symbols that can be perceived in both modes. Selfobjects are neither "inner" or "outer," but are experienced simultaneously in both worlds. However, the terms "inner" and "outer" still have a certain heuristic usefulness, as long as we remember that they refer to different modes of experience and not to anatomical or geographical locations. Similarly, the term "internalization," so important and yet so troubling in psychoanalysis, refers to a reorganization and reintegration of perceptions and their associated ideas, and not to any location in a space-occupying mind.

The data that we use, whether introspectively or extrospectively organized can be erroneous. For example, I may see my friend Joe in the distance coming toward me, but as he gets closer I realize that the man is a stranger. Or vice versa. Similarly, I may introspectively perceive myself to be sad, but as the experience gets more intense it becomes clear that I am exhausted. Or vice versa. In an analogous manner I can make mistakes when I try to imagine what another person is experiencing. For instance, an analysand tells me about the large crowd at the great mass celebrated by the Pope on his recent visit, and I imagine the noise of all those people. In fact, as I learned, it was remarkably quiet. This is an example of erroneous vicarious extrospection. I made an error in imagining what somebody's extrospective experience was like. Similarly, my introspective imagination, that is, my empathy for someone's subjective experience, can be in error. Many times I have been wrong in imagining an analysand to be feeling, for example, tired or irritated or angry, when longer scrutiny of my empathic data revealed the patient to have been depressed. I want to stress that the errors are usually not important, and that prolonged empathic immersion into the mental life of another yields introspective data just as reliable as the extrospective data that we depend on in ordering our daily lives. It is well to remember that both introspective and extrospective perception improve with training and experience. The fledgling medical student peering through a microscope for the first time will see little more than a confusing chaos of colors, spots, and irregular shapes. The same student, a few months later, will recognize patterns of cellular structure in an almost three-dimensional space. Similarly, the fledgling psychoanalyst first listening to a patient's associations will hear mainly a disorganized chaos of fleeting impressions, while the trained and experienced analyst will have become quite skillful in recognizing patterns of mental life by immersing himself or herself empathically into the analysand's experience.

Of course all the vicissitudes that can befall human intentions can also happen to perception. We can resist seeing, we can resist feeling, we can resist hearing, we can resist becoming aware of any perceptive mode, whether extrospective or introspective. And just as we can use reason in the service of resistance—that is, in the defense of rationalization—so we can put empathic understanding to the service of resistance. All these resistances occur at times, but the greatest obstacle to the proper use of introspective empathic data is the bias that sees such data as unscientific, animistic, or even mystical. I hope this discussion will contribute to lessening such prejudices.

I would say that any analyst, whether Freudian, Jungian, Kleinian, or Kohutian, will, with prolonged empathic immersion, obtain very similar vicariously introspective data about the analysand; in other words, sooner or later any analyst who is willing to listen and observe empathically will apprehend the same introspective empathic data. But what the analyst does with these data, the kind of explanation he or she gives them, depends on the theoretical framework that guides the processing of the empathically perceived data into an interpretation. For instance, I might interpret a patient's anxiety as apprehension about my unempathic intrusion into his self which threatens him with self fragmentation, while a colleague might interpret the same anxiety in the same patient as apprehension resulting from a perception of the analyst as a threatening castrator.

Different theories lead to different interpretations. The superiority of one theory over another is an empirical question. Clinical observations accumulated over prolonged periods will yield the experience that can demonstrate the practical usefulness, the explanatory power to make sense out of chaotic data, and the effectiveness as a treatment method of each competing theoretical approach. I have found in my clinical experience that the addition of a self-psychological theory to my armamentarium of traditional psychoanalytic theories has vastly increased my explanatory power in making sense out of psychoanalytic data, has significantly increased my therapeutic effectiveness, and has considerably increased the range of nonneurotic psychopathological conditions that I can now treat effectively. As a physician, a scientist, and as a responsible human being I cannot ethically ignore the vistas opened up by self psychology. But this does not mean that classical psychoanalytic theory is wrong. Rather, classical theory is merely another way of looking at and organizing data, and for some patients it is the most useful and effective way of doing so.

There is one other frequent misunderstanding about empathy that I would like to discuss. The experience of being listened to attentively and especially of being properly understood is a gratifying one, since it fulfills one of the primary aims of communication. Almost universally, feeling really understood is synonymous with feeling good. Inevitably, then, analysands respond to an empathically listening analyst with an increased feeling of well-being. No doubt there is some gratification in this, as there is in being in the presence of an interested and respected human being. Still, this is far removed from attempts to be kind, sympathetic, or compassionate. Yet, analysts who seriously attempt to get empathic introspective data are said to overgratify their patients by expressing attitudes of sympathy, if not loving concern, thereby preventing the analysis of hostile transference. Aside from pointing out that raging hostility is not a rarity in the analysis of self disorders, let me also state categorically that empathy is only a mode of data collection and not a mode of expression for the analyst. I have heard colleagues speak about ''expressing empathy'' to their patients, which is a complete misconception of the empathic process. Indeed, a similar misconception might be implicit in the coupling of the topics of empathy and countertransference. Empathy and countertransference are not terms for opposing influences on patients. Empathy is a method for collection of data and can be used for the patient's good as well as against it. Countertransference is not a method of data collection but an expression of needs, like transference itself. What distinguishes transference from countertransference is very simple: transference is based on the analysand's needs, countertransference is based on the analyst's needs.

Countertransference

My approach to the issues of countertransference is fundamentally different from my approach to empathy. Empathy, as an introspective perceptual mode yielding data that can be processed by any psychoanalytic theory, comes prior to theory. Empathy is the same in classical analysis or in psychoanalytic self psychology. In contrast, countertransference phenomena defined within classical drive-and-defense psychology, or within Kleinian psychoanalysis, or within separation-individuation theory are observed and formulated differently. I propose, therefore, to conceptualize and discuss these phenomena only within the specific framework of the psychoanalytic psychology of the self.

I shall include in my conceptualization of countertransference all the psychological needs mobilized in the analyst's subjective experience by virtue of participating in the analytic process with the analysand. In other words, the analyst's countertransference is the exact counterpart and natural complement of, but not necessarily a reaction to, the analysand's transference.

Transference, conceptualized within a self-psychological framework, represents the experience and perhaps also the enactment of needs that demand specific selfobject functions for their satisfaction. In other words, certain functions performed by the needed selfobjects—for example, the functional presence, the mirroring-echoing function, or being available to be idealized—are necessary for the self to experience itself and to function as a whole, cohesive unity. In short, selfobject transferences represent the mobilization and enactment within analysis of the analysand's selfobject needs. The mobilization of these needs by the analyst—that is, the analyst's transferences—are here designated as countertransferences.

The source of the analyst's countertransferences—whether they are exacerbations of his own psychopathology, whether they are evoked by the vicissitudes of the present situation, or whether they are responses to the analysand's transferences—are not in the focus of the present discussion. Furthermore, I shall not concern myself with neurotic transferences, whether libidinal or aggressive, or with analogously mobilized reactions of the analyst. Nor shall I attempt to classify these countertransference phenomena according to whether they are spontaneous or reactive, whether they are initiated by analyst or analysand, or whether they are identifications or projections or projective identifications. (While I cannot deny that such schematizations have a certain charm, they appear to me to be clinically useless and even misleading in that they give the appearance of solid scientific knowledge when, in fact, there is conceptual chaos.) In short, I shall limit myself to a consideration of the selfobject countertransferences with which we are becoming familiar in the analysis of selfobject disorders, i.e., disorders of the self characterized by selfobject transferences.

What is the relationship of selfobject transferences (including, of course, selfobject countertransferences) to empathy? Empathy is a method of data collection about another person's "inner" life and experiences based on introspective modes of perception that rely more on affective *gestalten* than on linear verbal patterning. Like all perceptions, these are subject to the vicissitudes that can befall mental processes. Empathic perceptions can be reduced by repression or disavowal, they can be enhanced by attention-focusing processes, or they can be distorted in numerous ways in the service of the expression or defense of the self. Thus, the selfobject needs designated transferences or countertransferences may likewise sharpen, dull, or distort empathically derived data. For example, the mobilization of a self's intense archaic needs for mirroring is likely to be accompanied by a dulling of the self's empathic sensitivity for nonselves. Conversely, empathically derived data may influence and distort transferences and countertransferences by evoking or discouraging the emergence and mobilization of certain selfobject needs. For example, the empathically mediated awareness of unconscious and subtle narcissistic rage in the other often evokes intense and specific transference and countertransference responses derived from one's archaic psychogenetic heritage. Empathy and transferences thus mutually influence each other.

Let us consider the analytic situation from the point of view of the psychology of the self. Certain rules structure this situation for each of the two participants. Moreover, the analysand in this psychoanalytic situation tends to regress; and this regression, in conjunction with the patient's hopes and fears, leads to a mobilization of his or her split-off, disavowed, or repressed archaic selfobject needs. These needs will be manifested as more or less hidden demands on the analyst, depending on the nature of the defenses. To the extent that these demands are the mobilized and revived residues of archaic selfobject frustrations, they are termed selfobject transferences. We often forget, however, that the analyst is in a situation very similar to that of the analysand. Though the analyst is privileged to be sitting up, he or she still experiences constraints entailed by the psychoanalytic situation. In particular, the analyst feels constraints on self-expression and the injunction to dismiss customary ways of thinking in favor of evenly hovering attention. These limitations combine to foster a regression in the analyst, which, one hopes, is not as intense as that of the analysand, but is its counterpart. The analyst's selfobject needs, therefore, also are mobilized into what I have termed selfobject countertransferences.

Of course, I am not talking about severe regressions or uncontrolled countertransferences on the analyst's part. I am talking about the inevitable and useful limited regression that results in a loosening of the analyst's self structure and an increased permeability of the boundaries of the analyst's self. In Freud's words, the analyst "must turn his own unconscious like a receptive organ towards the transmitting unconscious of the patient" (1912, p. 115). This implies an increased receptivity, especially for introspectively organized perceptions, that is, increased empathic "in-tuneness." It does not mean that the analyst's self has regressed to fragmentation or loss of boundaries. Controlled regression in the context of a psychology of the self is not synonymous with control of the id by the ego. Rather, control means that in a cohesive self the constituents are present in a balanced integration which constrains the constituent parts, just as the balanced integration of atoms bonds them into a molecule.

A major benefit of the analyst's countertransference—that is, of controlled regression—is increased empathic perceptiveness. Schaefer has noted that he is often capable of empathizing with an analysand more sensitively, in a more complex and sustained manner, and over a broader range of subjective experiences than he is with others in his personal, nonprofessional relationships. I have made similar observations. I believe the increased empathic sensitivity within the analytic situation reflects the analytic regression of the analyst, his or her analytic regressive countertransference, and the mobilization of the analyst's selfobject needs. It also follows that defenses against regression would interfere with the analyst's empathizing. I have often observed this with candidates in training, and I can well recall how my own anxieties as a fledgling analyst made the appropriately regressive empathic stance very difficult for me.

With the analyst's regression comes a mobilization of archaic selfobject needs. The analyst will experience the appropriate revival of these mobilized selfobject needs as a tendency to make demands on the patient. Again, I am talking about controlled regressions that allow a mature and well-trained analyst to become aware of these newly mobilized deep needs. Among the revived selfobject counter-transferences will be a need for idealized selfobject responses from the analysand. In other words, the analyst will experience a slight over-estimation of the analysand, which will probably be communicated in subtle ways. Is this destructive to the analysis? On the contrary, I think it is a necessary condition for the analytic process to unfold. The analysand experiences this idealizing countertransference as a confir-mation of his or her unrealized potential and as a stimulus to live up to. This countertransference corresponds to normal parents' narcissistic overestimation of their children, which is necessary for the children's healthy development.[1]

The analyst's controlled regression will also result in the mobi-lization, within limits, of certain archaic needs for self-aggrandize-ment. The exalted status of the physician in our culture, as expressed by the patient in seeking help, is usually experienced as a response to these needs for mirroring and echoing selfobject responses. Here, as I have noted elsewhere (Wolf, 1979), as well as in the mobilization of needs for idealizable selfobjects, it is to be expected,

> that the analyst's own analysis has allowed him to work through the more archaic forms of his needs for selfobject responses, and

---

[1] I want to comment briefly on motivation for analysis. We often hear that patients' psychological pain and discomfort are the forces behind their seeking psy-choanalytic treatment, and that certainly is true for most. However, we don't very often hear about another motivational force, which is perhaps best described under the general heading of hopeful anticipation. I do not mean only the hope for gratification of infantile instinctual drives and pleasures, but also the hope for recognition, affir-mation, and an ambience in which the self may find the means for expression. Once an analysis has progressed, and the pains that precipitated the analysis have amelio-rated, it is often the hopes and anticipations of fulfillment of the self that keep the analytic process going.

that he has internalized sufficient structure to give cohesion, vigor and harmony to his self. Moreover, it is to be hoped that the analyst in his professional and in his private life finds the opportunity for relationships of intimacy and creativity commensurate to his needs. Still, after all is said and done, there always remain unfulfilled longings to be mirrored and unfulfilled strivings to merge into an idealized imago [pp. 585–586].

So far I have only mentioned aspects of the analyst's countertransference that enhance empathy and facilitate the analytic process. Sometimes, however, countertransferences can interfere with, inhibit, or even totally derail the analytic process. This is the sense in which the term countertransference has usually been understood. Most of the psychoanalytic literature on countertransference deals with its origins in unanalyzed or persisting conflicts of the analyst and its deleterious effects on the treatment. Freud's initial comments at the Second Nuremberg Psychoanalytic Congress (1910) describe countertransference as arising in the physician as a result of the influence of the patient on the physician's unconscious feelings. Countertransference clearly is an important topic, but its discussion, in general, has been rather circumspect and focused mainly on issues of proper classification. This is not surprising when one notices that a notion of health as the primary moral value (and thus sickness as immoral) has subtly infiltrated our culture and psychoanalysis as well. It takes courage to write about one's countertransferences when they are thought to denote some pathological flaw that carries the flavor of moral opprobrium. Nevertheless, during the last decade one can discern in the psychoanalytic literature a growing recognition of the inevitability of countertransference and of its potential usefulness in influencing the psychoanalytic process.

Kohut (1971) has called attention to two types of countertransferences that correspond to two types of selfobject transferences. The analysand's intense archaic mirror transferences, for example, may deprive the analyst of the minimal recognition and response he or she needs for optimal experience and functioning of the self. For in these archaic mirror transferences, the analysand experiences the analyst as a part of him- or herself that is totally merged into the patient's self experience and does not acknowledge the analyst's existence as a separate person. Analysts, of course, differ in their vulnerability to such assaults on the boundaries and autonomy of their self. Some find themselves feeling bored or sleepy, the consequences of a defensive withdrawal of the analyst's self from the engulfing propensities of the analysand's merger transference. I have already referred to the analyst's remobilized need for an idealized selfobject—in other words, the need to see the patient as having some degree of potential. A prolonged, demanding encounter with an analysand in an intense archaic mirror transference may so disappoint the analyst's idealizing expectations that it evokes a bitter disillusionment, which may precipitate therapeutic pessimism and a premature termination. On the other hand, an analysand's idealizing selfobject transference, with its excessive admiration of the analyst, may become uncomfortably stimulating to the analyst's self, threatening the analyst's vulnerable defenses against his or her own gradiosities. In this case, the analyst is likely to become defensively self-deprecating or may attempt to escape the discomfort by inappropriately shifting the analytic focus from the analysand's admiring fantasies to cold reality.

One could supply manifold examples like these. Every analyst's experience is rich in clinical vignettes that highlight the varieties of selfobject transferences and the countertransferences evoked by them. Many times it is not at all clear how much a particular transference or countertransference—in other words, a particular selfobject need of either analyst or analysand—are the result of (1) residual archaic selfobject needs mobilized in the analytic situation; (2) selfobject needs evoked by the empathic resonance with the needs of the other participant in the analytic situation; (3) selfobject needs evoked in defense against the selfobject demands of the other; or (4) selfobject needs mobilized in defense against the demands of the analytic process itself. Classifications like this can be clinically useful, but our fascination with them should not distract us from the main analytic task, which is to keep the analytic process going.

The analytic process in treating disorders of the self can be described in five steps, each of which will take place only if certain conditions pertain. These can be outlined as follows:

1. Analysis of defenses against the analytic process, that is, of

defenses against regression and defenses against selfobject transferences. Conditions: ambience of acceptance and understanding, which encourages regression and mobilization of transference.

2. Unfolding of the selfobject transference; that is, the patient's mobilized archaic selfobject needs focus on the analyst as a potential need-satisfying selfobject. The result is a harmonious, sustaining self-selfobject transference that is experienced as a strengthened self with relative feeling of well-being. Condition: noninterference with the unfolding self-selfobject relationship.

3. Inevitable disruption of this sustaining self-selfobject relationship when the selfobject fails to fulfill the mobilized selfobject needs. Condition: the failure to fulfill must be optimal, i.e., nontraumatic. (The unanalyzable borderline patient will here experience even the slightest failure as unbearably traumatic.)

4. Appropriate interpretation of the observed disruption, restoring mutual understanding by explanation. According to Kohut, the self-selfobject merger is thereby replaced by an empathic resonance. The reestablished empathic bond substitutes for the fulfillment of the frustrated selfobject need. Condition: an honest and plausible explanation of the experienced disruption as blamelessly unintentional and probably unavoidable.

5. The patient's self, now strengthened by its bonds of empathic resonance, continues the deeper unfolding of more archaic selfobject needs in the transference. And the process repeats in ever-widening spirals of self expansion.

It is clear that the analyst's function consists of taking appropriate actions to facilitate and not to hinder this analytic process. To reiterate, that means (1) attempting to create the proper ambience; (2) not interfering in the unfolding of the transference; (3) recognizing when transference has been disrupted; (4) correctly explaining the dynamics of the disruption, including, eventually, interpreting and reconstructing appropriate genetic precursors; and (5) pointing out and interpreting failures *and* successes in the attempts to strengthen the self through the self's attempt to integrate into the surround and establish better empathic resonance.

The analyst's selfobject needs, i.e., countertransferences, can help or hinder at every one of these steps. Creation of the analytic ambience is helped if the analyst's selfobject needs facilitate this regression in the service of the analysis and in particular facilitate the analyst's enhanced empathic in-tuneness. It would not be helpful if the analyst's defensive rigidity prevented adequate (i.e., flexible and controlled) participation, which is an essential aspect of an analytic ambience. Nor would it be helpful if the analyst's vulnerable self had led him or her to be overly self-assertive either emotionally, intellectually, or morally, so that the analyst's archaic selfobject needs required a compliant analysand who would be expected to confirm the analyst's self, brilliant interpretations, and moral righteousness. As the transference unfolds the analysand's selfobject needs, now transferred to the analyst, will create tensions that the analyst recognizes as the analyst's mobilized selfobject responses—i.e., as countertransference—and which alert the analyst to various transference possibilities. If the analyst's selfobject needs intensify beyond this function as signals, they may lead to untoward interference in the analysand's unfolding transference. However, the harmoniously sustaining selfobject transference will inevitably become disrupted with the subsequent intensification of the selfobject needs of both analysand and analyst. The latter will become aware of his increased needs, experienced as mildly tension-producing, and usefully motivating the necessary search for the explanations which restore the cohesion of his own self. On the other hand, if this disruption results in urgent selfobject needs, the excessive tensions associated with them are likely to produce erratic behavior and perhaps even hostile acting out by the analyst.

To summarize, those countertransferences that can be used as signals and alert the analyst to threatened derailment of the therapeutic process are useful; and those countertransferences that cannot be monitored by the analyst because they have never been clarified in the analyst's own analysis or because their intensity is out of proportion to the firmly integrated cohesion of the analyst's own self are likely to interfere with the curative process.

These selfobject needs of the analyst may be unconscious or, if they are conscious, may escape the analyst's attention. Nevertheless, the practicing analyst usually develops not only increased self-awareness, but also an increased sensitivity to the sings of impending or actual disruption of sustaining selfobject relationships. When these persist, and when the analyst cannot explain them, he or she ought to think of possible countertransference possibilities before thinking of the patient as resisting the analysis. This may sound like heresy, as if I were blaming the analyst for anything that interferes with the analytic process. But, on the contrary, it is just these interferences in the analytic process that become the most fruitful points for investigation and thus the most useful tools for moving the analysis forward.

When Freud first discovered transference he saw it as a resistance to the analytic process. Today the analysis of the transference has become an absolutely essential aspect of conducting an analytic treatment. The discovery of countertransference should have led to the analogous use of countertransference analysis as a similarly essential aspect of the therapeutic process. Understandably, the proper appreciation of countertransference has been delayed by the narcissistic vulnerability of analysts. We have reached the point in the history of psychoanalysis, however, where we can stop being defensive about our narcissism—just as, with Freud's help, we stopped being defensive about our sexuality—and begin to assign to countertransference its proper place in psychoanalytic treatment.

References

Freud, S. (1905), Jokes and their relation to the unconscious. *Standard Edition*, 8. London: Hogarth Press, 1960.

——— (1910), The future prospects of psychoanalytic therapy. *Standard Edition*, 11:139–151. London: Hogarth Press, 1957.

——— (1912), Recommendations to physicians practising psycho-analysis. *Standard Edition*, 12:111–120. London: Hogarth Press, 1958.

——— (1913), On beginning the treatment (Further recommendations on the technique of psycho-analysis I). *Standard Edition*, 12:121–144. London: Hogarth Press, 1955.

——— (1921), Group psychology and the analysis of the ego. *Standard Edition*, 18:67–143. London: Hogarth Press, 1955.

Goldberg, A. (1981), On internalization. Unpublished manuscript.

Kohut, H. (1959), Introspection, empathy, and psychoanalysis. In: *The Search for the Self*, ed. P. H. Ornstein. New York: International Universities Press, 1978, pp. 205–232.

——— (1971), *The Analysis of the Self*. New York: International Universities Press.

Lee, V. (1904), Diary of February 20. In: *Beauty and Ugliness and Other Studies in Psychological Aesthetics*. New York: John Lane, 1912.

Lipps, T. (1903), *Leitfaden der Psychologie*. Leipzig: Wilhelm Engelmann Verlag.

Schaefer, R. (1979), The psychoanalyst's empathy. Presented at the Chicago Psychoanalytic Society, October 23.

Titchener, E. B. (1909), *Lectures on the Experimental Psychology of the Thought-Processes*. New York: Macmillan.

Trosman, H., & Simmons, R. D. (1973), The Freud Library. *J. Amer. Psychoanal. Assn.*, 21:646–687.

Wolf, E. S. (1979), Transference and countertransference in the analysis of disorders of the self. *Contemp. Psychoanal.*, 15.

The Negativism of the Negative Therapeutic Reaction and the Psychology of the Self

BERNARD BRANDCHAFT

> . . .there was nothing left for me but to remember
> the wise saying that there are more things in heaven
> and earth than are dreamed of in our philosophy.
> Anyone who would succeed in eliminating his pre-
> existing convictions even more thoroughly could no
> doubt discover even more such things.
> —Sigmund Freud (1918, p. 12).

Almost sixty-five years have elapsed since Freud (1918) described the clinical manifestations of what he was later to identify as the negative therapeutic reaction. Writing of his experience with the Wolf Man, Freud described the syndrome as follows: "He never gave way to fresh ideas without one last attempt at clinging to what had lost its value for him" (1918, pp. 68–69). Freud went on to relate how the Wolf Man produced negative reactions in the form of exacerbation of symptoms each time Freud had succeeded in conclusively clearing something up.

In "The Ego and The Id," Freud (1923) gave the syndrome further definition and its name. In the years that have followed, analytic

327

investigators of widely varying theoretical persuasions have written
about the negative therapeutic reaction. Such interest attests to the
clinical and theoretical importance of the syndrome. Indeed, one would
expect nothing less, inasmuch as this configuration defined the limits
of psychoanalytic influence and understanding as Freud and the libido,
dual instinct, and structural theories had thus far extended it.

Freud's formulations tied the clinical symptomatology of the negative therapeutic reaction to unconscious guilt and the need for punishment. This has been accepted so completely that subsequent
controversy has revolved around whether the description should not
be reserved for cases in which a disorder of the superego can be inferred
or identified as the primary causative factor. Abraham (1919) described
patients who would fit into the subsequently delineated nosological
categories of narcissistic personality and/or borderline personality disorder and who exhibited similar clinical negative responses to analysis.
As Olinick (1964) noted, although Abraham did not use the term
negative therapeutic reaction, the essence of the reaction he described
was the same. Subsequent psychoanalytic literature up to the present
day abounds with descriptions of patients who react negatively and
relentlessly refuse to yield to analytic interpretation. As advances in
psychoanalytic conceptualization have increased our knowledge of
possible impediments to analytic change, authors have attributed these
negative reactions to a variety of "resistances." It therefore seems
plausible to me to utilize the term negative therapeutic reaction in
considering all cases where there is an exacerbation of symptoms
following interpretations that are evidently correct (in the sense that
they identify elements or processes that can be verified or logically
inferred); in cases in which the reaction is not so dramatic but instead
is more covert and chronic, as in those who fear success and flee from
it; and in cases in which a nodal symptom or functional impairment
remains terminally resistant or recurrent despite the analytic process
and the analyst's insight. All these I would classify as *chronic negative
therapeutic reactions*. Together they define the depths beneath which
psychoanalysis has thus far been unable to penetrate.

It remains essential, as it was for Freud, to understand these
persistent adverse clinical reactions to psychoanalysis and its insights.
How are these limitations ultimately to be explained? Has our under-

standing reached immutable bedrock? Or are there still serious limitations in the conceptual tools of psychoanalysts, which are open to change? Reconsideration of the problem of the negative therapeutic reaction which defines these limits is thus timely. In this paper I propose to (1) review some of the more important contributions to the understanding of the negative therapeutic reaction; (2) describe some clinical experiences with these reactions and some observations derived from them; and (3) set forth some tentative conclusions drawn from these experiences that bear on the place of self psychology within psychoanalysis. I hope to contribute to the controversy over whether the new findings of self psychology enable us to extend our psychoanalytic knowledge and influence significantly beyond its previous limits.

Review of the Literature

It is proper that a review of the literature on negative therapeutic reaction should begin with Freud's (1918) account of his treatment of the Wolf Man. Jones (1955, p. 274) calls this "assuredly the best" of all Freud's case reports for "Freud was then at the very height of his powers, a confident master of his method." The Wolf Man also stands out because he was observed by a succession of psychoanalysts through his long life, following his analysis by Freud. As Gardiner (1971, p. vii) suggested, it was the case of the Wolf Man more than any other which established "for the lay person as well as the scientist" that psychoanalysis was capable of treating seriously disturbed persons.

Freud's (1918) fascinating record of this analysis consists of a detailed reconstruction of the childhood neurosis, beginning with an account of his patient's childhood and of a change which came over him following his parents' absence on a summer holiday. From a good-natured, tractable, pleasant boy, "he had become discontented, irritable and violent, took offence on every possible occasion, and then flew into a rage and screamed like a savage" (p. 15). Following this he developed an animal phobia, which was reproduced in the famous "Wolf Dream," one of the major landmarks in Freud's conception of childhood development. The understanding Freud arrived at through detailed analysis of this dream and through the recovery of memories in association to it were particularly valuable to him since they confirmed and expanded his theories of the importance of infantile sexuality and its vicissitudes.

In consonance with the libido theory, Freud attributed the resistances he noted and the reactions he refers to in the quotation at the beginning of this paper as emanating from an unconscious sense of guilt and castration fears. These resistances were mainly directed against the uncovering of fresh material, and were not described by Freud as specifically *transference* resistances. A reference to the transference resistance, however is contained in the following passage:

"The patient . . . remained for a long time unassailably entrenched behind an attitude of obliging apathy . . . His unimpeachable intelligence was . . . cut off from the instinctual forces which governed his behaviour in the few relations . . . that remained to him." Freud went on to describe his efforts to enlist a more active co-operation from his patient. However, the Wolf Man appeared to be comfortable only with Freud and consequently avoided the pursuit of any interests that could make him self-sufficient. "Only one way was to be found of overcoming it," Freud continued, and he thereupon set a date for termination.

> I was resolved to keep to the date; and eventually the patient came to see that I was in earnest. Under the inexorable pressure of this fixed limit his resistance and his fixation to the illness gave way, and now in a disproportionately short time the analysis produced all the material which made it possible to clear up his inhibitions and remove his symptoms. All the information, too, which enabled me to understand his infantile neurosis is derived from this last period of the work, during which resistance temporarily disappeared and the patient gave an impression of lucidity which is usually obtainable only in hypnosis [p. 11].

It is not lack of appreciation of Freud's enduring genius or accomplishments that leads me to suggest that there were influences in the case of the Wolf Man, especially in the patient's relationship to Freud, of which the conceptual tools that Freud had available could take no account. Indeed, a latter-day expansion of such tools is supported by Freud's own prescient words, which are a mark of his true genius: "Naturally, a single case does not give us all the information that we would like to have. Or, to put it more correctly, it might teach us everything, if we were only in a position to make everything out, and if we were not compelled by the inexperience of our own perception to content ourselves with a little" (p. 10).

The Wolf Man has written his own story of his treatment with Freud (Gardiner, 1971, p. 147). It is a fascinating and, for modern day analysts, indispensable addition to Freud's account. The Wolf Man offers us his own perceptions of Freud and of his relationship to Freud as his patient. It enables us to assess the factors beyond those described by Freud which played a significant role in the therapeutic result and in its limitation. In his recollections the Wolf Man describes the "storm and stress" period of psychoanalysis in which his own analysis took place: "[Freud's] views, as well as his whole theory, were so new that they were bound to meet with the most violent opposition everywhere. Freud was furiously attacked from all sides." The Wolf Man clearly regarded himself as a favorite of Freud and believed that he occupied a special place in Freud's life and in the history of psychoanalysis. In fact, this proved to be the case, as Anna Freud wrote in the foreword to the Wolf Man's book:

> The Wolf Man stands out among his fellow figures by virtue of the fact that he is the only one able and willing to cooperate actively in the construction and follow-up of his own case. . . . His grateful respect for and ready understanding of analytic thinking lifted him, . . . from the status of a patient to that of . . . a collaborator with 'an experienced explorer setting-out to study a new, recently discovered land.' . . . What he proudly reports as his analyst's acknowledgement of his first-class intelligence not only stood him in good stead throughout his personal life but was instrumental also in benefitting the psychoanalytic community as a whole in an unprecedented manner [Gardiner, 1971, p. xi].

In describing his experiences the Wolf Man emphasized his disappointment with a succession of therapists before he met Freud. He took special note of the ability he felt to speak freely about whatever troubled him. He stated "Freud's appearance was such as to win my confidence immediately. . . . At my first meeting with Freud I had the feeling of encountering a great personality.'' Modern-day psychoanalysts could hardly fail to recognize the immediate beginnings of a powerful idealizing transference, a transference which Freud was to leave unanalyzed in the Wolf Man for later explorers to chart.

The Wolf Man continues his description of his experiences with Freud in a similar vein. ''It was a revelation to me to hear the fundamental concepts of a completely new science of the human psyche, from the mouth of its founder'' (Gardiner, 1971, p. 138). ''It will be easy to imagine the sense of relief I now felt when Freud asked me various questions about my childhood and about the relationships in my family, and listened with the greatest attention to all that I had to say. Occasionally he let fall some remark which bore witness to his complete understanding of everything I had experienced.'' Once Freud spoke of the Wolf Man as a ''thinker of the first rank, which filled me with no little pride, since in my childhood I had suffered in competition with my sister, who is two and a half years older than I and far ahead of me'' (p. 139). ''My new knowledge, the feeling that I had, so to speak 'discovered' Freud, and the hope of regaining my health made my condition rapidly improve'' (p. 139).

Although Freud never identified an idealizing transference, it is clear from the Wolf Man's record that he responded to it intuitively and empathically. In so doing he kept it alive and nurtured it. As the Wolf Man describes it: ''I can only say that in my analysis with Freud I felt myself less as a patient than as a co-worker, the younger comrade of an experienced explorer setting-out to study a new, recently discovered land'' (p. 140). ''This feeling of 'working together' was increased by Freud's recognition of my understanding of psychoanalysis, so that he even once said that it would be good if all of his pupils could grasp the nature of analysis as soundly as I.'' The following incident indicates that Freud was responding to and encouraging in the Wolf Man a transference revival of archaic yearnings for an idealized father. The Wolf Man reports that once during an analytic hour Freud said he had just received word that his youngest son had broken a leg while skiing. Freud went on to say that of his three sons, the youngest was most like him in character and temperament. Subsequently, the Wolf Man became occupied with the idea of becoming a painter.

"Freud advised me against this," (p. 145) the Wolf Man recalls, with the suggestion that painting would not be sufficiently asorbing intellectually. And Freud went on to relate to the Wolf Man that his own youngest son had also wanted to be a painter but had given up the idea to become an architect.

In the remarks quoted earlier, Freud refers to the "long education" (p. 472) needed to facilitate the analysis of the Wolf Man. The Wolf Man records several instances of these educational procedures.

> [Freud] believed that culture develops under the iron pressure of the reality principle, which requires giving up the immediate gratification of instinctual drives for a later, more realistic satisfaction. . . . I need hardly emphasize the fact that Freud practiced this educational task in the most tactful way, and that his purely human influence on his patients, by virtue of the greatness of his personality was bound to be profound and lasting.

Again, he noted: "Human intelligence and the triumphs of the mind were for Freud the highest excellence; important is not what man does, but what he thinks." Through much of the analysis the Wolf Man recognized in Freud "the wistful consciousness that intellectuality can be purchased only by sacrifice: the renunciation of immediate instinctual satisfaction."

Powerful motivational forces are to be found here in the Wolf Man's recognition of the importance Freud placed on instincts and their renunciation; in the need to maintain himself in Freud's eyes as a "thinker of the first rank"; in the pridefulness of his position as a "co-worker," a "younger comrade of an experienced explorer" undertaking an historic voyage together; in the passionate concern for a revered colleague besieged on all sides by relentless opposition. These forces are more powerful, perhaps, than the instincts or even than Freud's brilliant insights. Freud provided the Wolf Man with a potent source of self-esteem, which enabled the patient to integrate himself. From a position of obscurity, a nonentity lost in a welter of symptoms designed to frantically maintain a tenuous and primitive psychological organization at whatever cost—to keep the wolves from his door—the Wolf Man acquired, with Freud's active assistance, a healing sense of his own importance and uniqueness, a feeling of being cared about, listened to, and understood. In short, the Wolf Man obtained (as Ferenczi might well have maintained) what he had longed for, needed, and been deprived of as the son of his own father. No wonder the Wolf Man sought so tenaciously to maintain his tie with Freud, and then sought from a succession of others reenforcement of what he had experienced with Freud.

In 1917 Freud described a major and special resistance to analysis. At the time, Freud noted that all his conceptions—the nature of morbid mental states, as well as all therapeutic measures to relieve them—were based on the libido theory. This is the first indication that Freud had come to regard narcissism as a resistance to analysis. It foreshadowed Abraham's 1919 paper which was to identify the narcissistic resistance as the primary source of the negative therapeutic reaction. The special resistance that Freud referred to was humanity's narcissism. This narcissism—already injured by Copernicus' destruction of the narcissistic illusion of the centrality of earth and by Darwin's assault on the narcissistic illusion of the superiority of humankind—was to undergo an even more devastating blow from Freud's discoveries of infantile sexuality and the unconscious. Today we might recognize that where challenges to omniscience or omnipotent control are regarded as seriously threatening, a disorder of narcissistic development is present; and that the threat posed by psychoanalysis in its discovery of infantile sexuality and the unconscious is not primarily due to the concepts, but to the vulnerability invited by the regressive situation of analysis. At the time, Freud's own "libidinal" investment in the libido theory was evident. He had not yet developed the conceptual tools that might indicate that the intractable "resistance" was not to psychoanalysis—the in-depth understanding of the mind—but was a response to the presentation of a limited, if important, aspect of human experience and development as central.

Freud expresses his ideas about the negative therapeutic reaction most clearly in "The Ego and The Id" (1923); there he states expressly that his concept of the superego and its relation to the ego rests on the clinical fact of this reaction. Thus, alternative explanations of the negative therapeutic reaction entail the possibility, indeed the necessity, of reconsidering this concept and this relationship.

There are certain people who behave in a quite peculiar fashion during the work of analysis. When one speaks hopefully to them or expresses satisfaction with the progress of the treatment, they show signs of discontent and their condition invariably becomes worse. One begins by regarding this as defiance and as an attempt to prove their superiority to the physician, but later one comes to take a deeper and juster view. One becomes convinced, not only that such people cannot endure any praise or appreciation but that they react inversely to the progress of the treatment. Every partial solution that ought to result, and in other people does result, in an improvement or temporary suspension of symptoms produces in them . . . an exacerbation of their illness; they get worse during the treatment instead of getting better. They exhibit what is known as a ''negative therapeutic reaction.''

In the end we come to see that we are dealing with . . . a ''moral'' factor, a sense of guilt, which is finding its satisfaction in the illness and refuses to give up the punishment of suffering. We shall be right in regarding this disheartening explanation as final. But as far as the patient goes this sense of guilt is dumb; it does not tell him he is guilty; he does not feel guilty, he feels ill. . . . It is . . . particularly difficult to convince the patient that this motive lies behind his continuing being ill; he holds fast to the more obvious explanation that treatment by analysis is not the right remedy for his case (pp. 49–50).

Freud goes on to suggest that this description applies to the most extreme instances, ''but in a lesser measure this factor has to be reckoned with in very many cases, perhaps in all comparatively severe cases of neurosis'' (p. 50). And he took his difficulty in convincing his patients that herein lay the ''final explanation'' for the persistence of their symptoms as itself the final proof of the inexorability of his patients' need to suffer.

There is no doubt that Freud's speculations about the ''final'' motivating forces—the unconscious sense of guilt and need for punishment—played an important part in the treatment of his patients. They were also to play an important part in the direction that psychoanalysis itself, following Freud's lead, was to take.

In the succeeding paragraphs, Freud indicates that direction. In discussing pathological forms of guilt that are conscious, as in obsessional neurosis, he suggests that it is the repressed unconscious impulses about which the patient knows nothing, that are really at the bottom of the patient's sense of guilt. "It would be folly to acquiesce," Freud states, in the patient's rebellion against the implication of guilt and to support the patient's repudiation of that guilt. The therapeutic task is to uncover the instinctual sources that feed the guilt and thus free the sufferer once and for all. The sense of guilt is itself unconscious and can only be inferred from the persistent "refusal to get well." The therapeutic task therefore involves winning the patient's agreement to this view that the negative reactions stem from an unconscious need for punishment. Any disbelief on the part of the patient thus becomes part of the "resistance" and, if accompanied by an intensification of symptoms, of the negative therapeutic reaction. The subsequent course of the analysis involves a continuing process against understandable "resistance," designed to uncover its instinctual sources in oedipal and subsequently in preoedipal relations, presumed to be feeding the resistance and at the same time keeping it from consciousness.

The theoretical deductions that arose from Freud's clinical findings are also outlined in "The Ego and the Id." They include (1) "that a great part of the sense of guilt must normally remain unconscious, because the origin of conscience is intimately connected with the Oedipus complex" (p. 52); (2) that the superego contains the transformations and, in some cases, the pure culture of the death instinct; (3) that the ultimate fear that causes the ego to submit masochistically to the demands of the superego—including the demand to continue to suffer and to fail—is a threat of castration. Freud subsequently (1933) stated that "masochism . . . affords us a guarantee of the existence of a trend that has self-destruction as its aim" (p. 105). Only in recent years have we become aware that masochism affords no such guarantee, but instead reveals itself as a means to maintain an urgently needed selfobject tie under the conditions that have been subjectively established to preserve that tie (Asch, 1976; Goldberg, 1975; Kohut, 1971; Stolorow, 1975). It will be shown later that the need of a patient with a vulnerable self to maintain a tie with an analyst experienced as a relentlessly failing archaic selfobject lies at the root of the negative therapeutic reaction.

Freud returns to the negative therapeutic reaction in the *New Introductory Lectures* (1933). He again emphasizes the signal importance of negative therapeutic reactions by stating that his clinical experiences with them were the starting point of all his reflections and gave rise to the theoretical foundations of the whole metapsychology of psychoanalysis (p. 108).

"Our first purpose, of course, was to understand the disorders of the human mind, because a remarkable experience had shown that here understanding and cure almost coincide, that a traversable road leads from one to the other" (p. 145). Implicit in this statement is the likelihood that negative therapeutic reactions do not arise from intrapsychic sources strictly within the patient, as "a need to fail," but from a failure of understanding of the interaction between patient and analyst.

Abraham's seminal paper, "A Particular Form of Neurotic Resistance," was the first paper to describe clinical reactions to analysis stemming from narcissistic sources, in particular what for a long time were regarded as narcissistic transference resistances. The special characteristics Abraham noted in patients who manifest these resistances include (1) a concealed "unusual degree of defiance" (p. 305) originating in the relationship with the father and evidenced by a refusal to free associate; (2) an unusual sensitivity to "anything which injures their self-love" (p. 305); an inclination to feel "humiliated by every fact that is established in their psychoanalysis" (p. 305); and thus to be continually on their guard; (3) an attempt to convert the analysis from its objective of self-understanding to one of narcissistic enhancement; and (4) an inability to form "true" transference—the patients "begrudge" the analyst "the role of the father"; they are easily disappointed, and they quickly react with "a withdrawal of libido" (p. 306). "They wish to be loved and admired and since the analyst cannot satisfy their narcissistic needs, a true positive transference does not take place" (p. 306).

Applying the conclusions of his research on obsessional neuroses, Abraham attributed these narcissistic characteristics to a regressive anality, as a retreat from oedipal love, disappointment, and envy. Abraham's description formed the basis for the newly emerging concept of negative transference, which he linked with and regarded as a source of the negative therapeutic reaction. Abraham advocated ana-lyzing this resistance by tracing it to its sources. These patients would then accept the analyst's view of the outmoded, defensive, and self-defeating nature of their anally rooted narcissistic wishes and reactions and renounce them in order to face their oedipal wishes and conflicts. They would thus ultimately be able to achieve more mature, reality-oriented goals. Many analysts now take a different approach, viewing these narcissistic characteristics that Abraham attributed to regression as rooted instead in a *primary* narcissistic deficiency. Thus analysts are able to undertake the analysis of the narcissistic need to be loved and admired which appears in the form of narcissistic transferences in the same manner as they have previously analyzed oedipal wishes.

Indeed, Balint's (1936) paper raised this same issue. In this paper, Balint makes a number of significant observations while questioning the final goal of analytic treatment and, by inference, the primary pathology. Balint had regularly observed in the final phase of treat-ment—including that of patients who had already undergone long and presumably successful treatments with other outstanding analysts—the emergence of long-forgotten, infantile wishes and a demand for "grat-ification from their environment." His empathic investigation of these wishes persuaded him that they arose because of object failures throughout childhood development.

Balint suggested that pathological structures are built up devel-opmentally as a means whereby the child accomodates to the reality of his objects. He observed that some analytic patients were content with extending the sway of their consciousness over the id and the unconscious superego. Others, however, more severely damaged in childhood, needed to utilize analysis for a "new beginning" (p. 215) in order to overcome the damage they had sustained. Balint also sug-gested that anal sadistic and phallic phases were not normal stages of psychosexual development but were the products of faulty environ-mental responses, especially empathic failures. He stressed his em-phatic disagreement with the emphasis psychoanalysis was placing on endopsychic factors, especially sadism and pathological superego, which were being identified most frequently as the cause for negative therapeutic reactions. Balint decried the grave neglect of the study of the effect that faulty object responses had both on the developing child, and also in the analytic situation. Thus Balint's contribution anticipated the thesis of this paper that negative therapeutic reactions are caused by situations in which the analyst insists on the correctness of well-intended interpretations and explains negative reactions as arising solely within the patient's mental apparatus; and thereby severely narcissistically traumatic developmental object failures are repeated.

Riviere's (1936) important article on the negative therapeutic reaction described it as present in all especially refractory character cases. She took as her starting point Freud's conclusion that in such cases the primary pathogenic factor is a pathologically severe superego, which could be placated only by a persistent need to suffer. She considered the complaint that adverse circumstances caused the suffering (when the complaint was also made about the analysis) indicative of the operation of a projection. Referring to Abraham's (1919) paper, she connected the negative therapeutic reaction directly with "narcissistic resistances," emphasizing, however, that when a patient does not respond, it is still the responsibility of the analyst to "discover the cause of his reactions" (p. 306).

Applying the insights gained from Melanie Klein's investigations, Riviere combined and extended Freud's and Abraham's contributions. She suggested that when narcissistic resistances are very pronounced, they are "part of a highly organized system of defense against a more or less unconscious depressive condition in the patient and are operating as a mask and disguise to conceal the latter" (p. 307). In this way she extended the classical theory to indicate a more basic and deeply lying primary source of pathology, residing in a superego formed in the earliest relationship to the mother. This was a significant departure from the more generally accepted thesis of the centrality of the Oedipus complex, which viewed "narcissistic" resistances as a retreat from and defense against its conflicts. Riviere saw as central in the defensive pathology of narcissistic disorders (and of negative therapeutic reactions) the "manic reaction"—defense by omnipotent denial of psychic reality. "This relates especially to the ego's *object relations and its dependence on objects, as a result of which contempt and depreciation . . .* is a marked feature, together with attempts at inordinate and *tyrannical control* and *mastery of its objects*" (p. 308). Riviere elaborated on Abraham's description of typically refractory patients—the omnipotent control of the analyst, frequently masked; the refusal to associate freely; the denial of anything that discredited themselves; the refusal to accept any alternative point of view or interpretation; defiance and obstinacy; the absence of any generosity; the acceptance of help from the analyst while refusing to help the analyst or acknowledge his value; and, above all, the trait of deceptiveness. All this, in Riviere's view, was not sufficiently recognized as a highly organized system of defense and resistance. It arises from an imperative need at all costs to avoid dependence and thus maintain the status quo in order to guard the patient's self and the analyst against the outbreak of depressive anxieties—the fear of having destroyed his primal objects and of a repetition of this in the analysis'' (p. 312). The patient will not permit the analysis to make this psychic truth real, for ''he does not believe it possible that any change on his part can bring about anything but the realization of disaster for all concerned'' (p. 312). In Riviere's view, it is the patient's underlying love for his internal objects, ''which lies behind and produces unbearable guilt and pain, the need to sacrifice his life for theirs, and so the prospect of death, that makes this resistance so stubborn'' (p. 319).

One notes with interest Riviere's claim that the fundamental task in analysis is to permit the patient's underlying subjective reality to emerge. Implicit in this is the recognition that the patient's experiences are determined by the structuralization (in the form of projectively distorted and defensively split internalized objects) of the patient's subjective world. She expressed the opinion that ''A great deal of therapeutic success in former years . . . actually rested, and still may do, on the illusion of cure rather than the fact'' (p. 320). She believed there was a collusion between patient and analyst that covered over the patient's more deeply buried anxiety situations and psychic reality, so that ''the instances of success Freud quotes seem to be last minute evasions'' (p. 320).

Riviere also drew attention to a transference relation that could remain virtually concealed, which was a product of narcissistic factors operating in the analyst. In attempting to account for far more undiscovered negative therapeutic reactions than were recognized, Riviere called attention to a ''false transference'' (p. 320) which frequently escaped notice because it constituted a blow to the analyst's narcissism.

To us analysts both the full true positive and true negative transferences are difficult to tolerate, but the false transference, when
the patient's feelings for us are all insincere and are no feelings
at all . . . seems to be something the analyst can see through only
with difficulty. A false and treacherous transference is such a
blow to our narcissism, and so poisons and paralyzes our instrument for good (an understanding of our patient's unconscious
mind), that it tends to rouse strong depressive anxieties in ourselves. So the patient's falseness often enough meets with denial
by us, and remains unseen and unanalyzed by us, too (p. 320).

Riviere's observations raises the question of how often patients'
falseness about their own authentic aims, feelings, and experiences
may be fostered unconsciously and unwittingly by responses from the
analyst which indicate that these feelings are defensive, outmoded,
destructive, or obstructive. Kohut (1971) has also described how countertransference reactions, rooted in the analyst's narcissism, impair the
emergence and analysis of narcissistic (selfobject) transferences.

Two contemporary papers (Olinick, 1964; Asch, 1976) and one
national symposium (Olinick, 1970) confirm that the negative therapeutic reaction continues to challenge psychoanalysts—although sometimes disguised under different aliases.

As Riviere attempted to apply the newer findings of object relations psychology of Melanie Klein to the negative therapeutic reaction, so Olinick (1964) attempts to apply the findings of ego
psychology. His focus is on the negativism inherent in the negative
therapeutic reaction. Olinick attempts to distinguish between the negativism rooted in the patient's character that is typical of the negative
therapeutic reaction and "the effect of an economically and structurally
wrong interpretation" (p. 543). He notes that "the negativism is directed not so much at the issue raised by the confrontation or interpretation as at the person of the confronter or interpreter in an
intensification of transference"; adding that although the "transference
is overtly negative and hostile, . . . it is latently or unconsciously
positive." He attributes the sequence of "defensive rejection, self-
punishment by symptom-exacerbation, and alloplastic attack upon the
therapist" (p. 543) to the pressure of the drives and affects which are

part of the underlying positive transference. Thus, he sees the negativism as a defense against the positive transference. Olinick subscribes to the theory that the resistance arises from pathological superego dominance within a generally sadomasochistic orientation.

Olinick refers to Spitz's findings on the normal developmental significance of phase-appropriate negative head-shaking and asserts that normal negativism subserves the functions of self-affirmation and assertiveness, and establishes the distinction between self and nonself. He postulates from reconstructions that the following sequence results in patients' development of the negative therapeutic reaction. These patients are constitutionally endowed with an overly intense oral and anal sadism (a position similar to that of Abraham and of Riviere). This intensifies their need for nonstressful mothering and insures that it will fail. The resentful helplessness and overcompensating need to control that the child's behavior engenders in the mother increases the child's aggressiveness and intensifies the ambivalence of the conflict around dependency. The father in this situation is unavailable, thus failing to provide a mitigating influence on the intense enmeshment. The superego conflict is preoedipal and arises from the introjection of an ambivalent, depressed preoedipal love object.

Olinick cites Riviere's (1936) formulation that these patients are defending against an underlying depression, dreaded as death and destruction. To this he adds the fear of regression to a stage of "primary identification with a love object" (A. Freud, 1952)—a fear of loss of intactness, or annihilation of the self.

Olinick endorses a therapeutic maneuver similar in its essentials to that described earlier by Riviere. It involves establishing a therapeutic milieu in which the patient can "attempt to enact his intrapsychic conflicts of omnipotence versus dependent gratification" in the transference. "It is only when the patient has recognized the importance of the other person as a vehicle for his own projections and provocations that the sadomasochism, having become ego-dystonic can yield to psycho-analysis" (p. 546). The therapeutic process entails replacing the patient's hated and hateful introjects with a new and more benevolent set.

In light of experiences with a similar patient which I will recount later, it is interesting to read Olinick's description of a patient who kept attacking the analyst as incompetent and malicious. The patient, according to Olinick, was defending against feeling guilty and helpless. The patient's intensity and his skill caused Olinick to be apprehensive that the patient might be right. When the analyst momentarily felt guilty and helpless, he concluded that the patient had forced him to introject something. The analyst was then able to find a suitable opportunity to interpret this defense. The patient's subsequent positive responses are the clinical basis for Olinick's thesis that the negativism in the negative therapeutic reaction is employed defensively against the positive transference.

In contrast, in my own experiences the crucial turning point in overcoming negative therapeutic reactions was my acceptance of the feelings that Olinick immediately rejected. I came to proceed in the opposite direction, abandoning Olinick's comforting notion that what I was experiencing at such times was the projection of "something bad" from the patient. I recognized that the patient was subjectively experiencing and communicating some essential traumatic event, and that what was called for was an intensified effort to identify and recognize the kernel of truth within the patient's complaint. This made possible the analytic investigation of such failures and their broader (and largely unconscious) current and genetic meanings to the patient. In my experience, the persistent negativism noted by Olinick generally arises within two contexts: (1) as an initial and sometimes continuing defense against the mobilization of the archaic selfobject longings systematically charted by Kohut (1971), and (2) in response to a persistent negativism in the patient's subjective experience of the analyst in response to some aspect of the patient's nuclear self—its strivings or demands, angry assertiveness or complaints, necessary protective structure or autonomous developmental step.

Asch (1976) approached the problem of the negative therapeutic reaction by attempting to apply the insights of Mahler's developmental psychology. He defines negative therapeutic reaction as the "paradoxical increase in symptoms that may follow a correct interpretation" (p. 383). He notes that "Freud's early concepts of 'unconscious guilt,' 'need for punishment,' and 'masochistic ego,' remained abstractions because of insufficient development of theory about intrapsychic structure" (p. 384). Citing Mahler's research into early infancy, Asch indicates that the major anxiety in masochism is not castration but loss of the mothering object. Thus, he says, some patients with a negative therapeutic reaction "attempt to maintain a relationship with a special kind of powerful mother by internalizing her. Their characteristic 'need to suffer' seems to reflect libidinal strivings toward the internalized object in the ego ideal" (p. 386). In this regard, Asch also cites Berliner (1947), who expressed the opinion that moral masochism was not primarily an instance of a person's own sadism directed against the self, but rather a persistent search for love from a primary object who is sadistic rather than loving. Thus the suffering and renunciation that Freud attributed to an "unconscious sense of guilt" can be more correctly understood as a condition of a continuing tie to a needed object.

Asch cites clinical material in which two patients reacted violently to his attempt to educate them to the way they contributed to their own pathology by clinging to an old maternal relationship. He considered these interpretations correct and the reactions to them indications of the need to maintain a masochistic internal object relation. I do not doubt that they were descriptively correct. I have found in similar cases, however, that the need to maintain such a tie is directly dependent on the extent to which archaic needs, which have remained congealed upon their original objects, are defended against in the analytic transference. If the resistance can be gradually surmounted, a transference will develop along masochistic channels. The analysis of this transference and its resolution results in a release from the masochistic tie to primal objects, which cannot be relinquished by direct analytic focus because there is as yet nothing to take its place.

In considering further Freud's concepts of unconscious guilt, Asch supports a host of investigators who have demonstrated that the most frequent and significant superego formations occur preoedipally. He incorporates Mahler's findings to indicate that guilt is usually stimulated or fortified by specific characteristics in the maternal relationship, especially with mothers who have difficulty in separating from their children. Asch, following Mahler, connects the resultant guilt which such patients feel about the demarcation of their own boundaries to their "experience of this wish as overt expression of . . . hostile destructive impulses towards the object" (Asch, 1966, p. 156). He also regards the resultant self-defeating compliance as unconsciously motivated by the need to triumph over a hated and envied figure, rather than as an act of submission serving to maintain a tie to a selfobject upon which the cohesion of the self depends.

In the 1969 panel on the negative therapeutic reaction (Olinick, 1970), Lucia Tower cited two papers by Kohut (1966, 1968) as containing significant new insight into the psychopathology of the negative therapeutic reaction. At the time, the psychology of the self was in its rudimentary stages. Kohut has recently summarized his work in two articles (Kohut, 1979; Kohut & Wolf, 1978). Together these constitute a statement of the current status of the new self psychology. The publication has stimulated searching questions (Rangell, 1979; Stein, 1979; Valenstein, 1979; Rothstein, 1980; Wallerstein, 1981). Among these questions, two recur in different forms. First, does the psychology of the self constitute a really new and distinctive contribution to psychoanalysis? And second, are the results that have been claimed for self psychology due to a better use of the essential tools of psychoanalysis and its methods of observation, data-gathering, and concept formation rather than to a new manipulation of the transference? No area is more suited than that of the negative therapeutic reaction to assess the merits of this new self psychology and to test its claims.

Clinical Experiences

My observations have been drawn largely from a group of five patients whose treatment was divided into two phases. In four, each of the phases occupied from three to five years. The fifth patient of this series terminated a nine-year treatment in which his homosexuality had successfully been overcome. After an interval of some five years, he returned to analysis because of severe, persisting impediments to his writing. In the first phase of the treatment of these patients, the focus was on disturbances in object relations, especially as observed in the transference. All showed marked evidence of such disturbances. One kept his relationships constricted, superficial, and transient by his absolute insistence that other people cater to his wishes, needs, and restrictions. "I want what I want when I want it," he would insist, together with a frequently repeated determination not to change. In three patients, all greatly talented, a particularly strong masochism dominated their object relations and severely constricted their pleasure and success. The fifth maintained an aloof and distanced posture, covered by a superficial friendliness and pretense at intimacy. His analysis was characterized for many years by one consistent and predictable activity. His response to virtually every interpretation showed a compulsive need to "fix" it and thereby to make it and me more perfect.

My understanding and the explanatory concepts on which my interpretations were based in this first phase were influenced by the view that the criterion for mature object relations and for development as a whole is the achievement of concern and love for other people. I was especially sensitive to the influence of unconscious guilt as an impediment to progress. In the second phase, I utilized observations drawn from an enforced empathic immersion[1] together with explanatory concepts derived from this experience. These were supplemented, revised, and reinforced by the knowledge I was acquiring from reports of the new self psychology.

The causes traditionally ascribed to negative therapeutic reactions proved not to be decisive for my patients. For the most part, the patients accepted for a time the formulations based on these concepts. Frequently, in fact, they would greet these insights with feelings of enthusiasm as they joined with me in my recognition that we had arrived at last at the "final" basis for their disorders. A kind of resignation would inevitably set in, however, together with renewed dissatisfaction with analysis, with life, and with themselves. In the later stages of treatment I frequently thought, as had Kohut (1979) in the treatment

---

[1] I would deliberately force myself into the position of the patient within the experience he was describing and counter my tendencies to emerge from that position until I was able to recognize the basis in subjective reality for what he was describing. This process led me to observe relationships that had hitherto been obscure to me or that I had entirely overlooked, and to explore new explanations for the sequences that were unfolding before me.

I believe that enforced empathic immersion involves the application of the principle of negative capability as it was described by Keats (quoted in Bion, 1977), and the analogue of that process that Hill (1966) had in mind when he wrote, "To empty one's mind of all thought and refill the void with a spirit greater than oneself is to extend the mind into a realm not accessible by conventional processes of reasoning" (quoted in Edwards, 1979).

of Mr. Z., that we were seeing the outcome of analysis after the conflicts, the omnipotent expectations behind them, and their genetic roots had been laid bare, and the processes of working through were coming to a close. I thought I could recognize the signs of the patients reluctantly giving me up as a transference object and relinquishing as well the cherished illusions of the pleasure principle as the reality principle inexorably asserted its sway. After all, the price of civilization has always been discontent!

In most of these patients I saw evidence of massive guilt (or, more properly, self-reproach) becoming more apparent as the curtain, signaling the end of the analysis, was descending, and this led me to surmise that the mood of depressed resignation was being sustained from still untapped sources of unconscious guilt. I thought I could detect the influence of an entrenched moral opposition to getting well and to benefiting from analysis, as from childhood and from life in general. If these patients were able to enjoy life, I conjectured, then I and the parents whom I had come to represent could hardly have been as bad as the patients had insistently made us out to be. I believed that the suffering and the disillusionment were regular and necessary aspects of the analysis. The patients complained about them because of the regressive pull of a narcissistic nirvana; resented them because of a refusal to relinquish narcissistic or oedipal claims; intensified them because of their superegos that surpassed in cruelty the patients' unconscious assessment of their own.

I gradually came to observe, however, that the cases of negative therapeutic reaction I was encountering were the consequences of failures on my part to recognize the narcissistic disorders as primary and the defective self as the core. These disorders were not used to deny me and the patient success, or to defend against oedipal or preoedipal conflicts and anxieties or depressions. The reactions were not to be counted as failures of psychoanalysis indicating innate constitutional factors in the patient and a need for more careful selection procedures and criteria. Rather, they represented unintentionally misdirected and therefore incomplete and interminable applications of psychoanalytic procedures. I came to accept that the goals I sought in each case were incompatible with the goals the patient was pursuing. I had to conclude that I must abandon my goals when they were incongruous with those of my patients and stop insisting that in their opposition they were defeating both themselves and me.

My experience with negative therapeutic reactions has caused me to give new emphasis to distinguishing between primary and secondary factors, for in psychoanalysis only concentration on the primary can yield durable, structural change. (I except, of course, the analysis of secondary factors as resistances and defenses to permit the emergence of the primary.) Only enforced and prolonged empathic immersion and introspection into the subjective experience of the patient can enable one to make such distinctions consistently. I believe that observation is being obscured and progress obstructed in psychoanalysis by continuing to regard primary factors as defensive or secondary, while secondary factors are installed as primary.

The primary factors in these patients proved to be the particular self disorder emerging within the transference in the forms of archaic, intensified, distorted longings, now out of phase, which originally should have formed the basis of sound psychological structure; the propensity for fragmentation; the anxiety of a disintegrating self; and the almost infinite variety of compensatory and defensive measures employed in attempts to insure the maintenance and recovery of self-esteem, self cohesion, and homeostatic stability. The factors that proved to be secondary in these cases were drives; conflicts; disorders of love; appreciation and concern for others; and castration, separation, and superego anxieties.

"The first thing I had to get across to you," said Mrs. J. in the second phase of her analysis,

> was how important what you thought of me was. Until that happened nothing else could happen. I couldn't disagree with you because I was afraid of worse consequences—that you would think I was resisting when I wanted so much to cooperate. So I tried to see and use and apply what you said. And I tried to think you were opening up a whole new world for me, a new way of seeing things that would work out better in the end. And I could never be sure that it wouldn't!

She recalled how often my interpretations revived the most painful experiences of her childhood. She had looked to her father for acceptance and for some reliable support to enable her to acquire a positively toned self-image, and he would say "Take her back to the store and get another one!" She recalled the dreadful, sinking feeling she would have, so frequently replicated in the analysis.

I have widely observed such situations, and not only in my own practice in which patients attempt to revive archaic bonds in the form of selfobject transferences, or experience, within these bonds, archaic states of mind in which these primary configurations are interpreted over and over again as defenses or as resistances. This is all the more dangerous because the appearance of truth is created, and in the face of reactions one can easily resort to the notion, advanced by Freud and hallowed by generations of psychoanalytic tradition, that the patients' narcissism is at work, so they are unwilling or unable to face the truth. The analyst must stand fast, it is said, however distasteful his role. The situation is repeated over and over, because the patient in some unseen part depends on the analyst as the upholder of truth. However, the appearance of truth is only an appearance, for it involves truth that is also a distortion. "You took one corner of my personality and held it up to me, with the implication that the corner was me," another patient told me. Such experiences, the relentless insistence on the correctness of the analyst's view, are regularly followed by responses from patients of the sort that Freud (1923) reported as characteristic of the negative therapeutic reaction: "Psychoanalysis is not the treatment for me!" But it would be far more accurate to say, "These particular psychoanalytic concepts are not right, because they are irrelevant, trivializing, and damaging and, perhaps most important, they are keeping me from having an analysis!"

A specific factor regularly accounted for the therapeutic impasse and exacerbation of symptoms in these patients. In each case the patient had sustained a significant injury to the self immediately prior to the reaction. Similar injuries had occurred earlier in the analysis, but I had failed to recognize their significance to the patient, for my eye had been fixed determinedly on what the patient was doing intrapsychically, as my analytic needle hovered evenly between the patient's id, ego and superego. Meanwhile, I had blinded myself to a different significance of what the patient was experiencing and to my part in it. When

narcissistic injuries are repeatedly ignored or attributed to some fault
("too sensitive") or to some perceptual distortion, projection, or other
"defensive" maneuver on the part of the patient, insult is added to
an already traumatized self. Chronic despair and the feeling of "not
counting" (being dis-counted) ensue. In analysis, the need to count
and to be understood reoccupy the status they had in childhood (as
can be seen in the Wolf Man's account, described earlier, of his analysis
with Freud). Having one's subjective experience confirmed and validated by empathic understanding is absolutely indispensable if one is
to establish the conviction of having a self at all. And this validation
is a precondition for children to develop the increasing discernment
that enables them to distinguish between injuries that are inevitable
and unintended and those that arise from the superimposition of the
needs or objectives of others. Without such validation early on, children
remain deprived of the means of protecting themselves in the widening
engagements that lie before them. They remain dependent on the assessments and perceptions of others or, alternatively, on rigidly maintained defensive and protective structures. Repeated failures on the
part of early selfobjects to provide this validation imparts and struc-
turalizes feelings of being a nonperson, an outcast—that is, feelings
of invalidation.

Thus, in the analyses I am describing, the stage was set for the
revival of a crucial derailment of the developmental process that had
first taken place in childhood. Consequently, as similar fragmenting
experiences recurred, similar defensive and reactive elements were
mobilized—negativism, distancing, rage, and acting out. In the first
phase of the treatments, I responded to such behavior by seeing it in
a rejection of me and of the analysis. I thought I recognized the
emergence of the concealed "negative transference," with its endog-
enous elements of instinctual ambivalence or its archaic, object-related
aspects. In this I took a view similar to that described by Olinick (1964)
and many others. I failed to appreciate the urgent signs of traumatic
injury and the beginning of the breakup of a damaged self reacting to
severe and chronic rejection (if unintentional) of the patient's most
urgent needs. Viewing these signs as "negative transference," I felt
challenged to maintain my position (or retreat from it only tactically)
and thereby serve the "larger interests" of my patients and "their"

analysis. So at various times as circumstances seemed appropriate, I interpreted a need to deny dependence on me as part of the transference, a hostile and denigrating envy, a need to triumph over me as a stand-in for a parent, and an unconscious guilt that stood in the way of the patient's getting well.

I reluctantly came to recognize, however, that whenever this point was reached, the procedure had gone awry. Whatever my intentions, interpretations that in effect blamed these patients for the difficulties in the analysis and in their childhood were neither constructive nor correct and never could be, no matter how delicately and ingeniously they were fashioned and presented. It was not sufficient for me to back off and allow these patients to recover, only for me to return to similar observations, concepts, and interpretations. Nor was it sufficient that I demonstrate my ability to cope with the patients' destructiveness without turning against them, being destroyed, or abandoning them (measures subsumed in the literature under "holding function" or "object constancy"). These measures were necessary under the circumstances, perhaps, but not sufficient. For these patients, in their depths, were far more concerned with what I was staying around *for* than in my mere staying power.

Behind the precipitating injury, an old and decisive one had been exacerbated. The intense drama reenacted before me was a condensed, encapsulated, and updated version of a host of earlier nuclear experiences in which these patients, as children, had desperately attempted to get a parent to see things from their point of view. These were efforts to salvage and restore a needed and cherished part of a sinking self and to keep open a developmental channel. The parents, however, had insisted that these children see things from the parents' more "objective" view, always for the children's own ultimate good.

One patient reported that his mother kept a leather belt available for use when he refused to take "his" castor oil, and she would beg him not to "force" her to use it. The mother had been as disturbed because her son's bowels had previously failed to follow her commands in the matter of soiling, as she was subsequently by the constipation with which he then reacted. She regarded the latter symptom as proof of his willful defiance, as she regarded most needs or characteristics that did not correspond closely to her own. This conflict between his needs and those of his mother occupied the center of the boy's development for his entire childhood. An army induction notice enabled him to tear himself away, and he welcomed it as another would a reprieve. He later recalled his military years as among the freest and most pleasurable of his life. A succession of marriages returned him to earlier and more familiar psychological territory. In both his childhood and in the analysis, the conflict situation was produced by the same forces. These were not the intrinsic intrapsychic energies and agencies, but rather the insistent supraordination of the pathological selfobject needs of his objects (including me in the transference replication) to the legitimate selfobject needs remaining from childhood to define an authentic self and to initiate its own intrinsic pattern of development within a supporting and confirming setting.

These observations have enabled me to understand more clearly what Freud (1923) described as the negative therapeutic reaction: "Every partial solution that ought to result . . . in an improvement or temporary suspension of symptoms produces in them for the time being an exacerbation of their illness" (p. 49). In my cases, however, it was not "something in these people that sets itself against their recovery [so that] its approach is dreaded as though it were a danger" (p. 49). It was not the need for illness that had gotten the upper hand. Instead it was my failure for a long time to understand the functions that my patients had assigned to me so that I was unable to see the essence of their disorder: a failure to have acquired in childhood a cohesive and vigorous self and the psychological resources to sustain them in the fulfillment of an internally generated and centered program to realize their innate potential. I believe this to be the deepest source of the depression and despair of these patients—not an inability to love, an inability to make reparation for their destructiveness toward damaged objects, or the imperatives and sequellae of unrequited oedipal love or oedipal rivalry.

In those cases where I was able to appreciate in good time the deeper meaning of the therapeutic impasse and disrupted functioning, as well as my own contribution, we were able to alleviate and move beyond the obstruction. The exacerbation of symptoms rapidly subsided and the patient's resistances to free associations[2] disappeared.

---

[2] Abraham (1919) and many other analysts have noted that narcissism is the most frequent cause of interferences with the basic rule, but insufficient attention has been paid to the role of the analyst's stance and interpretations in promoting self-protective withholding and other interferences that lead to such violations.

We could now calmly explore the precipitating transference experience, together with the nodal conflict centering around it, by the familiar and time-honored methods of psychoanalysis. No parameters were needed.

Frequently the free associations led in the direction of previous injuries that patients had not felt free to discuss before. "You encouraged me to associate freely," one patient recalled, "but when I did, you always told me something else that was wrong with me. Or else I got the impression that what I was saying wasn't the right thing and that I must be hiding something. But I could never figure out what it was that would make you satisfied with me." Each of these memories had to be carefully worked through in detail as to the specific failure involved, what it meant to the patient, and what sector of childhood experience it revived. The recall, exploration, and reconstruction of genetic traumata came to occupy the center of the analysis, as fresh memories appeared and old ones were reexamined from a broader and more constructive perspective. New energies appeared, new interests developed, and new possibilities opened up as the lethargy, dullness, and anhedonia disappeared as preeminent states.

An additional component of the negative therapeutic reaction appeared quite consistently in these cases, and it indicated the necessity for a thoroughgoing reconsideration of existing psychoanalytic theories of guilt and the formation of the superego. These patients suffered throughout their lives from marked lack of pleasure. Two spoke repeatedly during the first phase of feeling imprisoned, and described the boredom of their existence. They also spoke of feeling crushed under some enormous weight, and both dreamed of prisons, concentration camps, and crimes—communications I had come to consider pathognomonic for disorders of the superego.

Case Illustration

One of these patients was L., a man of great talent who, in his early twenties, fled from a promising opportunity to enter an artistic career, and settled down in a different area to a life of prosperous but routine commercialism. Approaching age fifty when he entered analysis, he kept longing for the career he had never had, despite the fact that it would have kept him chained to a life of poverty in a garret. He berated himself mercilessly and seemed to derive a certain almost exquisite pleasure from it. He had devoted himself to earning a large sum of money in a desperate attempt, as it turned out, to increase his "net worth." But he could not hold on to any of it, and until late in his analysis he remained imprisoned in debt. The more he spent, the less increment of pleasure he derived from each new acquisition, and the more he continued to spend. His relationship with his wife was similarly marked by a singular lack of pleasure. He constantly yearned for a different partner and engaged in extramarital affairs with some frequency. Each of these quickly became as denuded of pleasure or benefit as the relationship with his wife from which he was fleeing. Only occasionally would he show any indication of radiant enthusiasm, and this would be in relation to the prospect of some fresh sexual encounter or, briefly, when his fantasies took him along the path of "if I had only" and carried him to the heights of ecstatic glory in his abandoned artistic career. Then the curtain of self-loathing would again descend.

In the first part of the treatment I proceeded along the familiar lines Freud suggested long ago for dealing with those who are afraid of success. But I observed that my attempts to focus on the patient's guilt and his fears of my condemnation (as a projected aspect of his cruel superego) did nothing to brighten his mood or enlist his enthusiasm. We spent a great deal of time unmasking the unconscious roots of his guilt, particularly as they appeared in the transference and in relation to his sexual exploits and his wife, and tracing these to their genetic origins. His father was a physician, but was as unsuccessful in earning money as his son had become successful. Exploration of L.'s disparagement and envious rivalry with his father was followed by the emergence of feelings and memories of an intense relationship with his mother. The pall that had hung over his head for a lifetime had begun with her. The whole story of his childhood was that of a running battle. Here, it seemed, were the deepest roots of his repressed guilt. But the most careful and painstaking work brought about no essential change in his condition. The patient seemed determined to remain wedded to his suffering.

Somewhere in the process I began to notice that he experienced his most crushed feelings after I made interpretations. He would then "drift off" or revile himself or complain that he was getting nowhere. Sometimes he would miss the next few sessions, and in these periods he was likely to have another sexual encounter. He would seem to be reacting as Freud (1918) described, repeating the prohibited behavior once more before stopping it. Then he would be afraid to return because of the interpretations of "resistance" that he had come to expect, just as he had been loathe to return home after being truant from school for fear of the hysterical scoldings that awaited him.

Gradually I became aware that his withdrawals, masochistic outbursts, and missing of sessions were not due to a determination to suffer, nor to the hostility that presumably had caused his difficulties when it was first directed toward his mother and then was turned back upon his self. The analysis had unwittingly reproduced the conditions of his childhood, and I began to see how much of his behavior was a self-protective reaction to damage to his self-esteem. His sexual behavior could now easily be seen to reflect imperative needs to restore his fallen self-esteem in a variety of symbolic ways. In order to preserve the relationship with me that he needed if he was to retain his hope of psychological survival and future fulfillment, he had no alternative but to temporarily withdraw or to join in what he experienced as my criticisms of him. I began to draw his attention to the states of disorganization that followed unempathic responses to him. And I suggested to him my increasing recognition of the part played by my failure to understand him sufficiently in impasses in the analysis and in the disturbed states of mind that would follow injuries to his self in his relationship with me. After acknowledgements of this kind from me, his mood changed dramatically. Slowly, he emerged from his lethargy, and a new phase in the analysis was opened. An old dream of L.'s recurred. In it, he brought me a tape. We were listening to it together, and the tape was playing in the reverse! The dream of listening to a tape together was old—what was new was the reversal of the tape. This indicated to him that a shift had just taken place and that I had at last acknowledged my own part in intensifying his feelings of guilt.

The cultural interest which he had abandoned began to return, slowly and fleetingly at first, and then with an intensity that consumed him as he tried to make up for lost time. He had no time for or interest in extramarital sexuality. Each step along the path toward the revival and continuation of his artistic aims was accompanied by intense anxiety that would cause him again to abandon his project as a hopeless task, too long postponed. Through a now engaged selfobject transference, the analysis led back to his childhood and to the contempt which his father showed for his artistic interests when he was a child. "They're waiting for you!" was a sarcastic comment he heard again and again. His anxiety states also led back to the relationship with his mother, which he now saw differently. Details emerged of her desperate need to control him. She promised undying devotion to him, dreaming that he would make a lot of money when he grew up and would take her to live with him away from the entombment of her neighborhood and her marriage. He recalled how she would bemoan her misfortune ("just my luck") when he fell and hurt himself or when he was sent home from school with a persistent nosebleed. He told of how she would go to bed for days if he got engrossed in his play and failed to come home for supper "on time" or if he strayed outside of the three-block limit she had set for him. This was the prison of his dreams, and these were his childhood crimes.

The anxiety he felt, we came to see, was not the anxiety of a cruel superego, but a revival over and over again of childhood experiences in which the initial establishment of an internally centered program and design for a self of his own confronted him with the lack of any confirmation of his existence. Only his repeated apologies, accompanying self-condemnations, and reimposed constrictions on himself would bring his mother back to life. The violence of his self-reproaches would increase the benevolent smile, the reassuring pat, as no other achievements could.

His masochistic fixation was both the consequence of his entrapment and the sole condition under which his psychological survival was possible. His guilt was not due to hostility toward his mother or father—though there was enough of that—but to the fact that he was forced over and over again to accept responsibility for the psychological defects of his mother in order to restore and maintain her functioning, upon which his own depended. His deepest anxiety was that of the isolating effect upon a self that cannot maintain its organization and cohesion without a sustaining environment, no matter what the price.

The change that has subsequently taken place in L.'s life is dramatic. Whereas before he felt that his life was over, he now looks forward with pleasure and pride to the experiences that lie ahead. He seems firmly set on his own path in his creative work and in his marriage.

In the analysis of L.'s self disorder, I found that I could escape from the dilemma of having to either gratify directly his emergent selfobject (narcissistic) needs as they were mobilized in analytic transferences or, alternatively, attempt to disabuse him of these needs or his efforts to pursue them. Four major prerequisites for analytic work in this area then became clear to me: (1) continuous extension of the capacity for empathic immersion in the subjective experience of my patients; (2) awareness of the positive developmental significance of idealizing and self affirming needs; (3) continuous extension of my capacity for recognition and acceptance of my own shortcomings in my responses to the remobilized archaic selfobject needs of my patients; and (4) increased understanding of the nature and therapeutic approach to the states of psychological disruption that occur in response to the injuries, frustrations, and disappointments that follow such inevitable shortcomings.

The work of Kohut in the emergence, analysis, and resolution of selfobject transferences has proved to be crucial in the further understanding and treatment of the negative therapeutic reaction. It illuminates basic elements in the interacting, intersubjective field that have hitherto been obscured or isolated. According to this view, selfobject transferences represent revived attempts at acquisition of previously unacquired basic psychological structure and revivals of previously thwarted developmental steps. When these attempts—emanating from an inadequately cohesive, precarious, and developmentally stunted self—encounter an analytic environment that in its consistent and relentless failure repeats a signal characteristic of the developmental milieu, the stage is set for negative therapeutic reactions. These reactions comprise all the symptomatology described in the analytic literature. They represent, in any particular patient, the recrudescence and intensification of symptoms that marked the original derailments of self development in relation to subjectively experienced and subjectively interacting primal selfobjects.

References

Abraham, K. (1919), A particular form of resistance against the psycho-analytic method. In: *Selected Papers*. New York: Basic Books (1953), pp. 303–311.

Asch, S. (1966), Depression: Three clinical variations. *The Psychoanalytic Study of the Child*, 21:150–171. New York: International Universities Press.

——— (1976), Varieties of negative therapeutic reaction and problems of technique. *J. Amer. Psychoanal. Assn.*, 24:383–407.

Balint, M. (1936), The final goal of psychoanalytic treatment, *Internat. J. Psycho-Anal.*, 67:206–216.

——— (1937), Early developmental stages of the ego: Primary object-love. In: *Primary Love and Psychoanalytic Technique*. London: Hogarth Press, 1952, pp.

Berliner, B. (1947), On some psychodynamics of masochism. *Psychoanal. Quart.*, 16:459–471.

Bion, W. (1962), Learning from Experience. London: Heinemann.

——— (1977), Seven Servants Book IV Attention and Interpretation. New York: Jason Aronson.

Edwards, B. (1979), Drawing on the Right Side of the Brain. Los Angeles: J. P. Tarcher, Inc.

Freud, A. (1952), A Connection between the States of Negativism and of Emotional Surrender. Author's abstract. *Internat. J. Psycho-Anal.*, 33.

Freud, S. (1914), On narcissism: An introduction. *Standard Edition*, 14:67–102. London: Hogarth Press, 1957.

——— (1917), A Difficulty in the Path of Psycho-Analysis. *Standard Edition*, 17:135–144. London: Hogarth Press, 1955.

——— (1918), From the history of an infantile neurosis. *Standard Edition*, 17:1–122. London: Hogarth Press, 1955.

——— (1923), The ego and the id. *Standard Edition*, 19:1–66. London: Hogarth Press, 1961.

——— (1933), New Introductory Lectures. *Standard Edition*, 22:3–182. London: Hogarth Press, 1964.

Gardiner, M., ed. (1971), *The Wolf-Man by the Wolf-Man*. New York: Basic Books.

Goldberg, A. (1975), A fresh look at perverse behavior. *Internat. J. Psycho-Anal.*, 56:335–343.

Hill, E. (1966), *The Language of Drawing*. Englewood Cliffs, N.J.: Prentice-Hall.

Jones E. (1955), Life and Work of Sigmund Freud, 2. New York, Basic Books.

Kernberg, O. (1975), *Borderline Conditions and Pathological Narcissism*. New York: Aronson.

Koestler, A. (1959), *The Sleepwalkers*. London: Hutchison.

Kohut, H. (1966), Forms and transformations of narcissism. In: *The Search for the Self* ed. P. Ornstein, New York: International Universities Press, 1978, pp. 427–460.

——— (1968), The psychoanalytic treatment of narcissistic personality disorders: Outline of a systematic approach. *The Psychoanalytic Study of the Child*, 23:86–113. New York: International Universities Press.

——— (1971), *Analysis of the Self*, New York: International Universities Press.

——— (1979), The two analyses of Mr. Z. *Internat. J. Psycho-Anal.*, 60:3–27.

———— & Wolf, E. (1978), The disorders of the self and their treatment: An Outline. *Internat. J. Psycho-Anal.*, 59:413–424.

Olinick, S. (1964), The negative therapeutic reaction. *Internat. J. Psycho-Anal.*, 45:540–548.

———— Reporter (1970), Panel on Negative therapeutic reaction. *J. Amer. Psychoanal. Assn.*, 18:655–672.

Rangell, L. (1979), Contemporary issues in the theory of therapy. *J. Amer. Psychoanal. Assn.,*. 27 (suppl.):81–112.

Riviere, J. (1936), A contribution to the analysis of the negative therapeutic reaction. *Internat. J. Psycho-Anal.*, 17:304–320.

Rothstein, A. (1980), Toward a critique of the psychology of the self. *Psychoanal. Quart.*, 49:423–455.

Stein, M. (1979), Review of *The Restoration of the Self. J. Amer. Psychoanal. Assn.*, 27:665–680.

Stolorow, R. (1975), Addendum to a partial analysis of a perversion involving bugs. *Internat. J. Psycho-Anal.*, 56:361-365.

Valenstein, A. (1979), The concept of "classical" psychoanalysis. *J. Amer. Psychoanal. Assn.*, 27 (suppl.):113–136.

Wallerstein, R. (1981), The Bipolar Self. Discussion of alternative perspectives. *J. Amer. Psychoanal. Assn.*, 29:377–394.

Winnicott, D. (1960), The theory of the parent-infant relationship. In: *The Maturational Processes and the Facilitating Environment.* New York: International Universities Press, 1965, pp. 37–55.

Part IV

DEVELOPMENT

Corrective Emotional Experience: A Self-Psychological Reevaluation

MARIAN TOLPIN

Kohut's work, according to recent ego psychological critiques (for example, Stein, 1979; Valenstein, 1979; Rothstein, 1980; Richards, 1981), erroneously emphasizes structural deficits instead of structural conflicts, and leads to instinctual gratifications and active efforts to cure instead of thorough-going psychoanalytic treatment. In particular, Kohut's theory and technique for the treatment of disorders of the self is compared to Alexander's (1956) corrective emotional experience, and to the active techniques he employed with "his later drift away from 'traditional' [ego psychology] psychoanalytic thought" (Stein, 1979, p. 677).

The comparison of self psychology and Alexander's idea of the analyst actively trying to counter obstacles to cure highlights a salient point which the critiques overlook—namely, that psychoanalysis has been in search of a theory with which to overcome obstacles to analysis from 1913 on (Oberndorf, 1947). Alexander, like Freud before him, was part of this search. After initial enthusiasm with the newly emerging ego psychology (to which he was an important contributor) Alexander again became increasingly concerned with negative therapeutic results. While experimenting with active analytic technique as Ferenczi had done, he remained a strict ego psychologist and continued to share the prevailing view that tenacious structural conflict was responsible for therapeutic difficulties. Corrective emotional experience was designed to correct such conflict by counteracting pathogenic parental influences.

Further, the comparison of Kohut's theory and technique with Alexander's idea of corrective emotional experience overlooks the fact that far from being a "deviation" Alexander's ideas are in a line of thought strongly advocated by Freud in 1919. Freud thought then that the future of psychoanalytic therapy lay with active techniques, and he particularly recommended those of Ferenczi. These techniques, later repudiated by Freud, are the direct precursors of Alexander's (Oberndorf, 1947). Although Freud rejected Ferenczi's methods, he himself advocated "after education" (1940) for patients who (paraphrasing) were not reared properly. It is noteworthy that psychoanalytic pioneers (Alexander, et al, 1966) recognized the importance of pathogenetic parental attitudes while they continued to hold the "traditional" view that these attitudes led to particularly refractory conflicts. Thus, while retaining the drive-defense-conflict theory which sufficed for neurosis, they tried unsuccessfully to alter their techniques to bring about the cure that analysis proper failed to effect.

In my opinion, a self-psychological reevaluation of the idea of corrective emotional experience is in order, in my opinion, because the process of transmuting internalization, set in motion by the analysis of selfobject transferences, is indeed a corrective for structural deficits; and because the process of analyzing the deficits does indeed take place in connection with the patient's profound emotional experience of being understood and assisted. This form of corrective experience, ongoing throughout the analysis, is a new edition of the "corrective developmental dialogue" of childhood, the dialogue between self and selfobject with which I shall continue.

The Corrective Developmental Dialogue: "Building-in" Self-supports

With the help of his mother and father, five-year-old Mike learned to ice skate. Both parents served as needed selfobject—an encouraging, admiring audience, idealized source of strength and support, ally, mentor, partner all rolled into one. Mike threw himself into his latest pursuit with enthusiastic abandon, literally as well as figuratively. He gave his all, and he made steady progress, undaunted by collapsing ankles, innumerable falls, bruised knees, and hurt pride. Halfway through the winter the balance shifted: Mike managed to stay up more than he fell down. He began to need little more than occasional encouragement from the sidelines, or a helping hand up from a particularly hard fall. Mike was proud of himself and his parents were proud of him. They enjoyed his enjoyment of himself.

One day he ran home from school to announce with great excitement that his teacher was going to take the whole kindergarten class to the school skating rink. She would ask some parents to accompany the children. He seemed to take it in stride that neither of his parents would be able to go. On the appointed day Mike was in high spirits, swinging his skates as he set off for school. He returned home down and dejected. Expectably responsive selfobject which she was, Mike's mother noticed that he was crestfallen and asked, ''What's wrong?'' Tearfully, Mike informed her, ''My legs didn't work right; my ankles wouldn't stand up.'' He had not been able to wait to get out on the ice to show what he could do, and then he floundered and fell. He had been a total flop! Expectably responsive and supportive, his mother protested, ''But Mike, you've been skating so well. What happened to you?'' Without a moment's hesitation Mike replied sadly, ''You weren't watching.'' For the moment, the missing firming functions of his selfobjects and the missing firmness of his own ankles and his entire self experience were one and the same thing.

There is nothing out of the ordinary either about a five-year-old's mother not watching him all the time, or about his being a temporary flop; and there is nothing out of the ordinary about this bit of ''talking cure'' taking place between child and parent. They are partners here in an ongoing corrective developmental dialogue, the dialogue that puts the fallen hero to rights. What was unusual, however, was this budding psychologist's capacity for introspection and empathy with his own state, his grasp of the link between his inability to stand up and the missing selfobject functions of his mother, and his capacity to put the whole thing into words. Mike was able to lay his finger on the factor Freud (1926) was searching for in ''Inhibitions, Symptoms, and Anxiety.'' Increasingly occupied with the kinds of patients for whom analysis failed (see for example, his 1919 discussion of failures of psychosynthesis), Freud asked why some people acquire the capacity to subject their anxiety (psychic pain and distress) to the normal workings of the mind, and why others come to grief over that task. The exchange between mother and child is an example of the innumerable exchanges which go on throughout the entire course of development. It is these innumerable exchanges between the expectably attuned parent and the child who is not "working right," which serve as the corrective emotional experience I refer to as the ongoing corrective developmental dialogue. The corrective dialogue works to enable the child to restore his faltering equilibrium and failing self-esteem, to recover from his anxiety and shaken belief in his own capacities. The example, then, illustrates the normal workings of the self-selfobject unit. Although the 5-year-old is reasonably buoyant and self-confident on his own he temporarily comes apart because he still needs the extra boost provided by the actual "gleam" of the mirroring selfobject. After his failure he is put back together again via the latter's renewed support, through repeated nontraumatic failures, such as the one I illustrated, and the repeated reaffirmation now provided by the corrective developmental dialogue.

Normally, the nuclear self organization is reasonably well established by the time the child comes of oedipal age. The more or less firm establishment of a center which holds together with expectable parental care is the precondition for the normal oedipal phase. When self-cohesion is faulty the child's uppermost concerns are with ways of holding himself together. By the same token, then, normal infantile sexuality (including normal oedipal sexuality), affectionateness, and assertiveness "splinter up" when the child suffers from unrelieved fragmentation (disintegration) anxiety. Remnants of the normal oedipal configuration are then in evidence as isolated sexual (libidinal) and aggressive drives. The child frequently turns to these remnants—to his erogenous zones and capacities for aggression—in an attempt to fill in for missing continuity and cohesion. The fact that neither parent can watch the child's performance can be experienced by the oedipal-aged child as no more than a tolerable in-phase frustration, one among many. When inevitable tolerable frustrations are coupled with reasonable satisfaction of legitimate developmental needs, the modulations and transformations of the child's nuclear grandiosity and idealization into the normal workings of the mind take place as though of their own accord. That is to say, by the oedipal period, an endless number of experiences of need for support (of the grandiose self, for example) have been coupled with expectable selfobject response to the need. These responses have been preserved ("internalized") as the normal self-supporting workings of an integrated body-mind-self. The "grandiose exhibitionistic self," the "idealized parent imago," and the "partnering (alter-ego) selfobject" have undergone the developmental modulations and transformations which make for the "grandiose [oedipal] delusion" (Ferenczi, 1913, p. 217) of the normal five-year-old; and for the normal workings with which he recovers from inevitable oedipal failures and disappointments. With these workings the child begins to support himself and recover his own balance.

Failures like Mike's are a fact of life in childhood, and they are repeated over and over again (a fact of childhood life relevant to the working-through phase of analysis). For children's failures to be "transmuted" into tolerable disappointment in themselves and their own performance, and into sustained capacities to recover and try again, there must be continued parental participation in a corrective exchange. Mike had suffered the relatively minute loss of selfobject supporting functions which he had not yet quite made into his own psychological substance. Along with this, he suffered a relatively minute but reversible loss or collapse of his own effective functioning and his confidence in himself. One might say he had received an immunizing dose of disintegration anxiety through the transient disruption of a newly acquired skill and the proud feeling that went with it—the proud feeling of being a big boy who could stand on his own two feet.

However, like most five-year-olds who live in a world with enough psychological oxygen and calcium—the selfobjects' contribution to the formation of a cohesive self—Mike recovered his bounce and remastered the art which had eluded him.

The toddlers' experience of the humiliating, enraging fall—from being proudly erect one minute, to being down and out the next, and their recovery from the fall—being lifted up by their selfobjects (at first), or by themselves, must have a profound effect on the developing psyche. The feelings about the fall and the recovery—the state of the self these feelings create—reverberate throughout a lifetime, and go from the sublime to the ridiculous. Starting with the sublime, the fall is an enduring symbol of the human condition. The metaphor is woven throughout centuries of literature, from the Bible to Camus' novel *The Fall*. Proceeding to the ridiculous, whenever adults literally stumble and fall, they experience automatic signals of disintegration anxiety, depression, and/or rage, and they "feel ridiculous." In short, the highs and lows experienced with everyday falls like Mike's are part and parcel of the psychology of everyday life, part of the infinite number of ups and downs human beings experience from birth to death. There are all of the literal ups and downs in the self experience, which start with being picked up and put down by the idealized, mirroring self-object and continue with the toddler's standing proudly erect one minute and falling flat the next; and there are the countless figurative ups and downs, like the heightened self-esteem of success and the lowered self-esteem of failure.

When parents in the role of selfobjects constitute an expectable psychological environment, the child who flops and fails is put to rights. The older child then holds on to the renewed parental supports, just as the younger child holds onto the parent's hand in order to hold himself or herself up. Speaking in self-psychological terms, the child mentally holds onto an "impersonalized," transformed intrapsychic replica of the fall and drop in self-esteem, and also mentally holds onto an "impersonalized" and transformed intrapsychic replica of the supportive verbal and nonverbal exchanges after the fall. These intrapsychic replicas ("structures" and "functions") are built up into the child's own capacities and these help the child to recover his or her emotional balance and to stand firm again. The corrective sequence I have described is experienced as a veritable repetition compulsion—it is the way the childhood self is held together, put back together, built up, and strengthened. A bit more of a self-righting capacity is built in and built up in connection with each in-phase repetition of the sequence.

Classical psychoanalytic theory does not account for the fact that certain parents cannot constitute an expectable psychological environment. Then essential ingredients needed for a child to remain psychologically alive and well, the ingredients that enable the child to replace parental workings with his or her own, are insufficient. Pathogenetic faults and failings in the everyday responsiveness of parents as selfobjects lead to pathogenetic faults and failings in the formation of psychic structure. There are thus deficiencies in the capacities that enable the child to grow up and recover from failures and injuries, to keep ensuing threats of disintegration anxiety, depletion, and rage to expedient signals. The acquisition of the capacities that enable the child to become "self-supporting" is not satisfactorily explained by theories based on the primacy of drives and drive objects. That is why most of these theories were buttressed by the idea of the analyst as an ally, partner, new object, real person, sustaining object, or diatrophic function (see Tolpin, 1979); and that is why all the supporting-confirming functions of the analyst are subsumed in self-psychology under the concept of the selfobject whose workings are experienced as precursors of the psychic structure needed for the filling in, firming, and consolidation of the self. The chronic failures of parents to respond to the child's normal needs to be watched, enjoyed, and encouraged, to be reaffirmed and given a lift when he or she falters and fails, inevitably lead to the chronic struggle of the injured self to recover as best it can. The child begins to resort to pathogenetic defensive measures to fill in for missing selfobject functions—to firm himself or herself, to hold himself or herself up (Tolpin, 1978; Tolpin and Kohut, 1980). From there, if substitute selfobjects do not step into the breach to assist the faltering child, disintegration anxiety leads to the nightmare world of the precariously balanced childhood self. The child and later the adult cannot "outgrow" the driven need for selfobjects. And, from the world of the child lacking expectable psychological responses to legitimate needs, a distorted developmental line can lead to the nightmare world of the child with an irreversibly shattered self who permanently reconstitutes himself or herself around nonhuman, fetishistic, sexualized delusional supports. This is not the psychological world of Oedipus. It is the shattered world of Kafka and Ionesco and Beckett (Tolpin, 1968).

The New Edition of the Corrective Developmental Dialogue

In essence, psychoanalytic treatment for analyzable disorders of the self involves the establishment, interpretation, reconstruction, and working through of a new transference edition of the self-selfobject unit. These latter-day editions are derivatives of formative psychological ties with either or both parents. Although the transference ties reverberate with childhood depths, they do not, cannot, and need not reproduce the mother-infant tie. Analyzable selfobject transferences do, can, and must reactivate a persisting core of normal childhood expectations—expectations that one or both parents, or substitutes for them, can and will respond to legitimate needs in an *expectable psychological way*. The reactivation of childhood expectations in a selfobject transference, and the analyst's understanding, interpretations, and genetic reconstructions of the persisting expectations and of the deficits in the self they express, are the necessary conditions for the corrective analytic treatment of disorders of the self. Patient and analyst repeatedly engage in new versions of the "talking cure"—reciprocal exchanges like those which led to Mike's capacity to bounce back from a fall.

It cannot be emphasized strongly enough that it is the patients' needs and the transferences of these needs that put the analyst in the role of selfobject. When analysts actively try to put themselves into this role, by playing prophet, savior, or redeemer (Freud, 1923), they are resorting to the active analytic techniques with which Freud, Ferenczi, and Alexander tried to fill a clinical-theoretical gap. By the same token, it cannot be emphasized strongly enough that while the transference tie to the analyst as reinstated selfobject fosters improved cohesion, vitality, etc., the new edition of a selfobject tie is also inevitably disrupted. Interpretations and genetic reconstructions of both the cohesion-fostering and cohesion-disrupting dimensions of the reactivated self-selfobject tie are the vehicles for the bit-by-bit psychic work which eventually leads to transmuting internalization and the strengthened self-supports that are the basis for the restoration of the self. Thus, the corrective-curative factors in resumed development in analytic therapy are analogous to the corrective factors in childhood development that normally lead to the establishment and consolidation of the self. The needed cohesion-fostering self-selfobject tie is reestablished, often against intense resistances stemming from chronic characterologic defensive measures. There are innumerable, inevitable disruptions of the tie—frequently latter-day versions of the pathogenetic childhood disruptions that led to the failure to acquire needed self-maintaining capacities. With each disruption that is understood and explained, the cohesion-fostering tie is reestablished; and with the reestablished tie there is a "corrective" recovery. In contrast to childhood, when dialogue is between child and parents, the transference edition of the developmental dialogue is between patient and analyst; the dialogue unfolds and deepens in connection with understanding and explaining, interpreting and reconstructing the present-day state of the self and its vicissitudes in reconnection with the selfobject. (These vicissitudes of self and selfobject include the defensive measures used in renewed pathogenetic attempts to avoid the reinjury that comes with) the inevitable deflation by and disappointments in the reinstated selfobject. For children and adults with developmental momentum still intact—those whose nuclear self was intact in childhood although insufficiently established—the repetition of the corrective sequence once again sets in motion the inherent process that accounts for normal childhood development: The patient little by little begins to take over the "lost" functions of the selfobject, and begins to right himself or herself when the selfobject leaves off.

In other words, bit-by-bit transmuting internalizations of the self-righting, self-restoring function of the selfobject transference are the essence of the corrective-curative factor for patients with self disorders. These internalizations, and the psychosynthesis and unification of the self-organization they maintain and restore, are the essence of the patient's chance for further development with a "different ending." To put this metaphorically, the corrective-curative factor is the reactivated psychological tendency of the normally endowed child to automatically take in what is needed from the environment, the way the lungs take in oxygen or the way bony structure takes up and utilizes calcium. When the psychological calcium has been ingested, absorbed, and transformed by the person's own workings, the insufficiently established self organization is firmed up; the selfobject transference is resolved in the form of strengthened self-corrective, self-supporting structures.

Case Example

A patient with deficits in self-righting capacities she needed to acquire for herself started a second analysis with nightmares similar

to those she had in her earlier analysis. For example, soon after starting
in treatment again, she had a dream that turned into a nightmare. She
was going up a mountain road in a jeep, riding with an attentive man.
She was not sure if his attentions were sincere. They came to a lovely
medieval town with a charming square, an inviting market, and an
ancient church that was being rebuilt. She was enjoying herself. At
the critical moment when she wanted to go home, she discovered that
the driver and the jeep were gone, the attentive man was gone, and
the rest of the party with whom she came were gone. She was lost,
unable to find her way home. She started running through deserted
streets in a panic, unable to find her way out. This dream-turned-
nightmare (and the beginnings of the selfobject transference it heralded)
reminded her of a recurrent nightmare she had during her first analysis:

> I am trying to get a bus to get to my analytic hour. I am
> desperate to get there. Either the bus doesn't come, or it doesn't
> stop, or it's going in the wrong direction, or it lets me out at the
> wrong place. I'm in this desolate area. I don't know whether it's
> a neighborhood which was bombed out by war and full of rubble,
> or whether it's an urban renewal area. The buildings are either
> down or coming down, or maybe they're being rebuilt. Anyway,
> it's getting later and later and I never get to the analyst's office.

This patient's nightmare gave representation and mental content
to an unrecognized psychological state, persisting from childhood,
which was reactivated now in an analyzable selfobject transference.
The self-state dream expressed the persisting childhood psychic reality
of the deficits in her own self organization, and in the pathogenetic
selfobject environment—the erratic bus and bus driver, the desolate,
unsupportive landscape. She was trying urgently to get the reactivated
parent imago (bus-bus driver) to pick her up because she was still in
need of a strengthened amalgam of self-righting, self-directing capacities and workings of her own. Without this complex amalgam of
internalized parental functions, children and adults can be literally or
figuratively lost. Psychologically speaking, they are unable to recover
their equilibrium, to get their bearings, to go in the right direction, to
find their own way.

In the first analysis, the nightmare of failing to get the bus and reach the analyst's office for her appointment was interpreted to the patient as an unconscious resistance. She was told she was ambivalent that unconsciously she did not wish to get there. The analysis was conducted in the ego psychology–structural conflict framework. The injured self and thwarted developmental needs were not yet recognized as the driving force for an analyzable transference. By the same token, specific needs to acquire additional psychic structure went unrecognized. Instead, the injured self was seen and explained much as Freud and Abraham saw it and explained it (see, for example, Freud, 1916; Abraham, 1919). Injuries and structural deficits resulting from real parental deficiencies were overlooked, and the results of both were ascribed to unconscious conflict and compromise formations. The patient's feelings of being injured were attributed to fixations on infantile claims for specialness, failures to come to terms with being born without a penis, unconscious guilt and need for punishment, and a narcissistic tendency to be insulted by the analyst's insights into her neurotic conflict. The curative factor was held to lie in correcting faulty conflict solutions and in facing and relinquishing infantile wishes for magical greatness. Thus, the corrective work of building up and strengthening the crumbling self of her nightmares remained incomplete.

The patient undertook the second analysis in a renewed effort to get where she was trying to go. The recurring dream which she then recalled expressed her continued need to reach the selfobject to overcome the depression which threatened the self (represented by the desolate neighborhood); to overcome the chronic sense of crumbling, insufficiency, and incompleteness (represented by the rubble and the buildings, which were part coming down, part going up); and to overcome the chronic feeling of being lost or going in the wrong direction. (For example, the patient experienced rising panic at the mere thought of changing direction and shifting to a field of endeavor more suited to her talents and interests.) The bus dream was a Rosetta Stone (Kohut, 1977, p. 144) when it was looked at from the point of view of the self as a driving force struggling to reach a selfobject with whom to complete the building up of a cohesive organization. It preserved the record of chronically recurring failures of the corrective childhood dialogue.

For very different reasons, neither of the patient's parents was sufficiently available or responsive in their roles as expectable admiring
audience to her display, as partner, ally, or participant in her acquisition
of new skills, as an admired source of strength she could temporarily
borrow.

The patient's mother was a decent woman and had a pleasant
enough relationship with the patient as an adult. However, the mother
was physically and emotionally distant during her childhood. She
shrank from physical contact with all her children, and literally did
not pick them up or hold them. Possessing little vitality of her own
she revolved around her attractive, dynamic husband. She could not
assist the patient to get to where she was going, since she herself relied
wholly on her husband to set directions. Self-centered and wholly
absorbed in his own pursuits, successes, and failures, he had little
patience and interest in his child's struggles to get somewhere. Both
parents functioned as the unempathic driver from whom she was unable
to acquire the self-directing capacities she needed to make her own.
It was to obtain these capacities that she urgently needed a psychologically reachable selfobject with whom rebuilding and strengthening
psychological work could be carried out.

As in this case, many patients' deficits in self-organization are
heir to the deficits in their selfobjects, and it is these deficits that are
in need of correction. It is no more possible to cure such structural
deficits by designing a "corrective emotional experience" intended
to counteract parental distance, indifference, coldness, and unavaila-
bility than it is to effect cure by attributing the deficits to faulty conflict
resolution. Deficits are cured and corrected by working through a
selfobject transference. Working through the tie to the selfobject and
preserving the functions of the tie through transmuting internalization
are one and the same thing.

Two additional self-state dreams of the patient provide glimpses
into the corrective internalizations that preserved the analyst-selfobject's strengthening role. The first of these dreams took place about
a month before the second analyst was to leave for a four-week vacation, and reflects the beginning of change in the self:

We [the patient and the analyst] were in a car on a winding

mountain road with a lot of twists and turns. You [the analyst] were driving. There were hairpin turns. I wasn't frightened, but as we went around the bends I was flung back and forth—against the steering wheel and then against the door, toward you and away from you. I was trying to brace myself for the turns. It was hard to do, but I didn't get hurt—it was just uncomfortable. Then we were at this beautiful home. There was a party and a lot of people. Then you weren't there anymore. The walls of the house began to move, the rooms got huge. I was trying to drive home on the same road. The road disappeared, I was lost, running through fields. I was in a panic.

Two years of analytic work had led back over and over again to the patient's persisting need to be seen and stopped for by the selfobject—to be picked up, psychologically speaking, when she was again feeling passed by and threatened by depression, disorganization, and losing her way. As on numerous earlier occasions, the "talking cure," the "corrective developmental dialogue" between analyst and patient, focused on her recurring psychological experience of beginning disorganization (fragmentation, disintegration) as she unconsciously anticipated being without the selfobject-driver and having to find her way on her own. Specifically, interpretations and reconstructions focused on the cohesion-disrupting aspects of the childhood tie reactivated in the transference, and on the beginning of the reexperience of the traumatic states of disintegration anxiety she could not yet stem on her own. This time the analyst recognized explicitly that with the impending vacation interruption she began to feel again as though she were going from a world in which she was firmly anchored (because her needs for support were recognized) to an indifferent world in which she was tossed about. Specifically, the analyst explained to the patient that she felt tossed about by the analyst's comings and goings, as she had felt tossed about in childhood when her parents were unable to remain in touch with her need for them to be the "drivers," before she could learn to drive herself.

Nevertheless, the self-selfobject unit had changed. The bus and the bus driver of the nightmare childhood universe were experienced now as a "real person"—the selfobject-analyst-driver; and she was getting ready for the coming separation by trying to brace herself. Still, the self as an independent center did not yet hold, and the current disruption of the selfobject tie threatened her with the recurrence of the old traumatic states. Understanding her continued need for the bracing effects of the selfobject and for psychological support while she was trying to get her bearings on her own now became a part of the working-through process. With each repetition of the sequence of restored equilibrium following disruption, a bit more of the selfobject's righting function "went inside."

The second example of the many dreams reflecting further internalizations and changes in the patient's self organization followed another year of the joint psychic work. (This work involved understanding of the continuing need for the reinstated selfobject and the disrupted psychological state that resulted when the need was thwarted; of the continuing "resistance" of the adult who was ashamed of her out-of-phase needs for continuing encouragement, recognition, and support; and of the fear of the persisting, intensified childhood needs intruding into an adult world in which they might once again be impatiently rebuffed, ridiculed, and misunderstood instead of recognized and explained.) The dream was as follows: "I was in a strange, unfamiliar neighborhood in the city where I grew up. I don't think I'd ever been there. I was on roller skates. It was beginning to get dark. I didn't know exactly where I was, and I didn't know my way home. But, I didn't panic. I figured I'd find my way." The immediate day residue was that the patient had noticed a pair of roller skates at her door. The background for the dream was her own improved psychological equilibrium and her growing self-confidence. The inner balance had shifted, and with the shift the self and the object world had changed again. Although there was still a long way to go in the corrective psychological work, she could begin to subject her anxiety to augmented "self-righting workings" of her own. The lift from the roller skates, like the lift from the driver-selfobject, was still partly from the transference and partly from the strengthened self-organization that was heir to the transference. The patient and her world were no longer in danger of crumbling.

The Fate of the Selfobject Transference: A Change in the Self

The last dream of the patient's analysis illustrates the fate of the analyst after analysis of a selfobject transference. In the dream the patient was huge with child. She was not sure whether she was pregnant and nearing labor, or whether she was carrying a small child. However, she was alone and she was struggling to get up a hill. She kept trying to shift the weight of the child in order to keep going (in contrast to the earlier dream, in which she was tossed about). The effort was tremendous. She was awkward and uncomfortable, and the weight of the child seemed enormous. She ended her account of the dream: "It was all I could do to keep on walking." It was an uphill struggle to take over the analyst-driver's multiple psychological functions. She was in considerable psychological pain as she terminated the analysis and, as it were, picked up and carried her child-self. Nevertheless, the dream of the uphill struggle was not a return to a nightmare world. Her resumed development had a different ending because she was now self-steering and self-propelling. In short, the fate of the new edition of the selfobject is an augmented and strengthened amalgam of self-supporting capacities or "structures"—the selfobject's functions "go inside."

To recapitulate the main point of this self psychological reevaluation of active techniques such as Alexander's "corrective emotional experience": Certain analyzable patients who fail to improve when correction of faulty conflict solution is the goal of the techniques applied to analytic work are actually suffering from structural deficits. The deficits are "inside" the patients themselves, regardless of their origins in pathogenetic selfobject failures; and it is the deficits, as well as their psychological aftermath (such as defensive measures employed in attempts to recover from lack of feeling real, alive, or continuous or from feelings of depression, anxiety, rage, or shame) that are in need of correction. The curative-corrective factors in the analytic treatment rest solely on the joint psychic work carried out in the analysis and the working through of the selfobject transference. When the work is correctly carried out, the inherent process of transmuting internalization is reactivated. As the end result of this process, the patient metabolizes needed functions of the analyst-selfobject and makes these into his or her own psychological substance.

References

Abraham, K. (1919), A particular form of neurotic resistance against the psycho-analytic method. *Selected Papers on Psycho-Analysis.* New York: Basic Books, 1953, pp. 303–311.

Alexander, F. (1925), A metapsychological description of cure. *Internat. J. Psycho-Anal.*, 6:13–34.

——— (1933), On Ferenczi's relaxation principle. *Internat. J. Psycho-Anal.*, 14:183–192.

——— (1950), Analysis of the therapeutic factors in psychoanalytic treatment. *Psychoanal. Quart.*, 19:482–500.

——— (1954), Some quantitative aspects of psychoanalytic technique. *J. Amer. Psychoanal. Assn.*, 2:685–701.

——— (1956), *Psychoanalysis and Psychotherapy: Developments in Theory, Technique and Training.* New York: Norton.

——— & French, T. M. (1946), *Psychoanalytic Therapy.* New York: Ronald Press.

——— Eisenstein, S. & Grotjahn, M. (1966), *Psychoanalytic Pioneers.* New York: Basic Books.

Ferenczi, S. (1913), Stages in the development of the sense of reality. In: *Sex in Psychoanalysis.* New York: Basic Books, 1950.

——— (1919a), Technical difficulties in the analysis of hysteria. In: *Further Contributions to the Theory and Technique of Psychoanalysis.* New York: Basic Books, 1952, pp. 189–197.

——— (1919b), On the technique of psychoanalysis. In: *Further Contributions to the Theory and Technique of Psychoanalysis.* New York: Basic Books, 1952, pp. 177–188.

——— & Rank, O. (1925), *The Development of Psychoanalysis.* New York: Nervous and Mental Diseases Publishing Co.

Freud, S. (1916), Some character-types met with in psycho-analytic work. *Standard Edition*, 14:309–333. London: Hogarth Press, 1957.

——— (1919), Lines of advance in psycho-analytic therapy. *Standard Edition*, 17:157–168. London: Hogarth Press, 1955.

——— (1923), The ego and the id. *Standard Edition*, 19:3–66. London: Hogarth Press, 1961.

——— (1926), Inhibitions, symptoms and anxiety. *Standard Edition*, 20:77–178. London: Hogarth Press, 1959.

——— (1940), An outline of psycho-analysis. *Standard Edition*, 23:141–207. London: Hogarth Press, 1964.

Kohut, H. (1977), *The Restoration of the Self.* New York: International Universities Press.

Oberndorf, C.P. (1947), "Book Review of *Psychoanalytic Therapy* by Alexander & French." *Psychoanal. Quart.*, 16:99–102.

Richards, A. (1981), Self theory, conflict theory and the problems of hypochondriasis. *Psychoanal. Quart.*, 36:319–338.

Rothstein, A. (1980), Toward a Critique of the Psychology of the Self. *Psychoanal. Quart.*, 49:423–455.

Stein, M. H. (1979), Review of *The Restoration of the Self* by Heinz Kohut. *J. Amer. Psychoanal. Assn.*, 27:665–680.

Tolpin, M. (1968), Eugene Ionesco's *The Chairs* and the theater of the absurd. *Imagos*, 25:119–139.

——— (1978), Self-objects and oedipal objects: A crucial developmental distinction. *The Psychoanalytic Study of the Child*, 33:167–184. New Haven: Yale University Press.

——— (1979), Discussion of "the sustaining object relationship," by Howard B. Levine. In: *The Annual of Psychoanalysis*, 7:219–225. New York: International Universities Press.

——— & Kohut, H. (1980), The psychopathology of the first years of life: Disorders of the self. In: *The Course of Life*, ed. S. Greenspan & G. Pollock. Washington, D.C.: U.S. Government Printing Office.

Valenstein, A. F. (1979), The Concept of "classical" psychoanalysis. *J. Amer. Psychoanal. Assn.*, 27:113–136.

Winnicott, D. W. (1970), The mother-infant experience of mutuality. In: *Parenthood: Its Psychology and Psychopathology*, ed. E. J. Anthony & T. Benedek. Boston: Little, Brown, pp. 246–256.

Fantasy or Reality? The Unsettled Question in Pathogenesis and Reconstruction in Psychoanalysis

ANNA ORNSTEIN

The reciprocal feedback between the technique of psychoanalysis and the theory of the illnesses analysis is intended to cure requires periodic reexamination. Progress in psychoanalysis can only be assured when the relationship between these two aspects of psychoanalysis is carefully preserved. Should they become out of tune with each other, the discrepancy between them signifies that the particular theory guiding the treatment process has to be revised. As Kris put it: "Progress in psychoanalysis tends to manifest itself by a gradual, sometimes imperceptible shading of our views and procedures, as a process of sifting, of constant adjustment of theory and practice" (Kris, 1956, p. 55).

The relationship between the theory of analyzable psychological illnesses and psychoanalytic technique is of particular importance during "transitional periods" in the evolution of psychoanalysis as a science of depth psychology. We are currently in such a transitional period. For some time, only the psychoneurotic conditions — psychological conditions that can be related to the unresolved conflicts of the oedipal phase of development—had been considered analyzable. Object relations theory and the various developmental theories have

381

extended the boundaries of psychoanalysis beyond the oedipal into the preoedipal area of development, but these extensions have not occurred without serious controversies. Analysts remained preoccupied with the distinction between "oedipal" and "preoedipal" forms of psychopathology as an indication of important differences in the expected course and expected outcome of a particular analysis. In terms of the course, "preoedipal issues" were considered more likely to indicate the need for parameters (Eissler, 1953), and the outcome in such an analysis was not considered likely to be as favorable as in cases where the patient developed a "true" transference neurosis—the transference reproduction of an infantile neurosis. Increasingly, analysts have been unable to identify the presence of a true transference neurosis because preoedipal issues had been mobilized in such analyses and changed the configuration of the transference. These changes have had important effects on the practice of psychoanalysis. The technique was no longer in harmony with the theory of the illness that analysis claimed to be able to cure. This divergence interrupted the all-important reciprocal feedback between practice and theory.

A case in point is Greenacre's (1975) observation that reconstructions in their original form are neglected by the current generation of psychoanalysts; that instead of periodic, comprehensive reconstructions, present-day analysts simply include this aspect of psychoanalysis in the interpretive process. Does the omission of comprehensive reconstructions in the course of analysis indicate a neglect of the genetic point of view? Or does this change in technique indicate that uncertainty has developed about what is genetically significant and therefore about what should be included in a psychoanalytic reconstruction? Greenacre's regret about the fate of reconstructions in the present-day practice of psychoanalysis is related to the fact that reconstruction is not only an important technical tool of psychoanalysis but is its major scientific tool as well. Genetic reconstructions of his original cases provided Freud with an outline of the various libidinal phases of psychosexual development, which served as the basis for the evolution of psychoanalytic developmental theory as we know it today.

I would suggest that Greenacre's observation of the neglect of reconstructions in their original form is related to a gradual and imperceptible change in the thinking of the current generation of analysts about the pathogenesis and symptom formation of the psychological conditions they have been encountering in their analytic practices. In other words, this change in technique is related to the increasing frequency with which analysts have been encountering preoedipal conditions and the decrease in their ability to identify a transference neurosis.

In this paper, I shall examine the relationship between the theory of pathogenesis of analyzable psychological conditions and the content of reconstructions. It is in this relationship that theory and technique in psychoanalysis most clearly intersect.

Fantasy or Reality?

The controversy over whether unconscious, drive-related fantasies or actual traumatic events are responsible for the development of a psychological disorder is not new to psychoanalysis. The significance of *actual events* in pathogenesis was revised in Freud's own mind several times during his lifetime. He gave five successive accounts of the changes in his views about the reality of infantile sexual traumata (Schimek, 1975). "The seduction theory," which lasted from 1892 to 1897 and held actual events of sexual seduction in the patient's childhood to be responsible for later neurotic developments, was changed drastically in the course of Freud's self-analysis. With the discovery of the Oedipus complex and infantile sexuality, he related the endopsychic conflicts responsible for hysterical symptoms primarily to sexual and aggressive *fantasies*; actual events were of little or no significance in these conflicts. When Freud introduced the concept of "psychical reality" (1914, 1916–17, 1925), *he replaced the factual reality of unconscious memories with the psychic reality of unconscious fantasies.*

In terms of reconstructions, this meant that it was not sufficient for the analyst to recover a certain number of fragments of forgotten memories of actual events. Rather, to arrive at a genetically meaningful "construction" (Freud, 1937), sexual and aggressive fantasies related to these events had to be recovered in the course of analysis as well. These fantasies were responsible for the original distortions of the childhood reality and were now held responsible for the distorted perception of the analyst in the transference. The goal of reconstruction derived from this theory of pathogenesis was to undo the childhood *distortions* of reality and to help the patient recognize and accept the sexual and aggressive wishes and fantasies of childhood as they have now become reactivated in the transference.

Let me describe two representative examples: First, a female patient's memory of the mother of her childhood as unempathic, overtly hostile, or competitive with the little girl would require uncovering the patient's unconscious hostility and rivalry toward the mother in order for the patient to accept the distortion of her childhood perception of the mother. Another example would be a male patient's report of a tonsillectomy between the ages of four and six having been experienced as an act of castration. A genetically meaningful reconstruction would have to uncover the child's own castrating wishes toward his father, which had distorted the experience of the tonsillectomy so that it was experienced as if it had been an act of castration. The importance of reconstructing these pathogenic unconscious fantasies has been most clearly stated by Arlow (1963): "In clinical practice, it is most important to be able to uncover the precise way in which the unconscious instinctual wish is given form in the fantasy" (p. 21).

I am suggesting that a relatively innocuous change in technique—that analysts no longer offer periodic, comprehensive reconstructions of unconscious fantasies—signaled a change in the theoretical perspective of practicing analysts regarding the pathogenesis of analyzable psychological conditions. Specifically the change in technique signaled a change in perspective on symptom formation from a view of it as the result of an instinctual conflict with its origins in fantasy to a greater appreciation of the pathogenic influences of the environment. This shift occurred under the influence of discoveries made via analytically sophisticated observations of infants, toddlers, and their families, as well as reports from the offices of child analysts who recognized the importance of the environment for those developmental needs of children that are not drive related. This "psychoanalytic developmental view" could not be systematically included in the practice of psychoanalysis, however, because (1) these observations were made *outside* the analytic situation and (2) the defects and deficits created by the environment *by definition* were not considered analyzable.

Failures in Parental Empathy and the Nature of Psychic Trauma

In view of the direction in which psychoanalytic practice has been heading, it is not farfetched to say that the discovery of the selfobject transferences (Kohut, 1971) was a most welcome and timely development in the history of psychoanalysis. Selfobject transferences reactivate subjective emotional states of childhood, the sources of which are to be found in faulty parental responses to the child's non-drive-related (mirroring and idealizing) developmental needs.

At first, the discovery of the selfobject transferences retained the relatively sharp demarcation between the pathogenesis and etiology of the disorders of the self (Kohut, 1977) on the one hand—that is, the "deficiency illnesses"—and the psychoneuroses on the other. M. Tolpin (1978) affirmed this delineation and convincingly pointed out the essential differences between structural defects or deficits (which may be camouflaged by a "neuroticlike superstructure") and the neurotic symptomatology. In terms of reconstruction, this means that what has to be reconstructed in the psychoneuroses are the unconscious sexual and aggressive fantasies, while in the "deficiency illnesses," the analyst has to reconstruct the impact of nonempathic or partially empathic environment.

This distinction cannot be maintained unless failures in the self-object functions of parents are considered pathogenic only when they occur early in development, that is, prior to the oedipal phase; and unless only these defects and deficits are considered to give rise to selfobject transferences. We would now maintain, however (Kohut, 1977; A. Ornstein, in press), that even with the relatively advanced structuralization of the psyche that is present at the time of the Oedipus complex, parents and other important people in a child's environment continue to have structure-building selfobject functions. The absence or partial absence of these functions can still be potentially traumatic and have pathological consequences. This is in keeping with Kohut's (1977) view that emotional maturity is not characterized by absolute independence from objects; rather, selfobject needs exist throughout life, even though these needs change from archaic to more mature forms.

The traumatic potential of chronic parental failure in empathy (which is ultimately responsible for the execution of parental selfobject functions) is akin to Khan's (1963) description of the "cumulative trauma." According to Khan, cumulative traumata do not necessarily distort ego development in a gross way as much as they "*bias* it." He states: "In this context it would be more accurate to say that these breaches [in the mother's protective shield] over the course of time and through the developmental process cumulate silently and invisibly. Hence the difficulty in detecting them clinically in childhood. . . . They achieve the value of trauma only cumulatively and in retrospect" (p. 291). This perspective on the nature of psychic trauma helps us appreciate further the shift from a periodic comprehensive reconstruction to an ongoing interpretive one. Instead of attempting to reconstruct a single pathogenic event and the unconscious drive-related fantasies that would correspond to these events, analysts have become responsive to the cumulative traumatic effect of parental failures in empathy, which may have encompassed long periods of time in the child's development.

Clinical Example

Just how profoundly the theory of pathogenesis of analyzable conditions affects reconstructions is demonstrated in a case reported by Kris (1956). Kris, as a child analyst, was eager to integrate the developmental point of view into psychoanalytic technique. His attempt to do so was supported by his in-depth knowledge of children who were attending the Yale Child Study Center and their parents. With his report of the case of Dorothy, Kris raised a similar question to my own regarding the relationship between pathogenecity and reconstruction.

In his discussion of Dorothy, Kris indicates the complexities involved in genetic reconstructions and how developmental considerations may aid the process. Kris challenges the reader to predict how Dorothy's analyst twenty years later might go about reconstructing the potentially traumatic events in the child's life. Fortunately, in addition to describing these events, Kris also shares with the reader important observations about the parents' personalities and their relationships with each other and with the child. I emphasize the point about the parents' personalities because Kris's theoretical bias regarding fantasy or reality in pathogenesis appears most obvious in this regard.

Dorothy's parents had a stormy marriage, Kris tells us, and the little girl positioned herself skillfully between her two parents. While behaviorally she remained attached to her mother, she did not follow her "into her phobic tendencies," but rather shared her father's love for animals and the outdoors. Kris also records the mother's intense jealousy of Dorothy—specifically that the child did not share her apprehension of dogs with her. In a somewhat paranoid vein, the mother experienced the child's close attachment to her father as if the two of them were "ganging up on her."

Dorothy suffered a series of potentially traumatic events between the ages of two and three: A brother was born, her grandfather died, and a beloved dog was accidentally killed. When Kris projected the meaning these events would be given by Dorothy's future analyst, he interpreted the events in terms of their oedipal-sexual significance: "the wish for a child from the father, the death wish against the mother, the fear about both sexual and destructive impulses, and finally the fear of castration which seems age adequately added and superimposed" (pp. 75–76).

This strictly instinctual view of the pathogenesis of Dorothy's future neurosis is particularly significant, since Kris had commented earlier on the importance that "peculiarities of the parent's personality" (p. 68) have on the child's development. It appears that he could consider the parents' personalities as important in relation to the child's psychosexual development or as possibly pathogenic in a general sense, but not as a specific cause of neurosis—that is, as a cause of the only psychological condition that was at that time considered analyzable. If Kris expected Dorothy to develop an analyzable condition, her illness had to be understood and explained in terms of sexual and aggressive *fantasies* related to the Oedipus complex. And since, in keeping with this theory, a neurosis can only be reversed if the drive-related fantasies are made central to the working-through process, it was these fantasies that Kris projected as important for reconstruction in Dorothy's future analysis. Kris's predictions about the meaning of the potentially traumatic experiences in Dorothy's life were in keeping with the generally accepted neurosogenic effects of such fantasies.

But what is the pathogenic importance of Kris's description of the mother's jealousy of Dorothy's attachment to her father? This jealousy apparently antedated the time at which we would expect a child to be developmentally engaged in the oedipal conflict. But whatever meaning the mother's jealousy had for the child preoedipally, it would have to be of *special neurosogenic significance* during the oedipal phase itself. The mother who is jealous of her little girl's ability to secure her father's special attention because she is *his* little girl, is unable to mirror—that is, openly delight in—this particular progressive move in the child's psychological development. Such a failure in parental selfobject responsiveness can severely affect a girl's self-perception in terms of her femininity and sexual functioning.

It is important to stress that I am not speaking of an interpersonal conflict between a child and a mother who is jealous. There indeed may be many behavioral manifestations of conflicts between a sexually maturing girl and a jealous mother. But I am rather stressing the developmental significance of the mother as an oedipal selfobject. When the mother fails to respond to the girl's legitimate developmental need to be mirrored in her phase-appropriate rivalry, competitiveness, and sexual flirtatiousness, the mother *actively* participates in the genesis of a psychological condition that the child may develop later in life. This condition may then be erroneously traced to the child's unconscious oedipal fantasies; that is, her memory of her mother as having been jealous would be considered as a projection of the child's own jealousy and hostility toward her.

In our classical conceptualization of the Oedipus complex, the child experiences the same-sex parent primarily in terms of the unconscious conflicts that emanate from the child's unconscious rivalrous and hostile feelings. The resolution of these conflicts is supposed to occur through identification with the same-sex parent. However, when self-psychological considerations are included in this developmental event, we recognize that failure (or partial failure) on the part of the same-sex parent to respond to the child's active engagement in the oedipal experience results in a structural deficit. Identification with the same-sex parent under these circumstances will serve the function of filling in these deficits. Identification serves defensive purposes, then, and cannot be considered a primary psychic structure (A. Ornstein, in press).

The difference between identification and maternal mirroring self-object functions can be highlighted with a simple example: A mother who is secure in her feminine identity and in the attractiveness of her own feminine self is an ideal figure for a girl of oedipal age to identify with. However, the same mother may be unable to mirror the little girl's own, unique ways of expressing her emerging femininity. The child's oedipal passions and the rivalry, jealousy, and possessiveness of the same-sex parent require a particularly sensitive response from the parents, who are the targets of these very same affects (Kohut, 1977). When the little girl, in response to her developmental needs, actively turns to her father, it is then that she needs her mother's delight and affirmative mirroring, and it is then that she can be traumatized either by the absence of such a response or by a response of rivalry and jealousy.

Considering the updated view of the nature of the Oedipus complex, would we give a different answer now to Kris's question regarding reconstruction if Dorothy should undergo analysis later in life than she did in 1956? I believe we would. For example, Dorothy's regressive transferences and their working through might produce memories in which she remembers feeling distant from her mother, feeling her mother was hard to please, and feeling not totally acceptable to her mother. These memories could now be utilized to reconstruct the pathogenic aspects of the mother's personality in order to fully appreciate Dorothy's intrapsychic childhood experiences. If they are interpreted only as the child's distorted view of the mother resulting from the child's hostile, rivalrous impulses toward the mother in the context of the oedipal struggle for the father, the reality of the mother's reaction toward Dorothy as Kris observed it would not be given full consideration.

Anthony (1970) comments on the one-sided view of analysts on the Oedipus complex. As Kris did earlier, Anthony draws attention to Freud's description of the parents of Little Hans. "Both parents, in their several ways, were responding to the boy's oedipal provocations and pressures in expectable ways that have been replicated in subsequent studies. *Nevertheless, it is rare in any of these for the analyst's attention to be focused on the parental reaction*" (p. 279, italics added). One such "replication" was the analysis of seven-year-old Paul, reported by Leo Rangell (1950). The mother in this case was described as suffering from anxiety symptoms, "but little more is said about the reactions of the parents" Anthony concludes from Rangell's report; "the analysis of the oedipal conflict is confined to the boy" (Anthony, 1970, p. 280).

Returning to Dorothy, what advantages would a present-day analyst have in predicting the manifestations of Dorothy's transferences and the course of her analysis? The analyst would be aware of the fact that "the presence of a firm self is a precondition for the experience of the Oedipus complex" (Kohut, 1977, p. 227). This means that the presence of sexual themes or triangular configurations in the patient's associations does not indicate that the psychopathology is related to a faulty resolution of the Oedipus complex. Rather, in the case of an originally poorly consolidated self, such manifestations are likely to be efforts—through sexualization of various mental functions—to establish or to maintain a self that is threatened in its cohesion.

Today we would also be aware of the effect that the gender of the person who serves primary selfobject functions has on the child's oedipal experiences. In Dorothy's case, the primary selfobject was the father, not the mother. From the report we learn that at age 2½ Dorothy had already successfully "escaped" an identification with her mother's phobic attitudes and had established instead a strong emotional bond with her outgoing and carefree father. The question is, was this early identification with the father a primary or compensatory psychological structure or a defensive one? In the latter case, the identification with the father would be covering up defects related to failures in the early merger experiences with the mother.

This question naturally could only be answered by studying the nature of the regressive transference that Dorothy would develop in the course of the analysis. From our current state of knowledge, however, we would be able to predict that a genuine object-instinctual transference would only be possible if the psychological structures Dorothy had originally developed in relationship to her father were primary in nature. But if these structures were defensive, a regressive transference would expose the defects related to failures in the early merger experiences with the mother.

If Dorothy entered the oedipal phase with relatively severe or moderate degrees of preoedipal structural deficits, then this developmental phase, instead of making crucial contributions to the consolidation and enrichment of her self, would be utilized to ward off serious or moderate forms of fragmentation. Clinically, these are the pseudo-oedipal forms of self pathology (Kohut, 1972) that in psychoanalysis give rise to one or another form of selfobject transferences.

I wish to emphasize, however, that even if Dorothy entered the oedipal phase with a relatively cohesive self, the experiencing of her oedipal passions would still require appropriate parental responses in order for this developmental phase to make full contributions to her developing self and specifically to her feminine self.

Reconstruction: A Self-Psychological Perspective

The reconstruction of the pathogenic aspects of parents' personalities presents a special problem in psychoanalysis, even in instances where the parents' pathogenic effect on the adult disturbance is not too difficult to discern. The concern of analysts in attempting such reconstructions is related to the fear of "parent-blaming"—that the analysand, instead of becoming introspective and self-analytical, will externalize his or her anxieties and problems.

Kris (1956), in the same paper in which he discusses the case of Dorothy, warns about the difficulties in reconstructing the parents' personalities in the course of the analysis:

> In my experience we succeed only in the course of long and on the whole successful analytic treatments, since interpretations which take the nature of the parents' personality into account obviously require particular caution and a wealth of affirmative impressions, such as in this instance only the prolonged analysis of reactions in the transference situation can provide. Only this caution can protect us against the distorting element of memory which is hardly ever deeper ingrained than in the changing facets which characterize the report of adult patients on their parents [p. 68].

The empathic immersion into the patient's subjective experiences in the psychoanalytic treatment process provides the circumstance that Kris described as necessary for gathering "affirmative impressions" in the reconstruction of the parents' personalities.

It would be a mistake, however, to consider the reconstruction of the parents' personalities (or peculiarities) as *the* central aspect of the interpretive-reconstructive process as this is informed by self-psychological considerations. Rather, the central aspect in this process is the recovery of complex childhood emotional states and their behavioral concomitants, as these were experienced within—and in relationship to—the original selfobject environment. When the patients' childhood self states—such as a profound sense of loneliness, the sense of being isolated, compulsive daydreaming, or grandiose and revengeful fantasies—are reconstructed in the course of an analysis, patients frequently experience a "that's me" feeling, a sense of being understood longitudinally, as it were—an experience that constitutes a powerful motivation for ongoing analytic work (A. Ornstein, 1974). These childhood emotional states (self states) have to be considered "the precursors of the adult disturbance" (Kohut, 1971, p. 95), which may or may not be "preserved" in the form of a visual memory. When they are, memories such as banging one's head against the floor in helpless rage or pressing a tear-streaked face against the windowpane in anxious anticipation serve as screen memories, around which a host of childhood affects and fantasies have crystallized. The analysis of these memories follows the well-known principles of the analysis of screen memories.

In recovering these intrapsychic experiences of childhood, based on transference affects and recovered memories, the traumatic aspects of the parents' personalities become progressively clarified. The analyst can then reconstruct the pathogenic aspects of the parents' personalities (most frequently moderate to severe degrees of self pathology, latent schizophrenia, or chronic depression), that interfered with their "average expectable" selfobject functions. In this process, the analyst does not aim at an accurate reconstruction of the parents' total personalities any more than the analyst would aim at accuracy in reconstructing anything else which is "external" to the patient's internal experiences. In reconstructing the failure (or partial failure) of the environment to have responded to the child's narcissistic developmental needs in a phase-appropriate fashion, we recognize the "strain" or cumulative traumatic effect on the growing child's psyche, resulting in structural deficits of varying severity. Technically, "parent-blaming" is avoided by recognizing that the intrapsychic experiences of childhood have characterological and behavioral consequences that profoundly affect the parents' attitude toward the child and the child's ultimate perception of the parent. Reconstructive interpretations focus as much on childhood character and behavior patterns and the effect of these on the environment, as they do on the parents' failure in empathy in responding to the child's developmental needs. When the analysand's character defenses are included in the process of interpretive reconstructions, the parents' failures are not viewed in isolation but in relationship to the childhood solutions that continually reinforced or provoked subtle or overt forms of parental rejections. These patterns become reactivated in the transference, and their reconstruction establishes the continuity between the past and the present.

Reconstructions based on selfobject transferences, then, do not aim to recover actual single events as pathogenic, nor do they aim to recover unconscious fantasies related to the drives. Rather, they aim to recover intrapsychic experiences of childhood and their attendant behavioral consequences, which *in the context of the original selfobject relationships* give meaning to the analysand's current symptoms and transference manifestations.

Reconstructing the past, however meaningfully, does not in itself constitute the essentially curative aspects of psychoanalysis. By bringing about changes in the analysand's current psychic reality, however, such reconstructions make important contributions to the curative process. "In our clinical work, we hope that the patient-analyst interaction will help the patient construct a new representation of his past, a more complete and interpreted personal history, with a sense of continuity of the motives that make him an active agent in his present life, neither helpless nor omnipotent" (Schimek, 1975, p. 862).

Summary

This paper attempts to clarify the relationship between the theory of pathogenesis of the currently analyzable psychological conditions on the one hand, and the practice of reconstruction on the other. Complementarity, in which it is theorized that what is pathogenic in a given case is the manner in which an external event "complements" a drive-related fantasy, has not been discussed here. Complementarity as an explanataion of pathogenesis was omitted because the intent of this paper was not to reemphasize the role that actual experiences have in the pathogenesis of analyzable conditions. Rather, the specific issue raised was the pathogenic significance given to unconscious oedipal (sexual and aggressive) fantasies and to the empathic or partially empathic parental responses to the child's legitimate selfobject (mirroring and idealizing) needs. The difference between the view of pathogenesis in these two theories becomes most obvious when questions are raised regarding the content of reconstructions is closely examined.

An example of the way in which the theory of pathogenesis affects the content of reconstruction is the case of Dorothy reported by Kris in 1956. Although Kris had known the child and her parents intimately and had made note of the mother's jealousy of the little girl, his prediction was still that Dorothy's future analyst would reconstruct the child's unconscious oedipal fantasies as having been pathogenic for her. This is understandable, since at that time in the history of psychoanalysis only unresolved oedipal conflicts were considered analyzable. Kris could not then have predicted that Dorothy could develop selfobject transferences that would expose the structural deficits related to faulty maternal mirroring of her oedipal attachment to her father.

But the reconstruction of parental psychopathology has been problematic for present-day analysts even when their pathogenic effect on the adult disturbance is not difficult to discern. Reconstruction of parental psychopathology has been feared probably because it is viewed as "parent-blaming," which promotes externalization on the part of the patient rather than introspection and a self-analytic attitude.

However, the reconstruction of parental failures in empathy is not the central aspect of reconstruction of selfobject transferences. Rather, it is the reconstruction of childhood self states that constitutes the essential aspect of reconstruction. It is in relationship to these childhood self states that childhood memories, including those related to the parents, can be recovered. This emphasis on the reconstruction of childhood self states and their attendant behavioral manifestations requires that the view of the pathogenesis of analyzable conditions that has been implicit in the practice of psychoanalysis now be made explicit. Such an explicit statement would reestablish the reciprocal feedback system between the technique of analysis and the theory of the illnesses that analysts are now capable of analyzing—a reciprocity that is central for the continued development of psychoanalysis as a depth-psychological science.

References

Anthony, E. J. (1970), The reactions of parents to the oedipal child. In: *Parenthood: Its Psychology and Psychopathology*, ed. E. J. Anthony & T. Benedek. Boston: Little, Brown, pp. 275–288.

Arlow, J. (1963), Conflict, regression and symptom formation. *Internat. J. Psycho-Anal.*, 44:12–22.

Eissler, K. (1953), The effect of the structure of the ego on psychoanalytic technique. *J. Amer. Psychoanal. Assn.*, 1:104–143.

Freud, S. (1914), On the history of the psycho-analytic movement. *Standard Edition*, 14:3–66. London: Hogarth Press, 1957.

——— (1916–17), Introductory lectures on psycho-analysis. *Standard Edition*, 16. London: Hogarth Press, 1963.

——— (1925), An autobiographical study. *Standard Edition*, 20:3–74. London: Hogarth Press, 1959.

——— (1937), Constructions in analysis. *Standard Edition*, 21:255–269. London: Hogarth Press, 1964.

Greenacre, P. H. (1975), On reconstruction. *J. Amer. Psychoanal. Assn.*, 23:693–712.

Khan, M. (1963), The concept of cumulative trauma. *Psychoanalytic Study of the Child*, 18:286–306.

Kohut, H. (1971), *The Analysis of the Self*. New York: International Universities Press.

——— (1972), Thoughts on narcissism and narcissistic rage. In: *The Search for the Self*, ed. P. H. Ornstein. New York: International Universities Press, 1978, pp. 615–658.

——— (1977), *The Restoration of the Self*. New York: International Universities Press.

Kris, E. (1956), The recovery of childhood memories in psychoanalysis. *The Psychoanalytic Study of the Child*, 11:54–88. New York: International Universities Press.

Ornstein, A. (1974), The dread to repeat and the new beginning: A contribution to the psychoanalysis of the narcissistic personality disorders. *The Annual of Psychoanalysis*, 2:231–248. New York: International Universities Press.

——— (in press), Oedipal selfobject transferences: A clinical example. In: *Reflections in Self Psychology*, ed. J. Lichtenberg & S. Kaplan. New York: International Universities Press.

Rangell, L. (1950), A treatment of nightmares in a seven-year-old boy. *The Psychoanalytic Study of the Child*, 5:358–390. New York: International Universities Press.
Schimek, J. C. (1975), The interpretation of the past: Childhood traumas, physical reality, and historical truth. *J. Amer. Psychoanal. Assn.*, 23:845–865.
Tolpin, M. (1978), Selfobjects and oedipal objects: A crucial developmental distinction. *The Psychoanalytic Study of the Child*, 33:167–187. New Haven: Yale University Press.

Development of Verbal Self-Expression

BONNIE E. LITOWITZ and NORMAN S. LITOWITZ

Psychoanalytic evidence regarding the development of the individual has come from reconstructions of the past in analytic settings, for example, from the free associations and dreams of patients. Based on this retrospective evidence, psychoanalytic theoreticians have constructed developmental progressions for the individual from infancy to adulthood. The question arises, then, whether evidence from studies of early childhood supports these posited developmental progressions. The two most likely sources for such *in situ* evidence are developmental psychology and developmental psycholinguistics. This paper will concern itself with the latter and, more specifically, with the verbal self-expression by children.

There are two ways one can refer to oneself as differentiated from another: one can use proper names, or one can use personal pronouns (*I, me, mine*). We will suggest in this paper that these two forms of self-expression are not substitutes for each other but represent sequential developmental stages. Furthermore, we will suggest that these linguistic entities correspond to, represent, and perhaps influence the simultaneously occurring development of the individual as object and as subject or self, respectively. We are using Goldberg's (1980) definition of self as "the representation of [an individual] in terms of a multitude of functional and lasting relationships with others" (p. 5). There is no single term uniformly used to refer to the individual as object, in contrast to self. "Object" is not used here in the usual psychoanalytic sense of terms such as, "external object" or "internal object representation," but rather in the sense that a person is an object in the world and an object to others—that is, is animate, visible to others, has arms and legs, has a name, etc. Proper names, which are acquired earlier than pronouns, are names for particular objects; and the acquisition of a proper name is the way a child indicates his or her difference from other objects ("Billy" versus both "Tommy" and "chair"). The later acquisition of personal pronouns is related to the development of an individual as a subject in object relationships.

The development of the individual as object and as self are stages in the development of object relations. By object relations we mean the affective investment by others in an individual and by the individual in significant others (such as the mother). We will review several theorists who are concerned with object relations theory, in particular, those who mention use of proper names and pronouns as instrumental in or representative of evolving object relations. These authors do not always use a uniform set of terms to refer to what we have termed the individual as object and as self, so when necessary, we will note the authors' particular distinctions.

All psychoanalytic theories stress that the individual's psychic structure develops out of the matrix of the mother-child dyad. The notion of this period as a "precursor of the dialogue" (Spitz, 1963b) emphasizes not only certain aspects of the mother-child interaction but also focuses attention on those aspects that are important for later language development: reciprocity, internalization, and symbolization. Just as psychic structure develops out of interaction with another, language develops only in the context of communication with another. The axiom of the Soviet psychologist Vygotsky (1962, 1978) that all the functions of language that are intrapsychic were originally interpsychic is similar in some aspects to the concept of internalization as it was first described by Freud (1914, 1917, 1923). A major difference between Freud's explanations and Vygotsky's lies in whether this process originates from within the child or from within the dyadic relationship. Klein and Tribich (1981) suggest there has been a shift in post-Freudian schools of object relations theories (e.g., Kernberg, Guntrip, Fairbairn, Winnicott) from Freud's original within child focus (instinctual discharge through objects) to an emphasis on the attachment of the child to the mother.

Vygotsky stresses that language allows the internalization of cognitive structures, while psychoanalysts have focused on the process of internalization that underlies psychic structure. The process of the mother holding the child and performing functions, such as stimulus control and soothing, until the child can internalize these functions has been well documented by Khan (1974) and particularly by Kohut (1971) and M. Tolpin (1971). These authors and others have described the devastating effect of a partial failure to internalize these self-regulatory functions. In addition, as we will see below, various object relations theories are attempts to delineate the exact nature and sequence of the internalization process.

It is not our intention to cover the vast literature on the role of language in psychoanalytic theory. Forrester (1980) has meticulously documented the role of language in the origins of psychoanalysis. The role of particular linguistic theories in the development of psychoanalytic theory has been noted elsewhere (Litowitz and Litowitz, 1977). Moreover, we are not concerned here with detailing the works of psychoanalysts who discuss the role of symbolization either as a consequence or as an instrument of early psychic development (Klein, 1975; Drucker, 1979). We will confine our review to the works of psychoanalytic authors whose views of early object relations utilize the specific parts of language development we are interested in: proper names and personal pronouns. Prior to that review, however, it is necessary to describe the differences between proper names and pronouns and the differences in the development of their usage by the individual.

The Nature of Proper Names and Pronouns

Proper names and pronouns are two of the three classes of "paradigmatic referring expressions in English" (Searle, 1969, p. 28). In some languages, personal pronouns are not separate lexical items but are carried as inflections on verbs and constitute part of syntax (for example, hablo español; cognito ergo *sum*). Whatever subsystem of language they fall into for a particular language (and it may be more than one), pronouns and proper names are linguistically unusual elements in ways that have long intrigued philosophers and linguists. An examination of the differences between them may shed some light on the distinction between types of self words that we are proposing.

Although they are nouns, proper names differ from other nouns in critical ways. Proper names do not denote a class of objects, that is, have a designatum, even though they refer to individuals (denotata). Weinreich (1968) states: "A theory of signs must also allow for a more 'stunted' type of sign which has an extensional class as its designatum. Such signs are generally called '(proper) names.' The individuals, whether one or many, which are truly denoted by a proper name have no common property attributed to them except 'answering' to that name" (p. 166).

Whether proper names have "intensions" (Lyons, 1977, p. 159) or sense is a contested issue. Searle (1971) reviews the argument that "we use a proper name to refer and not to describe; a proper name predicates nothing and consequently does not have a sense" (p. 135). Another way of making the same point is that proper names are not defined in a dictionary; they serve as pointers to individuals. Yet, proper names, Searle notes, do have some connection to general terms like *person, city*, or *mountain*. In addition, while proper names cannot be said to describe or specify characteristics of objects, they do consist of the logical sum (i.e., inclusive disjunction) of "some set of identifying descriptions" (1971, pp. 138–140). A common noun, *dog*, is definable in terms of a more general class to which it belongs, *animal*, as well as describable by the properties that all animals share plus those that distinguish *dog* from *cat* or *rabbit*, for example. In contrast, while proper names are defined in terms of *person* and inherit the general class properties of *personhood* (has a body, sees, hears, etc.), the distinguishing properties are not clear. These properties or attributes Searle calls "descriptive backings" of the individual to whom the proper name uniquely refers.

Although person concepts, which are labeled by proper names, differ from other concepts that are represented by common nouns, there is no need to hypothesize that the course of development for descriptive backings differs from that for the intensions of other concepts. Both may be first sensorimotoric and later perceptual, descriptive, and logical. In some ways, person concepts may be more similar to Piagetian concepts that connect "varied appearances of a single exemplar of a class" and rely on psychological identity and conservation (Elkind, 1969, p. 176).

Miller and Johnson-Laird (1976, pp. 306, 310) claim that person concepts are semantically different from other concepts. They suggest that a "person memory," closer to episodic memory for experiences lived through than to hierarchically and contrastively organized semantic memory, might rely on associative linkages. These authors state: "It is characteristic of associative memory that a whole entry can be recovered from any part of it—no single part is an indispensable 'address' for retrieval—and it is just this property of memory that enables people to substitute descriptions for proper names" (p. 307). They add: "A proper name for a person can give access to information retrievable from person memory, whereas a generic term (e.g., animal) gives access to information from semantic memory" (p. 311). Thus, it is possible that children learn proper names as self labels much as they learn other labels for objects, but the information is stored and organized differently depending on what kind of objects are being labeled.

The distinction between episodic and semantic memory made originally by Tulving (1972) has been expanded by some theorists to explain developmental changes in memory—Petrey's (1977) "episodic-semantic shift." Early memory is seen as episodic and characterized as associative—events are embedded in time and place and are always autobiographical. Although episodic memory does not disappear, it gradually becomes increasingly supplanted by semantic memory, which is abstracted from events and dominated by hierarchic and contrastive semantic structures. While the episodic-semantic distinction has been criticized by some, it would seem that the memory for persons is different from and developmentally earlier than abstract conceptual memory. Proper names as unique labels for person-objects seem to be available to very young children along with their earliest labels for other objects.

Labeling activities by children have been studied by psycholinguists; and the nonequivalent "extensional" (Lyons, 1977, p. 158) use of terms by children and adults is well documented in the literature.

Sometimes children overextend "mama," for example, to include other women or underextend "baby" to include only themselves, but not other babies (Anglin, 1977). Much developmental cognitive as well as psycholinguistic literature envisions young children as making hypotheses concerning their physical, social, and linguistic environment. In this view, concepts, as hypotheses, are like prototheories about the world, some of which become disproved and thereby lead to altered hypotheses (Miller and Johnson-Laird, 1976). In this way, the child would work out what members are incorporated into "mama," "baby," and "Johnnie." It is interesting, however, that there are no reports in the literature of misusing one's proper name; and only *I, you* reversals are reported, not the misuse of *I* or *you* for others or inanimate objects. Perhaps self words do not evidence the same extensional confusion as other words because the uniqueness of the referent is clear to the child from the beginning. The child need only learn the proper forms of the linguistic system, not the coordination of intensional properties and extensional reference, which are the major factors to reckon with in the development of other concepts and vocabulary (Anglin, 1977; Inhelder and Piaget, 1964).

In comparison to proper names, whose reference is restricted to one unique referent, pronouns are relatively unrestricted. The stability of proper name reference can be contrasted with the contextual dependency and therefore shifting reference of personal pronouns (Maratsos, 1979, p. 227). For this reason, Jakobson (1957) called these pronouns "shifters." (Peirce [1931] calls them "indexical expressions"; others label them "egocentric particulars" or "token-reflective" words.) More generally, pronouns are part of a class of lexical items known as deictics, whose sole function is to connect elements within discourse and to anchor elements of discourse to the communicational situation in which the discourse is transpiring. Pronouns refer not to objects but to relationships.

Traditional grammars have always defined pronouns as "a word used in place of one or more nouns" (Warringer and Griffith, 1973, p. 5). However, as Peirce (1931) points out, one is mistaken to speak of pronouns as substituting for an already mentioned or apparent noun.

There is no reason for saying that *I, thou, that, this*, stand in place of nouns; they indicate things in the directest possible way. It is impossible to express what an assertion refers to except by means of an index. A pronoun is an index. A noun, on the other hand, does not *indicate* the object it denotes. . . . Thus, a noun is an imperfect substitute for a pronoun. . . . A pronoun ought to be defined as *a word which may indicate anything to which the first and second persons have suitable real connections, by calling the attention of the second person to it.* Allen and Greenough say, "Pronouns indicate some person or thing without either naming or describing" (p. 128, edition of 1884). This is correct [p. 163].

Developmentally, then, children are not simply learning alternate ways of referring to themselves—first proper names and then pronouns which substitute for these names. They are, instead, learning two very different kinds of signs—one a label for them as a particular kind of object, the other an indicator of their participation in discourse.

The structure of the personal pronoun system has typically been characterized in either of two ways: (1) by semantic components which combine to form individual members of the system; or (2) separate aspects of the communicational act, which are designated by different pronouns. The first way can be called semantic, the second, pragmatic.

In a semantic analysis of pronouns, atomistic components such as number (singular, plural, dual) and gender (masculine, feminine, neuter) are identified and combined with syntactic information: first person, second person, third person; subjective/nominative, objective/accusative; pronominal adjective, nominal pronoun, reflexive pronoun, etc. The results of analyses of various intersecting components yield, for example, the definition of *I* as first person singular nominative male or female nominal pronoun. The difference between *I* and *You* would be characterized as one of person (first versus second). Experimental studies of the semantic organization of the English pronoun system reveal the following: (1) differences between nominative and accusative cases (e.g., *I, me*) are less significant than differences of person or number; (2) the primary distinction in person is between first person (*I*) and "other," with a subsequent differentiation of "other" into second (*you*) and third persons (*he, she, it*); (3) gender and number are also significant (Fillenbaum and Rapoport, 1971, pp. 85–99).

Pragmatic analysis of pronouns begins from the Peircian perspective of these words as deictic or indexical and proceeds to decompose them into components, not of semantic or syntactic features, but of the communicational act. (Some analyses combine both, for example, Huxley, 1970.) Pragmatic components include participant or nonparticipant roles (speaker, addressee, other); number; gender; inclusion/exclusion; status of participants; and degree of distance (proximal, distal). In such an analysis, *I* would be defined in terms of speaker; *tu/vous* distinctions would be discussed in terms of status of addressee relative to speaker; *this/that* differ in terms of distance from speaker, and so forth. Each speech act (Searle, 1969) is viewed as having at least a speaker and an addressee as participants in the communication. Therefore, *I* and *you*, or some other expressions that refer to speaker and addressee, assume preeminent importance in pragmatic analysis. In a semantic analysis, however, fewest number of components or most inclusive components would differentiate some pronouns from others. One might predict that the most important pronouns, as defined by either type of analysis, would be learned earliest by children. Indeed, as we shall see, developmental psycholinguistic studies use these notions of either semantic or pragmatic complexity to explain children's acquisition of *I* and *you* before other aspects of the pronominal system.

Review of Developmental Psycholinguistic Literature

Under the influence of Chomsky's model of an innate faculty for language, for a long time only the emerging language competence of children was investigated. Recent studies, however, have rediscovered the mother's speech as important language input to the child. The importance of the early dialogue between the mother/caretaker and child is increasingly emphasized by developmental psycholinguists, as well as communicational precursors of language development. Bruner (1974–75, 1978) has stressed the importance of joint attention and reciprocal games, such as peek-a-boo or patty-cake, for the later development of topic and comment and turn-taking in verbal dialogue.

Stern (1974), Kaye (1977), Bullowa (1979), Brazelton and Tronick (1980), Trevarthan (1980), and others have undertaken microanalyses of mother-child interactions, illustrating how the "basic dialogue" (Freedman & Grand, 1977, pp. 84–85) provides the necessary surround and structure for later verbal dialogues, out of which the child's language competence evolves.

This section of the paper looks at the development of two specific linguistic entities: proper names and pronouns. We will examine the child's early use of the former and the various strategies or stages in acquiring the latter.

All reports indicate that proper names are the earliest words of self-reference used by children. "Baby," favorite names, and other nouns of endearment that are used by the mother may alternate with the child's proper name. These function in the same way as a label used by the child for himself or herself. Proper names used for self-reference always precede pronouns used for the same purpose. As discussed in the preceding section, of the two forms of self-reference, the pronominal system is the more complex. Proper names as labels for unique referents are available to young children, whereas pronouns as labels for relationships, with their shifting referents, are acquired more slowly.

Developmental psycholinguistic literature on the acquisition of personal pronouns views the child as progressing from global to increasingly differentiated distinctions. That is, the inherent complexity of the linguistic system to be mastered is considered the primary factor in earlier or later acquisition of specific parts of that system. Maratsos (1979) lists the following as criteria in the learning of distinctions among pronouns (and determiners): "conversational role, distal-proximal relations around the speaker [more important for *this, that, these, those*], and the specificity of references for both himself and his listener" (p. 229). He lists the earliest pronouns as *you, it, I* and *my*. (Other authors also often include *your, me* and *mine*.)

In an analysis of spontaneous use of pronouns by ten mothers and their children aged nineteen months or older, Wales (1979, p. 254) found the most frequently used pronouns are *I, you* (in subject position); *we, he* (*him, she* and *her* not as often); *it* (in both subject and object position); *they, mine* (by children); and *your* (and *yours*) and *his* (by mothers). Both Wales and Maratsos corroborate other theorists' analyses of *you* and *I* as being acquired early and as essentially different from other pronouns in the system, with *he, she, they* being much closer to demonstrative deictics like *this* and *that*. These other pronouns have a pointing and a contrastive function, distinguishing gender and distance from speaker, etc. This argues for their full acquisition being later than *you* and *I*, that have only the single function of pointing out speaker and addressee (self and other).

Developmental psycholinguists look only at the linguistic system per se, without connecting proper names and pronouns to the early mother-child relationship. Still, developmental psycholinguists have amassed considerable data concerning at what age and in what sequence various parts of that linguistic system appear. Eve Clark (1978) reviews the literature on the acquisition of deictic terms, of which pronouns are a subset, by looking for the kinds of strategies children display in the task of making sense of shifting references and shifting boundaries within the communicational setting. (Her total analysis includes *here-there, this-that, come-go,* and *bring-take,* as well as *I-you.*) She notes that *I-you* distinctions are difficult for children because the acoustic image (label or name) does not always designate the same class of objects, as is the case with *table* or *chair,* or the same object, as with proper names. *I* designates the speaker, but the speaker shifts with each turn taken in communication. All the pronouns are not equally difficult, however, since there is a continuum of shifting reference: *I* may shift, but it is always the speaker; *you* is always a nonspeaker, but may include many; *he, she,* and *they* are even more variable.

According to Clark, children bring a series of strategies to the mastery of shifting references: (1) a *no contrast* strategy, where the child uses one of a pair; (2) a *partial contrast* strategy, where both members of the pair are used but either incorrectly or incompletely (compared to adult usage); and (3) *full,* adult *contrast.* In language data from normal children, the first deictic contrast between *I* and *you* appears between ages two years, six months and three years. Usually one term of reference, *I* or *me,* alternates with the child's own name or *baby* (or some other common noun or term of endearment used as a name). There is some controversy in the literature about whether this early *I* is syncretic, that is, formulaically frozen within phrases such as "I wanna—," "I gonna—." Early forms—*I, me, John, baby*—all refer to the child-speaker.

At the next stage, *you* is adopted. A simple strategy would seem to be to keep *I*, etc., for the self and to use *you* to designate the "other." Yet the strategy adopted by children is the reverse. *You* is used to designate themselves and *I*, the adult, usually the mother. Perhaps this is because this is the pattern of utterances children hear most often, although such an explanation would not tell us why children initially take *I* to refer to themselves and actually switch at this second stage. For children who choose this strategy, *I* seems to name an adult and *you*, themselves, equivalent to their proper names or *baby*. Clark's analysis is intriguing, since the use of *you* for self-reference and *I* for reference to others has been reported as a hallmark of the disturbed communication (especially echolalia) of the autistic (Aug, 1974), and of the delayed competence in communication of blind children (Fraiberg and Adelson, 1972).

Alternatively, Clark claims that some children seem aware from the very beginning that *I* and *you* are not object names, but rather designate the shifting communicational relationship of speaker and addressee. For children to move from the former strategy to this adult one, can take as long as four to six months. Both these strategies have been noted in children acquiring Danish, Dutch, and Serbian; all seem to learn the adult *I-You* distinction of shifting reference by three years of age. It is interesting that of all the deictic terms Clark has explored, these are learned earliest. Although all deictic terms appear early in children's utterances, full adult contrasts for *here-there* and *this-that*, are not mastered until age five, and for deictic verbs (*come-go, bring-take*), not until eight years, eight to eleven months.[1] Clark's explanation is that shifting boundaries, in addition to shifting reference, complicate the latter contrasts.

Linguistic evidence suggests that children often refer to themselves as "me" rather than "I." Psycholinguistic research on nomi-

---

[1] The ages given for acquisition of, for example, deictic terms may seem late, but one should remember that comprehension of terms usually precedes their expression. Psycholinguists mark not just the appearance of a term but its contrastive use in obligatory and/or novel contexts—that is, evidence of productive use and not just imitation of words or sentences. In addition, ages are often estimated conservatively to include the wide range of individual variation in children's verbalizations.

native and accusative errors among children has produced conflicting findings. Tanz (1974) found that errors in English always tended toward overuse of the objective or accusative case, rather than the nominative, because the former has greater frequency of occurrence (see also Maratsos, 1979, p. 233). Kaper (1976), however, found that errors in Dutch and German go in the opposite direction. Possibly, errors in correct grammatical case continue to occur because this is a surface syntactic phenomenon and does not involve the more fundamental speaker-addressee dimension. For example, "me go, too" or "carry I" can both be interpreted as a self-reference to the speaker. As noted earlier, differences in *me* and *I* are superficial and less significant than the basic person difference of *I* and *You*.

The acquisition of correct pronominal usage is seen by psycho-linguists, then, as the child's mastery over the complexity of the linguistic system. These theorists do not focus on the social relationship of the mother and the child or how self-reference is instrumental in or reflective of the internalization of that relationship. There is, however, some interest in the language of the mother as this provides data on which the child can base his or her emerging linguistic system. When we leave the development of expressive language in children and look at the language mothers (or other caretaking adults) use with them—that is, the language input available to children—we find a perplexing situation. Wills (1977) examined baby talk used by adults in talking to children. Baby talk register is a particular manner of speaking to children. It is used across languages by adults as well as by children as young as four years old in speaking to younger children and baby dolls. Wills's study showed the way adults distort the pronominal system, providing linguistic input for children in a way that differs radically from usage between adults. One would think that the effects of obscuring pronominal systemic distinctions would confuse children and make pronouns harder to learn; yet, as we have seen, this is not the case. For example, a mother often uses *we* to include both herself and the child in an activity that only one of them is performing. In this way, she signals that she and the child are a unit. For example, "We'll put on our shoes now," means "I'll put on your shoes now"; or "We want to go night-night; we're sleepy," means "You're tired; I'll put you to sleep." Sometimes the mother will use an impersonal pronoun to refer to the child; for example, "Somebody is tired" or "somebody has been up to a lot of mischief." And often mothers use proper names or common-proper nouns (e.g., "baby," "a little boy"), as in, "I know a little boy who's getting cranky."

Besides baby talk, mothers routinely take the child's perspective in person-labeling activities. In addition to imitating the child's incorrect usage ("Me go, too"), a mother may call herself "mommy," her husband, "daddy," her brother Tom, "Uncle Tom," her father, "Grandpa." Fillmore (1975, p. 82) reports that in some languages, such as Arabic, symmetrical labeling occurs between parents and children. A woman calls her child "mama" as the child calls her; a father calls his child "baba," as the child calls him. In general, developmental psycholinguists focus on the presence of the mother in terms of her language input to the child, which is the source of the child's own knowledge of the language system he or she must acquire. As stated above, the fact that mothers alter their language (and thus the available data) for babies has perplexed linguists. They are divided into two camps—the innatists and the empiricists—over whether or not input is therefore necessary for language development.

A contrast to the developmental psycholinguistic focus on linguistic complexity is the diary observation of Cooley (1908) on the emergence of the meanings of self words for his third child. In this study Cooley distinguishes the notion of "self feeling" (sometimes termed "self-assertive feeling") from the "physical, visible, or tangible body." He charts expression of the former through the acquisition of the pronoun *I* (also, *she, you, me, my,* and *mine*) used by his daughter to refer to herself. The stages Cooley suggests are (1) inarticulate self feeling; (2) correct understanding as used by others (i.e., comprehension); (3) imitative use of *I* in phrases (syncretic *I*); and (4) true or subjective meaning of *I*. In contrast, he claims, the notion of physical body is tied to the "shadow on the wall and the reflection in the looking-glass" (p. 232) and is expressed by *baby*. In the latter case, the label is connected to the child's physical presence in a manner similar to all other labels or names for physical objects. These two concepts develop side by side and ultimately are interrelated, but, Cooley adds, "It is noteworthy how comparatively late self-feeling seems to connect itself with these images [physical reflections, etc.]"

(p. 232). Cooley's interest in self words focuses on whether the use of *I* by children is necessarily social. He concludes that *I* develops and makes sense only in communication with and as distinct from an "other" and is, therefore, social.

In an attempt to combine Cooley's distinction with Clark's analysis, Charney (1980) claims that there are two preferences in learning to use pronouns. Some children, she notes, seem to focus on the communicational role (*I*), while others focus on the person (the proper name). Those who prefer the role strategy use *I* to mean "primarily, a self-assertive feeling," while those who use their name signify "physical body." Charney terms the former the nonreferring function of pronouns. This is deceptive, since *I* is indeed used for referring to the speaker. What Charney may mean is that *I* does not have a single constant referent object, being rooted purely in social communication between speaker and hearers. Charney hypothesizes that children must pay careful attention to certain aspects of the language they hear and to the situations in which learning of language takes place.

Analyses like Charney's would require that children be capable of cognitively sophisticated analyses of language input, involving detection of complex features. Alternatively, arguments based on privilege of occurrence (for example, children use *me* because it occurs in more contexts than *I*) would require sophisticated syntactic judgments on the part of children. Charney, Clark, and others are concerned with alternative strategies for mastering the linguistic system. In contrast, Cooley's point is that two forms of self-reference represent the development of two different meanings for the child—physical presence and self—which are initially separate but ultimately connect. Cooley, however, does not relate his daughter's development of these two meanings to specific aspects of her relationship to others (mother, caretakers), beyond noting the social role of the child in communication. In contrast, psychoanalysts who are concerned about early object relations provide a different focus, in which the major emphasis is placed on the child's changing relationships to objects. We now turn to these authors, especially to those whose theories touch on forms of self-expression as reflective of or instrumental in such changes.

Review of Psychoanalytic Literature

Although anecdotes and case studies sometimes report specific difficulties in self-reference and often mention that a poor maternal environment leads to deficiency in later communicative performance, there has been little research on the interdependence of psychic and communicative structures. The collection by Freedman and Grand (1977) is one recent attempt to illustrate the importance of the development of psychic structure to the development of communicative structure. Articles in that book stress the centrality of object relations for the establishment of the initial dialogue between mother and child as well as the place of the search for reestablishment of those early object relations in later verbal and gestural dialogues. Many articles mention René Spitz, a pioneer in research on the role of dialogue in the establishment of psychic structures. More than any other psychoanalyst until Lacan, and taking a position close to that of Vygotsky on cognition, Spitz stressed the central place of dialogue, which is for him "an attempt at a more sophisticated approach to our usual concept of object relations" (1963b, p. 172). He eschews the latter term because

> when you speak of *object relations* you are moving in the shadowy realm of abstract terminology. To visualize what one means by such abstract terms, one has to remember definitions. . . .
>
> I would like to try to use terms which require no definition, because they belong to our everyday speech. Dialogue is such a term. When we say "object relations" nothing compels us to visualize a process going on between a child and a live partner [1963b, p. 173].

Spitz (1957) details three stages of psychic development in children. The first stage, which builds upon congenital equipment, is the maturation of the perceptive system and the development of its cathexis. This stage results in an "I"–"non-I" differentiation and is indicated by the smiling responses (the first organizer). The infant is aware, however, only of the "non-I," not the "I." (Note that "I" is a label for a stage and does not imply that the infant can use the word *I* in discourse.) In the second stage, indicated by the second organizer, eight-month stranger anxiety, the child separates the animate from the inanimate. Spitz (1963a, 1963b) has written about the importance of dialogue for the formation of this latter distinction and for all "species-specific adaptation." The last stage is a result of the establishment of language or, more specifically, the "semantic no gesture," which for Spitz symbolizes the child's awareness of the self as distinct from another. These stages represent the child's movement from a physical to a psychological and finally to a social entity. In using the term "social entity," Spitz is not denying that the predialogue stage is social. Instead, he is calling attention to the separate individual who can say "no" to another.

For Spitz, the self is a precipitate that evolves out of earlier ego development or "I," which in turn develops later than the body ego or "non-I." Spitz states: "The self, which is a continuation of the 'I' on a higher level, is the product of intrapsychic processes which take place as a result of the vicissitudes of object relations" (1957, p. 121). He emphasizes that *"through this awareness of the ego the 'I' now achieves identity as the self"* (p. 121). Spitz claims to differ from Jacobson, for whom the self is not present before the second year, by placing the emergence of the self at fifteen months (p. 119). At eighteen months, the child refers to himself or herself in the third person, representing, Spitz claims, evidence of beginning self-awareness (p. 130). (Note that the third person reference includes proper names or designations like "baby" "son," or "daughter," as well as "he," "her," and "it.") The child's accomplishment is to reconcile several sets of polarities: "I" and "non-I"; "yes" and "no"; self and other.

Spitz's writings on the preverbal dialogue, which predates actual verbal dialogues, is echoed by recent theoretical statements in developmental psycholinguistics, as noted in the previous section. Spitz, however, keeps the original Freudian emphasis on the instinctual investment in objects in his first stage. Spitz's later stages establish the self as basically reflexive, based on self-awareness. The child's use of his or her proper name (third person) is a first form of that self-awareness which will be fully represented by *I*. Spitz does not comment on the different natures of these two linguistic entities. It is interesting that, in spite of his stress on the mother-child dialogue, Spitz does not explain the sequential appearance of these terms to refer to the self as reflecting changes in participation within that dialogue. That is, that the mother carries the child in the dialogue as an object (expressed by the child by his or her name) until the child is ready to participate equally with her as an "I." It is unfortunate that in calling attention to behavioral markers (the smiling response, the "no" gesture) of the emerging individual, Spitz does not consistently make use of linguistic evidence as traces of the individual's progressive development.

Since for Spitz the self arises out of the ego at the end of the individual's separation-individuation, his perspective can be viewed as a variant of other ego psychologists such as Mahler. Mahler (1968) describes the development of object relations as a process of separation and individuation between the child and mother/caretaker. This process involves four stages, one of which has several substages. The end result is the differentiation of self and object representations and the beginning of self and object constancy. Attempts have been made to correlate affective object constancy with cognitive object permanence (Piaget, 1954), although the latter takes only eighteen to twenty-four months as opposed to thirty-six for the former (McDevitt, 1975, p. 714). The end result of self-object differentiation—object constancy—would then coincide with full mastery of the *I-You* language distinction. The earlier object permanence, on the other hand, would be reflected in the acquisition of object labels, including person labels, that is, proper names.

During the phase of separation-individuation, the child can tolerate successively greater absences from the mother because he or she has acquired a permanent and separate image of the mother whose previously external comforting and nurturing functions are then internally represented, available for self-comforting and self-nurturing. There is a striking similarity here to Vygotsky's interpsychic-intrapsychic developmental progression. Language is implicated as a means of keeping contact with the mother at a distance prior to completing the process of separation. For example, the child's calling out "Mama" with anxiety follows simple screaming in panic when the mother leaves the room, but precedes the use of "Mama" without anxiety as a symbolic tie to the absent mother (McDevitt, 1975). Tolpin (1971), in an attempt to unify Mahler's notion of object relations and Kohut's concept of self psychology, cites a similar example in which a child uses the words, "clock ring" to maintain contact with the distant mother.

Although "individuation centers around the child's developing self-concept" (McDevitt, 1975, p. 715), there is little in the object relations literature about how that self-concept is expressed verbally by the child. Bergman (1971) details the treatment of a four-year-old with arrested object relations development. The effects of this developmental arrest could be seen in the child's language usage: she is echolalic, with pronoun reversals, referring to herself as "you," and never expressing a wish directly. Bergman notes: "Rachel demonstrated her denial of herself as a separate person in a number of different ways. In her speech patterns, she not only avoided the use of personal pronouns, but also left gaps in her communications that would have to be filled in by the mother" (p. 333). That is, the mother had the responsibility of structuring the discourse, signaling that the child could not fully participate in the dialogue as an equal. In addition, the child chewed up all the letters *I*'s from several sets of plastic alphabet letters. As she progressed in treatment, Rachel referred to herself as "Nice baby" and to a doll as "Ah baby, sweet little Rachel." Proceeding through the rapprochement period, Rachel's use of *I* and *you* became increasingly consistent and appropriate. Bergman claims that the rapprochement period—roughly eighteen to twenty-four months of age—is the time of rapid language development, but it is not clear whether *I* and *you* are representative of that period or only possible following object constancy (achieved at about thirty-six months).

The role of language in Mahler's theory is not clear. On the one hand, language may be seen to emerge only after the formation of specific psychic structures, products of her phases and substages of separation and individuation. In that case, the absence or presence of an *I-you* distinction could mark progressive developmental stages in the "psychological birth of the human infant" (Mahler, Pine, and Bergman, 1975). It is unfortunate, then, that the use of proper names as a marker of an earlier stage and its relationship to later use of pronouns is not elaborated by this theory. It is not clear what specific differences in object relatedness these two distinct forms of self-reference denote, even though some authors have noted that the use of one and not the other marks a failure or arrest in object relations. On the other hand, language may be implicated in Mahler's theory as instrumental in the process of individuation by allowing the verbal presence of the absent (real) object/mother. A source for this role of language in object relations can be found in Freud's *fort-da* example.

In "Beyond the Pleasure Principle," Freud (1920) introduced into his explanation of children's play an anecdote about a young boy (1½ years old) who alternately throws away and pulls back a small toy, and who accompanies these actions with the words *fort* ("gone") and *da* ("there"), respectively. For Freud, the active control that the child experiences in this game contributes to his mastery over his mother's absence, which he passively suffers. At the same time the game affords him revenge on her for his abandonment. Subsequent theorists have generalized the *fort-da* example, making it prototypic of the functions of language in the mastery of separation. Cahn (1976), for example, describes a young boy who, having suffered the traumatic hospitalization and illness of his mother at ten months, enters treatment as a mute, hyperactive 3½ year old who does not relate to people or objects in his environment. Cahn illustrates how in treatment the child uses the repetition characteristic of the *fort-da* experience to master developmentally successive dialectical conflicts. The working through of these conflicts in therapeutic play is accompanied by the emergence of related vocabulary items. Thus, the primary conflict of full versus empty is followed by the boy's first utterance, *boi*[*re*] ([to] drink). A second conflict between the presence of the object in a light, known space versus its absence in a dark, unknown place is accompanied by *noir* ("black"), *coucou* ("cuckoo"), and *suis là* ("am there"). A third conflict between giving and rejecting, love and hate, is accompanied by *oui* ("yes"), *non* ("no"), and *dedans* ("within"). A fourth conflict over appearance and disappearance, played out by the child with a spool toy (as in Freud's example) is accompanied by the emergence of *voilà* ("here it is"), *éteint* ("put out"), and *porte* ("door"). Following experiences controlling the appearance and disappearance of his image in a mirror (which again parallels Freud's anecdote), the child is able to master *au revoir*. (In French, *au revoir* contrasts with *adieu* as "gone but will return" contrasts with "gone forever.") Here again we see the notion that specific language emerges as evidence that conflicts have been mastered.

Three themes emerge from the preceding material: (1) mastery over and revenge for separation through repetitive actions and words;

(2) the instrumental use of language to master separation by maintaining verbal contact with the absent (real) object; and (3) the emergence of language as a consequence of (and therefore a reflection of) stages of psychic structure formation. These themes show up in the theoretical writings of many psychoanalysts. For example, language is implicated in Winnicott's (1971) notion of the transitional object. In the process of maturation, the transitional object is situated somewhere between the inner world of the subject and the outer world. The outer, objective world includes the (objective) object and the objective subject. Winnicott defines the latter as "the idea of a self, and the feeling of real that springs from the sense of having an identity" (p. 80). Winnicott discusses infant babbling and presleep monologues as transitional phenomena and notes that children can use early organized sounds ("words") to designate transitional objects (pp. 2, 5). For Winnicott, then, language is useful in the process of becoming separate and subjective.

Weich (1978) extends the idea of children's creative use of sounds as transitional phenomena to encompass "transitional language," an essential stage between one- and two-word utterances in all normal language development. He sees this occurring in children's repeated use of favorite words, which appear for a while in children's language development and then disappear, as well as in generalized language play. Thus, repetitive activity (play) accompanied by language becomes a part of language itself. Therefore, for many psychoanalysts, language is implicated in the ability to establish stable object relations, whether one sees it as the instrument or the consequence.

There is some provocative evidence from case studies that ties disturbed object relations to general delays in the development of language as well as to disturbances in the acquisition of specific linguistic structures. In a modern study (Curtiss, 1977) of a "wild child" supervised by psychologists and linguists, the researchers blame Genie's nearly total isolation over a period of thirteen years for her lack of competence in communication and the attendant gaps in her knowledge of any language devices that solely mark communicational exchange (for example, pronouns or *yes* and *no*). Genie did not indicate any comprehension or expression of correct pronoun use or any communicative use of language in general, such as, initiating conversations. She may have had the use of *I*, or perhaps only syncretic *I*, and usually referred to herself by her proper name. After considerable contact (four to five years), Genie had begun to make *me-you* distinctions, although not without persisting confusion.

D. A. Freedman (1977) reports two cases of language delay. An eleven-year-old congenitally blind autistic boy was not able to differentiate human objects or to communicate even his basic wants. He referred to himself by proper name—"Peter not a bad boy"—and in Yiddish, as he had heard himself referred to by institutional workers: "*Der meshugene shlaft noch nit*" ("The crazy one isn't sleeping yet") (p. 62). In another case, two environmentally deprived children, discovered at ages four and six, were unable to develop discriminating affective ties to caring foster parents, used only echolalic language, and were never able to use the first person pronoun *I* (p. 65). The inability to acquire correct pronoun usage, often marked by pronoun reversals, is well documented in autistic children (Aug, 1974) and in the delayed communicational competence of blind children (Fraiberg and Adelson, 1972).

Fraiberg and Adelson (1972) describe the many cases of blind children whose language development proceeds normally until the point of learning the *I-you* distinction. This distinction, which usually takes four to six months to master at most, required an additional two years in a child described by the authors who was otherwise normal. The authors contend that the child's lack of vision prevented her from treating herself as an object (p. 185). Since one of the examples given in the article is of the blind child putting herself rather than her doll in the sink, and since she correctly used "Kathie" to refer to herself, it is perhaps more accurate to conclude that she did in fact view herself as an object. What she could not do is view herself as a subject. This latter explanation is consistent with delayed use of *I* as a subject or self marker.

Probably more than any other psychoanalytic theoretician, Lacan comments on the importance of language in the development of the individual as object and as subject. Although Lacan does not present (or is not aware of) the psycholinguistic evidence that we have reviewed in this paper, his notion that the child is at first primarily an object for another and only later develops subjectivity is close to our hypothesis.

Lacan comments on the use of proper names and pronouns as reflective of progressive subjectivity. Explicating Lacan, Lemaire (1977) states:

> Proper names do not take the place of the I and the Thou, but rather the reverse. Proper names designate the subject, but they do so by excluding the I-Thou relationship. . . . Young children who have not yet fully acquired the notion of "I" speak of themselves by using the third person together with their forenames. In this way they reproduce the language of their parents, who talk among themselves about children in a communication from which they are still excluded (p. 54).

Lemaire underscores the *instrumentality* of language in the formation of the individual, stating: "The grammatical category of the 'I' is the index of individuality because it cannot be conceived without the Thou. . . . It is the I-Thou dialectic, defining the subjects by their mutual opposition, which founds subjectivity" (p. 53). In this quote, "index" indicates the usefulness of *I* as a marker of the establishment of individuality, whereas later in the passage "founds" indicates the importance of language as an instrument in establishing true subjectivity.

For Lacan, like Spitz, the development of subjectivity involves a progression beyond ego development. Unlike Spitz, however, and contrary to other psychoanalytic views that the ego is an organ of adaptation to reality which utilizes language to this end and which must be strengthened in analysis, Lacan (1953, 1968) sees the ego as an illusion of unity and strength. Lacan is outspoken against identification of the ego with the self and denounces those who attribute to it "a reality of the order of being" (Lemaire, 1977, p. 180). This belief, Lacan claims, "arises from a failure to recognize the real nature of the ego as being completely derived from a dialectic of narcissistic identifications with external Imagos" (Lemaire, 1977, p. 180).

For Spitz, the self emerges out of ego development as the ego's awareness of itself. In contrast, Lacan defines the ego as "that nucleus given to consciousness, but opaque to reflection. . . . In other words, the ego is the conscious data we have upon ourselves" (Lemaire, 1977, p. 181). Therefore, there is nothing in Lacanian theory which would envision the self as arising out of the ego's self-awareness.

For Lacan a self is present earlier. But even though this incipient individuality may predate language (the symbolic), it is language that "actualizes and realizes this innate intuition by providing the grammatical categories for the individuality" (Lemaire, 1977, p. 53). Lemaire cites the many cases of psychotic children who never acquire the use of *I* and refer to themselves in the third person as evidence for the instrumentality of language in fully establishing the self. Language, for Lacan, is part of the symbolic order into which the child is born and by means of which the "world of words creates the world of things" (Lacan, 1966, p. 276). The symbolic order, with its ties to the oedipal complex, establishes "mediate relationships between things, . . . between self and others" (Lemaire, 1977, p. 7).

Lacan notes the differences between proper names and pronouns, which linguistic evidence supports. Further, he connects these two forms of expression of the self to the early child-other relationship. However, developmental psycholinguistic evidence places the sequential emergence of these forms at a significantly earlier date than Lacan's theory would predict. Another major difficulty in Lacan's theory is his insistence on the connection of language and the oedipal conflict. Research in developmental psycholinguistics has demonstrated the significance of the first three years of life for basic language acquisition. Lacan, in tying language to the symbolic order and the oedipal conflict, has failed to integrate the role of language in the preoedipal period.

One attempt to rectify the lack of consideration given this earlier period by Lacanians has been made by Brett (1981). Although she analyzes literary examples rather than developmental data, she hypothesizes that language is experienced differently by younger and older children. For Brett, very young children experience language as sound, the comforting and soothing voice of the mother. Tied to Lacan's imaginary order, this early linguistic experience is one of presence. For the older child, language, tied to the symbolic order, replaces the absent mother while simultaneously reminding the child of her absence. Since language marks absence, it intrudes into the oneness of the child's closed world and forces him or her into the more generalized sociocultural world. It is only through language that the child realizes the mother is not part of the self. The proper names of mother and child signify their differences. And proper names, like general names, illustrate to the child his or her general insignificance, "one amongst many" (Brett, 1981, p. 196), thus interrupting the magical fusion with the mother. Therefore, language for Brett symbolizes separation as loss. She ties this to the *fort-da* experience as interpreted by both Freud and Lacan.

Brett's emphasis is not on language as instrumental in overcoming separation or establishing individuation or as representing an individual identity, but rather on language as symbolizing the loss of the paradisiacal union with the mother. Brett assumes the self is present from birth, albeit merged with the mother, and therefore weak. She does not see language as constitutive in the development of the self, although "language becomes central to the cohesion of the self, able to fill up an empty self as it was once filled by the mother's presence." But, she adds, "like the mother [language] can withdraw, leaving the self empty and abandoned" (p. 198).

Unfortunately, Brett does not indicate the exact role of language in the cohesive self, whether it is part of the content of the self ("fill up," "empty") or its constituent structure. In this regard, how language could "withdraw" is not clear. Also, one cannot be sure whether Brett means language in some global sense or particular language structures. In differentiating earlier language, as sound, from later language, presumably as complex system (sound plus meaning combined by syntax), it would seem that specific parts of that system, such as proper names and pronouns, should reflect different aspects of self-cohesion. But these relationships between the language system and psychic development are not clarified.

Many psychoanalytic theorists agree that the child is first merged with the mother/caretaker and only gradually separates from that union into a separate individual. Most theorists agree that the ability to function as a separate individual requires the internalization of the representation of the mother/other. Some see the dialogue of the mother and child (Spitz) or the discourse of the other (Lacan) as critical in the developmental process. Theorists disagree as to whether this process involves only stages in ego development (Mahler) or whether there is a self (Spitz, Lacan, Kohut). If a self is posited, there is a question as to whether it is present from birth (Lacan, Kohut), needs language to articulate its presence (Lacan), or emerges out of ego development through the reflection of the ego on itself (Spitz).

We have only reviewed theorists who view the developmental process as involving language of a particular sort. Yet there are differences among these theorists concerning the role of language in a child's developing individuality. Most psychoanalysts, following Freud's example, emphasize the role of language in mastering the loss that separation entails. Some note the emergence of specific linguistic patterns following particular conflicts. Few psychoanalysts, however, consider differences in the form of the child's expression of the self, although evidence from deviance in early mother-child relationships indicates that differences exist.

Discussion

Two points emerge from this review. The first has to do with our hypothesis that the difference in self words reflects a difference in psychological development. The second concerns the usefulness of future collaboration between psychoanalysts and psycholinguists.

Proper names and personal pronouns are different kinds of referring expressions. The former refer uniquely to a particular object. Its usage is taken over by the child from the mother as an object label for the self. Pronouns, on the other hand, refer not to a static object (albeit of a particular type) but to a dynamic relationship and to the child's role in that relationship. Both proper names and pronoun usage develop out of the dialogue. In the case of the proper name, the child calls himself or herself what the mother calls him or her. In the case of the pronoun he calls himself the same thing the mother calls herself—*I*. In so doing, the child takes an equal part in the dialogue. In learning the linguistic system, not systemic complexity but the social relationship to the mother is the key to why one form and not another appears. The child can use the technically incorrect input from the mother because he or she is not using it to learn the linguistic system as has been supposed, but rather is using it to incorporate his or her ongoing participation in the relationship. The input is not incorrect for this purpose, since through it the mother identifies with the child and empathizes with him or her, taking the child's perspective, including the child in her *we*, etc. Pronouns are particularly suited to mark this process, since they are defined solely within the dialogue and have no specific reference outside of it.

In marking relationships rather then specific referents, pronoun usage provides clues to internal changes in those relationships. The early merged or symbiotic mother-child relationship that is hypothesized by many psychoanalytic theorists may be marked by the mother with *we*, but her *we* includes two separate individuals. For the child's part, he or she expresses union with the mother by *not* using pronouns. The child allows himself or herself to be carried in the mother's discourse, over which she has responsibility; she fills the gaps in these discourses until the child can participate more fully. The child first sees himself or herself through the mother's eyes, and therefore the child's initial self-reference is what the mother calls the child—his or her proper name. Only after this stage will the child begin the process of equal responsibility in the dialogic relationship, indicated by the use of *I*. The child's ability to use *we*, as the mother did originally, only follows the emergence of *I*. It is interesting to note that in data on children's actual use of language, the *me-I* distinction sometimes used in psychoanalytic literature to mark distinct structural psychic developments is insignificant in comparison to critical differences in use of proper names and pronouns.

All psychoanalytic theories of object relations stress the early mother-child relationship. They differ on the substages involved in the process of internalization. Nevertheless, all the theorists discussed here stress that correct pronoun usage (but not proper name usage) is involved in the process of internalizing the representation of the mother, which allows the child to become a separate individual. It would seem, therefore, that children refer to themselves as objects for another before they refer to themselves as subjects to another. Returning to Goldberg's definition of the self quoted earlier—"the representation of [an individual] in terms of a multitude of functional and lasting relationships with others" (1980, p. 5)—the self would seem to be embodied in the subjective *I*. *Self-* as a reflective epiphenomenon (e.g., "self-reflection," "self-awareness," "self-consciousness") would seem to occur even later, following proper names and pronouns in that order. What remains unclear among theories is whether the self is present from the beginning and only becomes evident as *I*; whether *I* is a precipitate of earlier ego development; whether the self is only created out of the last stages of object relations; whether language is the reflection or the instrument of the emergence of the self as *I*; and whether the concept of *self* and the concept of *physical person* are coterminous.

In representing the relationship of the child to another, proper names and pronouns signify changes that the relationship undergoes in development. Proper names represent an earlier phase in the developmental process and are not replaced by pronouns so much as joined by these signifiers of a new stage in the mother-child relationship.

In a recent article, Call (1980) has suggested a collaboration between developmental psycholinguists and psychoanalysts (see also Litowitz & Litowitz, 1977). To the careful descriptions and analyses of children's language by the former, the latter can add the theories of emotions that will provide insights into why and how language develops as it does. We have pointed out above how purely linguistic explanations of language development focus on the theoretically defined complexity of the linguistic system to the exclusion of the dynamics of the underlying relationship between child and mother, leaving these explanations devoid of psychological motivation.

In contrast, psychoanalytic explanations of early development that make global statements about the functions of language without full knowledge of the language system can also face difficulties. For example, Brett (1981) states: "Language penetrates the dyadic fusion of mother and child by giving both names, which, above all else are signs of their separate identity"; and since proper names are like general names, they "render that identity common" (p. 196). As we have seen, however, this cannot be the case for the following reasons: (1) Proper names are critically different from general names, and children's usage reflects these differences; (2) the penetration of language into the mother-child union is a more complex process, which develops over time and involves not only proper names but also pronouns; and (3) pronouns, not proper names, are the more crucial in the establishment of separate identities.

Many psychoanalytic writers do not treat proper names and pronouns as different entities in their theories of object relations, in spite of pathology suggesting a difference. For example, even though Spitz mentions this distinction, greater awareness of the differences we have discussed would have enabled him to add even subtler distinctions to the stages he proposed. Also, he might have avoided using confusing labels for his stages such as "I," which for him refers to the child's identity rather than the ability to use this pronoun in the dialogue. In contrast, Lacan does note the difference we have drawn, but he does not integrate it consistently into his theory. Integration, in turn, would necessitate taking into account the psycholinguistic evidence that early language development occurs largely in the preoedipal period. He would, therefore, have to reevaluate the interdependence that he posits between language and the Oedipus complex. Other analysts, such as Mahler, who have explored disturbed object relations, would benefit from an understanding of the role that language plays in development and therefore in the genesis of the conditions they describe.

One aim of this paper has been to provide some linguistic evidence that might inform the construction of progressions of psychic development hypothesized by psychoanalytic theorists. Another aim has been to provide psychological motivation for patterns of linguistic acquisition hypothesized by developmental psycholinguists. Finally, we have tried to provide an example of interdisciplinary collaboration, not just as the joining of two theoretical bodies of knowledge, but as the active cooperation of scholars in both fields. Toward that goal, this paper is only a beginning, raising questions for psychoanalysts and psycholinguists to address together in the future.

References

Anglin, J. (1977), *Word, Object and Conceptual Development*. New York: W. W. Norton.

Aug, R. G. (1974), The language of the autistic child. In: *Language and Language Disturbances*, ed. E. W. Straus. New York: Humanities Press, pp. 155–172.

Bergman, A. (1971), "I and you": The separation-individuation process in the treatment of a symbiotic-psychotic child. In: *Separation-Individuation*, ed. J. B. McDevitt & C. F. Settlage. New York: International Universities Press, pp. 325–355.

Brazelton, T. B., & Tronick, E. (1980), Preverbal communication between mothers and infants. In: *The Social Foundations of Language and Thought*, ed. D. Olson. New York: W. W. Norton, pp. 299–315.

Brett, J. (1981), Self and other in the child's experience of language: Hofmannstahl's "Letter to Lord Chandos." *Internat. Rev. Psycho-Anal.*, 8:191–201.

Bruner, J. (1974–75), From communication to language: A psychological perspective. *Cognition*, 3:255–287.

—————— (1978), Learning how to do things with words. In: *Human Growth and Development*, ed. J. Bruner & A. Garton. Oxford: Oxford University Press, pp. 62–84.

Bullowa, M., Ed. (1979), *Before Speech: The Beginning of Interpersonal Communication*. Cambridge: Cambridge University Press.

Cahn, R. (1976), De quelques conditions de l'apparition du langage: Une illustration. *Rév. Française Psychanal.*, 40:659–666.

Call, J. (1980), Some prelinguistic aspects of language development. *J. Amer. Psychoanal. Assn.*, 28:259–290.

Charney, R. (1980), Speech roles and the development of personal pronouns. *J. Child Lang.*, 7:509–528.

Clark, E. (1978), From gesture to word: On the natural history of deixis in language acquisition. In: *Human Growth and Development*, ed. J. Bruner & A. Garton. Oxford: Oxford University Press, pp. 85–120.

Cooley, C. H. (1908), A study of the early use of self-words by a child. In: *Sociological Theory and Social Research* (selected papers). New York: Henry Holt, 1930, pp. 229–247.

Curtiss, S. (1977), *Genie: A Psycholinguistic Study of a Modern-Day "Wild Child."* New York: Academic Press.

Drucker, J. (1979), The affective context and psychodynamics of first symbolization. In: *Symbolic Functioning in Childhood*, ed. N. Smith & M. Franklin. New York: Laurence Erlbaum, pp. 27–40.

Elkind, D. (1969), Conservation and concept formation. In: *Studies in Cognitive Development*, ed. D. Elkind & J. H. Flavell. New York: Oxford University Press, pp. 171–189.

Fillenbaum, S., & Rapoport, A. (1971), *Structure in the Subjective Lexicon*. New York: Academic Press.

Fillmore, C. (1975), *Santa Cruz Lectures on Deixis—1971*. Mimeographed, Bloomington: Indiana University Linguistics Club.

Forrester, J. (1980), *Language and the Origins of Psychoanalysis*. New York: Columbia University Press.

Fraiberg, S., & Adelson, E. (1972), Self-representation in language and play: Observations of blind children. In: *Foundations of Language Development*, Vol. 2, ed. E. H. Lenneberg & E. Lenneberg. New York: Academic Press, pp. 177–192.

Freedman, D. A. (1977), The influence of various modalities of sensory deprivation on the evolution of psychic and communicative structures. In: *Communicative Structures and Psychic Structures*, ed. N. Freedman & S. Grand. New York: Plenum Press, pp. 57–74.

Freedman, N., & Grand, S. (1977), ed. *Communicative Structures and Psychic Structures*, New York: Plenum.

Freud, S. (1914), On narcissism: An introduction. *Standard Edition*, 14:67–102. London: Hogarth Press, 1957.

—————— (1917), Mourning and melancholia. *Standard Edition*, 14:237–260. London: Hogarth Press, 1957.

—————— (1920), Beyond the pleasure principle. *Standard Edition*, 18:1–64. London: Hogarth Press, 1955.

—————— (1923), The ego and the id. *Standard Edition*, 19:3–66. London: Hogarth Press, 1961.

Goldberg, A. (1980), Introductory remarks. In: *Advances in Self Psychology*, ed. A. Goldberg. New York: International Universities Press, pp. 1–16.

Huxley, R. (1970), The development of the correct use of subject personal pronouns in two children. In: *Advances in Psycholinguistics*, ed. G. B. Flores D'Arcais & W. J. W. Levelt. New York: American Elsevier, pp. 141–165.

Inhelder, B., & Piaget, J. (1964), *The Early Growth of Logic in the Child*. London: Routledge & Kegan Paul.

Jakobson, R. (1957), *Shifters, Verbal Categories and the Russian Verb*. The Russian Language Project Department of Slavic Languages and Literature, Harvard University, Cambridge.

Kaper, W. (1976), Pronominal case-errors. *J. Child Lang*, 3:439–441.

Kaye, K. (1977), Toward the origin of dialogue. In: *Studies in Mother-Infant Interaction*, ed. H. R. Schaffer. New York: Academic Press, pp. 89–117.

Khan, M. M. R. (1974), The concept of cumulative trauma. In: *The Privacy of the Self*. New York: International Universities Press.

Klein, M. (1975), The importance of symbol-formation in the development of the ego. In: *Love, Guilt and Reparation and Other Works*. London: Delacorte Press.

Klein, M. & Tribich, D. (1981), Kernberg's object-relations theory: A critical evaluation. *Internat. J. Psycho-Anal.*, 62:27–44.

Kohut, H. (1971), *The Analysis of the Self*. New York: International Universities Press.

Lacan, J. (1953), Some reflections on the ego. *Internat. J. Psycho-Anal.*, 34:11–17.

——— (1966), *Écrits*. Paris: Éditions du Seuil.

——— (1968), The mirror-phase as formative of the function of the I. *New Left Rev.*, 51:71–77.

Lemaire, A. (1977), *Jacques Lacan*. London: Routledge & Kegan Paul.

Litowitz, B., & Litowitz, N. (1977), The influence of linguistic theory on psychoanalysis: A critical, historical survey. *Internat. Rev. Psycho-Anal.*, 4:419–448.

Lyons, J. (1977), *Semantics*, Vol I, Cambridge: Cambridge University Press.

Mahler, M. S. (1968), *On Human Symbiosis and the Vicissitudes of Individuation*. New York: International Universities Press.

——— Pine, F., & Bergman, A. (1975), *The Psychological Birth of the Human Infant*. New York: Basic Books.

Maratsos, M. P. (1979), Learning how and when to use pronouns and determiners. In: *Language Acquisition*, ed. P. Fletcher & M. Garman. New York: Cambridge University Press, pp. 225–240.

McDevitt, J. B. (1975), Separation-individuation and object constancy. *J. Amer. Psychoanal. Assn.*, 23:713–742.

Miller, G. A., & Johnson-Laird, P. N. (1976), *Language and Perception*. Cambridge: Harvard University Press.

Peirce, C. S. (1931), *Collected Papers*, Vol. 2. C. Hartshorne & P. Weiss, ed. Cambridge: Harvard University Press.

Petrey, S. (1977), Word associations and the development of lexical memory. *Cognition*, 5:57–71.

Piaget, J. (1954), *The Construction of Reality in the Child*. New York: Basic Books.

Searle, J. R. (1969), *Speech Acts: An Essay in the Philosophy of Language*. Cambridge: Cambridge University Press.

——— (1971), The problem of proper names. In: *Semantics: An Interdisciplinary*

Reader in Philosophy, Linguistics and Psychology, ed. D. D. Steinberg & L. A. Jakobovits. London: Cambridge University Press.

Spitz, R. A. (1957), *No and Yes*. New York: International Universities Press.

——— (1963a), The evolution of dialogue. In: *Drives, Affects, Behavior*, Vol. 2, ed. M. Schur. New York: International Universities Press, pp. 170–190.

——— (1963b), Life and the dialogue. In: *Counterpoint*, ed. H. S. Gaskill. New York: International Universities Press, pp. 154–176.

Stern, D. N. (1974), Mother and infant at play: The dyadic interaction involving facial, vocal and gaze behaviors. In: *The Effect of the Infant on its Caretaker*, ed. M. Lewis & L. Rosenblum. London: Wiley.

Tanz, C. (1974), Cognitive principles underlying children's errors in pronominal casemarking. *J. Child Lang.*, pp. 1:271–276.

Tolpin, M. (1971), On the beginnings of a cohesive self: An application of the concept of transmuting internalizations to the study of transitional objects and signal anxiety. *Psychoanalytic Study of the Child*, 26:316–352. New York: Quadrangle Books.

Trevarthan, C. (1980), The foundations of intersubjectivity: Development of interpersonal and cooperative understandings in infants. In: *The Social Foundations of Language and Thought*, ed. D. Olson. New York: W. W. Norton, pp. 316–342.

Tulving, E. (1972), Episodic and semantic memory. In: *Organization of Memory*, ed. E. Tulving & W. Donaldson. New York: Academic Press.

Vygotsky, L. S. (1962), *Thought and Language*. Cambridge: M.I.T. Press.

——— (1978), *Mind in Society*. Cambridge: Harvard University Press.

Wales, R. (1979), Deixis. In: *Language Acquisition*, ed. P. Fletcher & M. Garman. Cambridge: Cambridge University Press, pp. 241–260.

Warringer, J. E., & Griffith, F. (1973), *English Grammar and Composition: Complete Course*. New York: Harcourt, Brace, Jovanovich.

Weich, M. J. (1978), Transitional language. In: *Between Reality and Fantasy*, ed. S. A. Grolnick & L. Barkin. New York: Aronson, pp. 411–424.

Weinreich, U. (1968), Semantics and semiotics. In: *International Encyclopedia of the Social Sciences*. New York: Macmillan, pp. 164–169.

Wills, D. D. (1977), Participant deixis in English and baby talk. In: *Talking to Children: Language Input and Acquisition*, ed. C. E. Snow & C. A. Ferguson. Cambridge: Cambridge University Press.

Winnicott, D. W. (1971), *Playing and Reality*. New York: Basic Books.

Part V

APPLIED PSYCHOANALYSIS

Some Theoretical and Methodological Implications of Self Psychology

MICHAEL FRANZ BASCH

Self psychology is the name by which the work of Heinz Kohut and some like-minded colleagues and collaborators has come to be known among psychoanalysts. To explain why many of us feel that it represents not only an important evolutionary step for psychoanalysis but also a potential bridge to the other behavioral sciences is not a simple task. Self psychology and its significance for psychoanalytic theory can only be understood if one first finds one's way in the tangle of hypotheses that are incorrectly lumped together under the rubric "psychoanalytic theory" or "psychoanalytic metapsychology."

Long before Freud's treatment of neurotic disorders with hypnosis led to the discoveries that transformed cathartic or abreactive treatment into psychoanalysis, Freud took an even more momentous step. His introduction to the systematic investigation of the neuroses took place in the clinic of Charcot, in 1885. Charcot demonstrated that a neurotic symptom, which had previously been considered a form of malingering or worse, was an understandable phenomenon representing an involuntary reaction to a forgotten emotional stress of an earlier time. Since

Presented at a symposium on "Psychoanalytic Self-Psychology: A New Bridge to the Other Behavioral Sciences," at a Meeting of the American Association for the Advancement of Science, San Francisco, January 6, 1980.

no brain lesions could be found in neurotic patients that would account for this sequence, the only other cause that was imaginable at that time was a physiological one. A hereditary weakness of the brain was postulated that made it impossible for the neurotic's cerebrum to handle the discharge of emotions consciously, and the inadequate attempt of the lower centers to cope with that task without the benefit of consciousness resulted in otherwise meaningless symptoms. Freud (1888) disputed this, contending that (1) the high intelligence of neurotic patients argued against brain weakness being responsible for their symptoms and (2) the absence of consciousness did not rule out a cerebral contribution to the neurotic symptom He also disputed (3) the notion that neurotic symptoms were meaningless by demonstrating clinically that they represented a purposeful, albeit unconscious, compromise between the drive for the conscious expression of an idea, usually a sexual wish, and the moral barriers that made its acknowledgment unacceptable. With these three assertions, Freud dealt the definitive blow to Descartes' equation of thought with consciousness; took the neuroses out of neurology; and, by disputing the physical causation of the neuroses, established the need for a psychology that could explain them. In other words, Freud demonstrated the necessity for and laid the foundation of depth or dynamic psychology as we know it today.

The goal of establishing a general scientific psychology led Freud to first create what Andersson (1962) has called the ''brain mythology'' of the ''Project for a Scientific Psychology'' (1895) and to later attempt its transmutation into the various versions of the nonanatomical mental apparatus (Basch, 1975a, 1976c). These included the so-called picket fence model of Chapter VII in *The Interpretation of Dreams* (1900); the topographic model (Freud, 1915), with its division into unconscious, preconscious, and conscious mental states; and the final version of ego and id (Freud, 1923).

To understand what makes all these models of brain functioning and/or thought processing operational, we have to go back to a work that was never included in the various collections of Freud's psychological writings, *On Aphasia* (1891). In this book Freud first adopted the model for thought formation that remained throughout his lifetime the basis for his theory of cognition, and which he repudiated only in one of his last publications (1940). His hypothesis was that thought was made possible by a union of sensory images with the words that appropriately describe them, and, *per contra*, that without words sensory images were blocked from both consciousness and participation in cognitive maturation. He attributed motivation for action to the amount of instinctual force attached to a sensory image. Conflicts would spring up between the need to discharge instinctual tension and the restrictions placed on uninhibited behavior by conscience and convention. Unable to control the strength of the instincts, which were somatic givens, the brain or mind would withdraw the speech associations from forbidden sensory images. These images were then isolated both from thought, which precluded their maturation, and from consciousness, which blocked their direct fulfillment in action. This theoretical construct corresponded to the conflict Freud saw in his neurotic patients, which he cured by helping those patients find the words to espress their hidden desires and fears so that they could then either dismiss or sublimate them. For Freud, neurotics were essentially functional aphasics, and he made the error of thinking that the success of his therapy established the validity of his hypotheses regarding the development of thought. Unfortunately, Freud was studying the one psychological illness that seemed to corroborate his theory. In the long run, this success prevented the full implications of psychoanalysis from being appreciated by either Freud or the analysts that followed him.

It should be emphasized that none of the hypotheses I have mentioned so far are part of psychoanalytic theory, although they have come to be known as such. They were all formulated before Freud discovered the significance of dreams, psychic reality, and the transference, and before he deciphered the code of the preoperative (Piaget) or presentational (Langer) symbolism that he termed the primary process (Basch, 1977). Because Freud never published the Project and because the significance of *On Aphasia* went unrecognized until recently, analysts did not know the origin of these concepts. They assumed, as Freud's later writings had led them to believe, that these conclusions had somehow been reached through psychoanalytic investigation.

What, then, is psychoanalytic theory? If by psychoanalytic theory we mean (as I think we should) those hypotheses that can be inferred from data obtained by the psychoanalytic method, then psychoanalysis is a theory of the motivation for and meaning of human behavior (Basch, 1976b; Flew, 1954).

Psychoanalysis as an investigative method began when Freud realized (1) that much of what adult neurotic patients advanced as memory was actually childhood fantasy and that when it came to influencing later behavior, psychic reality was as significant as external reality; and (2) that the attempt to transform childhood fantasy into adult reality by projecting into the present situation what the patient had wished or feared was an ongoing process that manifested itself in the relationship between doctor and patient. In his practice, it was brought home to Freud that it was the interpretation of this transference, rather than emotional abreaction and catharsis or tracing of the symptom to its origin, that led to the cure of neurosis. It is the reliving of the old trauma in a new edition with the analyst that engages the emotional as well as the intellectual life of the patient and proves to be definitive. As Freud once said aphoristically, one cannot slay the devil in absentia.

The management, examination, and resolution of the transference became the basis for psychoanalysis and remains so to this day. It is what identifies the psychoanalytic method and is probably the one principle whose cardinal importance all analysts would accept.

As I noted earlier, the problem for psychoanalytic theory was that the psychoanalytic method worked too well, at least at first. It worked so well, in fact, that the theory whose formulation should have been stimulated by the application of the psychoanalytic method and that would truly have deserved the label ''psychoanalytic'' never came into existence. Instead, Freud felt that the success of the psychoanalytic method was the experimental proof for his general theory of the development of thought and his concept of how the mind or brain worked. He seems to have reasoned along the following lines: The vicissitudes of infantile sexuality are fundamental for the eventual onset of a neurosis. Dreams, slips of the tongue, and other errors of everyday life in healthy people show that infantile sexuality is a part of normal development. Therefore, development as reconstructed in the analysis of neurotic patients mirrors the development of all people: The neuroses show in bold relief what is ordinarily hidden from view by the resolution of the oedipal conflict in others. Similarly, Freud saw neurotic development as the result of a form of thought process that did not follow the rules of everyday adult logic. Everyone shows the universality of this type of thought process in dreams and errors of everyday life. On this basis Freud concluded that he had discovered the primary process, the earliest form in which the brain or mind attempted to adapt itself to the problems of life.

In retrospect, of course, such conclusions are non sequiturs. The insight into development offered by an analytic study of a neurosis does not in itself offer a guarantee that all infantile development or all that is significant about early development is now understood. Nor is it to be taken for granted that the ability to decode a manner of processing thought that precedes logic has put us in touch with the earliest or "primary" process (Basch, in press, b).

I will not go into my speculations as to why this circular reasoning was not effectively challenged for many years. Suffice it to say that the psychoanalytic view of development, which formed the basis for the causal explanatory theory that is called psychoanalytic metapsychology (Basch, 1973), rests on five postulates about general psychology. These postulates, which were developed by Freud before the discovery of the psychoanalytic method, are the following:

1. The goal of the brain or mental apparatus is to avoid stimuli, or at least minimize them to the greatest extent compatible with the preservation of life.

2. Thought development is linear; the infant's appreciation of self and the world, although less complex, is essentially based on the same principles of perception and cognition found in adults.

3. The intensity of thought—its affective component—is determined by the quantity of a postulated "psychic energy," which attaches itself to a wish and determines its influence on behavior.

4. Development of speech precedes and is essential for thought.

5. True thought is equated with verbal logic and is made possible by a union of sensory, pictorial images with the more sophisticated and later-acquired word images (Basch, in press, a).

We know today that every one of these postulates is false. True, the evidence that makes possible an alternative and more acceptable theory of development was, for the most part, not yet available to

Freud or the co-workers who eventually gathered around him. The experimental disproof of Freud's developmental hypothesis was to come shortly, however, although it was not recognized then and even now is not acknowledged as such by many analysts. In short, patients came for treatment whose symptoms should have been relieved by the investigation and interpretation of the vicissitudes of infantile sexual development, but were not. As people, these patients left much to be desired: They were not cooperative and, unlike neurotic patients, could not be depended on to have the necessary courage to stand back from their own suffering and, together with the analyst, look upon it objectively, at least, in part. Though chronologically adult, socially accomplished, and often quite successful by the world's standards, these patients behaved like demanding children in the analytic session. They seemed to require what Freud at one time called *Nacherziehung*, some belated upbringing, with the analyst acting *in loco parentis* to give that combination of understanding and discipline which leads children to eventually become reasonably mature persons (Basch, 1981b).

This turn of events could have been taken as an indication that a theory which equated the dynamics of development with the oral, anal, and phallic vicissitudes of infantile sexuality was not adequate to the burden assigned to it—but this is not what happened. Instead, the theory of development as advanced by Freud became a shibboleth and those who insisted on questioning it too vigorously soon found themselves unwelcome in psychoanalytic circles.

In the meantime, new evidence was accumulating from other branches of psychology—from biology, from physics, and from new fields such as cybernetics, linguistics, communication science, and semantics. This evidence indicated that the hypotheses Freud had advanced to explain the functioning of the mental apparatus, the process of thought, and the development of language were in error. Alternative explanations that could be experimentally validated were now at hand. Those few farsighted psychoanalysts who called for the reformulation of psychoanalytic metapsychology (Roy Grinker, Sr., and Lawrence Kubie come to mind) were given short shrift. Considerable effort went into trying to show either that these new hypotheses were really no different from what Freud had been saying or had meant to say, or that even if true they did not apply to development as seen by the psychoanalytic method. In any case, most analysts, having little if any background in epistemology and scientific philosophy, were content to let others argue about such issues, considering them to be of little relevance for their daily work. They did not realize that the clinical issues with which they were very much concerned depended precisely on the equitable resolution of these basic theoretical issues.

The clinical discoveries of Heinz Kohut offer a potential resolution for this impasse. His work forms the bridge that could unite psychoanalysis with its sister sciences, bring psychoanalytic explanatory theory into the twentieth century, and make what psychoanalysis has learned about human motivation useful to investigators in other fields.

Kohut, like Freud and Breuer before him, was led in his discoveries by a patient's insistence that he put aside his preconceptions and listen to her. Miss F., whose case is reported in *The Analysis of the Self* (1971), stubbornly refused to go along with Kohut's classical interpretation of her immature behavior as indicative of resistance to oedipal feelings in the transference. In doing so, she catalyzed his recognition that she was unconsciously attempting to recreate a very different and earlier period of development in the treatment. Kohut eventually recognized that Miss F. was not transferring to him the ambivalent love that a child mobilizes toward the parent of the opposite sex during the period of the oedipal conflict. Rather, she was manifesting a much earlier attitude, namely, the need to have the parent respond not as an identifiable individual but simply as a need-fulfilling extension of the child—a genie to her Alladin, so to speak. Once Kohut was able to accept his patient's wish to merge with him, and in doing so to eliminate him as an individual with feelings and an existence of his own, he ceased to think of himself as necessarily an object of either her love or anger. He was now sufficiently freed from theoretical preconceptions to let himself resonate empathically with the content and tone of what the patient was saying. Her associations, memories, and feelings and the reconstructions generated by them led Kohut to realize that she was expressing very different concerns from the ones he had assumed she was. When, at the opportune moment, he showed her these needs from early childhood, i.e., to be echoed in her significance and to be found worthwhile, the patient felt understood. Associative clarification and elaboration followed, and the transference deepened. What had been a stalemated analysis now moved forward to an essentially satisfactory conclusion.

Kohut's continued investigation of aspects of the transference other than the oedipal led him, over a period of years, to a concept of development that expanded and supplemented the one postulated on the basis of the analysis of the classic psychoneurotic patient. He realized that his patients were transferring to him their need for a structured, cohesive, viable, and stable sense of self. They could not themselves fulfill this need for validation of their existence and worthwhileness because of the less-than-optimal response to such needs during their formative years. These patients seemed to relate to the analyst in one of two ways, behaving either as if they were fused with the analyst, who then had no independent existence, or raising him to God-like status and attributing to him all virtues, knowledge, and power in which they then wished to share. If the analyst did not regard these attitudes as artifacts to be eliminated, and avoided confronting the patient with their supposedly unrealistic nature, they developed into the narcissistic or selfobject transferences on which the analysis of these heretofore often unanalyzable patients is based. Kohut has taught us that rather than repeating the conflict of the oedipal period in the transference, these patients repeat the longing and disappointments that accompanied an unsuccessful preoedipal attempt to establih a viable experience of the self—hence the label "self psychology" that is now attached to his discoveries.[1]

The implications of Kohut's work are as important for the causal explanatory theory of psychoanalysis, the so-called metapsychology, as they are for psychoanalytic practice. Kohut's retrospective reconstructions, based on observations made in the analysis of adult patients, corroborate and complement what is now known about early mental

---

[1] The practical or clinical consequences of looking at analytic patients' development from the viewpoint of the whole range of self development have been detailed in a number of books: *The Analysis of the Self* (Kohut, 1971), *The Restoration of the Self* (Kohut, 1977), *The Search for the Self*, a collection of Kohut's papers edited by Paul Ornstein (1978), and *The Psychology of the Self: A Casebook*, edited by Arnold Goldberg (1978). In a most interesting article, "The Two Analyses of Mr. Z," Kohut (1979) reports the analysis and reanalysis of a patient whose first treatment antedated the discovery of the selfobject transferences while the second was informed by them. Kohut and Wolf (1978) have written an excellent summary of the principles of self psychology.

development (Basch, 1977). Infant research has shown that babies seek stimulation rather than avoid it and that thought is not a product of speech. This agrees with Kohut's concept of the self as dependent on reasonably empathic communication between the baby and its parents. Only a theory which recognizes that infancy is a period of learning in which the baby lays down nonverbal memory traces that shape its problem-solving techniques can account for the lifelong influence of infantile experience on character formation. Piaget has shown that the learning process is not only one of simple accretion, but that superficially similar events are interpreted differently depending on the phase of cognitive development that has been reached by the experiencing person. Kohut's recognition that the manner in which patients relate in the selfobject transference reflects the particular time in their lives when empathic communication failed is in keeping with the hierarchical concept of cognitive maturation. The oedipal phase and its potential conflicts are only one phase of development, reflecting the child's newly acquired capacity for symbolic abstraction and concrete operations. It is a mistake to see all developmental problems in these particular terms. The communication between infants and their caretakers cannot be explained by what is essentially a closed-system concept, in which the goal is the discharge of instinctually derived psychic energy. An open system that permits error-correcting feedback and feedforward must be postulated to account for the complexities of maturation that are evident from the very first. Both motivation and its intensity can be accounted for by the vicissitudes of affective life, rather than by instinct and psychic energy—affect being understood as an inherited set of automatic and autonomic behavior patterns that serve as the basis for communication and cognition from the beginning to the end of life (Basch, 1976a).

The necessity for such revisions in psychoanalytic theory has been evident for some time, but analysts have been reluctant to accept them, preferring to isolate themselves from other sciences rather than risk what they felt might be damaging to their clinical work. Kohut's discovery of the broad range and scope of the transference is the first systematic exposition from within psychoanalysis that clearly demonstrates on the basis of clinical material the need to make the changes briefly sketched here. It should be emphasized that none of these revisions of metapsychology alter the significance of Freud's *clinical* discoveries in any way. What has changed is that what we can learn about development from the study of neurotic pathology is no longer paradigmatic for all of mental life. The oedipal phase and its vicissitudes form one aspect of maturation, and its importance is not diminished by the fact that it now fits into the larger schema for the evolution of character that is implicit in Kohut's concept of self-development.

In terms of epistemology and formation of scientific theory, it should be clear that Kohut has set psychoanalytic theory back on the track that it left so many years ago. The psychoanalytic method uncovers data regarding the meaning of human behavior, its motivation. Psychoanalysis alone can never generate a general psychology as Freud believed it would. On the other hand, general psychology needs an investigative method that will clarify unconscious motivation. In the past, the confusion about the nature of psychoanalytic theory has made it difficult, indeed impossible, for even those psychologists who appreciated the clinical achievements of psychoanalysis to coordinate what psychoanalysis has to offer with other aspects of their discipline. A psychoanalytic theory of motivation and meaning based on selfobject transferences is capable of probing the affective significance of relationships at any given time in development insofar as they are recreated in the transference of a particular patient. The accumulation of such data should prove very useful in the investigation of human behavior on all levels.

I have always objected to my psychoanalytic colleagues' call for a *psychoanalytic* theory of learning, or a *psychoanalytic* theory of affect, and so on. It seems to me that a viable learning theory would have application in all of psychology. Likewise theories of cognition, affect, and communication cannot have limited applicability. Interdisciplinary application and validation is essential if any theory is to be more than an ad hoc model illustrating some favorite preconception of this or that investigator or school. I have elsewhere tried to show that we are at a point where academic and experimental psychology have provided us with theories in those very areas that, while not perfect, are sufficiently refined and sophisticated to complement, enhance, and expand psychoanalytic findings (Basch, 1974, 1975b, 1976a, 1976b, 1977, 1981a). I would hope that clarification of the nature of psychoanalytic theory, combined with an investigation into the development of the concept of self as an open system, would build a bridge that would enable all students of human behavior to communicate with one another. Such a bridge would give psychology some hope of at long last attaining a theory that is both inclusive and unified.

References

Andersson, O. (1962), *Studies in the Prehistory of Psychoanalysis*. Norstedts: Svenska Bokförlaget.
Basch, M. F. (1973), Psychoanalysis and theory formation. *The Annual of Psychoanalysis*, 1:39–52. New York: Quadrangle.
———— (1974), Interference with perceptual transformation in the service of defense. *The Annual of Psychoanalysis*, 2:87–97. New York: International Universities Press.
———— (1975a), Perception, consciousness, and Freud's "Project." *The Annual of Psychoanalysis*, 3:3–19. New York: International Universities Press.
———— (1975b), Toward a theory that encompasses depression: A revision of existing causal hypotheses in psychoanalysis. In: *Depression and Human Existence*, eds. E. J. Anthony and T. Benedek. Boston: Little, Brown, pp. 485–534.
———— (1976a), The concept of affect: A re-examination. *J. Amer. Psychoanal. Assn.*, 24:759–777.
———— (1976b), Psychoanalysis and communication science. *The Annual of Psychoanalysis*, 4:385–421. New York: International Universities Press.
———— (1976c), Theory formation in Chapter VII: A critique. *J. Amer. Psychoanal. Assn.*, 24:61–100.
———— (1977), Developmental psychology and explanatory theory in psychoanalysis. *The Annual of Psychoanalysis*, 5:229–263. New York: International Universities Press.
———— (1981a), Psychoanalytic interpretation and cognitive transformation. *Internat. J. Psycho-Anal.*, 62:151–175.
———— (1981b), Selfobject disorders and psychoanalytic theory: A historical perspective. *J. Amer. Psychoanal. Assn.*, 29:337–351.
———— (in press, a), The concept of "self": An operational definition. In: *Psychosocial Theories of the Self*, ed. B. Lee. New York: Plenum Press.
———— (in press, b), The significance of self psychology for a theory of psychotherapy. In: *Reflections on Self Psychology*, ed. J. Lichtenberg & S. Kaplan. Hillsdale, N.J.: Analytic Press.
Flew, A. (1954), Psychoanalytic explanation. In: *Philosophy and Analysis*, ed. M. MacDonald. Oxford: Basil Blackwell, pp. 139–148.
Freud, S. (1888), Preface to the translation of Bernheim's *Suggestion*. *Standard Edition*, 1:75–87. London: Hogarth Press, 1966.
———— (1891), *On Aphasia*. New York: International Universities Press, 1953.
———— (1895), Project for a scientific psychology. *Standard Edition*, 1:283–397. London, Hogarth Press, 1966.

———— (1900), The interpretation of dreams. *Standard Edition*, 4 & 5. London: Hogarth Press, 1953.

———— (1915), The unconscious. *Standard Edition*, 14:159–204. London: Hogarth Press, 1957.

———— (1923), The ego and the id. *Standard Edition*, 19:3–66. London: Hogarth Press, 1961.

———— (1940), An outline of psycho-analysis. *Standard Edition*, 23:141–207. London: Hogarth Press, 1964.

Goldberg, A., Ed. (1978), *The Psychology of the Self: A Casebook.* New York: International Universities Press.

Kohut, H. (1971), *The Analysis of the Self.* New York: International Universities Press.

———— (1977), *The Restoration of the Self.* New York: International Universities Press.

———— (1979), The two analyses of Mr. Z. *Internat. J. Psycho-Anal.*, 60:3–27.

———— & Wolf, E. S. (1978), Disorders of the self and their treatment: An outline. *Internat. J. Psycho-Anal.*, 59:413–425.

Ornstein, P. H., Ed. (1978), *The Search for the Self: Selected Writings of Heinz Kohut: 1950–1978.* New York: International Universities Press.

Self, Other, and Free Association: Some Clinical Observations

PETER H. KNAPP

I. Psychoanalysis, Language, and Associative Discourse

The Task

Free association has been the subject of little systematic study. Clinical psychoanalytic writings all utilize associative material to some extent, but, despite a recent surge of interest in the interface between psychoanalysis and linguistics (Rosen, 1969; Schafer, 1976; Smith, 1978), scant attention has been paid to the exact features of thought and speech that enable us to recognize and utilize free association.[1]

Moreover, only a handful of workers (for instance Colby, 1960, 1961; Bordin, 1966; Dahl, 1972; Dahl et al., 1978) have used free association as a research tool. Yet in some ways, systematic examination of the process of free association would seem an ideal approach to some of the central questions facing psychoanalysis today. This

This work was supported in part by grants from the American Psychoanalytic Association and from the Boston Psychoanalytic Society and Institute.

[1] A notable exception, which appeared too late for systematic discussion here, is the recent volume by A. Kris, "Free Association," New Haven, Yale University Press, 1981.

paper will look at the potential contribution of such study to defining and studying aspects of those elusive entities, "SELF" and "OTHER." Their elusiveness stems partly from stylistic ambiguity, failure to clarify who is the observer and who the observed. Hence the convention used in this paper: "SELF" and "OTHER" refer to the actual participants in psychoanalytic discourse; "self" and "other(s)," refer to representations of the speaker and of the speaker's inner images, including those the listener, in the reported associations, remembers.

The Multiple Heritage

At the outset, one must ask whether the concept of free association is more than an outmoded relic of diverse therapeutic strategies, pulled together by the associationist vocabulary of the last century. Given the enormous variety of communicative styles we encounter between and within individuals, is there justification for singling out any of these as essentially "free association"?

Historically, Freud's clinical approach undoubtedly had a complex heritage (Zilboorg, 1952; Rapaport, 1938; Bellak, 1961; Seidenberg, 1971; Rosner, 1973). Four main strands can be discerned. Most important was the *introspective tradition*, dating at least to St. Augustine. This received intensified impetus in the nineteenth century, as the approaches of phenomenology and associationist psychology led to the obtaining of more secure knowledge from self-examination and self-report. Closely related was the *mystical tradition*, emphasizing the virtues of an altered state of consciousness aimed at bringing one into contact with a different, often hidden or higher form of reality. Lewin (1955) suggests that this tradition gave rise to the psychoanalytic couch as well as its original context, the hypnotic situation, and that both represent partial forms of "sleep therapies."

These two traditions of ostensibly private experience were joined by two currents that involved progressively more public, interpersonal communication. The *cathartic tradition*, which is epitomized by the Aristotelean notion of "purgation through pity and terror" and is also traceable to primitive rituals for "casting out" noxious influences, gave rise to the early approach of Freud and Breuer. It postulated relief through reexperiencing and "discharging" buried emotions, facilitated by a social setting and the person of a healer. Finally, the *confessional tradition*, extending far back into religious history, advocated the cleansing power of revealing sins to a forgiving figure.

Probably all contemporary dynamic therapies reveal varying mixtures of these traditions, depending on which may be uppermost as model or models and as short- or long-range strategies in the minds of the clinical participants. Psychoanalysis is unique in its insistence on integrating these traditions by way of a free associative contract. This leads, I contend, to the familiar phenomenologic and dynamic features of free association in psychoanalysis.

The Phenomenological and Dynamic Cores

The phenomenological features of free association can be recognized intuitively in literary creations, for example, the interior monologue of Virginia Woolf or James Joyce. An experiment soliciting free association from paid volunteers (Knapp, 1980; Knapp and Teele, 1981) revealed these aspects. They are subtle, often fleeting, but definite: a looseness in the habitual rational organization of discourse; evidence that obscure thematic influences are stimulating or blocking it; intrusion of fantasy, imagery, or concrete sense perceptions.

A full discussion of the taxonomy and structural complexity of free association would go beyond the scope of this paper. It is generally conceded that the process entails a degree of regression, the reemergence of modes of thought and experience ordinarily held in abeyance. Balter, Lothan, and Spencer (1980) developed a notion of Isakower's that the psychoanalytic situation is characterized ideally by parallel, partially controlled regression in both participants, who thus jointly form a transactional "analyzing instrument." Formal regression of this sort can be found in other altered states of consciousness.

Two other features of free association must be noted, which also appeared in our experimental material. Our subjects could not avoid emotional reactions to the listener, and they could not proceed without impediment. Put otherwise, they developed with striking regularity and rapidity manifestations of transference and resistance. These form the dynamic core of free association.

Psychoanalysis fosters and utilizes these dynamic elements; thus

it further distinguishes itself from purely introspective or phenomenologic approaches. Ricoeur (1970) remarks that the psychoanalytic unconscious, as a "center of *intentions*, of orientations-toward . . . is
inaccessible unless an appropriate *technique* is used" (p. 392, italics
added). Transference and the inevitable resistances that accompany it
not only are highlighted by free association, but also may be resolved
by it.

Readers familiar with concepts of communication undoubtedly
have noted that I am treating free association at two levels—the inner
and the outer, the intrapsychic and the dyadic. Partially corresponding
to these two levels are two traditional, more strictly linguistic levels—the semantic and the pragmatic. Semantics is defined by Morris
(1938) as the relation of signs to their referents. Semantic aspects of
free association pertain to decoding the primitive, nondiscursive, often
quasi-artistic symbolism that gives it both obscurity and richness (see
Leavy, reported in Seidenberg, 1971). Pragmatics is defined by Morris
(1938) as the relation of signs to their users. The importance of pragmatic aspects of therapeutic discourse and, indeed, of all speech, has
been increasingly recognized (see Watzlawick, Beavin, and Jackson,
1967; for discussions of the general theory of speech acts, see also
Austin, 1962; Searle, 1969).

The point that all utterances are acts has been emphasized for
psychoanalysts by Schafer (1976). In fact, Schafer has perhaps overemphasized that notion. To see communication only in terms of action
leads to difficulties; elaboration of these, again, would go beyond the
present argument. Let me merely state a preference for the general
view adopted by Bateson (1972), who spoke of two simultaneous
operations in all communication, that of "report" and that of "command." Applying these two simultaneous dimensions to free association, Knapp and Teele (1981) have spoken of the distinction between
reported contents and the *act of reporting*. Reported contents, on the
one hand, refers to the images, thoughts, and dreams that a speaker
brings to be decoded into the speaker's own personal semantic meanings. The act of reporting, on the other hand, includes the way the
speaker brings these images; how his or her discourse flows, is
impeded, or wanders; and the speaker's attitude toward the discourse
and toward the listener—all rich sources of inference about the purposes
and aims behind the speech.

Paradoxes

At both semantic and pragmatic levels we meet a further feature of free association, namely, *paradox*. Kelman (1962) said of free association: "A patient is admonished to follow a rule which he cannot and must circumvent." He argues that associations can never be fully "free"; the most we can hope for is to make them "freer." He goes a step beyond Freud (1912), who acknowledged the regularity with which, under the sway of transference, a patient "forgets the intentions with which he started the treatment" and "feels at liberty then to disregard the fundamental rule of psycho-analysis which lays it down that whatever comes into one's head must be reported without criticizing it" (p. 107).

The rule poses an obvious semantic paradox. There is a gulf between nondiscursive "referents," namely, unverbalized imagery or fantasy, and spoken "signs," namely, words. For an individual trying to report "whatever comes into his head" the gulf may seem like a chasm. James (1892) dramatized the dilemma, noting that introspective analysis of associations is "like seizing a spinning top to catch its motion, or trying to turn up the gas quickly enough to see how the darkness looks" (p. 175).

Pragmatic paradoxical aspects also emerge from the instruction to direct speech to the analyst, another, "without criticizing" or implicitly planning it. A subject in the experiment mentioned earlier (Knapp and Teele, 1981), an immature, extraordinarily blocked asthmatic, complained: "It's hard for me to say anything about something without saying anything, you know . . . stopping; saying, 'okay, don't think about what you're saying, just say it.' " Another subject compared the task to "shaking my own hand." These pragmatic difficulties are more obscure than the semantic, but, I shall argue, even more important.

SELF, OTHER, *and the Associative Process*

Clinical associations contain continual references to the communicative situation itself, some explicit, some progressively more allusive or metaphorical. Thus, Gill (1979) asserts that all associations are "transference associations." More broadly stated, they all in various ways reflect or are connected with the dyadic interaction that is generating them. We must ask, more specifically, What are the precise connections, and what do they tell us about the ongoing process?

We have learned to see a variety of levels in a patient's discourse, although our rules of inference are not always clear. A dream figure, an image arising within a session, a person or event brought into the associations all have their manifest content, behind which we discern latent meaning. More often than not, these are partial or complete representations of self or others. A patient may present us with the image of a wolf. Guided by a variety of cues, some having to do with context, some with symbolization, we "understand" that the patient's image is a self representation, perhaps of a savage pack leader, perhaps of a hungry, lonely roamer. We have performed an act analogous to translation; it may be called quasi-semantic decoding.

Simultaneously, we heed different cues, such as those having to do with the patient's execution of the communicative act, the patient's involvement in the associative relationship, the patient's coherence and self-possession as he or she speaks, the influences guiding his or her choice of content. Thus we may conclude that the patient's image of a wolf represents a murderous impulse toward the analyst, deeply hidden out of fear and guilt, or a longing disguised out of shame. Somehow it reflects the impact coming from, and the patient's intentions toward, the listening OTHER. Such inferences (the rules guiding them again to be elucidated) constitute what may be called a quasi-pragmatic decoding.

In strict linguistic studies, the two levels, semantic and pragmatic, are intertwined. So are their analogues, as these are conceptualized here. There is, however, an important hierarchical relation between them. Semantic translation yields information about the variety of representations of self and others present at some level in a patient's experience. Pragmatic translation reveals the SELF-in-action, or, more properly, in transaction with the world of key OTHERS. As these entities coalesce in the transference, we come to understand the deepest unverbalized strivings, fears, and conflicts of an individual, which are generating the flow of representations. The generative SELF, in this sense, represents a dynamically unconscious core. It becomes the focus of deepest concern to the psychoanalytic encounter.

II. A Sample Session: "The Fall"

A clinical fragment may clarify the argument. It has been chosen not to illustrate any crucial therapeutic or technical concept but because it shows clearly within one analytic session two common modes of involvement with the associative task: One can be called the mode of resistance, the other the mode of alliance. They are familiar forms of SELF-OTHER organization.

The patient in question has been described elsewhere (1980). Briefly, the young woman had entered treatment—first psychotherapy, later psychoanalysis—because of severe bronchial asthma of relatively recent origin. Articulate, sensitive, and highly intelligent, she nevertheless had specific difficulties in tolerating the analytic situation, particularly the couch. Her transference reactions reflected unresolved problems arising from a poignantly traumatic childhood. Her mother had herself suffered from a psychosomatic illness. The mother had been extraordinarily ambivalent, at times engulfing the patient with tenderness, at times attacking her with screaming rage.

In the hours immediately prior to the session described here, the patient had an unusual feeling of well-being, accompanied by guilt and anxiety. She was concerned about her sister and had guilty thoughts about a young woman who had killed herself recently. She also experienced diffuse anxieties about catastrophe following a wave of ambition that centered around Icarian dreams of flying triumphantly through space.

The patient started the hour in question by complaining of familiar symptoms of allergy, particularly a "splitting headache." She could not divert her attention from these symptoms and her sense of bitterness about them, which was mixed with thinly disguised frustrations over analysis.

She remarked, "Part of the irony is that last night I felt so good; and this is one of those 'falls.' "[2] She had attended a yoga class the previous evening. Only after it was over had she "realized that with severe allergies there might be a problem standing on your head for

---

[2] The patient was in a research analysis that was tape-recorded, subjected to repeated scrutiny in the analytic situation. In the report of this session, the quotations are taken from a transcript of the hour.

an hour . . . in an inverted position." She had hoped to attain relaxation from the yoga; instead "it had become this battleground personally of feeling so furious that I'm not allowed by myself to master it, to have any chance of—of versatility, of being able to relax."

The analyst tried to reconstruct the chronology of her "fall," but she became more upset, weeping and saying, "I'm just fighting to control my frustration and my anger [sobbing] my feeling that I never have the luxury right now—goddamnit, and I want to—to be able to talk about images and dreams and to think about where I was and how it all fits together."

She expressed a familiar resentment at the analyst and the rest of the world of healthy persons. Her distress reached a peak. She wanted "to run screaming, 'Help! I'm flooded with my own pain again.' [Sighs] I can't go on; I can't get outside myself. I can't be playful." And a moment later: "It's close to physically impossible to go beyond the physical discomfort."

Here, halfway through the session, the analyst made his longest intervention. He began by trying to express empathy, to understand "how absorbing the pain and the distress are." He called attention to the thread of enormous guilt that had run through the recent material, stressing his awareness of how hard it was for the patient to look at it. He also underlined the way her switch of mood switched her attitude toward him, making him become an enemy.

The patient responded by saying, "You should be using a term other than free association," continuing in a quieter, softer voice, "because free association right now is sheer rage." She amplified: Psychoanalysis had enabled her to "feel the freedom to say whatever was coming up"; but now it had thrown her into the "reverse position." The demand to associate had become a task-oriented one, to "stop wallowing . . . and get to work, which is the exact feeling you spent so long in helping me to undo." She added with a sigh, "There are dreams and there are images and I have no heart for them today."

Nevertheless, this proved to be a turning point in the session. The patient was able to give up her absorption in the immediate situation and her physical distress. She recalled wanting to talk to her sister in a distant city; then she thought about envying her fiance, whose family phoned often, in contrast to the puritanical stinginess of her own family.

She feared becoming like her mother, an ''angry, resentful, bitter person.''

She went on to talk of events in her daily life. She had met her mother for dinner, along with her aunt, who happened to have the same name as the analyst's wife and who had been a faithful visitor to her own mother's grave. The three of them had eaten together at a restaurant next to a theater that featured a film involving the ghostly power of a dead woman. The woman's name, actually the title of the film, was displayed on a marquee; it happened to be identical with the name of one of the analyst's daughters. The patient remarked on ''the spirit of the dead woman hovering over and flooding through current happenings.''

Later in the session she revealed that she had known quite clearly that the names from the previous evening were those of the analyst's wife and daughter; however, she had felt that it was ''inappropriate'' to mention this knowledge. In fact, she had actually had a dream about women with these names. As she left, she said that she might come back to the dream the following day. The analyst drew a smile from her by adding, ''If it happens to come up in your free associations.''

For the first half of this hour, the patient was openly struggling with the process of free association. She was feeling distressed, pleading for relief, overwhelmed with anger, both at the analyst and at herself. The two became mixed together in her painful perception of physical disease, further aggravated by the intolerable demand that she free associate. The focus of her attention was on bodily sensory experience and on the therapist and therapy.

The analyst tried to convey both his awareness of her suffering and his conviction that further psychological exploration might help it. His interpretations were not profound, but his empathy was clear, and a turning point resulted. The patient expressed awareness of the irrational nature of her anger, came to temporary terms with it, and embarked on a stream of associations in a more usual form.

Actually, this turning point led to a difference in general organization of discourse. In the first half of the session the patient adhered to a manifest theme: ''I feel pain; I resent it; and I need help, which you are not giving.'' There was little meandering, spontaneity, flow of ideas through time, or emergence of images other than the specific bodily sensations of distress.

In the second half of the hour, ideation and imagery moved smoothly from one scene or person to another. They centered around current events, but subordinated any immediate aims to the task of reporting them for an ultimate, collaborative goal.

The session illustrates two major, if not the only modes of psychoanalytic discourse; as noted earlier, these are resistance and alliance. Clinical intuition recognizes them easily, although clinical theory does not have a complete grasp of their varied structure. Using this excerpt as text, it may be profitable to look at them in ''self''-''other'' terms.

In the mode of resistance, we can discern, underlying the manifest physical distress, pervasive images of the self as inferior and damaged, along with slightly less obvious but even more pervasive representations of others as frustrating—unwilling or unable to bring about the necessary restoration. These others increasingly came into focus in the actual person of the analyst. At a deeper, unconscious level, was an alienated angry SELF separated from and tormented by a near-persecutory OTHER.

In the actual listener, the analyst, there was a parallel sense of tension, of being partly controlled, by being told only of the patient's absorption in illness, which was impeding progress toward its resolution. Undoubtedly, deeper and more primitive chords were struck, contributing to a partial sense of helplessness in the analyst.

In the mode of alliance, the patient's mood shifted, her sphere of attention broadened. The associative foreground was occupied by images of others—good and bad sister and mother figures. These contained multiple references to the analytic relationship, which became overt only at the end. Until then, the OTHER had been a benign and silent background figure. At the deepest level there was a rejoining, an identification with and partial idealization of the analyst. Undoubtedly, these deeper attitudes again contributed to the listener's state: a familiar sense of relaxation, a sense that the act of reporting was going forward as expected and that he could share in the gratification of discovering new meanings in the reported content.

At times we see cumulative tensions centering around the OTHER in the transference relationship, to be laid to rest as past and present are brought together in the mutative interpretation described by

Strachey (1934). At other times, as in the present example, the changes are subtler and do not fit his paradigm so well. But rhythmic oscillations of this kind are virtually inevitable. Closer examination of the paradoxes of free association may throw further light on these oscillations and on how they may contribute to growth in the psychoanalytic encounter.

III. Speaker-Audience Relationships and the Act of Free Association

Levels of Regression and Paradox

The regular components of free association, as already noted, involve obvious semantic paradox. Its instruction is to return to a state prior to verbalization—essentially, to verbalize the unverbalizable. Yet on the surface, this contradictory admonition does not interfere with one of the most obvious tasks of psychoanalysis, namely, reporting a dream. No one can actually describe the nonlexical, predominantly visual dream experience. Yet, undeterred, dreamers for the most part can readily and promptly provide a version of it in verbal retrospect. They go through a two-stage procedure, first experiencing, then reporting. Bellak (1961) described this as an inherent two-fold sequence in free association.

More pertinent, as the psychoanalytic relationship develops, associative collaboration itself gets caught up in the ebb and flow of conflicting transference impulses. The mutual formal regression outlined by Balter et al. (1980), operating in the service of alliance and semantic translation, becomes mixed with regression in the pragmatic sphere. In one or another way, patients echo the protest of the patient quoted earlier: "I never have the luxury right now . . . to be able to talk about images and dreams." Or they live out what she was finally able to say, "Right now free association is sheer rage."

A complete transference neurosis is not necessary for such an impasse. As mentioned earlier, some experimental subjects showed from the outset dramatic difficulties in adhering to a free association contract. Both clinical and experimental evidence point to the need for a more penetrating look at the pragmatic aspects of discourse in free association.

Developmental Pragmatics

Speech is pragmatic activity, originating in a social milieu, and carried out by a social creature involved with an audience, even if invisible or internalized. In ordinary discourse many aspects of this are dimly grasped: speech is directed at someone external. The speaker is at least preconsciously aware of this fact, of how he or she demonstrates, assuages, exhibits, leads, argues, demands, attacks, seduces, and engages in myriad other speech acts. The speaker is dominated by an aim; it may be more logical and discursive or more intuitive and nondiscursive, but the speaker is striving to influence an audience.

Speech, in turn, is guided by feedback of two sorts. Internally it is matched against a plan, used to monitor its meaning, partly semantic and partly pragmatic. Are the words an accurate reflection of underlying sense and purpose? Externally it is matched against the reactions of an audience, used to monitor attainment of meaning, principally in the pragmatic sense. Are the words achieving their purpose, including the purpose of maintaining the attention, good will, and collaboration of the listener?

Essential to the present argument is the paramount, continuing role of intention. Analysts have come to realize this in our interpretations of patients' behavior, including verbal behavior, as Leavy (1980) among others has emphasized. But we often lose sight of this fact in formulating our psychology and metapsychology; this despite Schafer's (1976) recent emphasis on language as action; despite, indeed, Freud's conceptual ancestry in act psychology, or his predecessors among poets. "Hope springs eternal," Pope told us, and added, in a phrase tailormade for future psychoanalyses, "Man never is, but always to be blest."

The internal agencies postulated by psychoanalysis, such as self and other representations, are formulated in human terms; they are organized and stored partly as composite images (Knapp, 1969). Basically, however, they are plans against which performance is evaluated—hence, the paramount role of feedback. Feedback provides information about the realization of these plans. The more it comes from the world outside the SELF, the greater the power of the feedback. Mere thought is pliable, evanescent; it can be readily glossed over or rationalized away. When anchored in words, it becomes less easily dismissed. When thought is finally uttered to a listener, it enters still another realm; the thought becomes part of a shared public universe and acquires a different, much more permanent, and inescapable existence.

It is important to see transactional guidance in developmental perspective. In its origins, speech is virtually nothing but activity and action, an immediate response to impact of the world and a direct effort to act on the world. These origins are reflected in a model of communication proposed elsewhere (Knapp and Teele, 1981). This model conceptualizes a "core" of SELF, permeated with drive and emotion and continually involved in pragmatic transactions with the world of key humans. In this primitive core, schemata of self and other are not well discriminated from one another. In the first years of life memory and planning are imperfect resources. As childhood progresses, maturation and learning slowly promote a sense of a separate self and fill in the schemata of a surrounding world; they shape discursive thought and language as necessary components of effective action.

Again, note the inclusive definition of thought and speech. It is recognized that thought is experimental action, the imagining of plans before executing them. By the same token, speech is social action, engaging the world with discursive symbols rather than physical force. To the extent that thought and speech are molded by reciprocity and social learning, that is, by feedback, there is truth in Lacan's view (1968) that the "unconscious is the discourse of the other." This discourse begins nonverbally, however, long before the beginnings of language as it is conceived in Lacan's Saussurian model (see Call, 1980). A view of the social nature of language, needless to say, does not contradict but complements Chomsky's that a thinking and speaking self also emerges along lines determined by neural organization.

Learning sets limits for possible and permissible plans. Conscious goals constrain and mold unconscious urges and impulses. Transactions with and feedback from the world of others provide models that permit differentiation of the SELF from OTHERS, and that provide external verification and sanction. Thus, a communicative matrix, having inner and outer poles, is a sine qua non of human existence. Aims, directed at an audience, are ineluctable constituents of speech. This necessarily social and intentional character of language has important implications for free association and in turn for a broader theory of SELF-OTHER organization.

Feedback: The Necessity to Invent an Audience

The stability of internal structures, or internalized plans, depends to a surprising extent on external feedback. Its absence in various forms of experimental deprivation has led to disturbance of the sense of reality and of many related functions concerned with self organization (Klein, 1970; Holzman and Rousses, 1971; Mahl, 1972). Rapaport (1951) reviewed earlier literature on sensory deprivation and suggested that autonomous ego functions readily became disrupted by interference with transactional relationships to the external world. If adults are so dependent on feedback, we can imagine its overarching importance to a child.

Most experiments in this area have measured cognitive variables, often precise ones, but not always ones that are vital in personality function. By contrast, the attenuation of feedback in psychoanalytic free association, attained by removing the analyst from view and giving him or her the powerful instrument of silence, powerfully influences the patient's deeper social and emotional spheres. More important still, in most experiments deprivation has been forced on the subject, who has been left free or even challenged to maintain or restore habitual functions. In free association, however, the individual is told to use his or her own initiative for the opposite goal: to demolish habitual internal and external guides, to impose deprivation upon himself or herself. The deprivation, it must be stressed again, is not just of gratification, but of feedback, or, to put it more comprehensively, of the crucial purposive dyadic ingredients of discourse.

The manifest communicative goal of an analysand's free association is to surrender his or her usual aims for the abstract one of collaborating in the process. This tells the patient to be essentially aimless. One might as well be told to drive an automobile without its steering equipment through a thick fog! The patient is assured that this uncontrolled trip through obscurity will ultimately be beneficial, an assurance that is met with understandable skepticism.

It is not simply that anxiety and shame tempts the patient to conceal as well as to reveal associative contents—a temptation to which the patient soon yields, as Freud (1913) remarked. Even more significant, the instruction, like the Zen instruction to suspend volition, is essentially impossible. The act of communication cannot proceed without semantic plan. Insofar as that is consciously suspended, unconscious fantasy supplies its own. Communication cannot proceed without pragmatic purpose. Insofar as that is suspended, unconscious urges supply their own.

These two aspects of communication are related in complex ways. Semantic ideation serves as a blueprint for pragmatic purpose. As both come under the sway of unconscious forces, they embody progressively more primitive cognitive structures. As the process succeeds, it leads to self and other representations that are progressively less well discriminated, and ultimately, in the semantic basis of experience, to a state of near fusion and confusion as to who is whom.

At the same time, the act of communication is given unlimited scope. The speaker is thrown into radical conflict: the supremely rational purpose of collaboration entails mobilizing the most primitive reactions to the speaker's immediate and ever-present audience. A split is inevitable: The listener becomes a benign audience, a listening, observing parental ally, with whom the speaker identifies; but the listener also becomes a primitive enemy, engulfing or abandoning. To collaborate and suspend "rational" (consciously planned, delaying, civilized) communicative activity, is to liberate one's primitive (unplanned, gratification-seeking, retaliation-fearing) aspects, aimed at the would-be collaborator. To fully experience and express "everything that comes to mind" not only is impossible in a semantic sense, but if it were possible, it would threaten in a pragmatic sense to put the relationship under intolerable strain.

Small wonder that the patient discussed earlier spoke indirectly of the psychoanalytic situation as "standing on your head for an hour . . . in an inverted position." Or that she protested because the freedom to say and feel "whatever was coming up" had thrown her into a "reverse position," so that association had become a virtually impossible "task to be accomplished."

Kelman's remarks (1962) on the rule that cannot be followed but must be circumvented may be further elaborated. The instruction to free associate entails the semantic paradox: translate what is untranslatable because ultimately you cannot know who is who; it entails the pragmatic paradox: express what is unexpressable because ultimately it will destroy the process.

Freud's self-described reluctance to be stared at (1913), coupled with his intuitive awareness of the guiding strength of his facial cues, plus his conviction that the talking cure depended on listening in relative silence all came together in a technical stroke of genius. His early metaphor of the blank screen scarcely does it justice. That metaphor suggests a passivity and detachment in collaborative viewing, rather than a reincarnation of primitive forces and involvement in an archaic struggle.

Freud's free associative method rang a change on Voltaire's dictum that if God did not exist, it would be necessary to invent him. By abjuring the active and prescriptive role of medical authority, Freud found himself to be the necessary invention of his patients, invested with pagan religious power, part deity, part demon.

Benefits: The Role of the OTHER

To cite Freud's ''genius'' implies more than creation of insoluble dilemmas. The therapeutic traditions described earlier as being at the root of free association all yield forms of ameliorating the distress of the individual. None is complete in itself; yet the ameliorating influences of these traditions go beyond the mere temporary comfort felt by patients or ascribed by them to the free association process.

Confessional relief may lead to lasting changes in superego structure, as Strachey pointed out (1934), although we may be less ready than he to accord such changes preeminence in changing the total personality.

Cathartic relief can promote outer trust and inner confidence, and perhaps even lead to a restabilization of inner structures. The spontaneous flow of free association may revive, as Scott (1955) has suggested, the earliest pleasurable relationship of infant prattling to its mother. Stone (1961) also states that free association in the psychoanalytic situation is analogous to the ''babbling of an infant . . . met with interpretation'' (p. 51). However, Southwood (1974) has re-marked in this regard that the patient must to some extent forego the reciprocity found in his or her earliest intimate interactions. Even when such skewed intimacy is attained, it probably should be considered more as a climate that favors change than as an actual instrument that produces it.

Linkage of free association to the sleep therapies may confer other advantages. Gray (1973) has remarked on the illusion that permits a patient to say to himself or herself at some level: I am immobile, as in a dream; therefore, I can freely experience the ultimate in threatening fantasy. Such dreams, however, tend to wake the sleeper. Impulses are then directly focused on a listener, who becomes not only the object of associative content derived from the past, but the immediate target of a terrifying verbal act. True, a related ameliorative function may derive from the overall ritual aspects of clinical psychoanalysis. Sessions become a regular routine, removed from the rest of life, promoting some sense of play acting, the feeling that the analysis is almost a game, as Shands remarks (1960). But it is a deadly game. The patient's whole affective life is at stake. The power of what is stirred up overrides awareness of limited participation in prescribed ritual. As our young woman patient said, ''I can't be playful.''

The most decisive, if also most complex, form of amelioration stems from the introspective tradition. This demands that the subject both experience and observe, at least in oscillating fashion, as Bellak put it (1961). It promotes a degree of splitting, of holding back, some preservation of a sense of reality and intellectual control. The very struggle against regressive forces insures that regression is not total. The determining factor is channeling emotion and action into speech (a point made by Balter et al., 1980). Speech itself entails maturation; it fosters integration and growth. By the same token, however, the paradoxical nature of free associative discourse dooms it to perpetual pragmatic unfulfillment. In attempting to suspend the aims of discourse, the speaker gives up obvious aims, but his or her discourse is still guided. The speaker substitutes subtler guidelines, efforts to please, to follow what he or she takes to be the goal of free association, whether producing dreams, or profuse memories, or exotic fantasies, or pseudo-affective experiences. Unconscious fears may lock the patient into these forms and steer him or her away from more revealing and relevant but also more disturbing areas that start to emerge. Such choices account for much of the diversity of associative styles. A full taxonomy of free association must also be a taxonomy of resistances.

The amplifying and penetrating role of the OTHER is vital. To pursue it in detail would go beyond the present focus into unsolved questions of technique. The present discussion, stressing feedback, bears on the analyst's role as mirror. That term, given a new richness by Kohut (1977), is also a metaphor that needs elaboration. The term carries connotations of a surface that automatically corrects distortions. Kris (1956) pointed out, as has Balter et al. (1980), that in a "good hour" the listener is actively involved in the stream of associations. Beres and Arlow (1974) illustrated this involvement in their lively account of empathy-in-action.

Thus, the OTHER not only reflects but also catalyzes. Together these functions counteract two of the greatest dangers of free association. By existing as target for projections, the analyst helps to disentangle projections from one another and helps the developing SELF to establish its boundaries. By resonating with the emotional storms of the patient through speech—informed, one hopes, by wisdom and compassion—the analyst's activity becomes a model for the patient's inner speech and self-observation.

But a mirror must reflect with candor, and a catalyst must activate. The analyst must press to deepen the process of free association. One way of doing this is by perpetual reanalysis of its meaning. Insofar as the analyst succeeds, he or she constantly remobilizes longing, rage, and terror.

Risks: The Role of the SELF

The essential burden of free association remains on the speaker. For the patient in psychoanalysis, this fact may in the long run account for lasting therapeutic gains. In the short run, it poses critical challenges. To the extent that free association sets aside the purposes of mature thought, it inevitably plunges the patient into primitive conflict for the abstract promise of uncertain future rewards. Adherence to such a task is an instance par excellence of Kris's (1950) "regression in the service of the ego." It represents a triumph of maturity.

Adherence requires more than disembodied faith in a process. It requires an activity from the patient that we may call "mutative experimentation"—parallel to the analyst's "mutative intervention" (Strachey, 1934)—and experimentation must be bold. The patient must suspend, in a semantic sense, his or her tested techniques of rational mastery. The patient must enter an altered state of consciousness and become immersed in a world of imagery without full knowledge of its meaning, in the hope that what to him or her seems nonsense will make ultimate sense, but also in the certainty that it must make sense first to an OTHER. This entails, pragmatically, a measure of helplessness. The patient must surrender control and knowledge to the OTHER, who becomes the target of the patient's most primitive impulses. The OTHER then embodies the inevitable dangers of retaliation, including a "falling from grace," as the patient in the sample session experienced it—a loss of the love everyone needs. Since both wishes and fears are unconscious, the dilemma is inevitable. To sustain such a contract requires the development and maintenance of deep basic trust and basic love. Seen from this perspective, successful free association is not only regression in the service of the ego, but—as I remarked once before (1960)—regression at the behest of another. It represents a triumph of human relationship.

Summary

Free association is a fundamental tool of psychoanalysis, yet it has received comparatively little systematic study. Although there are common phenomenologic elements in most subjects' attempts to describe their inner experience, the therapeutic procedure has a complex heritage, coming from the confessional, cathartic, mystical, and introspective traditions. Moreover, it contains (as noted by Kelman, 1962) intrinsically paradoxical features.

The present clinical study amplifies previous experimental observations of free association, which made the distinction between the contents reported and the act ᵒᶠ ᵣeporting, and applied distinction to self and other representations and transactions in the psychoanalytic situation.

A session from one patient's analysis revealed major paralysis of the basic process, partially resolved into a resumption of transference-tinged associations. Such paralysis is determined in part by a semantic paradox, the requirement to translate the untranslatable, but in greater measure by a pragmatic paradox—the injunction to obey a rule that forces disobedience. Adherence to an associative alliance in the face of these inevitable dilemmas promotes SELF growth. It represents a double victory: successful regression in the service of the ego and fruitful regression at the behest of another.

References

Austin, J. L. (1962), *How to Do Things with Words.* New York: Oxford University Press.

Balter, L., Lothan, S., & Spencer, J. S., Jr. (1980), On the analyzing instrument. *Psychoanal. Quart.,* 49:474–504.

Bateson, G. (1972), *Steps to An Ecology of Mind.* New York, Ballantine, 1972.

Bellak, L. (1961), Free association: Conceptual and clinical aspects. *Internat. J. Psycho-Anal.,* 42:9–20.

Beres, D. & Arlow, J. A. (1974), Fantasy and identification in empathy. *Psychoanal. Quart.,* 43:4–25.

Bordin, E. S. (1966), Free association: An experimental analogue of the psychoanalytic situation. In: *Methods of Research in Psychotherapy,* ed. L. A. Gottschalk & E. A. Auerbach. New York: Appleton-Century-Crofts, pp. 189–208.

Call, J. D. (1980), Some prelinguistic aspects of language development. *J. Amer. Psychoanal. Assn.,* 28:259–290.

Colby, K. M. (1960), Experiment on the effects of an observer's presence on the imago system. *Behav. Sci.,* 5:216–232.

——— (1961), On the greater amplifying power of causal-correlative over interrogative inputs on free association in an experimental psychoanalytic situation. *J. Nerv. Ment. Dis.,* 133:233–241.

Dahl, H. (1972), Quantitative study of a psychoanalysis. *Psychoanalysis and Contemporary Science,* 1:237–257. New York: Macmillan, 1972.

——— Teller, V., Moss, D., & Trujillo, M. (1978), Countertransference examples of the syntactic expression of warded-off contents. *Psychoanal. Quart.,* 47:339–363.

Freud, S. (1912), The Dynamics of Transference. *Standard Edition,* 12:97–108. London: Hogarth Press, 1958.

——— (1913), On beginning the treatment (Further recommendations on the technique of psycho-analysis I). *Standard Edition,* 12:121–144. London: Hogarth Press, 1958.

Gill, M. (1979), Assessment of transference. Presented at the Rapaport Study Group, Stockbridge, Mass., June.

Gray, P. (1973), Psychoanalytic technique and the ego's capacity for viewing intrapsychic activity. *J. Amer. Psychoanal. Assn.,* 21:474–494.

Holzman, P. S., & Rousses, C. (1971), Disinhibition of communicated thought: Generality and role of cognitive style. *J. Abnorm. Psychol.,* 77:263–274.

James, W. (1892), The stream of consciousness. In: *Psychology: Briefer Course*. London: Collier-Macmillan, 1962, Chapter 2.

Kelman, H. (1962), Freer associating: Its phenomenology and inherent paradoxes. *Amer. J. Psychoanal.*, 22:176–200.

Klein, G. S. (1970), *Perception, Motives and Personality*. New York: Alfred A. Knopf.

Knapp, P. H. (1960), in Panel Discussion: Criteria for Analyzability. S. A. Guttman, Reporter. *J. Amer. Psychoanal. Assn.*, 8:141–151.

——— (1969), Image, symbol, and person: The strategy of psychological defense. *Arch. Gen. Psychiat.*, 21:493–406.

——— (1980), Free Association as a Biopsychosocial Probe. *Psychosom. Med.*, 42:197–219.

——— (1981). Core emotional processes in the organizationof emotion. *J. Amer. Acad. Psychoanal.*, 9:415–434.

——— & Teele, A. S. (1981), Self, Other, and Free Association: Some Experimental Observations. In: *Object and Self: A Developmental Approach*. ed. S. Tuttman, C. Kaye, & M. Zimmerman. New York: International Universities Press, pp. 455–500.

Kohut, H. (1977), *The Restoration of the Self*. New York: International Universities Press.

Kris, E. (1950), On preconscious mental processes. In: *Psychoanalytic Explorations in Art*. New York: International Universities Press, 1952.

——— (1956), On some vicissitudes of insight in psychoanalysis. In: *Selected Papers*. New Haven: Yale University Press, 1975, pp. 252–271.

Lacan, J. (1968), *The Language of the Self*, transl. A. Wilden. Baltimore: Johns Hopkins Press.

Leavy, S. (1980), *Psychoanalytic Dialogue*. New Haven: Yale University Press.

Lewin, B. D. (1955), Dream psychology and the analytic situation. *Psychoanal. Quart.*, 24:169–199.

Mahl, G. F. (1972), People talking when they can't hear their voices. In: *Studies in Dyadic Communication*, ed. A. Siegman & B. Pope. New York: Pergamon Press.

Morris, C. (1938), Foundations of the Theory of Signs. In: *Foundations of the Unity of Science: Toward an International Encyclopedia of Unified Science*. Chicago: University of Chicago Press.

Rapaport, D. (1938), The recent history of the association concept. In: *Collected Papers*, ed. M. M. Gill. New York: Basic Books, 1967, pp. 37–51.

——— (1951), The Autonomy of the Ego. In: *The Collected Papers*, ed. M. M. Gill. New York: Basic Books, 1967, pp. 357–367.

Ricoeur, P. (1970), *Freud and Philosophy*. New Haven: Yale University Press.

Rosen, V. J. (1969), Sign phenomena and their relation to unconscious meaning. *Internat. J. Psycho-Anal.*, 50:197–207.

Rosner, S. (1973), On the nature of free association. *J. Amer. Psychoanal. Assn.*, 21:558–575.

Schafer, R. (1976), *A New Language for Psychoanalysis*. New Haven: Yale University Press.

Scott, W. C. M. (1955), A Note on Blathering. *Internat. J. Psycho-Anal.*, 36:348–349.

Searle, J. R. (1969), *Speech Acts: An Essay in the Philosophy of Language*. London: Cambridge University Press.

Shands, H. C. (1960), *Thinking and Psychotherapy*. Cambridge: Harvard University Press.
Seidenberg, R., Reporter (1971), Panel on The Basic Rule: A Reconsideration. *J. Amer. Psychoanal. Assn.*, 19:98–109.
Smith, J. H., Ed. (1978), *Psychoanalysis and Language*. New Haven: Yale University Press.
Southwood, H. M. (1974), The communicative relationship. *Internat. J. Psycho-Anal.*, 55:417–423.
Stone, L. (1961), *The Psychoanalytic Situation: An Examination of its Development and Essential Nature*. New York: International Universities Press.
Strachey, J. (1934), The nature of the therapeutic action of psycho-analysis. In: *Psychoanalytic Clinical Interpretations*, ed. L. Paul. London: Collier-Macmillan.
Watzlawick, P., Beavin, J. J., & Jackson, D. D. (1967), *Pragmatics of Human Communication*. New York: W. W. Norton.
Zilboorg, G. (1952), Some sidelights on free associations. *Internat. J. Psycho-Anal.*, 33:489–495.

Hope For the Self

NATHANIEL J. LONDON

I welcome the opportunity to contribute to a Festschrift in honor of Heinz Kohut. My topic lies in an area of little controversy: Kohut's organization of the data with respect to psychopathology and personality organization. His formulations of the themes of grandiosity and idealization, particularly as they emerge in the various selfobject transferences in the unfolding clinical process, have captured the interest of even those most critical of self psychology. It seems as if we have known these formulations all along. The sense of having "always known it" is not a denial of the originality of Kohut's contributions. It is rather like the frequent reaction of an analysand after working through a crucial interpretation. Not only does the patient feel that he or she has "known it all along," but it is even hard to remember what he or she was like before the valuable effects of the interpretation. Such is the case with many things once they are seen in a new way.

An earlier version of this paper, "Psychoanalysis and Narcissism: Implications for Political Science," was presented at Mankato State University, Mankato, Minnesota, November 3, 1975.

Grateful acknowledgement is made to the publishers to quote from *Hope Abandoned*, by Nadezhda Mandelstam, translated from the Russian by Max Hayward. Originally published in Russian in 1972. Copyright © 1972 by Atheneum Publishers; English translation copyright © 1973, 1974 by Atheneum Publishers. Used with the permission of Atheneum Publishers and Harvill Press.

Kohut's formulations were derived from the stuff of people's lives—the details of personal experiences in their public and private aspects, ranging from the readily observable to the unexpressed to the unconscious. My interest here is in published information about two outstanding twentieth century poets: Ossip Mandelstam and Anna Akhmatova. They were well known in prerevolutionary Russia as leaders of the Acmeist school of poetry. Both were seriously dedicated to their art and well equipped to pursue it. As with most committed artists, they were intensely involved with the intellectual and artistic life of their world. This was certainly true prior to the revolution, and the degree to which they maintained contact with a community of poets after the revolution is amazing. Both held to a fierce independence and devotion to their poetic ideals, which left them in opposition in their artistic work to the demands of the Soviet state. They endured the tumultuous years after the revolution—at times ignored, at times tolerated, occasionally accepted, and ultimately persecuted. Mandelstam died in a concentration camp in December, 1938. Akhmatova's works were banned in the Zhdanov Decree of 1946, but she survived to enjoy some measure of acceptance after Khruschev's reforms in 1956. She died, having found a degree of peace, in 1966. What is particularly impressive about these two poets is their integrity and devotion to the ideals of their creative work in the face of overwhelming and relentless opposition.

Personal information about these two poets is available from the writings of Mandelstam's wife and Akhmatova's friend, Nadezhda Mandelstam. Her book, *Hope Abandoned* (1972), provides a panoramic view of fifty years of postrevolutionary Russia from the viewpoint of a beleaguered intellectual and artistic segment of society. She died in Moscow on December 29, 1980 at the age of 81. It is awesome to note how this woman, even when evacuated to Tashkent during World War II, managed to keep in touch with the intellectual and artistic streams of the twentieth century. She certainly knew something about psychoanalysis. It is to our advantage that she could hardly have known of Kohut's self psychology: She is an independent witness.

Nadezhda Mandelstam viewed herself as a frivolous, immature girl, although she was well educated and demonstrated an astounding intellect, perseverence, and strength of character. She believed that her life would have mattered little except for her marriage and devotion to M. (as she referred to her husband in her book). She managed, against overwhelming odds, to preserve his works for thirty years and see to their ultimate publication. Except for losing her husband, Mrs. Mandelstam fared better than millions of others during the Stalin Era and World War II. As she notes:

> There was nothing exceptional about my case. There were untold numbers of women like myself roaming the country—mute, cowed creatures, some with children, some without, timidly trying to do their work as best they could and constantly "improving their qualifications," which meant joining study groups to sweat year in, year out, over the single "Fourth Chapter" [of the history of the Communist Party], including the story of how the ape turned into Homo Sapiens by learning to distinguish left from right [p. 3].

Nevertheless, her account of physical, emotional, and intellectual deprivation, the constant sense of terror, and the dissolution of social bonds is overwhelming. The reader has no difficulty in accepting her statement that over these years, she lost her sense of identity. Having lost herself in this way, she notes:

> My aim was to justify M.'s existence by preserving the things that gave it meaning. My own life was mutilated and robbed of meaning—apart from the aim which had been forced upon me. Instead of living my life, all I did was wait until its two severed parts could be joined together again. In such periods of waiting an aim in life is all that matters: while hardly enriching, it at least keeps some flicker of the soul alive. . . . I was lucky; it could have been much worse: I could also have ended in a mass grave with a tag on my leg, and then all my papers would have moldered away or been burned [p. 184].

As an expert on the loss of self, Mrs. Mandelstam observed that it "leads either to self-effacement (as in my case) or to blatant individualism with its extremes of ego-centrism and self-assertiveness" (p.

6). In other words, she reacted with an overwhelming sense of failure and disappointment, sustained only by the hope of saving her husband's poetry for posterity, while others reacted with grandiosity and a protective selfishness. It was only in writing her book that she began to recover her *self*:

> The fact that I have begun to ponder whether I had a task, and how well I have acquitted myself, is a sure sign that I have begun to recover my "self." . . . I came back to life only when my main task was at an end. It is clear that, crushed as it was, my "self" had survived and needed only a short breathing space to come into its own again—it is particularly active in old age when a certain peace of mind has been achieved, but before the pain of past years has died away. Later, the pain too no doubt goes and gives way to senile complacency, but I have not reached this stage yet. Then it will be too late to write—pain acts like a leaven for both word and thought, quickening your sense of reality and the true logic of this world. . . . What we do with our lives is to some extent socially conditioned, since we all live at a particular moment in history, but the realm of inevitability is confined to our historical coordinates—beyond them everything depends on us. Freedom is boundless, and even the personality, one's own "self," is not something "given" once and for all; rather it takes shape in the course of one's life, depending to a large extent on the path one has chosen [pp. 11–12].

To provide a sense of the repeated insults that led to a loss of "self," Mrs. Mandelstam describes a conversation she had with a fellow evacuee during World War II:

> "You have a strange way of talking about your family," I said to the man. "Don't they mean anything to you? Don't you love them?" He was a Pole who had only just been released from a camp. He laughed and replied: "I haven't lost only my family, I've lost myself as well. If I find myself again, I shall know what I think of my family." This had happened to him after two unhinging years in the camps. In the delirium of our existence we

had lost ourselves, no longer hearing our own voices or seeing the road ahead [p. 231].

Another example is drawn from an incident that occurred in 1929:

Just before we set off for the Caucasus, a curious incident took place. Feeling in poor shape, M. went to the polyclinic for a checkup, but the doctors immediately passed him on to a psychiatrist. . . . M. asked me to go and have a word with the psychiatrist, who proved to be a very crude and cocksure type. His diagnosis was that M. had the illusion of being a poet and of writing verse, though in fact he was only a minor employee who did not even hold a post of any responsibility and harbored all kinds of grudges, speaking badly, for instance, about the writers' organizations. This was a well-known psychosis: persecution mania based on an exaggerated idea of one's own importance. The clinics were full of people who imagined they were Napoleon. . . . M.'s case, he went on, was completely uninteresting, since his delusion took a dull and tedious form. Some cases were more interesting than others, and the general level of a person's development was reflected in the quality of his delusion. M.'s delusion was, moreover, a very deep one: it was impossible to convince him that he was not a poet. The psychiatrist advised me not to succumb to this psychosis . . . and in the future to cut short all my husband's talk about writing verse. I went home in a rage. . . . But quite unexpectedly, M. disagreed and said the doctor was not all that stupid. "I wrote you, didn't I, that I shouldn't make such a great point of being the poet Mandelstam? I noticed the swine when the other doctors took me to task and was even indignant about it. This is always happening: why do I think I'm better than others?" [p. 263].

M. reacted differently from Nadezhda to this crass assault on his identity as a poet because he was so sure of himself—because his commitment to poetry was part of an inner identity and his ideals; no longer dependent on social recognition for confirmation. Furthermore, he accepted the psychiatrist's demeaning attack because he was ashamed of strivings within himself to assert superiority over others as a poet. He viewed these strivings as a kind of shameful grandiosity that ran counter to his profound allegiance to Christian morality and Christian ideals of humility.

Ossip Mandelstam and Anna Akhmatova courageously held to their artistic ideals and artistic identity in the face of overwhelming opposition. Nadezhda Mandelstam is precise in her descriptions of her husband:

M. very easily got on friendly terms with both men and women, but he just as quickly lost interest in them. It even frightened me, the way he visibly cooled toward people whom he had only recently been talking with, seeing a great deal, or looking forward to meeting again. He admitted that his attitude to people was predatory: he took what he could and then dropped them [p. 228].

But this predatory attitude yielded to a fierce loyalty when it came to Akhmatova and to M.'s love for Nadezhda:

But what mattered most to him in all circumstances was to preserve his relations with me and his friendship with Akhmatova. With her he talked, joked, laughed, drank wine; most important of all, they were travelling the same road, taking the same view of essential things, supporting each other in work and misfortune. They were allies in the literal sense of the word: two people standing up for the same thing [p. 230].

Mandelstam adds:

Nobody should imagine that we thought of nothing but work and poetry. It was all quite different: we lived intense, boisterous lives, making merry, playing games, having fun, drinking wine and vodka, going on a spree, seeing friends, quarreling, jeering at each other, gloating over each other's follies, many times trying to run in opposite directions, but never managing, for some reason, to part even for a single day. I cannot explain why myself [p. 236].

There is more to it than that M. and Nadezhda never separated, even for a single day:

While he was still alive, incidently, I had no thought of "finding myself." We lived too intensively and intimately to think of "searching" for ourselves . . . but he could always forsee what shape his relations with women—including me—would eventually assume. Actually he not only forsaw what they would be like, but worked to make them that way, always taking what he thought fit from any relationship, with men or women. From me he wanted only one thing: that I should give up my life to him, renounce my own self, and become a part of him. That was why he so stubbornly dinned his own ideas into my head, getting me to see things his way. Once, while he was telling me that I not only belonged to him but was a part of his own being, I remembered a poem about Leah. . . . Leah's love for a Jew came from the very depths of the consciousness. . . . Even in the smallest things he was always to expect the same from me as from himself, and he could make no distinction between my life and his own. . . . He firmly believed that I should die when he did—or that if by any chance I died earlier, he would follow me very soon afterward. He was upset if I knew something in which he was not interested, or if I was lazy about reading the Italians and the Spaniards together with him. In the last years I read a lot of Shakespeare, and he was jealous; in the end he wrote and asked me to teach him how to read my "Englishman." He had immediately taken over my love of painting—since it could not be eliminated—and decided on the same policy with regard to Shakespeare. Loving different things was the same as separating, and he just could not bear the thought. He behaved in exactly the same way with my friends: he either adopted them himself or—which was more often the case—"eliminated" them. If he was awake, he expected me to be awake too, going to sleep only when he did. My brother used to say to him: "Nadia doesn't exist—she is just your echo." "That's how we like it," he replied gleefully. At the same time, he believed I could read his thoughts and hear the same words going through his head that he did. Both he and Akhmatova had an uncanny way of replying to a question just as it crossed your mind, before you had spoken it. "It's witchcraft," I used to say to Akhmatova, astonished that she had intercepted some thought before it had barely had time to form in my mind. M. literally read my thoughts and was astonished if I didn't know what he had been thinking at a given moment. Perhaps I just didn't take enough trouble to penetrate his thoughts and gave him good reason to be angry with me for not "sitting in his head."

Occasionally, withdrawing into himself, or into his friendship with someone, he would let me be for a while. I liked these breathing spaces. . . . It was hard because of the incredible intensity with which he lived; I was always having to run to keep up with him. . . . I tried not to show how hard it was for me to keep pace with him and his thoughts. I didn't want him to stop in his tracks for my sake, but I was upset when he failed to see that I was out of breath. What made life with him easy, on the other hand, was that I was never bored—and also, perhaps, the fact that I loved him. I can't say exactly [pp. 232–235].

Nadezhda Mandelstam felt trapped by Akhmatova's special needs for a selfobject just as with M.:

M. just failed to understand why I could not remember a poem he already had in his head, or why I did not automatically know what he knew. Because of this we had umpteen rows a day. With Akhmatova it was the other way around: she could not bear me to know things she did not know. She was particularly incensed by my knowledge of English. . . . Both M. and Akhmatova, the one as temperamental as the other, were thus constantly taunting poor me, though alone with either of them I gave as good as I got. When they were together, on the other hand, I was careful not to offer provocation, in case they joined forces to attack me. On these occasions I had to take avoiding action. This is a difficult art. If I had been allowed to go on living with M., I should have mastered it. I am not without talent—as M. recognized [p. 478].

It appears, then, that M. and Akhmatova would join forces to tyrannize

Nadia in exactly the way young twins often forge a team that exasperates their family and the neighborhood. This capacity to form a twinship also appeared in Akhmatova's preoccupation with doubles:

> This preoccupation with "doubles," however, was not a mere literary game with Akhmatova; it was something rooted in her psychology, a result of her attitude to people—in whom, as in mirrors, she always sought her own reflection. She looked at people as one might look into a mirror, hoping to find her own likeness and seeing her "double" in everybody. She described Olga Sudeikina as "one of my doubles" and Marina Tsvetayeva as a "mocking double, out of sight"; and she once dedicated a book to me with the words: "To my second self." But how many "second selves" can a person have, and how can they be so unlike each other? . . . In her final years Akhmatova also began to see "doubles" in the men she knew—not of herself, of course, but of each other. All of them, dead or alive, had one thing in common: namely, that they were, or had been, in love with her and had written poems to her. In her middle years there was nothing of this in Akhmatova, and it was only a feature of old age—though, I suspect, from what M. told me, that she may have been the same in the early, still-unclouded days of her youth. The self-centeredness typical of both youth and old age finds an outlet in this game of "doubles." In fairness to Akhmatova, however, I must say that, apart from the element of self-centeredness, it was due as well to another quality which she displayed in high degree: a capacity to become so passionately involved in others that she had the need to tie them to herself as closely as possible, to merge herself in them. This was particularly so in the case of those many women on whom she conferred the status of "beauties" [p. 437].

While Nadezhda Mandelstam documents so well a dimension of archaic selfobject relationships with respect to M. and Akhmatova, she has little to say about the developmental origins of such behaviors. She does provide one clue that fits Kohut's theories, however. She indicates that M.'s father was totally preoccupied with grandiose intellectual fantasies and was incapable of empathic contact with his son:

He was something completely unique, utterly unlike a *Stetl* philosopher, a Jewish craftsman or merchant, or anybody else under the sun. As a manufacturer of suede leather, he apparently knew his job very well, but felt frustrated by an inner restlessness and craving to express himself. He used to quote Spinoza, Rousseau, and Schiller, but in such incredible combinations that people could only gasp. Not just a dreamer, but a spinner of fantasies—or, rather, phantasmagorias—he was the sort of person of whom one could not say whether he was good or bad, mean or generous, because the main thing about him was his quality of being totally abstract. It was beyond belief. Between preaching his own peculiar brand of deism, he would complain about his late wife for having taken his sons away from him but it was hard to imagine what else besides his "philosophy" he would ever have wanted to discuss with them. As far as I could make out, their mother had tried only to protect them from him [p. 507].

Another clue may be found in Nadezhda's discussion of M.'s brother. She attributes what appears to be a severe dyslexia to inheritance from the father. That the father and brother may have been dyslexic would not be irrelevant to Mandelstam's brilliant fascination with the written word.

Nadezhda Mandelstam, like Heinz Kohut, was in her own way an expert on self psychology. To say that she had a *cohesive self* would be a gross understatement. This woman's life story could be considered a triumph of the "self." True, in her writings, she tends to belittle herself and her idealization of M., and his ideals are preeminent. As for her devotion to M., she states:

I now understood that I could have had no better fate and quite see how it was that some of the dimwits who hung around us did not appreciate his brilliance. . . . if I had ever taken up with any of them, or branched off on my own to become a painter—as I had wanted in my youth—or if I had ever been anything but the language teacher I was forced to become in my later years, then my life would certainly have been frittered away in vain and I would indeed have turned into a mere cog, replaceable at will, in some vile institute or other [p. 235].

Yet, her passionate idealization of her husband, in my opinion, does not have the quality of a narcissistic personality disorder. I do not find evidence of a vulnerable self and whatever grandiosity may be inferred is well integrated into her personality. Her observations of others are subtle and sophisticated with a remarkable capacity for empathy; yet, she does not merge with others. Her extensive accounts of her relationship with M. consistently reveal an independent self.

Nadezhda Mandelstam does reveal a vulnerable self-esteem, as distinguished from a vulnerable self, which may be traced at least to her youth before she met M. I am inclined to place her vulnerable self-esteem on the level of the structured neuroses; although that is only an impression based on her account of herself in *Hope Abandoned*. While this book deals exclusively with Kohut's (1977, p. 206) "Tragic Man," there is reason to suspect that she avoids evidence of "Guilty Man" in the organization of her own personality. Specifically, she omits her early life history in a way that contrasts sharply with her moving and wise chapter on "Memory" (pp. 151–163). This repudiation of the past, which appears to me as a neurotic defense in support of the "repression barrier," is stated eloquently as she discusses the periods of her life:

. . . they were determined exclusively by external circumstances. My childhood was important only as a preparatory stage and in no other way. In general I fail to understand people's excessive interest in their own childhood; I believe it must have something to do with the desire to treat reality as an unbroken whole and to relive past experience. This is a feature of the age, connected no doubt with an increasing individualism—which hinders the attainment of maturity and the growth of the personality, and was much aided in our country by all the insuperable obstacles put in the way of really growing up, by the furtiveness of frightened people laboring under a feeling of their own inadequacy. Oddly enough—and though I do not like him—I can forgive only Nabokov's somnambulist excursion into his childhood. Separated from his native county, no longer immersed in its language and history—and having lost his father in the way he did—Nabokov re-creates the idyll of his childhood as his only link with the country of his forebears. Living the life of an expatriate, he was deprived of the chance of coming to maturity . . . My life really began when I met M., and the first period was our life together [pp. 181–182].

In rejecting the significance of early life, Nadezhda Mendelstam stands apart from Kohut. What she shares with him is a profound respect for the importance of selfobjects throughout life and of the devastating consequences of the social upheavals of the twentieth century.

As for M. and Akhmatova, I have sifted from Mandelstam's voluminous accounts evidence for their use of archaic selfobject relationships. That is consistent with Kohut's description of narcissistic personality disorders, but it does not establish that these two poets could be classified in such psychopathological terms. That they used archaic mechanisms in their thought processes and in the organization of their personalities may well be relevant to their creativity. Their situation may be similar to that observed among identical twins, who tend to use similar archaic mechanisms and whose behavior may be mistakenly interpreted as pathological.

Nadezhda Mandelstam's *Hope Abandoned*, regarded by many as among the outstanding literary achievements of this century, reverberates with the work of Heinz Kohut. Evidence of neurotic elements in her personality—of Kohut's "Guilty Man"—is likely, in my opinion, but beyond her intent to reveal. Her account is a panoramic view of Kohut's "Tragic Man," provided with eloquence, with rigor, with sensitivity, with fortitude, and most of all, with hope.

References

Kohut, H. (1977), *The Restoration of the Self*. New York: International Universities Press.
Mandelstam, N. (1972), *Hope Abandoned*, trans. M. Hayward. New York: Atheneum, 1973.

Fantasy, Self Psychology, and the Inner Logic of Cults

CHARLES B. STROZIER

1. Freud and Fantasy

The Oxford English Dictionary lists three different meanings of *fantasy* in the late Greek that have carried over into modern English: (1) appearance, especially that of spectral apparition or phantom; (2) the mental faculty of sensual perception; and (3) the faculty of imagination. A number of now obsolete meanings of *fantasy* in early English gave way in time to a modern conception of the term that stresses the imaginative process of forming mental representations of things that are not actually present. This definition usually carries the sense of extravagant or visionary fancy. This imaginative process may be creative, but it rests fundamentally on whimsical or visionary notions. Fantasy is a supposition resting on shaky ground.

The psychoanalytic use of the term, although varied and often confusing, emphasizes the connection of fantasy with primary process thinking. As it is most often used, fantasy seems to be a process under some ego control and modulation, yet one that draws its imaginative vitality from its proximity to dreams, wishes, and unconscious mental processes in general. In topographic terms, fantasy lies on the border

477

between the preconscious and the unconscious; in structural terms, between the ego and the id. As Ablon and Mack (1980) put it:

> Dreams and fantasy share many characteristics. Both involve symbolic expression of thoughts, images, emotions, memories, and unconscious impulses. Primary process thinking is usually less disguised or transformed in dreams than in fantasy. Dreams, fantasy, myth, poetry, and art reflect related creative and symbolic processes. Visual imagery, symbolism, prelogical thought, strong emotions, and immediacy are common characteristics of these diverse human activities [p. 190].

In this sense, fantasy can be highly adaptive and can serve as a bridge between the prelogical and the rational, between the antisocial, wishful impulses of the unconscious and the creative strivings of what most eloquently defines human experience. The conceptual problem with the psychoanalytic meaning of fantasy, however, lies in its grounding in the sexual drive. Libidinal energy somehow magically propels fantasy, just as ideas are cathected in the creation of dreams and libido is the psychic fuel that runs the engine of the mind. For Freud this economic perspective on fantasy was linked intimately with his genetic assumptions, first in the individual and then in the group. The drives, in his view, always filtered reality.

This conceptual problem began with Freud's belief in the actuality of parental seduction as the crucial event in the childhood of adult hysterics:

> The event of which the subject has retained an unconscious memory is *a precocious experience of sexual relations with actual excitement of the genitals, resulting from sexual abuse committed by another person*; and the *period of life* at which this fatal event takes place is *earliest youth*—the years up to the age of eight to ten, before the child has reached sexual maturity [1896a, p. 152].

In two other papers from the same year, Freud (1896b, c) hammered away at this theme. All his adult hysterics, it seemed, first thirteen cases, then eighteen (including two men), had been seduced as young children.

The theory of infantile seduction, however, proved untenable. As Freud (1887–1902) wrote Fliess on September 21, 1897, a number of considerations forced him to abandon the idea. The theory seemed to lack clinical relevance and led many of his patients to flee analysis. It also seemed too astonishing, in the last analysis, to put so much blame on the perverse acts of the father. If the theory were true, furthermore, perversion would have to be much more widespread than hysteria, "as the illness can only arise where the events have accumulated and one of the factors which weaken defence is present" (p. 216). Freud had also become troubled by the necessity in his theory for the unconscious "to distinguish between truth and emotionally-charged fiction." Finally, Freud now argued, if the seduction hypothesis were universally true, it would have to break through in psychotic states of delirium. So Freud admitted defeat, but in the next breath substituted a new idea on the role of fantasy to replace the old seduction hypothesis:

> So far was I influenced by these considerations that I was ready to abandon two things—the complete solution of a neurosis and sure reliance on its aetiology in infancy. Now I do not know where I am, as I have failed to reach theoretical understanding of repression and its play of forces. It again seems arguable that it is later experiences which give rise to phantasies which throw back to childhood [p. 216].

Freud's understanding of fantasy after 1897 proved remarkably productive. It focused his attention on unconscious mental processes, especially as expressed in dreams. Unconscious thought, Freud argued in *The Interpretation of Dreams* (1900), was itself wishful as well as infantile. As early as 1899 Freud had realized that what emerged as taboos in the human psyche began as wishes. Fantasy, he argued, profoundly influenced the way the young child experienced the tensions of the Oedipus complex. The idea of the fantastic and, in a sense, the unreal, as the basis for the most real psychological event in childhood—the Oedipus complex—suggests how far Freud had traveled in a few short years from the time he believed children had to be seduced in order to become adult hysterics. Freud's notion of fantasy, furthermore, prodded him to formulate a full-scale theory of psychosexual development. The theory falls apart without fantasy. In that mythical beginning point of psychological life, for example, the child cathects the memory traces of his or her first satisfaction at the breast in hallucinatory—that is, fantasy—form. The fantasy proves unsatisfactory, of course, for it fails to provide nourishment, but it defines the process of turning to fantasy as an experiential attempt to mold reality (1900, pp. 565–566). Furthermore, fantasy is the crucial link between unconscious impulses and action, and it is the turn from fantasy that explains neurotic symptoms:

> It is by no means only at the cost of the so-called *normal* sexual instinct that these [neurotic] symptoms originate—at any rate such is not exclusively or mainly the case; they also give expression (by conversion) to instincts which would be described as *perverse* in the widest sense of the word if they could be expressed directly in phantasy and action without being diverted from consciousness. Thus symptoms are formed in part at the cost of *abnormal* sexuality; *neuroses are, so to say, the negative of perversions* [1905b, p. 165].

Freud's new understanding of fantasy seemed to have an impact on his clinical work. Dora, for example (1905a), was beset with hysterical symptoms. The most famous was her cough, which expressed her displacement upward of the conflict over Herr K.'s penis pressing against her dress in the attempted seduction *and* the repressed wish to replace Frau K. performing fellatio on her father: "But the conclusion was inevitable that with her spasmodic cough, which, as is usual, was referred for its exciting cause to a tickling in her throat, she pictured to herself a scene of sexual gratification *per os* between the two people whose love-affair occupied her mind so incessantly" (p. 48). In the case history Freud also unraveled Dora's homosexual love for Frau K., which he felt inhibited her natural sexual response to Herr K.'s advances. To put that point somewhat differently, Dora's fantasies of homosexual seduction made the prospect of heterosexual contact repulsive. Even Erikson (1964), who has directed our attention to quite different aspects of the case, acknowledges that Freud's detective work into Dora's fantasy life was masterful.

And yet, in fact, Freud never really abandoned his hold on the primacy of reality over fantasy. It may be that when the complete correspondence with Fliess is published, it will reveal that Freud retained elements of the seduction hypothesis in his thinking, despite his repudiation of the idea (*New York Times*, August 18, 1981). In any event, his psychosexual theory of development, which gave so much weight to fantasy, was based on his notion of drives that propelled inner experience. Fantasy for Freud was a psychic representation of an instinct. Little Hans (1909), for example, fantasized often about the sights, sounds, and smells of his parents' intercourse after being moved from their bedroom, but in a sense he was also programmed to be deeply affected and overstimulated by the primal scene. The instinct provided the readiness for response, the potential that the specific family environment actualized. Fantasy mediated that process. Nothing stops the relentless push of the instinct, but it is as much, if not more, biologically based as psychologically expressive. To become a part of human experience, the drive (somehow) gets translated into thought as fantasy. Freud had this notion of the relationship between reality and fantasy from the beginning, but it assumed new significance in his general theory of psychosexual development only after he relinquished the role of external reality in shaping internal, psychological states—that is, after he relinquished the seduction hypothesis. Once he had cleared away that conceptual debris, Freud could clarify for himself the way reality in ontogeny (the drives) shapes fantasy and unconscious mental processes in general.

But in a very important sense Freud also never abandoned his idea that external events shape internal psychological processes. He simply shifted the concept from ontogeny to phylogeny. In *Totem and Taboo* (1913), Freud argued that the powerful father dominated the primal horde and retained for himself sole possession of the women, excluding the young males. Resentment and envy eventually drove the other males to band together and kill the father. This deed required massive repression and atonement, which Freud felt was the basis for religion and civilization. Freud's conclusion to the book stressed that these phylogenetic beginnings of civilization resulted in the neurotic's inhibition of action, in sharp contrast with primitive man, who is uninhibited and whose "thought passes directly into action." The last

sentence of the book, however, puts this idea somewhat differently:
"And that is why, without laying claim to any finality of judgement,
I think that in the case before us it may safely be assumed that 'in the
beginning was the Deed' " (p. 161). As Strachey reminds us in a
footnote to this passage, this idea was essential to three of Freud's
later works, "Group Psychology and the Analysis of the Ego" (1921),
"The Future of an Illusion" (1927), and *Moses and Monotheism*
(1939). First there is historical reality, which for various reasons requires repression and the creation of new psychological structures.
Culture and civilization as we know them evolve from this process.
The residue of the historical event, however, the "deed" in Goethe's
poem, appears imbedded ontogenetically in fantasy. The drives for
Freud activate ingrained phylogenetic memories which become for the
individual fantasies of what the human race once carried out.

II. Fantasy, Self Psychology, and the Group Self

Freud, it seems, always found recourse in phylogeny when he
could not explain ultimate beginnings in ontogeny. His myths were
not an incidental part of his explanation of human existence. But his
stories now seem rather stilted. To accept them as science requires one
to accept a decidedly teleological view of history, a view of primitive
man as quite different psychologically from civilized man, and, perhaps
most of all, an awkward model of the way reality merges into fantasy
over time. A more elegant and parsimonious framework for viewing
these issues is the work of Heinz Kohut.

To begin with the issue of fantasy, it is probably true that Freud
was closer to the truth with his seduction hypothesis than he realized.
As Kohut commented in an interview[1] held in 1981:

Freud often used the example of the hysterical patients whose
fantasies he originally believed. They all told him they had been
seduced by their parents. We now realize that the hysterical patients were right, in a way. Probably they did not describe real
seductions, it is true; Freud had to recognize he had been misled

[1] The author conducted a series of eight interviews with Heinz Kohut between
January and July 1981.

in his credulity. But he went too far in the other direction and said the parents had nothing to do with their children's hysteria, that all we have to look at is the child's drives and the child's conflicts about his drives and the rest is all fantasy. But that is preposterous.

Freud, in other words, mistakenly felt he had to choose between real seduction, which prematurely aroused libidinal desires, and pure fantasy, which became a psychic event that forced psychosexual fixation and, in severe cases, developmental arrest. The baggage of his drive theory blinded Freud to the subtleties of the interaction of parent and child. It is the nature of that interaction and its impact on development that Kohut has most clearly articulated in his theory.

For Kohut, psychological beginnings always occur in terms of the individual's earliest experiences with the selfobjects. These breathe psychological life into the baby, which is a complete self if seen in terms of an empathic idealizing and mirroring selfobject milieu. Minute frustrations of an infinite variety and form require the budding self to take shape, build cohesion, and create structure via transmuting internalization. As Kohut put it in a 1981 interview:

To speak in biological analogies, we need foreign protein in order to build up our own protein. The essence of our biological equipment is the protein molecule. The protein molecule is a highly complex and a very specific molecule; not only is it specific for each race but probably for each individual in its fine arrangement. Now, the protein molecule is composed of various shifts and combinations of amino acids, which are themselves molecules, but not as complex as the total protein molecule. The body apparently cannot build up protein molecules. It needs foreign protein, which it then takes apart into its constituent amino acids, and then reassembles these amino acids again to form its own protein. If we eat beef, we do not become oxen, but we do need meat or cheese or vegetables in order to take these proteins apart and reassemble them for our own purposes. This is a good analogy for transmuting internalization. You need other people in order to become yourself.

The residues of the earliest archaic needs for the selfobjects, however, remain intact, always capable of reappearing in dramatically primitive form under the pressure of fragmentation. Normally, the needs for confirmation from and merger with selfobjects is transformed into more socially useful and individually productive forms. The need for selfobjects is never lost, but the mature self goes beyond its original dependence on the selfobjects for psychological existence. The meaning of individual human life and the ties between it and the environment and culture in which it lives reflect the forms and transformations of selfobject strivings in the individual and the group.

On the individual level, the regressive process unravels the cohesive self. For example, the need for merger with an idealizable other can become so great that an external power can be experienced as an archaic prestructural selfobject, one whose overvalued magnificence entirely absorbs the vulnerable self. In the individual—Mr. E., for example (Kohut, 1971)—the search for the idealized selfobject may become sexualized. At the group level, a prolonged break in empathy between the group self and its political and cultural selfobjects may so fragment the cohesion of the group self that only the primitive certainties of the intensely idealized paranoid leader can allow people to merge into some secure greatness that holds them together. Thus, the confusions of Weimar Germany gave way to Hitler and Nazism, to mention one of Kohut's favorite examples. Such an explanation, it should be noted, posits neither the return of a phylogenetic, mythic heritage nor the eruption of a vaguely defined, largely biologically based instinct. On the contrary, Kohut's explanation is based solidly on the complex subjective states of people in crisis as empathically perceived by the investigator.

From a psychohistorical point of view, Kohut's most important methodological and conceptual step was to consider the group self as analogous to the individual self. As he noted in a 1981 interview:

A human being, of course, is born, lives, and dies, which gives corporeal structure to his psychological life. There is no exact analogue for the group. And yet, the beginnings of the individual self are not so easily determined either. I would think that the baby, when born, has an individual self. However, it takes shape only within the matrix of the selfobjects. How that is with groups is another story. But I would think that a group also surrounds itself with selfobjects, like artists, political seers, prophets, historians. The idea of the group self locates the group destiny, the ambitions of a group, the ideals of a group, the skills of a group. In that sense there is a parallel between the individual and the group. And we have another parallel in that the concept of the group self allows us to see whether a particular group is developing near its optimum capacity, supported by selfobjects, moving on to fulfill its ideals and what have you, or whether something has been seriously interfered with and there are regressive phenomena.

Again, on the individual level, the need for selfobject confirmation and merger takes complex forms. In the milieu of family and friends, selfobject strivings express themselves in a network of personal relationships as well as what Kohut (1966) called transformed narcissism: humor, creativity, empathy and, ultimately, wisdom. In the political world beyond the self, leaders and the inanimate symbols of the group provide important selfobject sustenance. A break in the continuity or integrity of these selfobjects can cause primitive, archaic needs to surface and become peremptory.

Selfobject needs are not drive-related fantasies based in the instincts. They are specific psychological strivings of the self for confirmation and mirroring from a variety of nurturing selfobjects. These needs remain imbedded in the maturing and adult self and become elaborately organized and institutionalized in the group self. Under the pressure of fragmentation, however, the adult self regressively fantasizes the earliest selfobject images. Freud's model leads the unwary psychohistorical investigator inward to an awkward nineteenth century theory of instinct, and backward in time to a mythical, phylogenetic beginning of history. Kohut's leads into real childhood experience, the family, the complexities of human relationships, politics, society, and culture. Kohut's world is one we can see and touch and feel. It is the real world caught in up fantasy.

III. Fantasy, Reality, and Cults

An example of this confluence of fantasy and reality is found in the psychohistory of cults. Much of the behavior attributed to these groups seems in fact to be the product of the fantasies of the larger society. For example, the early Christians seemed to the Romans to practice strange forms of worship. Minicius Felix, a Roman historian, recorded the Christian worship of their priest's genitals, the killing of children with "invisible blows," and polymorphous sexual activity of feast days. Around 168 A.D., Athenagoras codified these apparent practices in terms of "Oedipean mating" and the "Thyestean feasts" (after the children of Thyestes who were killed by his brother Arteus and served up to him at a banquet). Both fantasies were important to the cohesion of the group self as the Romans consolidated their political order. "Erotic orgies of a more or less perverted kind," states Cohn (1975), "belonged to the stereotype of a revolutionary conspiracy against the state." It was common then (and for at least the next millennium and a half) to extract confirming "confessions" of such practices through the systematic use of torture. In this way the fantasies of the larger group found confirmation in the cult's alleged behavior. The Knights Templars were crushed in early fourteenth century France by King Philip "the Fair," who unabashedly sought to appropriate the enormous wealth of this religious order. Throughout the Middle Ages, Jews suffered frequently from Christian fantasies. It was said the Jews kidnapped Christian babies and squeezed their blood out to make the Passover bread and inflicted widespread misery on Christian communities by giving Satan more than his due in strange forms of worship. In the sixteenth and seventeenth centuries the process of fantasy, torture, and confirmation had become ritualized; there seemed to be almost a script to the witch trials of those years. More recently, the "Protocols of the Elders of Zion" (the fraudulent document from the early twentieth century of a supposed Jewish conspiracy to overthrow Christianity) fed anti-Semitic fantasies and was an important "justification" for organized Nazi slaughter of the Jews.

A parallel theme in the history of cults, however, gives reasonable documentation for some of the practices so often attributed to them. The cult of Dionysus as first practiced in Thrace, for example, seemed to involve the eating of an infant. Throughout the Middle Ages, the Inquisition uncovered so many instances of perverse sexual behavior by members of cults or cultlike groups that it is difficult to believe there was no basis in fact for the accusations of the Church. The abundant descriptions of witches' sabbats in the sixteenth and seventeenth centuries, replete with scenes of copulation with Satan in the form of a donkey or whatever, have convinced most scholars that there was some real basis for the persecutions. It is fairly well documented that in the early twentieth century the secret society of "human leopards" killed and ate young people. And, of course, the scenes of carnage and sexual excess from Jonestown leaves little doubt that some cults actually enact some of the practices attributed to them.

It seems fairly clear that in the past confusion of practice and fantasy often fed fears of the cults. The Jews, for example, seemed to carry a heavy burden of interest in ritual infanticide as a result of the story in Genesis (22:2–10) of Abraham's near sacrifice of his son Isaac. The early Christians also were put on the defensive by the description of St. Paul in 1 Corinthians (11:24–25) of the Last Supper: "And when he has given thanks, he brake it, and said, 'Take, eat: this is my body, which is broken for you: this do in remembrance of me.' After the same manner also he took the cup, when he had supped, saying, 'This cup is the new testament in my blood: this do ye, as oft as ye drink it, in remembrance of me.' " In its turn, triumphant and dominant Christianity in the medieval world found orgiastic excesses and infanticidal practices among its own cultlike offshoots as well as among the Jews and the witches. Cohn (1975) feels the history of these phenomena is entirely fantastic; thus he titles his book *Europe's Inner Demons*. Undoubtedly, torture produced confessions; rampant anti-Semitism created out of whole cloth the notion that Jews killed Christian babies; and the Knights Templars succumbed to the rapacious designs of a ruthless French king. Still, the experience of Jonestown (Naipul, 1980; Reston, 1981) leaves gnawing doubts as to whether one can universally attribute cult excesses to fantasy alone. Some people in some cultlike situations seem capable of the most cruel and perverse behavior. In other cases, it seems, a colossal misperception of new and often creative experimental religious communities leads to unfair persecution.

The issue of fantasy and reality in the psychohistory of cults raises perplexing problems. An author like Cohn, whose point of reference is the Jewish Holocaust at the hands of the Nazis would have us understand all cults in terms of projected fantasies. From such a point of view, there is no reality to the charges of cult excesses; it is a problem in the mind of the beholder. This approach leads Cohn to a psychological "epilogue" that casts his topic in Kleinian terms. This approach to cults draws support from those, mainly in the fields of religion and theology, who see cults now and in the past as subject to abuse but basically as an expression of a creative attempt to define new, alternative modes of worship. All major world religions, it is often pointed out, began as cults.

This benign view of the cult experience contrasts sharply with a good deal of historical evidence that cults often engaged in perverse and cruel practices and not uncommonly degenerated into mayhem, as in Jonestown. It is often apparent that observers of cults choose their perspective to fit their bias. Facts then easily fall into place. The Romans saw the early Christians as a cult, which is a nice precedent for stressing whatever religious creativity may lie in the Moonies. The *Malleus Maleficarum* in 1384 described the horrors of witches and helped build a framework for persecution that has its modern equivalent in the Nazi use of the "Protocols of the Elders of Zion." For still others, Jonestown is the prototypical cult experience, and they see it as their responsibility to "uncover" abuses of cults and inform the young of their dangers. Conceptual and factual confusion reigns supreme in the field.

One longs for bearings. There are basic problems of definition and point of view in framing the issues of the study of cults. The *Oxford English Dictionary* defines cults as representing a particular form of religious worship, especially with regard to their external rites and ceremonies. Operationally, we generally think of cults as a small group within a larger social matrix. However, Kallen (1930) notes that the term "cult" is always used to describe the other person's worship, not one's own. Thus: "Protestants refer to Roman Catholicism as a cult, but not to Protestantism; Catholics deny Protestantism is Christian at all; and agnostics and infidels will decry all religions as cults" (p. 621). Most studies of cults express one of several points of view. The religious perspective on cults stress the way they pursue transcendent goals. The sociological perspective (for example, Bainbridge, 1978), notes especially the internal structure of a cult and how its practices define religious deviancy in relation to the society at large. The historical perspective complements both these points of view by telling the story of the evolution of cults over time. Yet, in the last analysis, only the psychological perspective addresses the inner experience of cult participation, the dynamics of group membership, the psychological appeal of the special rites of worship, and the diverse individual needs fulfilled by the organization itself, especially in the presence of a charismatic leader.

Kohut's work, by going beyond the issue of fantasy and reality as posed by Freud, permits us to approach these psychological issues. It allows us to get inside the world of cults and not see them simply as projected fantasies of the group. The self-psychological perspective on cults opens up debate rather then closing off dialogue. For example, cults have always been predominantly centered around a charismatic figure. This generalization is as true for Christ and his followers as it is for the devil who visited witches' sabbats or Hitler or Jim Jones. There are of course numerous exceptions to this generalization; my point is not to attempt a taxonomy of cults, but to focus on one important psychological characteristic of the cult experience. In Kohut's view, the idealized selfobjects that appear in response to desperate yearnings tend toward rigidity, certainty, perhaps even paranoia. Kohut (1976) noted quite specifically how Freud in his own period of loneliness and intense creativity turned to Wilhelm Fliess as an idealized selfobject into which he could merge. Fliess's limitations were severe: He was something of a scientific crackpot, a flaky physician, and deeply suspicious of Freud's yearnings. He needed to keep Freud in a kind of psychological bondage. Until Freud rediscovered his own cohesion, Fliess succeeded.

Fliess's complex characteristics equally fit the charismatic cult leader. Jim Jones, for example, became increasingly paranoid as he secured his hold on a dwindling but ever more loyal and needy following. Jones fed his fears with drugs as he staged elaborate rituals of the Götterdämmerung. It is interesting that the breaking point for him and his followers came in response to an "invasion" from outside—the visit of Congressman Leo Ryan. That visit shattered the fragile cohesion of the group, based as it was on the unraveling paranoia of its leader. The close parallels with Hitler and Nazi Germany hardly need elaboration. But perhaps one should temper the analysis by reflecting on the further parallel with Jesus of Nazareth. Clearly, paranoia was not the meaning of Jesus' teachings. But he did present himself to his followers as an idealizable figure of great significance—in fact, as the son of God. The inner logic of charisma, it seems, is based on this communicated sense of absolute rightness.

Communication is a process of exchange. The question of charismatic cult leadership leads naturally to what specific needs among followers are met in such a leader. Most obviously, the leader is an idealized selfobject into whose greatness humble followers can merge. It is sometimes difficult to realize, as Kohut has often noted, how desperately we need such figures of strength to bolster ourselves. But the cult leader also seems to fulfill mirroring needs in his followers that feeds on and in turn nourishes gradiosity in the group self. For example, sexual exhibitionism of the leader and followers build an often strange tie. In Jonestown a "Relationship Committee" ruled on all matters of intimacy in the group. Offenders were publicly chastized and ridiculed. Jones himself boasted repeatedly of both heterosexual and homosexual exploits. Women had to wail in public meetings about how monstrous Jones' penis was and what an incredible experience it was to be "fucked by Jim Jones." The lurid tales of the perversity of cults in earlier centuries seem to be cultural variants on this theme.

An interesting example of the way idealizing and mirroring elements blend inextricably in the cult is the staging of Hitler's party rally in September 1934. This event was filmed by Leni Riefenstahl (*Das Triumph des Willens*). In the beginning of the film, Hitler—strong, confident, relaxed, majestic—arrives in Nuremburg out of the starry heavens. His plane floats mistily through the clouds, only breaking through right over the city. Thousands of people in the streets below are marching toward the rally. The shadow of the plane is cast on the streets, the buildings, the people. A triumphant ride to the hotel follows. Thousands line the street and cheer. Women gasp, children wave. A smile of quiet joy suffuses everyone participating. Some cry. Hitler holds himself erect in the car, looking aloof, like a parent tolerating the whims of children.

This celebration of Hitler as an intensely idealized leader is complimented by elements of participatory grandiosity in the rally itself. The huge rallies in the stadium allow each participant to feel unified in the reflection of himself or herself in thousands of others behaving exactly alike. As captured by Riefenstahl, at least, they all look somehow the same. Strength seems to rub off and to be mutually reflected. There is joy and exhilaration—especially in the nighttime torchlit rally—that fuses with a colossal sense of strength in unity. As the men and boys wash up in the morning in the campgrounds, there is frolicking, touching, and holding. At the close of the festivities, the expression of ecstatic abandon on the face of Deputy Führer Rudolph Hess (whose nickname in homosexual circles was Fräulein Anna) testifies to the powerful sense of cohesion gained from participation in the week's activities. It is quite an image.

The fragility of such cohesion in the cult is apparent, however. There must be constant affirmations of the charismatic leader's strength and frequent opportunities for renewed merger, as well as ritualized forms of celebratory grandiosity, often sexualized. Cults thus evolve bizarre forms of worship. That these rituals may be creative goes without saying, but their psychological purpose seems more to build cohesion between the leader and his fragile followers. As such, the bond easily breaks, and fragmentation proceeds rapidly. In its wake comes furious, undirected, and dangerous rage. In Jonestown everyone was to die; Charles Manson and his followers killed. Curiously, the rage often spills over and is adopted by the larger social matrix in which the cult usually operates. It is as though the cult shatters some unspoken agreement within the larger group self. In seventeenth century New England, for example, the fragmenting experience of having witches in its midst elicited some examples of cruel punishment from the community. Mindless persecution by society at large thus can be seen as a group response to the rage generated by the fragmenting cult. In this sense, rage blends fragmentation and persecution.

IV. Conclusion

Cults provide a fascinating point of access for the psychohistorical observer to the complexities of leadership and human behavior in groups, but little can be gained without conceptual clarity. The classical psychoanalytic emphasis on drives and its understanding of fantasy leads only to blind alleys. Self psychology maps a more evocative terrain. The work of Kohut hardly provides easy answers. But it does orient the observer to ask historically meaningful questions, to probe the depths of otherwise baffling events, and defines a productive agenda for future research.

References

Ablon, S. L., & Mack, J. E. (1980), Children's dreams reconsidered. *The Psychoanalytic Study of the Child*, 35:179–217. New Haven: Yale University Press.

Bainbridge, W. S. (1978), *Satan's Power: A Deviant Psychotherapy Cult*. Berkeley: University of California Press.

Cohn, N. (1975), *Europe's Inner Demons: An Inquiry Inspired by the Great Witch-Hunt*. London: Sussex University Press.

Erikson, E. (1964), *Insight and Responsibility: Lectures on the Ethical Implications of Psychoanalytic Insight*. New York: Norton.

Freud, S. (1887–1902), *The Origins of Psychoanalysis: Letters to Wilhelm Fliess, Drafts and Notes*, ed. M. Bonaparte, A. Freud, & E. Kris. New York: Basic Books, 1954.

——— (1896a), Heredity and the aetiology of the neuroses. *Standard Edition*, 3:141–156. London: Hogarth Press, 1962.

——— (1896b), Further remarks on the neuro-psychoses of defence. *Standard Edition*, 3:159–185. London: Hogarth Press, 1962.

——— (1896c), The aetiology of hysteria. 3:189–221. London: Hogarth Press, 1962.

——— (1900), The interpretation of dreams. *Standard Edition*, 4&5. London: Hogarth Press, 1953.

——— (1905a), Fragment of an analysis of a case of hysteria. *Standard Edition*, 7:3–122. London: Hogarth Press, 1953.

——— (1905b), Three essays on the theory of sexuality. *Standard Edition*, 7:125–245. London: Hogarth Press, 1953.

——— (1909), Analysis of a phobia in a five-year-old boy. *Standard Edition*, 10:3–149. London: Hogarth Press, 1955.

——— (1913), Totem and taboo. *Standard Edition*, 13:1–162. London: Hogarth Press, 1955.

——— (1921), Group psychology and the analysis of the ego. *Standard Edition*, 18:67–143. London: Hogarth Press, 1955.

——— (1927), The future of an illusion. *Standard Edition*, 21:3–56. London: Hogarth Press, 1961.

——— (1939), Moses and monotheism. *Standard Edition*, 23:3–137. London: Hogarth Press, 1964.

Kallen, H. M. (1930), Cults. *Encyclopedia of the Social Sciences*, Vol. 4. New York: Macmillan, pp. 618–621.

Kohut, H. (1966), Forms and transformations of narcissism. In: *The Search for the Self*, ed. P. Ornstein. New York: International Universities Press, 1978, pp. 427–460.

——— (1971), *The Analysis of the Self*. New York: International Universities Press.

———— (1976), Creativeness, charisma, group psychology: Reflections on the self-analysis of Freud. In: *The Search for the Self*, ed. P. Ornstein. New York: International Universities Press, 1978, pp. 793–843.

Naipul, S. (1980), *Journey to Nowhere: A New World Tragedy*. New York: Simon & Schuster.

Reston, J. (1981), *Our Father Who Art in Hell: The Life and Death of Jim Jones*. New York: Times Books.

Concluding Statement

ERNEST S. WOLF

One hundred years is really not a very long time span to allow one to judge the germination of a fundamentally new departure in the history of ideas. To some psychoanalysis may appear to have been an archaic and outmoded attempt to safeguard a dying vitalism from the victorious encroachment of modern science, particularly physics and chemistry. To many others, however, including the contributors to this book, psychoanalysis appears as a lusty and vibrant youngster among more venerable sister sciences. Indeed, one hundred years is a rather short time in the history of a branch of science—so short, in fact, that the most revolutionary departures, the most significant innovations in science, typically take much longer before even becoming widely discussed, not to speak of being generally accepted. Thus, the temerity of publishing a book on the future of psychoanalysis and of psychoanalytic self psychology in particular may evoke howls of derision. But at those moments in the heat of discussion when one's scientific credentials are challenged or one's motives pejoratively distorted, it is at least comforting to remember that we are in good company. The great Galileo was forced in 1633 to recant his assertion that the earth revolves around the sun, when that "new" idea had been conclusively proven by Copernicus in 1530, more than a hundred years earlier. In our own day, well over one hundred years after Darwin published the "Origin of the Species" in 1859, we see a renewed resurgence of blind fury

495

at those who would shake the old and dearly held beliefs about the creation of the world. Freud recognized that some of the contemporary hostility to science resulted from these two blows to naive self-love and human megalomania. Kohut has shown in more microscopic detail how the narcissistic injury is experienced as an unbearably insulting helplessness by the self, which reacts with narcissistic rage to wipe out the offending threat.

My purpose in this concluding statement is to attempt to put into broader perspective the accomplishments of psychoanalytic self psychology over the last decades and to venture some more or less well informed guesses regarding future trends. I shall do this undeterred either by traditionalists in science who cannot accept psychoanalysis as a genuine scientific method of inquiry or by traditionalists within psychoanalysis itself who cannot encompass self psychology within their narrow view of their field.

I can anticipate the protests: You're not being objective, I shall be told. You are biased by years of professional commitment and personal allegiance and see these problems in the particularly shaded light of your own prejudices. You are unable to perceive the true state of affairs with the clear vision of the trained but neutral observer, the true scientist.

Alas, I will concede this point. I cannot be truly neutral, objective, detached, and disinterested—but neither can any other human being. Yes, I do bring to this essay, as well as to all other activities that I engage in, a certain view of the world, a Weltanschauung, a value system, which certainly has been influenced by psychoanalysis and by self psychology, although, in essence, it precedes them both. But are neutrality, objectivity, detachment, and disinterest the only approach to the truth, especially the truth about human beings? Are human statements that do not pass the rigorous criteria of logical positivism therefore untrue?

I do not approach my task of reviewing Heinz Kohut's contribution to psychoanalysis innocent of values, that is, without awareness of choices and preferences. To do otherwise would be humanly impossible. How, then, am I different from those colleagues who aim at a scientific objectivity uncontaminated and uninfluenced by who they are and by what they feel? Simply, I differ only insofar as I acknowledge and, at times, even welcome those conscious and unconscious intentions of my self that in a more traditional scientific discourse would be passed over in silence, or denied, or even condemned. The pivotal point that makes our new psychoanalytic psychology of the self different, and in my judgment decisively advanced, is this: We do not attempt to deny or to silently bypass via mechanistic theories the fact that in depth psychology, a science defined by our method of inquiry, human beings are always concerned with human beings—nothing more, nothing less. As self psychologists, we know that while attempts to reduce the self to some objective definition, whether to patterns of instincts or to circuits of impulses, may bring forth an objective, scientific fact, perhaps an important biological or neurophysical finding, the result may be of great psychological triviality. Attempts to objectify the science of complex mental states by reducing it to prepsychological limits destroy any psychology of the human self.

We have to make a choice: do we study, at one extreme of reductionism, biology, or neurochemistry, or neurophysics? Or do we study the behavior of people, singly or in groups, under various social, cultural, anthropological conditions, at another extreme? Or, finally, do we study the inner life of human beings by the methods of psychoanalysis? Freud, guided by Breuer's Anna O., the first pure depth-psychological case history, took the first giant step in the development of a science of our inner life. But Freud stepped into the field with one foot only, so to speak. With the other foot he remained firmly planted on the solid ground of contemporary science. I believe that he was not fully aware of how an analysis of human behavior into quasi-biological components would tend to push the living complexity of the whole, human self into the background. Freud started one of the rare revolutions in the history of human ideas. It detracts nothing from his genius, therefore, to recognize that he did not complete the psychoanalytic revolution. Today we have embarked on the next leg of the journey toward self knowledge.

Kohut has provided the major impetus for moving psychoanalysis away from a mechanistic metapsychology, stressing the necessity of including empathic values in our conceptualizations as well as in data collection. To be sure, neither Freud nor any of his important followers conducted analyses with the objectivity of a computer. They tried, however, and in the post-Freudian era the aims of a pseudo-scientific objectivity led to the teaching and practice of a brand of psychoanalysis that tended to be sterile and mechanistic. The attempt for the sake of an outmoded model of science to make the analyst "neutral," "abstinent," and essentially nonparticipatory except as a commenting and interpreting observer is destructive of the analytic process. These are harsh words and they usually evoke a hot denial that good analysts were ever so cold and rigid and unresponsive. To be sure, Kohut did not invent empathy. Yet, those of us whose memories go back twenty or more years can well remember the distortion of Freud's rule of abstinence that was taught in many a classroom and reigned over many a couch. Indeed, such attitudes have been manifest as recently as March 1981. In a "Report of the Committee on Certification" in the *Newsletter* of the American Psychoanalytic Association, a leading analyst gives critical comments about recent applicants and calls attention to such problems as "hardly any mention of anger during the termination phase but, rather, an emphasis on feelings of gratitude and regret for terminating the analytic work" (pp. 11–12). No, he does not state explicitly that patients who feel good about their analysts and regret leaving them have not really been analyzed properly, but the message to candidates and young analysts is nevertheless clear and threatening. Perhaps, like many well-meaning and humane individuals among our colleagues, this analyst subscribes to the misguided view that to obtain the scientific truth through psychoanalysis means reducing complex mental states to their constituent parts, whether biological, prepsychological, or psychological—in other words by painfully fragmenting the patient's self. Thus, a patient who has experienced the analyst as empathically understanding and who thus has not felt the narcissistic rage attendant upon the helpless disintegration of the self in response to some particularly neutral or abstinent analytic response may not, in the view of some, have been properly analyzed at all. We have to make choices, and we have to choose what this thing called psychoanalysis is. Is it a method of psychological dissection only, or is it a fitting together of the fragmented parts that we find in our patients so that they may regain their wholeness?

Kohut was not, of course, the first analyst to recognize that the preservation or reconstruction of the analysand's wholeness—or as he has termed it, the restoration of the cohesion of the self—has to be an essential aspect of the therapeutic endeavor that goes hand in hand with the investigative aims of psychoanalysis. But it was Kohut who put the self in the center of the analytic enterprise, theoretically as well as clinically. He was the first to recognize that the child, like the adult, is not the victim of sexual impulses or aggressive drives only, whether those of the child or of others. Rather, Kohut demonstrated clinically and elaborated in his conceptualizations that children or adults never experience sexuality or aggression *in vacuo* or *in vitro*, so to speak, but always in the context of a complex organization—a self or, more precisely, a selfobject matrix. The vantage point of the psychoanalytic self psychologist is not that of the observing outsider but of the experiencing insider. All analysts, whether self-psychologically sophisticated or not, exclude the awareness of self and selfobjects only at the cost of impoverishing the analytic process through repression or disavowal.

The changes that self psychology has brought to psychoanalysis can be brought into focus by examination of the changed view of the clinical therapeutic process. It is here that theoretical modifications manifest themselves in a subtly altered analytic technique and a redefinition of the goals of therapeutic psychoanalysis in terms of a healthy self. Both therapists and patients, regardless of their psychoanalytic sophistication or their preference for one set of theories over another, are virtually unanimous in describing an almost dramatic change in what I have elsewhere designated the analytic ambience (Wolf, 1976). The change that came about as a result of Kohut's emphasis on the empathic-introspective approach to the collection of psychoanalytic data is the inclusion of the patient's perspective—that is, of the patient's subjective experience of the analytic situation objectively evaluated—in the conceptualization of the analytic ambience. Thus, an objective analytic neutrality can no longer be defined by criteria that ignore the patient's sense of whether the analyst is or seems to be for or against the patient.

Based on the insights and clinical experience gained from the treatment of narcissistic personality disorders illuminated by the insights of self psychology, I have elsewhere (Wolf, 1976) examined the deleterious effects on the analytic ambience resulting from an extreme uncritical application of the rule of abstinence, resulting in the patient experiencing the analyst as excessively critical. This stance produces the analyst who refuses to greet patients or to bid them good-bye at the end of a session, who refrains from the ordinary gestures and courtesies of social intercourse, who will neither smile nor frown, and who abstains from ordinary, expected human responses in a mis-guided, so-called neutrality. A good example is that of the analyst quoted by Malcolm (1981), who refused to acknowledge any sympathy with the grief of an analysand whose parent had just died. Such an analyst, I believe, is perverting Freud's meaning of the rule of absti-nence and interfering in the analytic process.

I will not look further at these deleterious influences on the an-alytic ambience but will focus on the positive contributions made by self psychology to our understanding of the analytic ambience as it facilitates the analytic process. Kohut (in press) in his last book, spelled out certain aspects of how psychoanalytic treatment heals that previ-ously had been left obscure. The most important of these new con-ceptualizations is Kohut's thesis that the goal of the therapeutic process is a shift from archaic modes of selfobject relationships, mostly merg-ers, to mature selfobject relationships. Kohut has designated these mature relationships as empathic resonance with selfobjects in the social surroundings of adult life. This therapeutic process constitutes a healing of the injury of the self. It proceeds in several steps.

The first is an analysis of the resistances against the spontaneous emergence of the selfobject transferences. This makes it possible for the selfobject transferences to mobilize and structure the relationship with the analyst in such a way that the analyst will be experienced as performing the needed selfobject functions. To overcome these re-sistances means that the injured self dares to open itself up to a potential experience of being injured again; in other words, the self entrusts itself to the analyst's capacity and willingness to perform the selfobject function. The analysand's self knows that the analyst not only can fail, but inevitably will fail, and new disappointment and injury will occur, as they have on numerous occasions in ordinary life. Yet hope springs eternal, and is encouraged by the analyst's professional commitment and self-revealing attitude. During the early phases of resistance anal-ysis, the analyst may reveal that he or she is ignorant or clumsy in attempting to understand the analysand, or perhaps, the analyst's own selfobject needs may seek some surcease in the psychoanalytic situation, even at times using the patient as a selfobject. Since in essence, resistance is nothing but fear of being traumatically injured again, the decisive event of its analysis is the moment when the analysand has gained courage from these self-revelations of the analyst to know that the analyst does not need to feed on the patient to achieve cohesion and harmony.

Let me illustrate with a vignette of a woman who came thirty-five minutes late for her first appointment and announced that she did not come for treatment but to have some things explained to her. I considered reminding her that I was an analyst, that I had chosen to do analytic work with people who desired such services, that I was not in the business of teaching or explaining psychoanalysis. In short, I came close to revealing my injured self, which was demanding certain patientlike behavior from my analysand. But my momentary outrage passed as I began to hear a desperately fragile self open itself up ever so slightly to being injured again, while ostensibly surrounding itself with a barrage of denials of its needs. So I said nothing, and soon we made another appointment to which the patient came only twenty minutes late. Suffice it to say that it did not take very long for a genuine treatment situation to evolve, which, however, could not be openly acknowledged by either one of us for a long time. Eventually, of course, it became appropriate to interpret the defensive behavior. I am sure that if on that first day I had felt a stronger need for appropriate patientlike behavior in order to feel myself an analyst, I would not have been able to treat this patient.

The second step in the therapeutic process is the spontaneous mobilization of the analysand's selfobject transferences. The selfobject transferences have already been much discussed, but I wish to stress the point that patients are in constant conflict. The conflict is between the need for selfobject responses, on the one hand, and the fear of self injury, on the other. Most of the time the fears are dominant, and they thwart movement toward the establishment of selfobject relationships. Consequently, patients coming into treatment are usually starved for the needed selfobject responses. When the analytic ambience in combination with analysis of resistance creates an experience of relative safety for the patient, the balance between need and fear shifts. The ever-present hope is encouraged, and the rising expectation that the selfobject needs will be heard and understood leads to an intensification of the needs which override the fear. And as these needs, at first revealed only haltingly, are understood by the analyst, the experience of being understood brings about a general mobilization and revival of archaic, repressed, and disavowed selfobject needs: in other words, the selfobject transference.

The third step, the opening of a path of empathic resonance between the analysand's self and the selfobject, represents the selfobject function of the analyst. This process can be seen most clearly if we divide it into a number of substeps. First, there is a disruption of the established, sustaining selfobject transference through nontraumatic, optimal frustration—usually one of the inevitable "failures" of the analyst to maintain total empathic in-tuneness with the analysand. This disruption causes a temporary return to previous, more archaic modes of relationship, which may be characterized by defensively distorted and exaggerated demands on the analyst or by a defensively motivated distancing and withdrawal. Note that defensiveness here does not mean defense against instinctual intrusion. On the contrary, the temporary regression of the self to a state of lessened cohesion is often accompanied by some disintegration and the emergence of distorted fragments of sexuality and aggression, such as perversion and other forms of acting out. The defensive nature of these more archaic modes of relating is evident from their use in the defense of the remaining self structure. The disappointing selfobject may be held at a safer distance by the often obnoxious quality of these defensive manifestations of disintegration, or it may be brought closer by the needy demandingness. Either way, the self, despite its pain, need, and reduced functional capacity, tries to marshal its resources, including the disintegration products, to influence the analyst to supply the needed selfobject function. It is the archaic and distorted nature of the revived selfobject need that often makes it counterproductive in ordinary social intercourse. The analyst, however, by virtue of his or her empathy and theoretical orientation, ideally can recognize the legitimate selfobject needs underlying the archaic and distorted manifestations, despite also experiencing some discomfort.

As the next substep in achieving empathic resonance, the analyst explains and interprets the sequence of events to the patient and corrects his or her own previous misunderstanding of the patient. Again, it is important to point out, the disruptions, like the preceding harmonious selfobject transferences, are not new experiences for the patient with a new object. What is new is that the analyst does not respond in the manner of an ordinary social situation but responds by explaining and interpreting on the basis of an empathically informed understanding. Such an explanation is not a gratification of a need—whether of a selfobject need or of an instinctual wish or need—except for the need to be understood. By allowing the patient to again feel understood, the empathic flow between analyst and analysand is restored. I believe this is what Kohut means by stating that archaic merger is changed into empathic resonance. As far as I know, Kohut did not further define the concept of empathic resonance. But I think it is useful to see how far this concept will lead us in furthering our understanding of the therapeutic process.

My impression is that empathy—the process of grasping the inner psychological state of another human being—is in clinical experience a reciprocal process. To be sure, we can talk about empathy as a means by which the analyst gets data about the analysand, and we can attempt to clarify philosophically or psychologically how such knowledge of other minds is possible. Theoretically, we can talk about empathy as if it were a one-way street. In clinical practice, however, I find it impossible to maintain for very long any real conviction of the correctness of my empathic insights without a particular kind of response from the analysand. This response, which gives my empathic understanding the persuasive depth of a lived experience rather than the shallowness of a mere impression, is neither the affirmation nor the negation of my interpretation by the patient. Instead, it is the analysand's empathic grasp of my psychological state and activity at that moment, not necessarily a verbal response, that engages my self in its depth and thereby evokes the conviction of correctness. In other words, at the moment that I really understand what is going on with the analysand, I also know that he or she really understands what I'm doing. Empathic resonance is reciprocal resonance.

For the analysand, then, the experience of being understood has become a mastered understanding of someone else, in this case the analyst. A passivity has been transformed into an activity of the patient's self, a capacity to act that remains as a part of the self. A selfobject function of the analyst has become a function of the analysand's self, a process that Kohut has called transmuting internalization.

Kohut describes how the empathic resonance with the analyst eventually leads to the analysand's discovery of empathic resonance is the most human aspects of his or her environment and to the development of a capacity to seek out available selfobjects in the social matrix of the surround. Most important, increasing self structure does not mean an eventual independence from selfobjects but an increased ability to find them and to use them. As obvious as this seems, particularly in the light of everyone's day-to-day experience of the world, it is one of the most controversial findings of psychoanalytic self psychology. Traditional psychoanalytic theory is not alone in its excessive stress on independence, self-sufficiency, self-directiveness, and self-responsibility as the goal of human development. It is part of a Western Weltanschauung of individuality, responsibility, and autonomy that informs our Judeo-Christian culture. I believe this view is grievously mistaken, because it is out of balance. It misunderstands the basic striving of the human soul, which is not just to save itself in its capacity for individual distinctiveness, but to find a resonant response in the cosmos.

Those fellow human beings who are universally recognized as the most human, the wisest, the most developed in the best sense of that phrase, are not those who succeed in giving maximum development and expression to the uniqueness of their individuality. What we value is not the bizarreness of their personality, not their crankiness or their eccentricity. Rather, we value as the heroes of our civilization those fellow sufferers who overcame their individualism in their striving for a universality of shared responsiveness through their arts and artifacts. Religion, art, philosophy, and literature are not primarily the expression of misdirected sexuality or thwarted aggression. Rather, they are created selfobjects whose selfobject function can be universally shared and with which lasting, reliable, fulfilling, and yet humanly alive empathic resonances can be established. It is this capacity for a living, human responsiveness by the artistically creating experience that distinguishes a work of art from another category of created selfobjects—the lifeless, mechanical, nonresonant selfobjects that are usually designated as fetishes.

The concept of empathic resonance has thus given us a powerful tool not merely for the better understanding of the therapeutic process, but also for the exploration of the arts and of that still mysterious and magical capacity that we call creativity. The future of psychoanalysis lies not only in the expansion of the theoretical basis and clinical application of our science, but also in establishing an empathic resonance between psychoanalysis and all the sciences of humanity including the *Geisteswissenschaften* as well as the *Naturwissenschaften*.

Among the many accomplishments of self psychology, the one that appears paramount to me is the renewal of our psychoanalytic creativity, a freeing up of our creative powers, both as individuals and as participants in a science that has reached a new level of creative discourse. For this we are all indebted to Heinz Kohut.

References

Kohut, H. (1972), Thoughts on narcissism and narcissistic rage. In: *The Search for the Self*, ed. P. Ornstein. New York: International Universities Press, 1978, pp. 615–658.
——— (in press), *How Does Psychoanalysis Cure?*
Malcolm, J. (1981), *Psychoanalysis: The Impossible Profession*. New York: Knopf.
Wolf, E. S. (1976), Ambience and abstinence. *The Annual of Psychoanalysis*, 4:101–116. New York: International Universities Press.

INDEX

507